Solutions Manual to Accompany

QUANTITATIVE METHODS FOR BUSINESS Fifth Edition

David R. Anderson
University of Cincinnati

Dennis J. Sweeney
University of Cincinnati

Thomas A. Williams
Rochester Institute of Technology

West Publishing Company
St. Paul   New York   Los Angeles   San Francisco

Contents

Preface

Chapter

Preface

The Purpose of *Quantitative Methods for Business* is to provide students with a sound conceptual understanding of the role quantitative methods plays in the decision making process. The text emphasizes the application of quantitative methods by using problem situations to introduce each technique. The text has been designed to meet the needs of nonmathematicians who are studying the fields of business and economics.

The solutions manual furnishes assistance by identifying learning objectives and providing detailed solutions for all problems and questions in the text. Specific sections of the manual are as follows:

Learning Objectives

Problem Solutions

Solutions to Case Problems

Answers to Questions for Quantitative Methods in Practice

Acknowledgements

We would like to provide special recognition to Catherine J. Williams for her efforts in typing the solutions manual and putting the final package together. We are also indebted to our editor Mary C. Schiller for her support during the preparation of this solutions manual.

David R. Anderson
Dennis J. Sweeney
Thomas A. Williams

Chapter 1
Introduction

Learning Objectives

1. Develop a general understanding of the role of quantitative methods in decision making.

2. Realize that quantitative applications begin with a problem situation.

3. Obtain a brief introduction to quantitative methods and their frequency of use in practice.

4. Understand that managerial problem situations have both quantitative and qualitative considerations that are important in the decision making process.

5. Learn about models in terms of what they are and why they are useful (the emphasis is on mathematical models).

6. Identify the step-by-step procedure that is used in most quantitative approaches to decision making.

7. Learn about basic models of cost, revenue, and profit and be able to compute the break-even point.

8. Obtain an introduction to microcomputer software packages and their role in quantitative approaches to decision making.

9. Understand the following terms:

model	infeasible solution
objective function	management science
constraint	operations research
deterministic model	fixed cost
stochastic model	variable cost
feasible solution	break-even point

Solutions

1.   Management science and operations research, terms used almost interchangeably, are broad disciplines that employ scientific methodology in managerial decision making or problem solving. Drawing upon a variety of disciplines (behavioral, mathematical, etc.), management science and operations research combine quantitative and qualitative considerations in order to establish policies and decisions that are in the best interest of the organization. The table of contents, as well as Tables 1.2 and 1.3, list many of the important quantitative procedures that have played significant roles in management science or operations research studies.

2.   Numerous methodological developments based on research into quantitative methods to decision making and advances in computer technology were two of the biggest reasons for the growth in the use of management science. In addition, an increase in the complexity of business operations and decisions provided new areas of application for the methods of management science.

3.   See section 1.2.

4.   A quantitative approach may be considered for the following reasons:

   a.   the problem is large and complex;

   b.   the problem is very important;

   c.   the problem is new and no past experience exists;

   d.   the problem is repetitive.

5.   Problem definition

   Model development

   Data preparation

   Model solution

   Report generation

         For further discussion see section 1.3

6.   Iconic - scale model of new building, memorial status or busts

   Analog - barometer, altimeter

   Mathematical - inventory cost equation, sales expressed as a function of price

7.   Models usually have time, cost, and risk advantages over experimenting with actual situations.

8. a.   maximize $10x + 5y$
        subject to

                             $5x + 2y \le 40$

                             $x \ge 0$

                             $y \ge 0.$

   b.   Controllable inputs: x and y
        Uncontrollable inputs: profit (10,5), labor hours (5,2) and labor-hour availability (40).

   c.

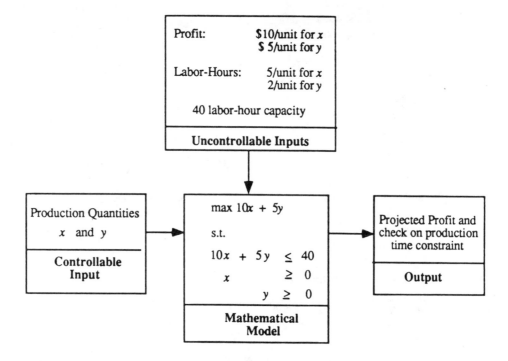

   d. $x = 0$, $y = 20$ Profit $= \$100$
        (Solution by trial-and-error)

9.   Deterministic - all uncontrollable inputs are fixed and known.

10.   If $a = 3$, $x = 13\ 1/3$ and profit = 133.
      If $a = 4$, $x = 10$ and profit = 100.
      If $a = 5$, $x = 8$ and profit = 80.
      If $a = 6$, $x = 6\ 2/3$ and profit = 67.

      Since a is unknown, the actual values of x and profit are not known with certainty.

11.a.   Total Units Received $= x + y$

b.   Total Cost $= 0.20x + 0.25y$

c. $x + y = 5000$

d. $x \leq 4000$ Kansas City Constraint
$y \leq 3000$ Minneapolis Constraint

e.   Min $0.20x + 0.25y$
s.t.

$$
\begin{array}{rclr}
x + & y & = & 5000 \\
x & & \leq & 4000 \\
& y & \leq & 3000
\end{array}
$$

$x, y \geq 0$

12.   Let $d =$ distance
$m =$ miles per gallon
$c =$ cost per gallon,

$\therefore$ Total Cost $= \left(\dfrac{2d}{m}\right)c$.

We must be willing to treat m and c as known and not subject to variation.

13.a.   at \$20 $d = 800 - 10(20) = 600$
at \$70 $d = 800 - 10(70) = 100$

b. $TR = dp = (800 - 10p)p = 800p - 10p_2$

c.   at \$30 $TR = 800(30) - 10(30)^2 = 15,000$
at \$40 $TR = 800(40) - 10(40)^2 = 16,000$
at \$50 $TR = 800(50) - 10(50)^2 = 15,000$
        Total Revenue is maximized at the \$40 price.

d. $d = 800 - 10(40) = 400$ units
$TR = \$16,000$

14.   Model (a) may be quicker to formulate, easier to solve, and/or more easily understood.

15.a. $TC = 1000 + 30x$

b. $P = 40x - (1000 + 30x) = 10x - 1000$

c.   Breakeven when $P = 0$
Thus $10x - 1000 = 0$
$$
\begin{array}{rcl}
10x & = & 1000 \\
x & = & 100
\end{array}
$$

16.a. max $6x + 4y$

b.
$$50x + 30y \le 80,000$$
$$50x \quad\quad \le 50,000$$
$$30y \le 45,000$$

$x, y \ge 0.$

17.a. $s_j = s_{j-1} + x_j - d_j$

or $s_j - s_{j-1} - x_j + d_j = 0$

b. $x_j \le c_j$

c. $s_j \ge I_j$

Chapter 2
Introduction to Probability

Learning Objectives

1. Obtain an appreciation of the role probability information plays in the decision making process.

2. Understand probability as a numerical measure of the likelihood of occurrence.

3. Know the three methods commonly used for assigning probabilities and understand when they should be used.

4. Know how to use the laws that are available for computing the probabilities of events.

5. Understand how new information can be used to revise initial (prior) probability estimates using Bayes' theorem.

6. Know the definition of the following terms:

    experiment   addition law
    sample space   mutually exclusive
    event   conditional probability
    complement   independent events
    Venn Diagram   multiplication law
    union of events   prior probability
    intersection of events   posterior probability
    Bayes' theorem

Solutions

1.   The sample points are: major defect, minor defect, no defect.

2. a.   52; one for each card.

   b.   Classical; each outcome is equally likely.

   c.   1/52 for each sample point or card selected.

   d. $0 \leq P(E_i) \leq 1$ since $P(E_i) = 1/52$ for each sample point.

$$\Sigma P(E_i) = 1/52 + 1/52 + \cdots + 1/52 = 1$$

3. a. $S = \{\text{ace of clubs, ace of diamonds, ace of hearts, ace of spades}\}$

   b. $S = \{\text{2 of clubs, 3 of clubs, ..., 10 of clubs, J of clubs, Q of clubs, K of clubs, A of clubs}\}$

   c.   There are 12; jack, queen, or king in each of the four suits.

   d.   For a: $4/52 = 1/13 = 0.08$
        For b: $13/52 = 1/4 = 0.25$
        For c: $12/52 = 0.23$

4. a.   0; probability is 0.05

   b.   4,5; probability is $0.10 + 0.10 = 0.20$

   c.   0,1,2; probability is $0.05 + 0.15 + 0.35 = 0.55$

5. a.   The relative frequency approach using the data available.

   b. $\text{P(never married)} = \dfrac{1106}{2038} = 0.5427$

        $\text{P(married)} = \dfrac{826}{2038} = 0.4053$

        $\text{P(other)} = \dfrac{106}{2038} = 0.0520$

   Note that the sum of the probabilities equals 1.

6. a.   Six, one for each possible number of refrigerators sold: 0, 1, 2, 3, 4, 5.

   b.   Relative frequency based on the historical data.

c.

E_1	=	0 sales	$P(E_1)$	=	6/50	=	0.12
E_2	=	1 sale	$P(E_2)$	=	12/50	=	0.24
E_3	=	2 sales	$P(E_3)$	=	15/50	=	0.30
E_4	=	3 sales	$P(E_4)$	=	10/50	=	0.20
E_5	=	4 sales	$P(E_5)$	=	5/50	=	0.10
E_6	=	5 sales	$P(E_6)$	=	2/50	=	0.04

The probabilities are all greater than or equal to zero and they sum to one so the two basic requirements are satisfied.

7. a. No, the probabilities do not sum to one. They sum to 0.85.

   b. Owner must revise the probabilities so that they sum to 1.00.

8. a. $P(A) = P(\$150 \text{ but less than } \$200) + P(\$200 \text{ and over})$

   $$= \frac{26}{100} + \frac{5}{100}$$

   $$= 0.31$$

   b. $P(B) = P(\text{less than } \$50) + P(\$50 \text{ but less than } \$100) + P(\$100 \text{ but less than } \$150)$
   $$= 0.13 + 0.22 + 0.34$$
   $$= 0.69$$

9.   Let: E = event patient treated experienced eye relief.
       S = event patient treated had skin rash clear up.

   Given:

   $$P(E) = \frac{90}{250} = 0.36$$

   $$P(S) = \frac{135}{250} = 0.54$$

   $$P(E \cap S) = \frac{45}{250} = 0.18$$

   $$P(E \cup S) = P(E) + P(S) - P(E \cap S)$$
   $$= 0.36 + 0.54 - 0.18$$
   $$= 0.72$$

10. Let: J = event student had a part-time job.
     D = event student made the Dean's list.

     Given:

$$P(J) \quad = \quad \frac{40}{100} = 0.40$$

$$P(D) \quad = \quad \frac{25}{100} = 0.25$$

$$P(J \cap D) \quad = \quad \frac{15}{100} = 0.15$$

$$P(J \cup D) \quad = \quad P(J) + P(D) - P(J \cap D)$$
$$= \quad 0.40 + 0.25 - 0.15$$
$$= \quad 0.50$$

11.a. $P(A) = P(E_1) + P(E_4) + P(E_6) = 0.05 + 0.25 + 0.10 = 0.40$

$P(B) = P(E_2) + P(E_4) + P(E_7) = 0.20 + 0.25 + 0.05 = 0.50$

$P(C) = P(E_2) + P(E_3) + P(E_5) + P(E_7) = 0.20 + 0.20 + 0.15 + 0.05 = 0.60$

b. $A \cup B = \{E_1, E_2, E_4, E_6, E_7\}$

$$P(A \cup B) = P(E_1) + P(E_2) + P(E_4) + P(E_6) + P(E_7)$$
$$= 0.05 + 0.20 + 0.25 + 0.10 + 0.05$$
$$= 0.65$$

c. $A \cap B = \{E_4\}$ $P(A \cap B) = P(E_4) = 0.25$

d. Yes, they are mutually exclusive.

e. $B^c = \{E_1, E_3, E_5, E_6\}$ $P(B^c) = P(E_1) + P(E_3) + P(E_5) + P(E_6)$
$$= 0.05 + 0.20 + 0.15 + 0.10$$
$$= 0.50$$

12.a. A and B are not mutually exclusive. There is not enough information to compute $P(A \cap B)$.

b. B and C are mutually exclusive assuming both could not be identified as the primary cause of death.

$$P(B \cup C) = P(B) + P(C) = 0.25 + 0.20 = 0.45$$

c. $P(C^c) = 1 - P(C) = 1 - 0.20 = 0.80.$

13.a. Let: A = event that the first car starts
       B = event that the second car starts

   Given: $P(A) = 0.80$, $P(B) = 0.40$, $P(A \cap B) = 0.30$

  b. $P(A \cup B) = P(A) + P(B) - P(A \cap B)$
      $= 0.80 + 0.40 - 0.30 = 0.90$

  c.

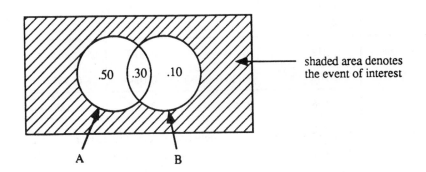

shaded area denotes
the event of interest

A   B

   $1 - P(A \cup B) = 1 - (0.50 + 0.30 + 0.10) = 0.10$

14.a. Yes; the person cannot be in an automobile and a bus at the same time.

  b. $P(B^c) = 1 - P(B) = 1 - 0.35 = 0.65$

15.a.

	Single	Married	Total
Under 30	0.55	0.10	0.65
30 or over	0.20	0.15	0.35
Total	0.75	0.25	1.00

  b. 65% of the customers are under 30.

  c. The majority of customers are single: $P(\text{single}) = 0.75$.

  d. 0.55

  e. Let: A = event under 30
       B = event single

$$P(B|A) = \frac{P(A \cap B)}{P(A)} = \frac{0.55}{0.65} = 0.8462$$

f. $P(A \cap B) = 0.55$

$$P(A)P(B) = (0.65)(0.75) = 0.49$$

Since $P(A \cap B) \neq P(A)P(B)$ they cannot be independent events; or, since $P(B|A) \neq P(B)$ they cannot be independent.

16.a.

	Reason for Applying			
	Quality	Cost/Convenience	Other	Total
Full Time	0.218	0.204	0.039	0.461
Part Time	0.208	0.307	0.024	0.539
Total	0.426	0.511	0.063	1.00

b. It is most likely a student will cite cost or convenience as the first reason: probability = 0.511. School quality is the first reason cited by the second largest number of students: probability = 0.426.

c. $P(\text{Quality}|\text{full time}) = 0.218/0.461 = 0.473$

d. $P(\text{Quality}|\text{part time}) = 0.208/0.539 = 0.386$

e. $P(B) = 0.426$ and $P(B|A) = 0.473$

Since $P(B) \neq P(B|A)$, the events are dependent.

17.a.

		Do you own a US car?		
		Yes	No	Total
Do you own a foreign car?	Yes	0.15	0.05	0.20
	No	0.75	0.05	0.80
	Total	0.90	0.10	1.00

b. 20% own a foreign car; 90% own a US car

c. 0.15

d. Let: A = foreign car
B = US car

$$
\begin{aligned}
P(A \cup B) &= P(A) + P(B) - P(A \cap B) \\
&= 0.20 + 0.90 - 0.15 = 0.95
\end{aligned}
$$

e. $P(A|B) = \dfrac{P(A \cap B)}{P(B)} = \dfrac{0.15}{0.90} = 0.17$

f. $P(B|A) = \dfrac{P(A \cap B)}{P(A)} = \dfrac{0.15}{0.20} = 0.75$

g. $P(A)P(B) = (0.20)(0.90) = 0.18$; since $P(A \cap B) = 0.15$, the events are not independent.

18.a. Let: A = event Ms. Smith gets the first job
B = event Ms. Smith gets the second job

Given: $P(A) = 0.50$, $P(B) = 0.60$, $P(A \cap B) = 0.15$

b. $P(B|A) = \dfrac{P(A \cap B)}{P(A)} = \dfrac{0.15}{0.50} = 0.30$

c. $P(A \cup B) = P(A) + P(B) - P(A \cap B)$
$= 0.50 + 0.60 - 0.15 = 0.95$

d.

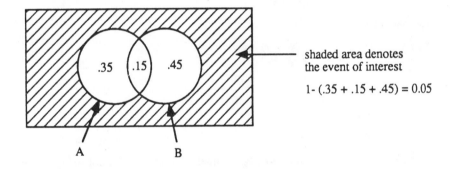

shaded area denotes
the event of interest

$1 - (.35 + .15 + .45) = 0.05$

e. $P(B|A) \neq P(B)$; the events are not independent.

19.a.

		Son		
		Attended College	Did Not Attend College	Total
Father	Attended College	0.2250	0.0875	0.3125
	Did Not Attend College	0.2750	0.4125	0.6875
	Total	0.5000	0.5000	1.0000

b. Son has a higher probability of having attended college.

c. Let: A = son attends college
B = father attends college

$$P(A|B) = \frac{P(A \cap B)}{P(B)} = \frac{0.2250}{0.3125} = 0.72$$

d. $P(A|B^c) = \frac{P(A \cap B^c)}{P(B^c)} = \frac{0.2750}{0.6875} = 0.40$

e. $P(A|B) \neq P(A)$; $\therefore$ the events are not independent.

20. Let: A = event of a well drilled in a Type A structure
B = event a well is productive

Given: $P(A|B) = 0.40$, $P(A) = 0.50$, $P(B) = 0.30$

a. $P(A \cap B) = P(A|B)P(B)$
$= (0.40)(0.30) = 0.12$

b. $P(B|A) = \frac{P(A \cap B)}{P(A)} = \frac{0.12}{0.50} = 0.24$

c. not independent

$$P(B|A) = 0.24 \neq P(B) = 0.30$$

21.a. $P(A \cap B) = 0$

b. $P(A|B) = \frac{P(A \cap B)}{P(B)} = \frac{0}{0.40} = 0$

c. No. $P(A|B) \neq P(A)$; $\therefore$ the events, although mutually exclusive, are not independent.

d. Mutually exclusive events are dependent.

22.a. $P(A \cap B) = P(A)P(B) = (0.55)(0.35) = 0.19$

b. $P(A \cup B) = P(A) + P(B) - P(A \cap B) = 0.90 - 0.19 = 0.71$

c. $1 - 0.71 = 0.29$

23.a. $P(T) = 0.50$, $P(B) = 0.30$, $P(T \cap B) = 0.20$

b. No since $P(T \cap B) \neq 0$.

c. $P(B \mid T) = \frac{P(T \cap B)}{P(T)} = \frac{0.20}{0.50} = 0.40$

d.   No, $P(B|T) \neq P(B)$.

e.   Probability of buying the product increases to 0.40.

24.a.

	Smoker	Nonsmoker	Total
Record of Heart Disease	0.10	0.08	0.18
No Record of Heart Disease	0.20	0.62	0.82
Total	0.30	0.70	1.00

b. $P(S \cap H) = 0.10$

c.   30% are smokers, 70% are nonsmokers; 18% have a record of heart disease, 82% have no record of heart disease.

d. $P(H|S) = \dfrac{P(H \cap S)}{P(S)} = \dfrac{0.10}{0.30} = 0.333$

e. $P(H|S^\circ) = \dfrac{P(H \cap S^\circ)}{P(S^\circ)} = \dfrac{0.08}{0.70} = 0.114$

f. $P(H|S) \neq P(H)$; $\therefore$ the events are not independent

g.   Smokers have a higher probability of having heart disease.

25.a. $P(B|S) = \dfrac{P(B \cap S)}{P(S)} = \dfrac{0.12}{0.40} = 0.30$

We have $P(B|S) > P(B)$.
Yes, continue the ad since it increases the probability of a purchase.

b.   Estimate the company's market share at 20%. Continuing the advertisement should increase the market share.

c. $P(B|S) = \dfrac{P(B \cap S)}{P(S)} = \dfrac{0.10}{0.30} = 0.3333$

The second ad has a bigger effect.

26.a. $P(B) = 0.25$

   $P(S|B) = 0.40$
   $P(S \cap B) = 0.25(0.40) = 0.10$

b. $P(B|S) = \dfrac{P(S \cap B)}{P(S)} = \dfrac{0.10}{0.40} = 0.25$

c. B and S are independent. The program appears to have no effect.

27. Let: A = lost time accident in current year
   B = lost time accident previous year

   ∴ Given: $P(B) = 0.06$, $P(A) = 0.05$, $P(A|B) = 0.15$

a. $P(A \cap B) = P(A|B)P(B) = 0.15(0.06) = 0.009$

b. $P(A \cup B) = P(A) + P(B) - P(A \cap B)$
   $= 0.06 + 0.05 - 0.009 = 0.101$ or 10.1%

c. $1 - 0.71 = 0.29$

28.a. $P(B \cap A_1) = P(A_1)P(B|A_1) = (0.20)(0.50) = 0.10$

   $P(B \cap A_2) = P(A_2)P(B|A_2) = (0.50)(0.40) = 0.20$

   $P(B \cap A_3) = P(A_3)P(B|A_3) = (0.30)(0.30) = 0.09$

b. $P(A_2|B) = \dfrac{0.20}{0.10 + 0.20 + 0.09} = 0.51$

c.

Events	$P(A_i)$	$P(B|A_i)$	$P(A_i \cap B)$	$P(A_i|B)$
A_1	0.20	0.50	0.10	0.26
A_2	0.50	0.40	0.20	0.51
A_3	0.30	0.30	0.09	0.23
	1.00		0.39	1.00

29. S_1 = successful, S_2 = not successful and B = request received for additional information.

a. $P(S_1) = 0.50$

b. $P(B|S_1) = 0.75$

c. $P(S_1|B) = \dfrac{(0.50)(0.75)}{(0.50)(0.75) + (0.50)(0.40)} = \dfrac{0.375}{0.575} = 0.65$

30. M = missed payment

   D_1 = customer defaults
   D_2 = customer does not default

   $P(D_1) = 0.05$ $\qquad$ $P(D_2) = 0.95$ $\qquad$ $P(M|D_2) = 0.2$ $\qquad$ $P(M|D_1) = 1$

a. $P(D_1|M) = \dfrac{P(D_1)P(MLINED_1)}{P(D_1)P(MLINED_1) + P(D_2)P(M|D_2)}$

$= 0.05/0.24 = 0.21$

b. Yes, the probability of default is greater than 0.20.

31. Let: A = event driver is 30 or older
    B = event driver has a traffic violation in a 12 month period

Given: $P(A) = 0.60$, $P(A^c) = 0.40$
$P(B|A) = 0.04$, $P(B \cap A^c) = 0.10$

$$P(A^c|B) = \frac{P(A^c)P(B|A^c)}{P(A)P(B|A) + P(A^c)P(B|A^c)}$$

$$= \frac{(0.40)(0.10)}{(0.6)(0.04) + (0.40)(0.10)}$$

$$= \frac{0.040}{0.024 + 0.040}$$

$$= \frac{0.040}{0.064} = 0.625$$

32. Let: H = event this game is at home
    W = event the team wins

Given: $P(H) = 0.55$, $P(H^c) = 0.45$
$P(W|H) = 0.80$, $P(W|H^c) = 0.65$

$$P(H|W) = \frac{P(H)P(W|H)}{P(H)P(W|H) + P(H^c)P(W|H^c)}$$

$$= \frac{(0.55)(0.80)}{(0.55)(0.80) + (0.45)(0.65)}$$

$$= \frac{0.4400}{0.4400 + 0.2925}$$

$$= \frac{0.4400}{0.7325} = 0.60$$

33.a. $P(\text{Oil}) = 0.50 + 0.20 = 0.70$

b. Let S = Soil test results

Events	$P(A_i)$	$P(S\,|\,A_i)$	$P(A_i \cap S)$	$P(A_i\,|\,S)$
High Quality (A_1)	0.50	0.20	0.10	0.31
Medium Quality (A_2)	0.20	0.80	0.16	0.50
No Oil (A_3)	0.30	0.20	0.06	0.19
	1.00	$P(S) =$	0.32	1.00

$P(\text{Oil}) = 0.81$ which is good; however, probabilities now favor medium quality rather than high quality oil.

34.a. & b.

Let: D = first part tested is defective
G = second part tested is good

Events	$P(A_i)$	$P(D\,|\,A_i)$	$P(A_i \cap D)$	$P(A_i\,|\,D)$
Correct Adjustment	0.90	0.05	0.045	0.375
Incorrect Adjustment	0.10	0.75	0.075	0.625
	1.00	$P(D) =$	0.120	1.000

$P(\text{Defect}) = 0.12 \quad P(\text{Incorrect}\,|\,\text{Defect}) = 0.625$
∴ check machine adjustment.

c.

Events	$P(A_i)$	$P(G\,|\,A_i)$	$P(A_i \cap G)$	$P(A_i\,|\,G)$
Correct Adjustment	0.375	0.95	0.356	0.695
Incorrect Adjustment	0.625	0.25	0.156	0.305
	1.000	$P(G) =$	0.512	1.000

Now probability of incorrect adjustment is 0.305. This is still high. Either check adjustment now, or perhaps preferred, continue sampling and revising probabilities until probabilities show a clear-cut decision.

35.

Events	$P(A_i)$	$P(D\,|\,A_i)$	$P(A_i \cap D)$	$P(A_i\,|\,D)$
Supplier A	0.60	0.0025	0.0015	0.23
Supplier B	0.30	0.0100	0.0030	0.46
Supplier C	0.10	0.0200	0.0020	0.31
	1.00	$P(S) =$	0.0065	1.00

a. $P(D) = 0.0065$

b. B is the most likely supplier if a defect is found.

36.a. A_1 = field will produce oil
A_2 = field will not produce oil
W = well produces oil

Events	$P(A_i)$	$P(W^c|A_i)$	$P(W^c \cap A_i)$	$P(A_i|W^c)$
Oil in Field	0.25	0.20	0.05	0.0625
No Oil in Field	0.75	1.00	0.75	0.9375
	1.00		0.80	1.0000

The probability the field will produce oil given a well comes up dry is 0.0625.

b.

Events	$P(A_i)$	$P(W^c|A_i)$	$P(W^c \cap A_i)$	$P(A_i|W^c)$
Oil in Field	0.0625	0.20	0.0125	0.0132
No Oil in Field	0.9375	1.00	0.9375	0.9868
	1.0000		0.9500	1.0000

The probability the well will produce oil drops further to 0.0132.

c. Suppose a third well comes up dry. The probabilities are revised as follows:

Events	$P(A_i)$	$P(W^c|A_i)$	$P(W^c \cap A_i)$	$P(A_i|W^c)$
Oil in Field	0.0132	0.20	0.0026	0.0026
No Oil in Field	0.9868	1.00	0.9868	0.9974
	1.0000		0.9894	1.0000

Stop drilling and abandon field if three consecutive wells come up dry.

Answers to Questions for Quantitative Methods in Practice

1. Indications are that it would have been too expensive to produce a product that would meet customer specifications 100% of the time. The customer made relatively small orders suggesting that Carstab would not have wanted to adjust production for the customer when some of Carstab's current production already meets the customer's specifications. In any case Carstab did not have the testing capabilities to verify customer specifications were met even if the production process was altered for the customer.

2. Probability was helpful in that it provided a measure of the likelihood Carstab's standard production operation could provide a product that would meet the customer's specification. In addition, probability helped Carstab evaluate the new testing procedure in that it identified the conditional probability the product would meet the customer's specifications given that the product passed the specially developed Carstab test. Thus, probability was a helpful measure of the service Carstab was able to provide for the particular customer.

3.
$$P(A|B) = \frac{P(A \cap B)}{P(B)} = \frac{0.30}{0.40} = 0.75$$

This probability indicates that the testing procedure would be an improvement but it is not as good as the procedure results presented in the application. Originally the probability of meeting the customer's specifications was 0.60. The above results show that passing the Carstab test would have increased this probability to 0.75. However, the results reported in the application show that the test procedure increases the probability if meeting the customer's specifications to 0.909.

Chapter 3
Probability Distributions

Learning Objectives

1.   Understand the concepts of a random variable and a probability distribution.

2.   Learn how random variables and probability distributions can be used to provide decision making information.

3.   Know the difference between a discrete and a continuous random variable.

4.   Be able to compute and interpret the expected value and variance of a discrete random variable.

5.   Be able to compute probability values using a binomial, a Poisson, a uniform, a normal, and an exponential probability distribution.

6.   Understand the following terms:

random variable	binomial distribution
probability distribution	Poisson distribution
discrete random variable	uniform distribution
continuous random variable	normal distribution
expected value	standard normal distribution
variance	exponential distribution
standard deviation	

Solutions

1. a. values: 0,1,2,...,20
           discrete

   b. values: 0,1,2,...
           discrete

   c. values: 0,1,2,...
           discrete

   d. values: $0 \leq x \leq 8$
           continuous

   e. values: $x \geq 0$
           continuous

2. a. Yes; $f(x) \geq 0$ for all x and $\Sigma f(x) = 1$

   b. $P(1200 \text{ or less})$ $= f(1000) + f(1100) + f(1200)$
                                   $= 0.15 + 0.20 + 0.30$
                                   $= 0.65$

3. a. Yes, since $f(x) \geq 0$ for $x = 1,2,3$ and $\Sigma f(x) = f(1) + f(2) + f(3) = 1/6 + 2/6 + 3/6 = 1$

   b. $f(2) = 2/6 = 0.3333$

   c. $f(2) + f(3) = 2/6 + 3/6 = 0.8333$

4. a. $f(200)$ $= 1 - f(-100) - f(0) - f(50) - f(100) - f(150)$
                  $= 1 - 0.95 = 0.05$
       This is the probability MRA will have a $200,000 profit.

   b. $P(\text{Profit}) = f(50) + f(100) + f(150) + f(200)$
                           $= 0.30 + 0.25 + 0.10 + 0.05 = 0.70$

   c. $P(\text{at least } 100) = f(100) + f(150) + f(200)$
                                  $= 0.25 + 0.10 + 0.05 = 0.40$

5. a, b, c.

x	$f(x)$	$xf(x)$	$(x - \mu)$	$(x - \mu)^2$	$(x - \mu)^2 f(x)$
-5	20/38	-2.63	-4.74	22.47	11.83
5	18/38	2.37	5.26	27.67	13.11
	1	-0.26			24.94

$\mu = E(x) = -0.26$. One could expect to lose 26¢ per bet on the average in the long run.
$\sigma^2 = 24.94$
$\sigma = 4.99$

d.   The expected winnings on 100 bets is

$$100\mu = 100(-0.26) = -\$26.00$$

Casinos like a high volume of betting because the percentages are on their side.

6. a.

x	$f(x)$	$xf(x)$
0	0.90	0.00
200	0.04	8.00
500	0.03	15.00
1000	0.01	10.00
2000	0.01	20.00
3000	0.01	30.00
	1.00	83.00

$E(x) = 83$. If the company charged a premium of $83.00, it would break even.

b.

gain to policyholder	P(gain)
-130	0.90
70	0.04
370	0.03
870	0.01
1870	0.01
2870	0.01

E(gain) $= -47$. The policyholder is more concerned with the big accident rather than the expected annual loss of $47.

7. a. $E(x) = \Sigma xf(x)$
    $= 300(0.20) + 400(0.30) + 500(0.35) + 600(0.15)$
    $= 445$

The monthly order quantity should be 445 units.

b.
$$\begin{array}{lll}\text{Cost:} & 445 @ \$50 = \$22,250 \\ \text{Revenue:} & 300 @ \$70 = \underline{21,000} \\ & \$\,1,250 \text{ Loss}\end{array}$$

c.

x	$f(x)$	$(x - \mu)$	$(x - \mu)^2$	$(x - \mu)^2 f(x)$
300	0.20	-145	21025	4205.00
400	0.30	- 45	2025	607.50
500	0.35	+ 55	3025	1058.75
600	0.15	+155	24025	3603.75

$$\sigma^2 = 9475.00$$

$$\sigma = \sqrt{9475}$$

8. a. Medium: $E(x) = \Sigma x f(x)$
$$= 50(0.20) + 150(0.50) + 200(3.0) = 145$$
Large: $E(x) = \Sigma x f(x)$
$$= 0(0.20) + 100(0.50) + 300(0.30) = 140$$
Medium preferred.

b. <u>Medium</u>

x	$f(x)$	$(x - \mu)$	$(x - \mu)^2$	$(x - \mu)^2 f(x)$
50	0.20	-95	9025	1805.0
150	0.50	5	25	12.5
200	0.30	55	3025	907.5

$$\sigma^2 = 2725.0$$

<u>Large</u>

x	$f(x)$	$(x - \mu)$	$(x - \mu)^2$	$(x - \mu)^2 f(x)$
0	0.20	-140	19600	3920
100	0.50	- 40	1600	800
300	0.30	160	25600	7680

$$\sigma^2 = 12,400$$

Medium preferred due to less variance.

9. a. $E(x) = 1.6$

b. $\$75 E(x) = \$120.$

10.a. $f(x) \geq 0$
       $\Sigma f(x) = 0.35 + 0.25 + 0.25 + 0.10 + 0.05 = 1.0$

  b. $E(x) = \Sigma x f(x)$
       $= 16(0.35) + 17(0.25) + 18(0.25) + 19(0.10) + 20(0.05)$
       $= 17.25$

  c. $E(\text{gain}) = E(x) - 16 = 17.25 - 16 = 1.25$
       or $1.25/16.00(100) = 7.8\%$

  d.

x	$f(x)$	$(x - \mu)$	$(x - \mu)^2$	$(x - \mu)^2 f(x)$
16	0.35	-1.25	1.5625	0.5469
17	0.25	-0.25	0.0625	0.0156
18	0.25	0.75	0.5625	0.1406
19	0.10	+1.75	3.0625	0.3063
20	0.05	+2.75	7.5625	0.3781
			$\sigma^2 =$	1.3875

  e. The first stock is preferred with the lower variance of 1.3875.

11.a. Yes. Since they are selected randomly, p is the same from trial to trial and the trails are independent.

  b. 0.0574 (from binomial probability tables)

  c. 0.3487 (from binomial probability tables)

  d. $1 - P(0 \text{ Women}) = 1 - 0.3487 = 0.6513$

12. We assume the properties of a binomial experiment are satisfied.

$$f(1) = \frac{4!}{1!3!} (0.3)^1 (0.7)^3$$

$$= 4(0.3)(0.343) = 0.4116$$

$$f(2) = \frac{4!}{2!2!} (0.3)^2 (0.7)^2$$

$$= 6(0.09)(0.49) = 0.2646$$

$$f(0) = \frac{4!}{0!\,4!}(0.3)^0(0.7)^4$$

$$= 1(1)(0.2401) = 0.2401$$

13.a.
$$f(12) = \frac{12!}{12!\,0!}(0.15)^{12}(0.85)^0 = 0$$

b.
$$f(12) = \frac{12!}{12!\,0!}(0.85)^{12}(0.15)^0$$

$$= 1(0.1422)(1) = 0.1422$$

c.
$$f(1) = \frac{12!}{1!\,11!}(0.15)^1(0.85)^{11}$$

$$= 12(0.15)(0.16734) = 0.3012$$

d. $P(\text{at least } 3) = 1 - P(2 \text{ or less})$
   $P(2 \text{ or less}) = f(0) + f(1) + f(2)$

$$f(0) = \frac{12!}{0!\,12!}(0.15)^0(0.85)^{12} = 0.1422$$

$$= 0.3012 \text{ from } (c)$$

$$f(2) = \frac{12!}{2!\,10!}(0.15)^2(0.85)^{10} = 0.2924$$

$\therefore P(2 \text{ or less}) = 0.1422 + 0.3012 + 0.2924 = 0.7358$

Hence $P(\text{at least } 3) = 1 - 0.7358 = 0.2642$

14.a. 0.90

b. $P(\text{at least } 1) = f(1) + f(2)$

$$f(1) = \frac{2!}{1!\,1!}(0.9)^1(0.1)^1$$

$$= 2(0.9)(0.1) = 0.18$$

$$f(2) = \frac{2!}{2!\,0!}(0.9)^2(0.1)^0$$

$$= 1(0.81)(1) = 0.81$$

$$\therefore P(\text{at least } 1) = 0.18 + 0.81 = 0.99$$

Alternatively

$$P(\text{at least } 1) = 1 - f(0)$$

$$= \frac{2!}{0!\,2!}(0.9)^0(0.1)^2 = 0.01$$

$$\therefore P(\text{at least } 1) = 1 - 0.01 = 0.99$$

c. $P(\text{at least } 1) = 1 - f(0)$

$$f(0) = \frac{3!}{0!\,3!}(0.9)^0(0.1)^3 = 0.001$$

$$\therefore P(\text{at least } 1) = 1 - 0.001 = 0.999$$

d. Yes; $P(\text{at least } 1)$ becomes very close to 1 with multiple systems and the inability to detect an attack would become catastrophic.

15.a. $f(0) = \dfrac{2!}{0!\,2!}(0.82)^0(0.18)^2 = 0.0324$

$$f(1) = \frac{2!}{1!\,1!}(0.82)^1(0.18)^1 = 0.2952$$

$$f(2) = \frac{2!}{2!\,0!}(0.82)^2(0.18)^0 = 0.6724$$

b. Similar to *a* except $p = 0.56$; $f(0) = 0.1936$, $f(1) = 0.4928$. $f(2) = 0.3136$

c. Yes, foul the player with the worst free throw percentage.

16.a. $f(1) = \dfrac{5!}{1!\,4!}(0.03)^1(0.97)^4 = 0.1328$

b. $1 - f(0) = 1 - 0.8587 = 0.1413$

17. Since the shipment is large we can assume that the probabilities do not change from trial to trail and use the binomial probability distribution.

a. $n = 5$

$$f(0) = \frac{5!}{0!\,5!}(0.01)^0(0.99)^5 = 0.9510$$

b. $f(1) = \dfrac{5!}{1!4!} (0.1)^1(0.99)^4 = 0.0480$

c. $1 - f(0) = 1 - 0.9510 = 0.0490$

d. No, the probability of finding one or more items in the sample defective when only 1% of the items in the population are defective is small (only 0.0490). We would consider it likely that more than 1% of the items are defective.

18.a. 5 minutes is 1/6 of a half-hour.

$$f(0) = \frac{(15/6)^0 e^{-15/6}}{0!}$$

$$= e^{-2.5}$$

$$= 0.0821$$

b. $f(8) = \dfrac{5^8 e^{-5}}{8!} = 0.0653$

c. $1 - [f(0) + f(1) + f(2) + f(3) + f(4) + f(5)]$
$= 1 - [0.0067 + 0.0337 + 0.0842 + 0.1404 + 0.1755 + 0.1755]$
$= 1 - 0.6160$
$= 0.3840$

19.a. Set $\mu = (1.5)(2) = 3$ and $x = 0$
$f(0) = 0.0498$

b. Set $\mu = (2)(2) = 4$ and $x = 2$
$f(2) = 0.1465$

c. $1 - [f(0) + f(1) + f(2) + f(3)]$
$= 1 - 0.6472$
$= 0.3528$

d. Set $\mu = 7$ and $x = 0$
$f(0) = 0.0009$

20.a. $f(0) = \dfrac{10^0 e^{-10}}{0!} = e^{-10} = 0.000045$

b. $f(0) + f(1) + f(2) + f(3)$

$f(0) = 0.000045$ (part a)

$f(1) = \dfrac{10^1 e^{-10}}{1!} = 0.00045$

Similarly, $f(2) = 0.00225$, $f(3) = 0.0075$
∴ $f(0) + f(1) + f(2) + f(3) = 0.010245$

c. 15 second period, ∴ 2.5 arrivals/15 second period

$f(0) = \dfrac{2.5^0 e^{-2.5}}{0!} = 0.0821$

d. $1 - f(0) = 1 - 0.0821 = 0.9179$

21. $\mu = 15$

prob of 20 or more arrivals $= f(20) + f(21) + \cdots$
$\qquad = 0.0418 + 0.0299 + 0.0204 + 0.0133 + 0.0083 + 0.0050 + 0.0029$
$\qquad + 0.0016 + 0.0009 + 0.0004 + 0.0002 + 0.0001 + 0.0001$
$\qquad = 0.1249$

22. $\mu = 1.5$
prob of 3 more breakdowns is $1 - [f(0) + f(1) + f(2)]$.

$1 - [f(0) + f(1) + f(2)]$
$= 1 - [0.2231 + 0.3347 + 0.2510]$
$= 1 - 0.8088$
$= 0.1912$

23.a. $f(8) = \dfrac{8^8 e^{-8}}{8!} = \dfrac{(16,777,216)(0.000335)}{40,320} = 0.1394$

b. 1/2 hour period: 4/period

$f(3) = \dfrac{4^3 e^{-4}}{3!} = \dfrac{64(0.0183)}{6} = 0.1952$

24.a.

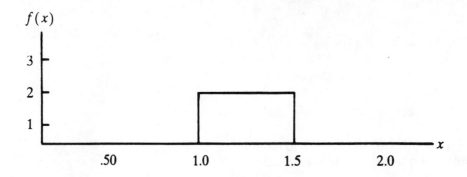

b. $P(x = 1.25) = 0$. the probability of any single point is zero since the area under the curve above any single point is zero.

c. $P(1.0 \leq x \leq 1.25) = 2(0.25) = 0.50$

d. $P(1.20 < x < 1.5) = 2(0.30) = 0.60$

25.a.

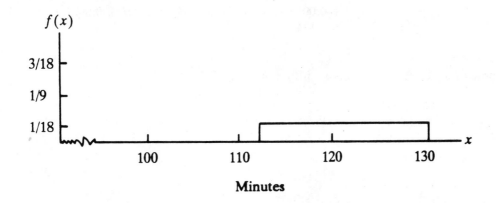

b. $P(x \leq 117) = \dfrac{1}{18}\ (5) = 0.2778$

c. $P(x > 122) = \dfrac{1}{18}\ (8) = 0.4444$

26.a.

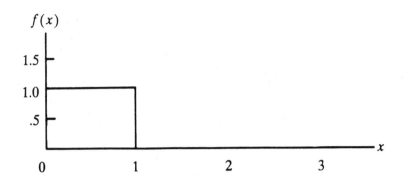

b. $P(0.25 < x < 0.75) = 1(0.50) = 0.50$

c. $P(x \leq 0.30) = 1(0.30) = 0.30$

d. $P(x > 0.60) = 1(0.40) = 0.40$

27.a. $f(x) = \begin{cases} 1/4 & \text{for } 3 \leq x \leq 7 \\ 0 & \text{elsewhere} \end{cases}$

b. $P(x < 3) = 0$

c. $P(x \leq 5) = \dfrac{1}{4}\ (2) = 0.50$

28.a. $P(12 \leq x \leq 12.05) = 0.05(8) = 0.40$

b. $P(x \geq 12.02) = 0.08(8) = 0.64$

c.

$$P(x < 11.98) \quad + \quad P(x > 12.02)$$

$$\downarrow \qquad\qquad\qquad \downarrow$$

$$0.005(8) = 0.04 \qquad\qquad 0.64$$

Therefore, the probability is $0.04 + 0.64 = 0.68$

29.a. $f(x) = \begin{cases} 1/5 & \text{for } 0 \leq x \leq 5 \\ 0 & \text{elsewhere} \end{cases}$

b. $P(x > 3.5) = 3.0$

c. $P(x \leq 0.75) = 0.15$

d. $P(1 < x < 3) = 0.40$

30.

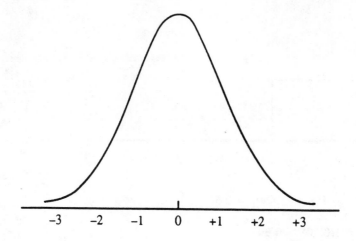

a.   0.3413

b.   0.4332

c.   0.4772

d.   0.4938

31.a.   0.2967

b.   0.4418

c.   0.5000 - 0.1700 = 0.3300

d.   0.0910 + 0.5000 = 0.5910

e.   0.3849 + 0.5000 = 0.8849

f.   0.5000 - 0.2612 = 0.2388

32.a.   Using the table of areas for the standard normal probability distribution, the area of 0.4750 corresponds to $z = 1.96$.

b.   Using the table, the area of 0.2291 corresponds to $z = 0.61$.

c.   Look in the table for an area of 0.5000 - 0.1314 = 0.3686. This provides $z = 1.12$.

d.   Look in the table for an area of 0.6700 - 0.5000 = 0.1700. This provides $z = 0.44$.

33.a. Look in the table for an area of 0.5000 - 0.2119 = 0.2881. Since the value we are seeking is below the mean, the z value must be negative. Thus, for an area of 0.2881, z = -0.80.

b. Look in the table for an area of 0.9030/2 = 0.4515; z = 1.66.

c. Look in the table for an area of 0.2025/2 = 0.1026; z = 0.26.

d. Look in the table for an area of 0.9948- 0.5000 = 0.4948; z = 2.56.

e. Look in the table for an area of 0.6915 - 0.5000 = 0.1915. Since the value we are seeking is below the mean, the z value must be negative. Thus, z = -0.50.

34.a. At x = 180

$$z = \frac{180 - 200}{40} = -0.50$$

At x = 220

$$z = \frac{220 - 200}{40} = +0.50$$

$$\underline{Area}$$
$$0.1915$$
$$\underline{0.1915}$$
$$P(180 \leq x \leq 220) = 0.3830$$

b. At x = 250

$$z = \frac{250 - 200}{40} = 1.25 \qquad Area = 0.3944$$

$$P(x \geq 250) = 0.5000 - 0.3944 = 0.1056$$

c. At x = 100

$$z = \frac{100 - 200}{40} = -2.50 \qquad Area = 0.4938$$

$$P(x \leq 100) = 0.5000 - 0.4938 = 0.0062$$

d. At x = 250

$$z = 1.25 \qquad Area = 0.3944$$

At x = 225

$$z = \frac{225 - 200}{40} = 0.625 \qquad Area = 0.2341$$

$$P(225 \leq x \leq 250) = 0.3944 - 0.2341 = 0.1603$$

35. a.   At $x = 800$

$$z = \frac{800 - 550}{150} = \frac{250}{150} = 1.67$$

From tables, $P(x \geq 800)$ is $0.5000 - 0.4525 = 0.0475$
or 4.75% of customers

b.   At $x = 200$

$$z = \frac{200 - 550}{150} = \frac{-350}{150} = -2.33$$

From tables, $P(x < 200)$ is $0.5000 - 0.4901 = 0.0099$
or 0.99% of customers

c. $P(300 < x < 700)$ is 0.7938.
or 79.38% of customers

d.   At $z = 1.645$ we have an area of 0.05 in the upper tail.

$$1.645 = \frac{x - 550}{150} \rightarrow x = 550 + 1.645(150)$$

$$= 550 + 246.75$$
$$= 796.75$$

The bank should not pay interest on balances below \$796.75. In practice this amount would probably be rounded off to \$800.00.

36. a.   At $z = -0.77$ we have an area of 0.2206 or approximately 0.22 in the lower tail.

$$-0.77 = \frac{x - 3.25}{0.5}$$

$\therefore x = 0.5(-0.77) + 3.25 = 2.865$
2.865 years is the manufacturer's advertised life.

b.   At $x = 3$

$$z = \frac{3 - 3.25}{0.5} = -0.5$$

At $x = 4$

$$z = \frac{4 - 3.25}{0.5} = 1.5$$

	Area
	0.1915
	0.4332
$P(3 \leq x \leq 4) =$	0.6247

37.a.   At $x = 4760$

$$z = \frac{4760 - 5000}{800} = -0.3$$

At $x = 5800$

$$z = \frac{5800 - 5000}{800} = 1$$

$$\begin{array}{r}
\underline{\text{Area}} \\
0.1179 \\
\underline{0.3413} \\
P(4760 \leq x \leq 5800) = 0.4592
\end{array}$$

b. $$z = \frac{6500 - 5000}{800} = 1.875 \approx 1.88$$

Area $= 0.5 - 0.4699 = 0.0301 =$ Probability of more than 6500 customers.

c.   At $z = -1.28$ we have an area of 0.1003 or approximately 0.10 in the lower tail.

$$-1.28 = \frac{x - 5000}{800}$$

∴ $x = 800(-1.28) + 5000 = 3,976$

The number of customers exceeds 3,976 90% of the time.

38.a. $\mu = 10,000$ $\sigma = 1500$

At $x = 12,000$

$$z = \frac{12,000 - 10,000}{1500} = 1.33 \quad \text{Area} = 0.4082$$

$$P(x > 12,000) = 0.5000 - 0.4082 = 0.0918$$

b.   At 0.95

$$z = 1.645 = \frac{x - 10,000}{1500}$$

∴ $x = 10,000 + 1.645(1500) = 12,468.$

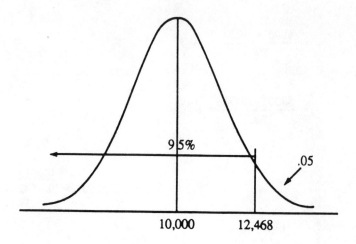

10,000   12,468

12,468 tubes should be produced.

39.a.   At 400,

$$z = \frac{400 - 450}{100} = -0.50 \qquad \text{Area} = 0.1915$$

At 500,

$$z = \frac{500 - 450}{100} = +0.50 \qquad \text{Area} = \underline{0.1915}$$

$$0.3830 \text{ or } 38.3\%$$

b.   At 630,

$$z = \frac{630 - 450}{100} = 1.80 \qquad \text{Area} = 0.5000 - 0.4641$$

$$= 0.0359 \text{ or } 3.59\%$$

3.59% do better and 96.41% do worse.

c.   At 480,

$$z = \frac{480 - 450}{100} = 0.30 \qquad \text{Area} = 0.5000 - 0.1179$$

$$= 0.3821 \text{ or } 38.21\%$$

38.21% are acceptable.

40. $\sigma = 0.6$
        At 2%

$$z = -2.05 \qquad x = 18$$

$$z = \frac{x - \mu}{\sigma} \qquad \therefore -2.05 = \frac{18 - \mu}{0.6}$$

$$\mu = 18 + 2.05(0.6) = 19.23 \text{ oz.}$$

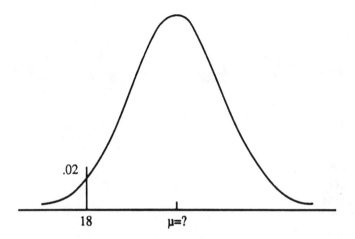

The mean filling weight must be 19.23 oz.

41.a.

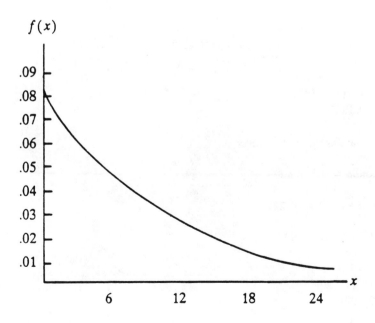

b. $P(x \le 12) = 1 - e^{-12/12} = 0.6321$

c. $P(x \le 6) = 1 - e^{-6/12} = 0.3935$

d. $P(x \ge 30) = 1 - P(x < 30)$
$$= 1 - (1 - e^{-30/12})$$
$$= 0.0821$$

42.a. 50 hours

b. $P(x \le 25) = 1 - e^{-25/50} = 0.3935$

c. $P(x \ge 100) = 1 - (1 - e^{-100/50}) = 0.1353$

43.a. 4 hours

b. $f(x) = \dfrac{1}{4} e^{-x/4}$ for $x \ge 0$

c. $P(x \ge 1) = 1 - P(x < 1)$
$$= 1 - (1 - e^{-1/4})$$
$$= 0.7788$$

d. $P(x > 8) = 1 - P(x \le 8)$
$$= e^{-8/4}$$
$$= 0.1353$$

44.a. $P(x \le 15) = 1 - e^{-15/36} = 0.3408$

b. $P(x \le 45) = 1 - e^{-45/36} = 0.7135$

Therefore $P(15 \le x \le 45) = 0.7135 - 0.3408 = 0.3727$

c. $P(x \ge 60) = 1 - P(x < 60)$
$$= 1 - (1 - e^{-60/36})$$
$$= 0.1889$$

45.a. $1/\mu = 0.5$ therefore $\mu = 2$ minutes

b. Note: 30 seconds = 0.5 minutes

$P(x \le 0.5) = 1 - e^{-0.5/2} = 0.2212$

c. $P(x \le 1) = 1 - e^{-1/2} = 0.3935$

d. $P(x \ge 5) = 1 - P(x < 5)$
$$= 1 - (1 - e^{-5/2})$$
$$= 0.0821$$

46.a. $f(x) = \dfrac{1}{1.2} e^{-x/1.2}$ for $x \geq 0$

b. $P(0.5 \leq x \leq 1.0) = P(x \leq 1.0) - P(x \leq 0.5)$
$$= (1 - e^{-1/1.2}) - 1 - e^{-0.5/1.2})$$
$$= 0.5654 - 0.3408$$
$$= 0.2246$$

c. $P(x > 1) = 1 - P(x \leq 1)$
$$= 1 - 0.5654$$
$$= 0.4346$$

Answers to Questions for Quantitative Methods in Practice

1. The simulation model provided a representation of the on-line computerized publication system. The probability distribution in ˉle 3.10 was used to determine how long each user who accessed the system would be on line. By knowing the length of time between sessions and the time a user was on line, the simulation model could determine the percentage of time the system was fully utilized and as a result, the probability that a new user would be refused access to the system.

2.

x	$f(x)$	$xf(x)$
10	0.05	0.5
20	0.06	1.2
30	0.08	2.4
40	0.20	8.0
50	0.25	12.5
60	0.20	12.0
70	0.08	5.6
80	0.06	4.8
90	0.02	1.8
	$E(x) =$	48.8 minutes

The average time a user is on the system is 48.8 minutes.

3.

x	$(x - \mu)$	$(x - \mu)^2$	$(x - \mu)^2 f(x)$
10	- 38.8	1505.44	75.2720
20	- 28.8	829.44	49.7664
30	- 18.8	353.44	28.2752
40	- 8.8	77.44	15.4880
50	+ 1.2	1.44	0.3600
60	+11.2	125.44	25.0880
70	+21.2	449.44	35.9552
80	+31.2	973.44	58.4064
90	+41.2	1697.44	33.9488
			322.5600

4. $P(35 \leq x \leq 65) = 0.20 + 0.25 + 0.20 = 0.65$

5. $\mu = 48.8$ $\sigma^2 = 322.56$ $\sigma = 17.96$

At 35,   Area

$$z = \frac{35 - 48.8}{17.96} = -0.77 \qquad 0.2794$$

At 65,

$$z = \frac{65 - 48.8}{17.96} = +0.90 \qquad 0.3159$$

$$0.5953$$

The normal distribution underestimates the probability given by the probability distribution in part 4.

Chapter 4
Decision Analysis

Learning Objectives

1. Learn how probability information and economic measures can be combined to arrive at decision recommendations.

2. Understand what is meant by the decision analysis approach to decision making.

3. Learn how to describe a problem situation in terms of its decision alternatives, states of nature, and payoffs.

4. Be able to analyze a decision analysis problem from both a payoff table and decision tree point of view.

5. Be able to use sensitivity analysis to study how changes in the probability estimates for the states of nature affect or alter the recommended decision.

6. Be able to determine the potential value of additional information.

7. Learn how new information and revised probability values can be used in the decision analysis approach to problem solving.

8. Be able to use a Bayesian approach to computing revised probabilities.

9. Understand what a decision strategy or decision rule is.

10. Learn how to evaluate the contribution and efficiency of additional decision making information.

11. Understand the following terms:

decision alternatives	prior probabilities
states of nature	posterior probabilities
payoff table	Bayesian revision
decision tree	decision strategy
optimistic approach	expected value of sample information (EVSI)
conservative approach	efficiency of sample information
minimax regret approach	marginal analysis
expected value approach	sensitivity analysis
expected value of perfect information (EVPI)	

Solutions

1. a.

Decision	Maximum Profit	Minimum Profit
d_1	14	5
d_2	11	7
d_3	11	9
d_4	13	8

Optimistic approach: select d_1

Conservative approach: select d_3

Regret or Opportunity Loss Table

	s_1	s_2	s_3	s_4	Maximum Regret
d_1	0	1	1	8	8
d_2	3	0	3	6	6
d_3	5	0	1	2	5
d_4	6	0	0	0	6

Minimax regret approach: select d_3

b. The choice of which approach to use is up to the decision maker. Since different approaches can result in different recommendations, the most appropriate approach should be selected before analyzing the problem.

c.

Decision	Minimum Cost	Maximum Cost
d_1	5	14
d_2	7	11
d_3	9	11
d_4	8	13

Optimistic approach: select d_1

Conservative approach: select d_2 or d_3

Regret or Opportunity Loss Table

	s_1	s_2	s_3	s_4	Maximum Regret
d_1	6	0	2	0	6
d_2	3	1	0	2	3
d_3	1	1	2	6	6
d_4	0	1	3	8	8

Minimax regret approach: select d_2

2. a.

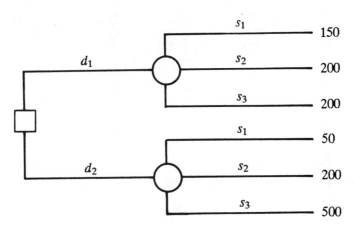

b.

Decision	Maximum Profit	Minimum Profit	Maximum Regret
d_1	200	150	300
d_2	500	50	100

Optimistic approach: select d_2

Conservative approach: select d_1

Minimax regret approach: select d_2

3. a.

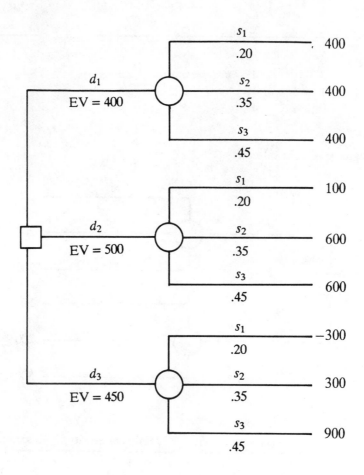

b.

Decision	Maximum Profit	Minimum Profit	Maximum Regret
d_1	400	400	500
d_2	600	100	300
d_3	900	-300	700

Optimistic approach: select d_3

Conservative approach: select d_1

Minimax regret approach: select d_2

Note: The maximum regret was obtained using the following regret or opportunity loss table.

	s_1	s_2	s_3
d_1	0	200	500
d_2	300	0	300
d_3	700	300	0

4. a. $EV(d_1) = 0.5(14) + 0.2(9) + 0.2(10) + 0.1(5) = 11.3$

$EV(d_2) = 0.5(11) + 0.2(10) + 0.2(8) + 0.1(7) = 9.8$

$EV(d_3) = 0.5(9) + 0.2(10) + 0.2(10) + 0.1(11) = 9.6$

$EV(d_4) = 0.5(8) + 0.2(10) + 0.2(11) + 0.1(13) = 9.5$

Recommended decision: d_1

b.   The best decision in this case is the one with the smallest expected value; thus, d_4, with an expected cost of 9.5, is the recommended decision.

5.   Let d_1 = develop a prototype
d_2 = do not develop a prototype
s_1 = failure
s_2 = moderate success
s_3 = major success

a.

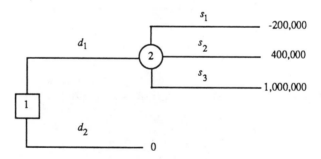

b. $EV(d_1) = 0.7(-200,000) + 0.2(400,000) + 0.1(1,000,000) = 40,000$

$EV(d_2) = 0$

Since the expected value of d_1 is \$40,000 and the expected value of d_2 is 0, JSI should develop the software.

6. $\quad\quad\quad\quad EV(d_1) = 0.2(-100) + 0.3(50) + 0.5(150) = 70$

$\quad\quad\quad\quad EV(d_2) = 0.2(100) + 0.3(100) + 0.5(100) = 100$

Recommended decision: d_2 (sell)

7. $\quad\quad\quad\quad EV(d_1) = 0.20(400) + 0.35(400) + 0.45(400) = 400$

$\quad\quad\quad\quad EV(d_2) = 0.20(100) + 0.35(600) + 0.45(600) = 500$

$\quad\quad\quad\quad EV(d_3) = 0.20(-300) + 0.35(300) + 0.45(900) = 450$

Recommended decision: d_2 (medium)

8. a. d_1 = invest $\quad\quad\quad\quad\quad\quad$ s_1 = heavy $\quad\quad\quad\quad\quad\quad$ $P(s_1) = 0.4$
$\quad\quad d_2$ = do not invest $\quad\quad\quad\quad$ s_2 = moderate $\quad\quad\quad\quad$ $P(s_2) = 0.3$
$\quad\quad\quad\quad\quad\quad\quad\quad\quad\quad\quad\quad\quad\quad$ s_3 = light $\quad\quad\quad\quad\quad\quad$ $P(s_3) = 0.3$

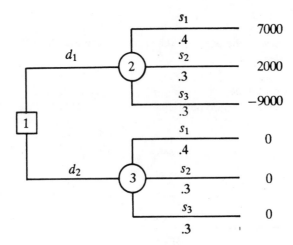

b. $\quad\quad\quad\quad EV(\text{Node } 2) = 0.4(7000) + 0.3(2000) + 0.3(-9000) = \$700$

$\quad\quad\quad\quad EV(\text{Node } 3) = 0$

c.   Recommended decision: d_1 (invest)

9. $\quad\quad$ Let $\quad d_1$ = sell the option
$\quad\quad\quad\quad\quad\quad d_2$ = purchase the property, clear the land, and prepare the site for building
$\quad\quad\quad\quad\quad\quad s_1$ = real estate market is down
$\quad\quad\quad\quad\quad\quad s_2$ = real estate market remains at the current level
$\quad\quad\quad\quad\quad\quad s_3$ = real estate market is up

$$EV(d_1) = 0.6(250,000) + 0.3(250,000) + 0.1(250,000) = 250,000$$

$$EV(d_2) = 0.6(-1,500,000) + 0.3(1,000,000) + 0.1(4,000,000) = -200,000$$

Doug should sell the option.

10.a.   Let p = probability of s_1

$$EV(d_1) = p(80) + (1 - p)50 = 30p + 50$$

$$EV(d_2) = p(65) + (1 - p)85 = -20p + 85$$

$$EV(d_3) = p(30) + (1 - p)100 = -70p + 100$$

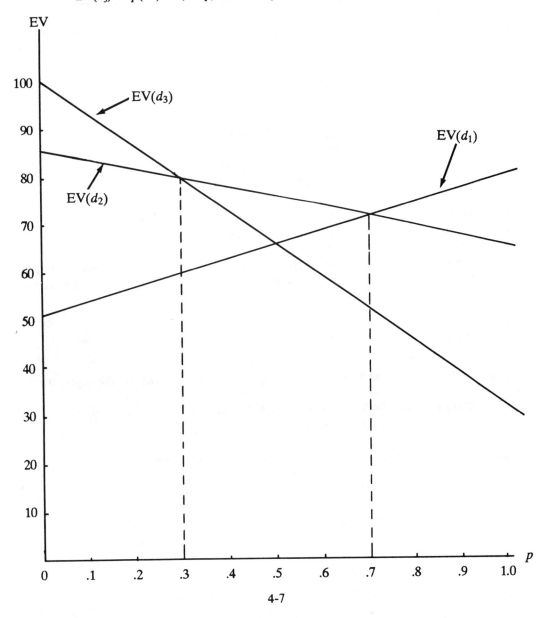

Solving for the point where EV(d_2) and EV(d_3) are equal

$$EV(d_2) = EV(d_3)$$
$$-20p + 85 = -70p + 100$$
$$\therefore p = 0.3$$

Solving for the point where EV(d_1) and EV(d_2) are equal

$$EV(d_1) = EV(d_2)$$
$$30p + 50 = -20p + 85$$
$$\therefore p = 0.7$$

Value(s) of p	Best Decision(s)
$0 \le p < 0.3$	d_3
$p = 0.3$	d_2 or d_3
$0.3 < p < 0.7$	d_2
$p = 0.7$	d_2 or d_1
$0.7 < p \le 1.0$	d_1

11.

Probabilities	Expected Value
0.5, 0.3, 0.2	$350,000
0.4, 0.4, 0.2	$600,000

These results suggest that the best decision is influenced a great deal by the probability of s_1. Problem 12 deals with how Doug can address this issue using sensitivity analysis.

12.   We are given $P(s_3) = 0.1$. First, let us determine the value of $P(s_1)$ that will result in an expected value for d_1 of $250,000, the expected value of selling the option. Denoting the unknown value of $P(s_1)$ as p, we know that
$$p + P(s_2) + 0.1 = 1$$
Thus
$$P(s_2) = 0.9 - p$$

Using p, $0.9 - p$, and 0.1 as the probabilities for s_1, s_2 and s_3, respectively, the expected value for d_2 is
$$EV(d_2) = p(-1,500,000) + (0.9 - p)(1,000,000) + 0.1(400,000)$$
$$= -2,500,000p + 1,300,000$$

Setting the expression equal to $250,000 and solving for p we obtain

$$p = 1,050,000/2,500,000 = 0.42$$

Thus, if the probability that the real estate market is down is equal to 0.42, EV(d_1) and EV(d_2) are equal. However, if $p < 0.42$, EV(d_2) will exceed $250,000 and d_2 will be the best decision.

13.a.
$$EV(d_1) = 0.4(2000) + 0.6(2000) = 2000$$

$$EV(d_2) = 0.4(2500) + 0.6(1000) = 1600$$

Recommended decision: d_1 (St. Louis)

b.   Let p = probability of s_1

$$EV(d_1) = 2000$$

$$EV(d_2) = p(2500) + (1 - p)1000 = 1500p + 1000$$

Solving for the point where $EV(d_1)$ and $EV(d_2)$ are equal

$$EV(d_1) = EV(d_2)$$
$$2000 = 1500p + 1000$$
$$\therefore p = 0.67$$

Value(s) of p	Best Decision(s)
$0 \leq p < 0.67$	d_1
$p = 0.67$	d_1 or d_2
$0.67 < p \leq 1.0$	d_2

14.   Optimal decision strategy with perfect information:

If s_1 then d_2

If s_2 then d_2

If s_3 then d_1

Expected value of this strategy is

$$0.2(100) + 0.3(100) + 0.5(150) = 125$$

EVPI = 125 - 100 = 25

15.   Optimal decision strategy with perfect information:

If s_1 then d_1

If s_2 then d_2

If s_3 then d_3

Expected value of this strategy is

$$0.2(400) + 0.35(600) + 0.45(900) = 695$$

$$EVPI = 695 - 500 = 195$$

16.a.   Let d_3 = purchase blade attachment. Recall that d_1 = purchase snowplow and d_2 = no purchase.

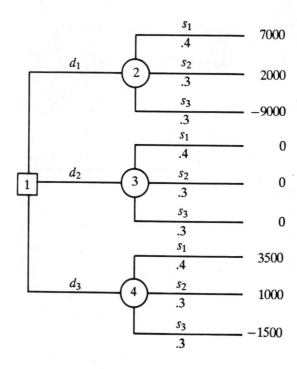

b.   From 10(b) we know that $EV(d_1) = 700$ and $EV(d_2) = 0$

$$EV(d_3) = 0.4(3500) + 0.3(1000) + 0.3(-1500) = 1250$$

Recommended decision: d_3 (purchase blade attachment)

c.   Optimal decision strategy with perfect information:

   If s_1 then d_1

   If s_2 then d_1

   If s_3 then d_2

Expected value of this strategy is

$$0.4(7000) + 0.3(2000) + 0.3(0) = 3400$$

$EVPI = 3400 - 1250 = \$2150$

17. Optimal decision strategy with perfect information:

      If s_1 occurs, then select d_2

      If s_2 occurs, then select d_1

Expected value of this strategy is

$$0.4(2500) + 0.6(2000) = 2200$$

From 9a we have

      Expected Value Without Perfect Information = 2000

Therefore,

      $EVPI = 2200 - 2000 = \$200$

18.

State of Nature	$P(s_j)$	$P(I \mid s_j)$	$P(I \cap s_j)$	$P(s_j \mid I)$
s_1	0.2	0.10	0.020	0.1905
s_2	0.5	0.05	0.025	0.2381
s_3	0.3	0.20	0.060	0.5714
	1.0	$P(I) =$	0.105	1.0000

19.a. $EV(d_1) = 0.8(15) + 0.2(10) = 14$

       $EV(d_2) = 0.8(10) + 0.2(12) = 10.4$

       $EV(d_3) = 0.8(8) + 0.2(20) = 10.4$

Recommended decision: d_1

b.   Let p = probability of s_1

       $EV(d_1) = p(15) + (1 - p)(10) = 5p + 10$

       $EV(d_2) = p(10) + (1 - p)(12) = -2p + 12$

       $EV(d_3) = p(8) + (1 - p)(20) = -12p + 20$

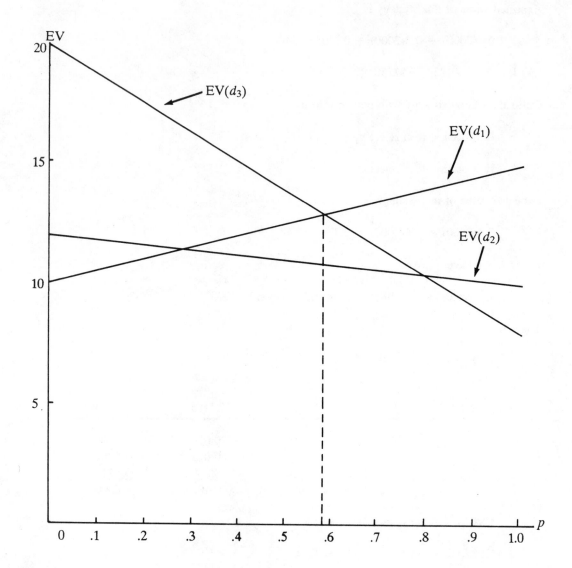

Solving for the point where EV(d_1) and EV(d_3) are equal

$$EV(d_1) = EV(d_3)$$
$$5p + 10 = -12p + 20$$
$$\therefore p = 0.59$$

Value(s) of p	Best Decision
$0 \leq p < 0.59$	d_3
$p = 0.59$	d_1 or d_3
$0.59 < p \leq 1.0$	d_1

c. Optimal decision strategy with perfect information:

If s_1 then d_1

If s_2 then d_3

Expected value of this strategy is

$0.8(15) + 0.2(20) = 16$

EVPI $= 16 - 14 = 2$

d.

State of Nature	$P(s_j)$	$P(I \mid s_j)$	$P(I \cap s_j)$	$P(s_j \mid I)$
s_1	0.8	0.20	0.16	0.5161
s_2	0.2	0.75	<u>0.15</u>	0.4839
		$P(I) =$	0.31	

$EV(d_1) = 0.5161(15) + 0.4839(10) = 12.5805$

$EV(d_2) = 0.5161(10) + 0.4839(12) = 10.9678$

$EV(d_3) = 0.5161(8) + 0.4839(20) = 13.8068$

Recommended decision: d_3

20.a. & b.

For I_1,

State of Nature	$P(s_j)$	$P(I_1 \mid s_j)$	$P(I_1 \cap s_j)$	$P(s_j \mid I_1)$
s_1	0.4	0.8	0.32	0.57143
s_2	0.6	0.4	<u>0.24</u>	0.42857
		$P(I_1) =$	0.56	

For I_2,

State of Nature	$P(s_j)$	$P(I_2 \mid s_j)$	$P(I_2 \cap s_j)$	$P(s_j \mid I_2)$
s_1	0.4	0.2	0.08	0.18182
s_2	0.6	0.6	<u>0.36</u>	0.81818
		$P(I_2) =$	0.44	

c.

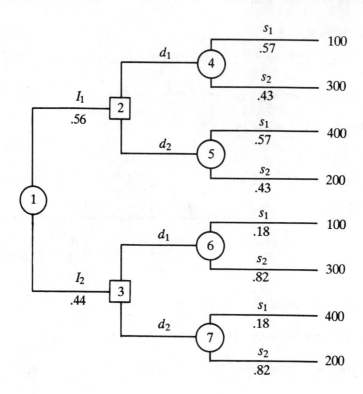

$$EV(\text{node } 4) = 0.5714(100) + 0.4286(300) = 185.71$$

$$EV(\text{node } 5) = 0.5714(400) + 0.4286(200) = 314.28$$

$$EV(\text{node } 6) = 0.1818(100) + 0.8182(300) = 263.64$$

$$EV(\text{node } 7) = 0.1818(400) + 0.8182(200) = 236.36$$

Decision strategy:

If I_1 then select d_2 since $EV(\text{node } 5) > EV(\text{node } 4)$

If I_2 then select d_1 since $EV(\text{node } 6) > EV(\text{node } 7)$

$$EV(\text{node } 1) = 0.56(314.29) + 0.44(263.64) = 292.00$$

21.a. $$EV(d_1) = 0.4(100) + 0.6(300) = 220$$

$$EV(d_2) = 0.4(400) + 0.6(200) = 280$$

Recommended decision: d_2

b. From 16(c) we know that the expected value of the decision strategy which used I_1 and I_2 is 292. Therefore, EVSI = 292 - 280 = 12.

c. Optimal decision strategy with perfect information:

If s_1 then d_2

If s_2 then d_1

Expected value of this strategy is

$$0.4(400) + 0.6(300) = 340$$

EVPI = 340 - 280 = 60

d. Efficiency $= \left(\dfrac{12}{60}\right)100 = 20\%$

22. If I_1 (recommendation to develop a prototype)

s_j	$P(s_j)$	$P(I_1 \cap s_j)$	$P(I_1 \mid s_j)$	$P(s_j \mid I_1)$
s_1	0.7	0.2	0.14	0.4000
s_2	0.2	0.6	0.12	0.3429
s_3	0.1	0.9	0.09	0.2571
		$P(I_1) =$	0.35	1.0000

In this case, ignoring for now the $5,000 fee,
$$EV(d_1) = 0.4(-200,000) + 0.3429(400,000) + 0.2571(1,000,000)$$
$$= 314,260$$

If I_1 (recommendation to not develop a prototype)

s_j	$P(s_j)$	$P(I_2 \mid s_j)$	$P(I_2 \cap s_j)$	$P(s_j \mid I_2)$
s_1	0.7	0.8	0.56	0.8615
s_2	0.2	0.4	0.08	0.1231
s_3	0.1	0.1	0.01	0.0154
		$P(I_2) =$	0.65	1.0000

In this case (ignoring for now the $5,000 fee)

$$EV(d_1) = 0.8615(-200,000) + 0.1231(400,000) + 0.0154(1,000,000)$$
$$= -107,660$$
$$EV(d_2) = 0$$

Decision strategy:

If I_1 then d_1

If I_2 then d_2

The expected value of this decision strategy is

$$0.35(314,260) + 0.65(0) = 109,991$$

Subtracting the fee of $5,000, we obtain an expected value of $104,991. Compared to the expected value of $40,000 using no information (problem 5), JSI's best decision is to hire the consultant.

Note: the consultant's fee of $5,000 could have been subtracted from the payoffs prior to computing $EV(d_1)$ and $EV(d_2)$; the results obtained will be identical to the approach shown.

23.a.

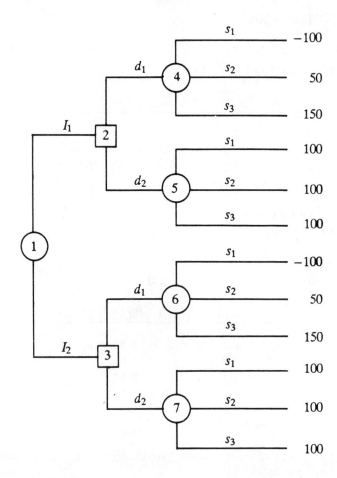

b. For I_1 - Favorable,

State of Nature	$P(s_j)$	$P(I_1 \mid s_j)$	$P(I_1 \cap s_j)$	$P(s_j \mid I_1)$
s_1	0.2	0.3	0.06	0.08696
s_2	0.3	0.6	0.18	0.26087
s_3	0.5	0.9	0.45	0.65127
		$P(I_2) =$	0.69	

For I_2 - Unfavorable,

State of Nature	$P(s_j)$	$P(I \mid s_j)$	$P(I \cap s_j)$	$P(s_j \mid I)$
s_1	0.2	0.7	0.14	0.45161
s_2	0.3	0.4	0.12	0.38710
s_3	0.5	0.1	0.05	0.16129
		$P(I) =$	0.31	

EV(node 4) = 0.087(-100) + 0.261(50) + 0.652(150) = 102.17

EV(node 5) = 100

EV(node 6) = 0.452(-100) + 0.387(50) + 0.161(150) = -1.7

EV(node 7) = 100

Decision strategy:

If I_1 then select d_1 since EV(node 4) > EV(node 5)

If I_2 then select d_2 since EV(node 7) > EV(node 6)

EV(node 1) = 0.69(102.17) + 0.31(100) = $101.50

c. From exercise 5, we know that the expected value of the best decision (d_2) is $100. Thus, EVSI = 101.5 -100 = 1.5, or $1500. The consulting information is not worthwhile; the cost of $2500 is worth more than the expected gain.

24.a. Revised Probabilities
For I_1,

State of Nature	$P(s_j)$	$P(I_1 \mid s_j)$	$P(I_1 \cap s_j)$	$P(s_j \mid I_1)$
s_1	0.20	0.6	0.120	0.39344
s_2	0.35	0.4	0.140	0.45902
s_3	0.45	0.1	0.045	0.14754
		$P(I_1) =$	0.305	

For I_2,

State of Nature	$P(s_j)$	$P(I_2 \mid s_j)$	$P(I_2 \cap s_j)$	$P(s_j \mid I_2)$
s_1	0.20	0.3	0.060	0.15789
s_2	0.35	0.4	0.140	0.36842
s_3	0.45	0.4	<u>0.180</u>	0.47368
		$P(I_2) =$	0.380	

For I_3,

State of Nature	$P(s_j)$	$P(I_3 \mid s_j)$	$P(I_3 \cap s_j)$	$P(s_j \mid I_3)$
s_1	0.20	0.1	0.020	0.06349
s_2	0.35	0.2	0.070	0.22222
s_3	0.45	0.5	<u>0.225</u>	0.71429
		$P(I_3) =$	0.315	

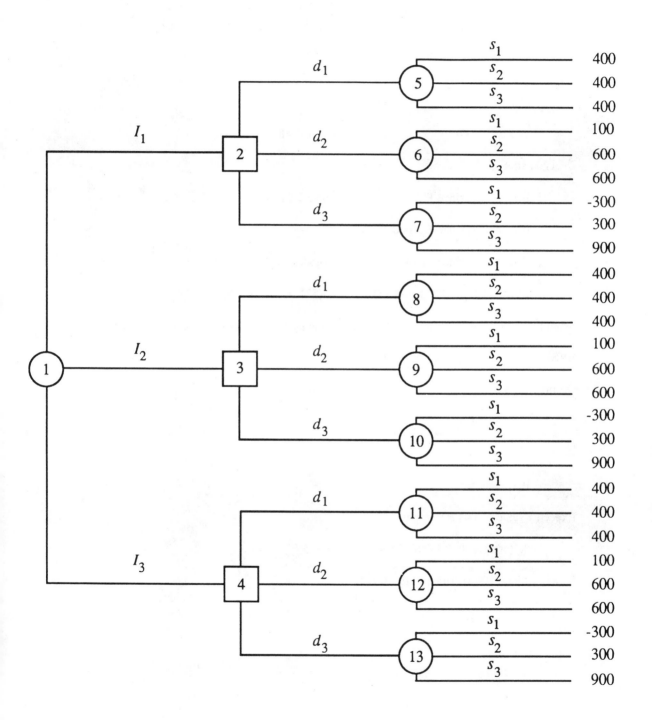

Summary of Calculations

Node	Expected Value
5	400
6	403.28
7	152.46
8	400
9	521.05
10	489.47
11	400
12	568.26
13	690.48

Decision strategy:

If I_1 then d_2 since EV(node 6) > EV(nodes 5 or 6)

If I_2 then d_2 since EV(node 9) > EV(nodes 8 or 10)

If I_3 then d_3 since EV(node 13) > EV(nodes 11 or 12)

EV(node 1) = 0.305(403.28) + 0.380(521.05) + 0.315(690.48) = $538.50

b. From problem 6 we know that the best decision is d_2 with an expected value of $500

EVSI = 538.50 - 500 = 38.5 or $38,500

c. Optimal decision strategy with perfect information:

If s_1 then d_1

If s_2 then d_2

If s_3 then d_3

Expected value of this strategy is

0.2(400) + 0.35(600) + 0.45(900) = 695

EVPI = 695 - 500 = 195 or $195,000

Efficiency $= \dfrac{38,500}{195,000}(100) = 19.7\%$

25. Let

I_1 = unseasonably cold September
I_2 = not an unseasonably cold September

For I_1,

State of Nature	$P(s_j)$	$P(I_1 \mid s_j)$	$P(I_1 \cap s_j)$	$P(s_j \mid I_1)$
s_1	0.4	0.30	0.120	0.615385
s_2	0.3	0.20	0.060	0.307692
s_3	0.3	0.05	0.015	0.076923
		$P(I_1) =$	0.195	

For I_2,

State of Nature	$P(s_j)$	$P(I_2 \mid s_j)$	$P(I_2 \cap s_j)$	$P(s_j \mid I_2)$
s_1	0.4	0.70	0.280	0.347826
s_2	0.3	0.80	0.240	0.298137
s_3	0.3	0.95	0.285	0.354037
		$P(I_2) =$	0.805	

4-21

Summary of Calculations

Node	Expected Value
4	4230.77
5	0
6	2346.16
7	-155.28
8	0
9	984.47

Decision Strategy:

If I_1 then d_1 since EV(node 4) > EV(node 5 or 6)

If I_2 then d_3 since EV(node 9) > EV(node 7 or 8)

Expected value of this strategy is

$$0.195(4230.77) + 0.805(984.47) = 1617.50$$

26.a. For I_1,

State of Nature	$P(s_j)$	$P(I_1 \mid s_j)$	$P(I_1 \cap s_j)$	$P(s_j \mid I_1)$
s_1	0.40	0.60	0.24	0.57
s_2	0.60	0.30	0.18	0.43
		$P(I_1) =$	0.42	

For I_2,

State of Nature	$P(s_j)$	$P(I_2 \mid s_j)$	$P(I_2 \cap s_j)$	$P(s_j \mid I_2)$
s_1	0.40	0.40	0.16	0.28
s_2	0.60	0.70	0.42	0.72
		$P(I_2) =$	0.58	

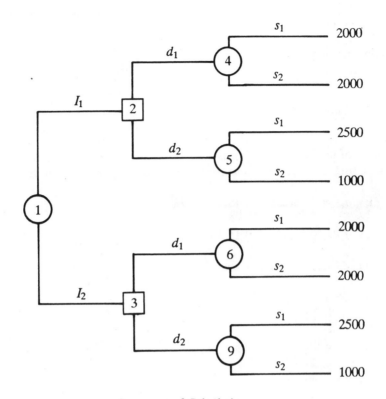

Summary of Calculations

Node	Expected Value
4	2000
5	1855
6	2000
7	1420

Decision strategy:

If I_1 then d_1 since EV(node 4) > EV(node 5)

If I_2 then d_1 since EV(node 6) > EV(node 7)

Expected value of this strategy is

$$0.42(2000) + 0.58(2000) = 2000$$

b. $P(s_1 \mid I_1) = 0.57$; nonetheless, Milford should take the St. Louis trip.

c. From problem 9 we know that with no information the recommended decision is d_1 with an expected value of 2000; in addition, EVPI = 200

EVSI = 2000 - 2000 = 0

$$\text{Efficiency} = \frac{0}{200}(100) = 0\%$$

27.a. An estimate of the probability of s_1 is 17/20 = 0.85. An estimate of the probability of s_2 is 3/20 = 0.15. Using the Expected Value Approach we obtain the following results:

$$EV(d_1) = 0.85(25) + 0.15(45) = 28$$

$$EV(d_2) = 0.85(30) + 0.15(30) = 30$$

Recommended decision: d_1 (expressway)

b. Let p = probability of s_1

$$\begin{aligned}
EV(d_1) &= p(25) + (1 - p)(45) \\
&= 25p + 45 - 45p \\
&= -20p + 45 \\
EV(d_2) &= 30
\end{aligned}$$

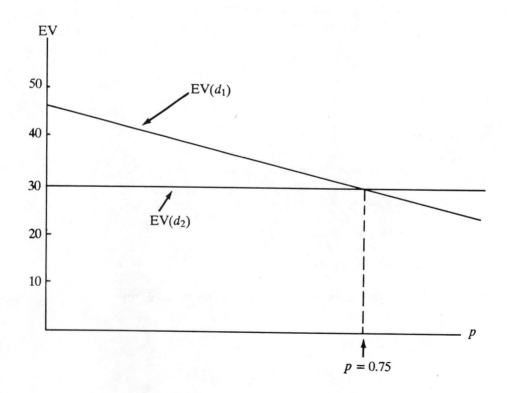

$$EV(d_1) = EV(d_2)$$
$$-20p + 45 = 30$$
$$20p = 15$$
$$p = 0.75$$

Thus, whenever $p = 0.75$ each decision alternative will provide the same expected value. If $p <$ 0.75 then d_2 is the recommended decision; if $p > 0.75$ then d_1 is the recommended decision.

c.   The expected value approach may not be the best approach for this problem since the recommended decision, d_1, also includes a 0.15 probability of a 45 minute trip; if this occurs, Rona and Jerry may be late for work. Thus, the consistent Queen City Avenue route, with a travel time of 30 minutes, may be preferred.

d.

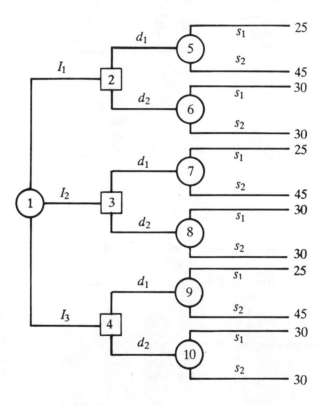

e.   For I_1,

State of Nature	$P(s_j)$	$P(I_1 \mid s_j)$	$P(I_1 \cap s_j)$	$P(s_j \mid I_1)$
s_1	0.85	0.8	0.680	0.9784
s_2	0.15	0.1	0.015	0.0216
		$P(I_1) =$	0.695	

For I_2,

State of Nature	$P(s_j)$	$P(I_2 \mid s_j)$	$P(I_2 \cap s_j)$	$P(s_j \mid I_2)$
s_1	0.85	0.2	0.170	0.7907
s_2	0.15	0.3	<u>0.045</u>	0.2093
		$P(I_2) =$	0.215	

For I_3,

State of Nature	$P(s_j)$	$P(I_3 \mid s_j)$	$P(I_3 \cap s_j)$	$P(s_j \mid I_3)$
s_1	0.85	0	0.000	0.0000
s_2	0.15	0.6	<u>0.090</u>	1.0000
		$P(I_3) =$	0.090	

Summary of Calculations

Node	Expected Value
5	25.43
6	30
7	29.19
8	30
9	45
10	30

Decision strategy:

If I_1 then d_1 since EV(node 5) < EV(node 6)

If I_2 then d_1 since EV(node 7) < EV(node 8)

If I_3 then d_2 since EV(node 10) < EV(node 9)

EV(node 1) = 0.695(25.43) + 0.215(29.19) + 0.09(30) = 26.65

f.   With no weather information:

EV(d_1) = 0.85(25) + 0.15(45) = 28

EV(d_2) = 30

Recommended decision:d_1

Optimal decision strategy with perfect information:

If s_1 then d_1

If s_2 then d_2

Expected value of this strategy is

$$0.85(25) + 0.15(30) = 25.75$$

$$EVPI = 28 - 25.75 = 2.25$$

$$EVSI = 28 - 26.65 = 1.35$$

$$\text{Efficiency} = \frac{1.35}{2.25}(100) = 60.0\%$$

28.a. d_1 = Manufacture component s_1 = Low demand
         d_2 = Purchase component s_2 = Medium demand
                                                  s_3 = High demand

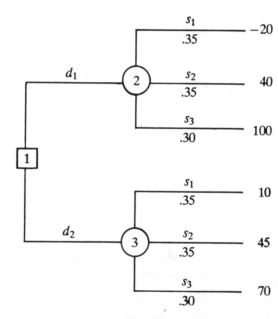

$$EV(\text{node 2}) = (0.35)(-20) + (0.35)(40) + (0.30)(100) = 37$$

$$EV(\text{node 3}) = (0.35)(10) + (0.35)(45) + (0.30)(70) = 40.25$$

Recommended decision: d_2 (purchase component)

b. Optimal decision strategy with perfect information:

If s_1 then d_2

If s_2 then d_2

If s_3 then d_1

Expected value of this strategy is

$$0.35(10) + 0.35(45) + 0.30(100) = 49.25$$

EVPI $= 49.25 - 40.25 = 9$ or \$9,000

c.　　For I_1,

State of Nature	$P(s_j)$	$P(I_1 \mid s_j)$	$P(I_1 \cap s_j)$	$P(s_j \mid I_1)$
s_1	0.35	0.10	0.035	0.09859
s_2	0.35	0.40	0.140	0.39437
s_3	0.30	0.60	0.180	0.50704
		$P(I_1) =$	0.355	

For I_2,

State of Nature	$P(s_j)$	$P(I_2 \mid s_j)$	$P(I_2 \cap s_j)$	$P(s_j \mid I_2)$
s_1	0.35	0.90	0.315	0.48837
s_2	0.35	0.60	0.210	0.32558
s_3	0.30	0.40	0.120	0.18605
		$P(I_2) =$	0.645	

The probability the report will be favorable is $P(I_1) = 0.355$

d.

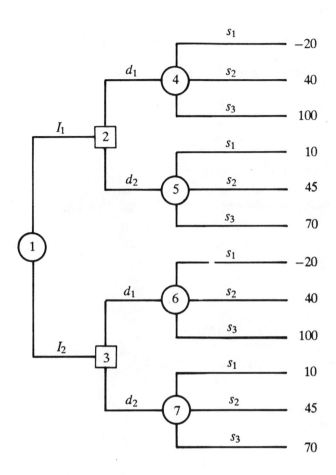

Summary of Calculations

Node	Expected Value
4	64.51
5	54.23
6	21.86
7	32.56

Decision strategy:

If I_1 then d_1 since EV(node 4) > EV(node 5)

If I_2 then d_2 since EV(node 7) > EV(node 6)

EV(node 1) = 0.355(64.51) + 0.645(32.56) = 43.90

e. With no information:

$$EV(d_1) = 0.35(-20) + 0.35(40) + 0.30(100) = 37$$

$$EV(d_2) = 0.35(10) + 0.35(45) + 0.30(70) = 40.25$$

Recommended decision: d_2

EVSI = 43.90 - 40.25 = 3.65 or $3650

f. Optimal decision strategy with perfect information:

If s_1 then d_2

If s_2 then d_2

If s_3 then d_1

Expected value of this strategy is

$$0.35(10) + 0.35(45) + 0.30(100) = 49.25$$

EVPI = 49.25 - 40.25 = 9 or $9,000

$$\text{Efficiency} = \frac{3650}{9000}(100) = 40.6\%$$

29.a.

		Demand (lbs)	
	1000	2000	3000
Amount 1000	50,000	10,000	-30,000
Produced 2000	-50,000	100,000	60,000
(lbs) 3000	-150,000	0	150,000

For example,

Sales	1000 @ $200 = $200,000	Sales	3000 @ $200 = $600,000
Mfr.Cost	2000 @ - $150 = -300,000	Mfr. Cost	2000 @ - $150 = -300,000
Shortage	0 @ - $240 = 0	Shortage	1000 @ - $240 = -240,000
Salvage	1000 @ $ 50 = 50,000	Salvage	0 @ $ 50 = 0
Net Profit	= -$50,000	Net Profit	= $ 60,000

b. d_1 = produce 1000 lbs. s_1 = demand is 1000 lbs.
    d_2 = produce 2000 lbs. s_2 = demand is 2000 lbs.
    d_3 = produce 3000 lbs. s_3 = demand is 3000 lbs.

Given:

$$P(s_1) = 0.3 \qquad P(s_2) = 0.5 \qquad P(s_3) = 0.2$$

$$EV(d_1) = 0.3(50{,}000) + 0.5(10{,}000) + 0.2(-30{,}000) = \$14{,}000$$

$$EV(d_2) = 0.3(-50{,}000) + 0.5(100{,}000) + 0.2(60{,}000) = \$47{,}000$$

$$EV(d_3) = 0.3(-150{,}000) + 0.5(0) + 0.2(150{,}000) = \$-15{,}000$$

Recommended decision: d_2 (produce 2000 lbs.)

c. Optimal decision strategy with perfect information:

If s_1 then d_1

If s_2 then d_2

If s_3 then d_3

Expected value of this strategy is

$$0.3(50{,}000) + 0.5(100{,}000) + 0.2(150{,}000) = 95{,}000$$

EVPI = 95,000 - 47,000 = \$48,000

Therefore, a discount of up to \$48,000 is acceptable.

d. For I_1,

State of Nature	$P(s_j)$	$P(I_1 \mid s_j)$	$P(I_1 \cap s_j)$	$P(s_j \mid I_1)$
s_1	0.30	0.10	0.03	0.10000
s_2	0.50	0.22	0.11	0.36667
s_3	0.20	0.80	$\underline{0.16}$	0.53333
		$P(I_1) =$	0.30	

For I_2,

State of Nature	$P(s_j)$	$P(I_2 \mid s_j)$	$P(I_2 \cap s_j)$	$P(s_j \mid I_2)$
s_1	0.30	0.40	0.12	0.24
s_2	0.50	0.68	0.34	0.68
s_3	0.20	0.20	$\underline{0.04}$	0.08
		$P(I_2) =$	0.50	

For I_3,

State of Nature	$P(s_j)$	$P(I_3 \mid s_j)$	$P(I_3 \cap s_j)$	$P(s_j \mid I_3)$
s_1	0.30	0.50	0.15	0.75
s_2	0.50	0.10	0.05	0.25
s_3	0.20	0.00	<u>0.00</u>	0.00
		$P(I_3) =$	0.20	

Summary of Calculations

EV(Decision)	I_1	I_2	I_3
$EV(d_1)$	-7,333	16,400	40,000
$EV(d_2)$	63,667	60,800	- 12,500
$EV(d_3)$	65,000	-24,000	-112,500

Decision strategy:

If I_1 then d_3

If I_2 then d_2

If I_3 then d_1

Expected value of this strategy is

$$0.3(65,000) + 0.5(60,800) + 0.2(40,000) = \$57,900$$

e. From (b), the best decision with no information is d_2 with an expected value of $47,000.

EVSI = 57,900 - 47,000 = $10,900

f. From (c), EVPI = 48,000

Efficiency $= \dfrac{10,900}{48,000}(100) = 22.7\%$

30.a.

Percent Defective	Number of defects in Batch of 500	Cost @ $25/defective
0%	0	0
1%	5	125
2%	10	250
3%	15	375

	Percent Defective			
	0%	1%	2%	3%
100% Inspect	250	250	250	250
No Inspection	0	125	250	375

b.
$$EV(d_1) = 0.15(250) + 0.25(250) + 0.40(250) + 0.20(250) = 250$$

$$EV(d_2) = 0.15(0) + 0.25(125) + 0.40(250) + 0.20(375) = 206.25$$

Recommended decision: d_2 (no inspection)

c.

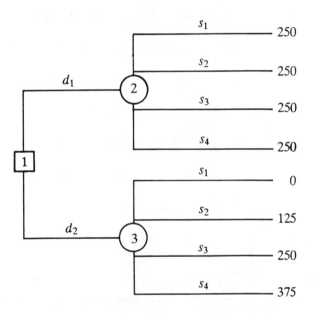

d.   Binomial: $P(x) = \dfrac{n!}{x!(n - x)!} p^x(1 - p)^{n - x}$

Since the event of interest (I) is one defective part in a sample of 5, $x = 1$ and $n = 5$.

$$P(1) = \frac{5!}{1!\,4!} p^1(1 - p)^4 = 5p^1(1 - p)^4$$

s_j	$p = P(s_j)$	$P(I \mid s_j) = 5p^1(1 - p)^4$
s_1	0.00	$5(0.00)^1(1.00)^4 = 0$
s_2	0.01	$5(0.01)^1(0.99)^4 = 0.048$
s_3	0.02	$5(0.02)^1(0.98)^4 = 0.092$
s_4	0.03	$5(0.03)^1(0.97)^4 = 0.133$

e.

State of Nature	$P(s_j)$	$P(I \mid s_j)$	$P(I \cap s_j)$	$P(s_j \mid I)$
s_1	0.15	0.000	0.0000	0.000
s_2	0.25	0.048	0.0120	0.159
s_3	0.40	0.092	0.0368	0.488
s_4	0.20	0.133	0.0266	0.353
		$P(I) =$	0.0754	

f. $\text{EV}(d_1) = 0(250) + 0.159(250) + 0.488(250) + 0.353(250) = \$250$

$\text{EV}(d_2) = 0(0) + 0.159(125) + 0.488(250) + 0.353(375) = \$274.25$

Recommended decision: d_1 (100% inspection)

g. cost saving $= \$274.25 - 250 = \$24.25$

31.a. $\text{EV}(d_1) = 0.20(500) + 0.20(200) + 0.60(-100) = 80$

$\text{EV}(d_2) = 0.20(-400) + 0.20(800) + 0.60(700) = 500$

$\text{EV}(d_3) = 0.20(-1000) + 0.20(-200) + 0.60(1600) = 720$

Recommended decision: d_3

b.

State of Nature	$P(s_j)$	$P(I_2 \mid s_j)$	$P(I_2 \cap s_j)$	$P(s_j \mid I_2)$
s_1	0.20	0.80	0.16	0.5333
s_2	0.20	0.40	0.80	0.2667
s_3	0.60	0.10	0.06	0.2000
		$P(I_2) =$	0.30	

$\text{EV}(d_1) = 0.5333(500) + 0.2667(200) + 0.2(-100) = 300$

$\text{EV}(d_2) = 0.5333(-400) + 0.2667(800) + 0.2(700) = 140$

$\text{EV}(d_3) = 0.5333(-1000) + 0.2667(-200) + 0.2(1600) = -267$

Recommended decision: d_1

32.a.

		s_1 Major	s_2 Minor	s_3 Failure
Fund	d_1	150,000	10,000	-100,000
Do Not Fund	d_2	0	0	0

$EV(d_1) = 0.15(150,000) + 0.45(10,000) + 0.40(-100,000) = -13,000$

$EV(d_2) = 0$

Recommended decision: d_2 (do not fund)

b.   Optimal decision strategy with perfect information:

If s_1 then d_1

If s_2 then d_1

If s_3 then d_2

Expected value of this strategy is

$0.15(150,000) + 0.45(10,000) + 0.4(0) = 27,000$

$EVPI = 27,000 - 0 = \$27,000$

Recommendation: Do not hire the consultants

c.   For I_1,

State of Nature	$P(s_j)$	$P(I_1 \mid s_j)$	$P(I \cap s_j)$	$P(s_j \mid I_1)$
s_1	0.15	0.70	0.105	0.552632
s_2	0.45	0.10	0.045	0.236842
s_3	0.40	0.10	0.040	0.210526
		$P(I_1) =$	0.190	

$EV(d_1) = 64,210.62$

$EV(d_2) = 0$

Recommended decision: d_1 (fund)

d.   For I_2,

State of Nature	$P(s_j)$	$P(I_2 \mid s_j)$	$P(I_2 \cap s_j)$	$P(s_j \mid I_2)$
s_1	0.15	0.25	0.0375	0.079365
s_2	0.45	0.70	0.3150	0.666667
s_3	0.40	0.30	0.1200	0.253968
		$P(I_2) =$	0.4725	

$EV(d_1) = -6,825.38$

$EV(d_2) = 0$

Recommended decision: d_2 (do not fund)

e.   For I_3

State of Nature	$P(s_j)$	$P(I_3 \mid s_j)$	$P(I_3 \cap s_j)$	$P(s_j \mid I_3)$
s_1	0.15	0.05	0.0075	0.022222
s_2	0.45	0.20	0.0900	0.266667
s_3	0.40	0.60	0.2400	0.711111
		$P(I_3) =$	0.3375	

$EV(d_1) = -65,111.13$

$EV(d_2) = 0$

Recommended decision: d_2 (do not fund)

Decision Strategy:

If I_1 then d_1

If I_2 then d_2

If I_3 then d_2

Expected value of this strategy is

$$0.19(64,210.62) + 0.4725(0) + 0.3375(0) = \$12,200$$

f.   From (b) we know that EVPI = \$27,000 and that with no information the best decision is d_2 with an expected value of 0.

EVSI = 12,200 - 0 = 12,200

Efficiency $= \dfrac{12,200}{27,000}(100) = 45.2\%$

33. $$c_u = \$1.50 - 1.10 = \$0.40$$
$$c_o = \$1.10$$

Optimal quantity Q^* must satisfy the following condition:

$$P(\text{demand} \leq Q^*) = \frac{c_u}{c_u + c_o} = \frac{0.40}{0.40 + 1.10} = 0.2667$$

From Appendix C we obtain the z value as shown below:

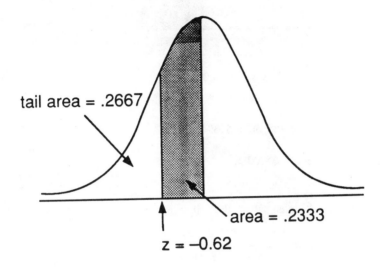

tail area = .2667

area = .2333

z = −0.62

Thus, $Q^* = 30,000 - 0.62(4000) = 27,520$

Recommendation: Carolina Times should not continue to print 30,000 copies; the optimal quantity is 27,520 copies.

34. $$c_u = \$14.99 - 4.99 = \$10.00$$
$$c_o = \$4.99 - 2.99 = \$2$$

Optimal order quantity Q^* must satisfy the following condition:

$$P(\text{demand} \leq Q^*) = \frac{c_u}{c_u + c_o} = \frac{10}{10 + 2} = 0.8333$$

From Appendix C we obtain the z value as shown below:

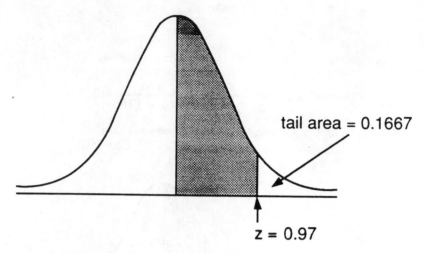

tail area = 0.1667

z = 0.97

Thus, $Q^* = 2500 + 0.97(200) = 2694$

Recommendation: Gerald should order 2,694 shirts.

35.a. $c_u = \$8.95 - 3.95 = \$5.00$
$c_o = \$3.95$

Optimal order quantity Q^* must satisfy the following condition:

$$P(\text{demand} \leq Q^*) = \frac{c_u}{c_u + c_o} = \frac{5.00}{5.00 + 3.95} = 0.5587$$

From Appendix C we obtain the value as shown below:

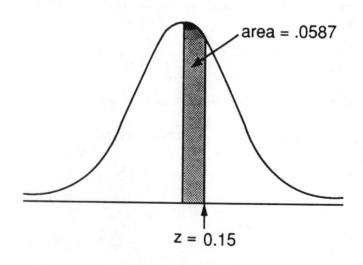

area = .0587

z = 0.15

Thus, $Q^* = 210 + 0.15(65) = 220$

Recommendation: MRT should order 220 box lunches

b.
$$c_o = \$3.95 - 1.95 = \$2.00$$
$$P(\text{demand} \le Q^*) = 5/(5 + 2) = 0.7143$$
$$z = 0.57$$

Thus, $Q_* = 210 + 0.57(65) = 247$

Recommendation: MRT should order 247 box lunches

36.a.
$$c_u = \$1.25 = 0.80 = \$0.45$$
$$c_o = \$0.80$$

Optimal order quantity must satisfy the following condition:

$$P(\text{demand} \le Q^*) = \frac{c_u}{c_u + c_o} = \frac{0.45}{0.45 + 0.80} = 0.36$$

From Appendix C we obtain the z value as shown below:

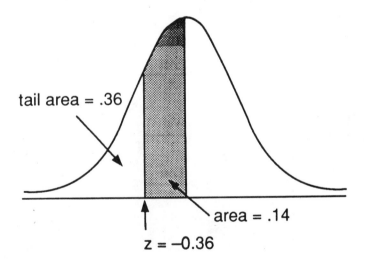

tail area = .36

area = .14

z = −0.36

Thus, $Q^* = 180 - 0.36(50) = 162$

Recommendation: Since 40 pieces are in the warmer, $162 - 40 = 122$ additional pieces should be prepared.

b.
$$c_o = \$0.80 - 0.50 = \$ 0.30$$
$$P(\text{demand} \leq Q^*) = 0.45/(0.45 + 0.30) = 0.60$$
$$z = 0.25$$

Thus, $Q_* = 180 + 0.25(50) = 193$

Recommendation: prepare 193 - 40 = 153 additional pieces.

Chapter 5
Utility and Decision Making

Learning Objectives

1. Know what is meant by utility.

2. Understand why utility could be preferred to monetary value in some decision making situations.

3. Know how to develop a utility function for money.

4. Learn about the role a lottery plays in helping a decision maker assign utility values.

5. Understand why risk avoiding and risk taking decision makers would assign different utility values in the same decision making situation.

6. Be able to discuss the relative merits of expected monetary value and expected utility as decision making criteria.

7. Understand the following terms:

    utility   risk avoider
    lottery   risk taker
    utility function   expected utility

Solutions

1. a.

$$EV(d_1) = 0.40(100) + 0.30(25) + 0.30(0) = 47.5$$

$$EV(d_2) = 0.40(75) + 0.30(50) + 0.30(25) = 52.5 \left.\right\} d_2$$

$$EV(d_3) = 0.40(50) + 0.30(50) + 0.30(50) = 50.0$$

   b.   Using Utilities

Decision Maker A		Decision Maker B	
$EU(d_1)$ = 4.9		$EU(d_1)$ = 4.45	Best
$EU(d_2)$ = 5.9		$EU(d_2)$ = 3.75	
$EU(d_3)$ = 6.0	Best	$EU(d_3)$ = 3.00	

   c.   Difference in attitude toward risk. Decision maker A tends to avoid risk, while decision maker B tends to take a risk for the opportunity of a large payoff.

2. a. $EV(d_1) = 10,000$

   $EV(d_2) = 0.96(0) + 0.03(100,000) + 0.01(200,000) = 5,000$

   Using EV approach $\rightarrow$ No Insurance (d_2)

   b.   Lottery:

$$p = \text{probability of a \$0 Cost}$$
$$1 - p = \text{probability of a \$200,000 Cost}$$

   c.

		s_1	s_2	s_3
		None	Minor	Major
Insurance	d_1	9.9	9.9	9.9
No Insurance	d_2	10.0	6.0	0.0

   $EU(d_1) = 9.9$

   $EU(d_2) = 0.96(10.0) + 0.03(6.0) + 0.01(0.0) = 9.78$

   $\therefore$ Using EU approach $\rightarrow$ Insurance (d_1)

   d.   Use expected utility approach.

3. a. $P(\text{Win}) = 1/250,000$ $P(\text{Lose}) = 249,999/250,000$

$EV(d_1) = 1/250,000(300,000) + 249,999/250,000(-2) = -0.80$

$EV(d_2) = 0$

$\therefore d_2$ - Do not purchase lottery ticket.

b.

		s_1	s_2
		Win	Lose
Purchase	d_1	10	0
Do Not Purchase	d_2	0.00001	0.00001

$EU(d_1) = 1/250,000(10) + 249,999/250,000(0) = 0.00004$

$EU(d_2) = 0.00001$

$\therefore d_1$ - purchase lottery ticket.

4. a.

$$EV(A) = 0.80(60) + 0.20(70) = 62 \left.\vphantom{\begin{matrix}a\\b\end{matrix}}\right\} \text{\textit{Route B}}$$
$$EV(B) = 0.70(45) + 0.30(90) = 58.5$$

b.   Lottery:

p = probability of a 45 minute travel time
$(1 - p)$ = probability of a 90 minute travel time

c.

		Route Open	Route Delays
Route A	d_1	8.0	6.0
Route B	d_2	10.0	0.0

$$EU(A) = 0.80(8.0) + 0.20(6.0) = 7.6 \left.\vphantom{\begin{matrix}a\\b\end{matrix}}\right\} \text{\textit{Route A}}$$
$$EU(B) = 0.70(10.0) + 0.30(0) = 7.0$$

Risk avoider strategy.

5. a.

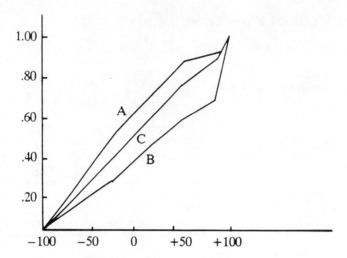

b. A - risk avoider
B - risk taker
C - risk neutral

c. Risk avoider A, at $20 payoff $p = 0.70$

$$\therefore \text{EV(Lottery)} = 0.70(100) + 0.30(-100) = \$40$$

$\therefore$ Will Pay 40 - 20 = $20

Risk taker B, at $20 payoff $p = 0.45$

$$\therefore \text{EV(Lottery)} = 0.45(100) + 0.55(-100) = -\$10$$

$\therefore$ Will Pay 20 - (-10) = $30

6. Decision Maker A

$$EU(d_1) = 0.25(7.0) + 0.50(9.0) + 0.25(5.0) = 7.5$$
$$EU(d_2) = 0.25(9.5) + 0.50(10.0) + 0.25(0.0) = 7.375$$
$\left.\right\} d_1$

Decision Maker B

$$EU(d_1) = 0.25(4.5) + 0.50(6.0) + 0.25(2.5) = 4.75$$
$$EU(d_2) = 0.25(7.0) + 0.50(10.0) + 0.25(0.0) = 6.75$$
$\left.\right\} d_2$

Decision Maker C

$$EU(d_1) = 0.25(6.0) + 0.50(7.5) + 0.25(4.0) = 6.175$$
$$EU(d_2) = 0.25(9.0) + 0.50(10.0) + 0.25(0.0) = 7.25$$

$\Bigg\} d_2$

7. a. $EV(d_1) = 0.60(1000) + 0.40(-1000) = \$200$

   $EV(d_2) = \$0$

   $\therefore d_1 \rightarrow$ Bet

   b.

   $$\text{Lottery: } p \text{ of winning } \$1,000$$
   $$(1 - p) \text{ of losing } \$1,000$$
   $\Bigg\}$ vs. $\Bigg\{$ \$0

   Most students, if realistic, should require a high value for p. While students will differ, let us use $p = 0.90$ as an example.

   c. $EU(d_1) = 0.60(10.0) + 0.40(0.0) = 6.0$
      $EU(d_2) = 0.60(9.0) + 0.40(9.0) = 9.0$

   $\therefore d_2 \rightarrow$ Do Not Bet (Risk Avoider)

   d. No, different decision makers have different attitudes toward risk, therefore different utilities.

8. a.

		s_1	s_2
		Win	Lose
Bet	d_1	350	-10
Do Not Bet	d_2	0	0

   b. $EV(d_1) = 1/38(350) + 37/38(-10) = -\$0.53$
      $EV(d_2) = 0$

   $\therefore d_2 \rightarrow$ Do Not Bet

   c. Risk takers, because risk neutral and risk avoiders would not bet.

d. $EU(d_1) \geq EU(d_2)$ for decision maker to prefer Bet decision.

$$1/38(10.0) + 37/38(0.0) \geq EU(d_2)$$
$$0.26 \geq EU(d_2)$$

∴ Utility of $0 payoff must be between 0 and 0.26.

9. a. $EV = 0.10(150,000) + 0.25(100,000) + 0.20(50,000) + 0.15(0) + 0.20(-50,000)$
$+ 0.10(-100,000) = \$30,000$

Market the new product.

b.   Lottery

$$p = \text{probability of } \$150,000$$
$$(1 - p) = \text{probability of -}\$100,000$$

c.   Risk Avoider.

d. $EU(\text{market}) = 0.10(10.0) + 0.25(9.5) + 0.20(7.0) + 0.15(5.0) + 0.20(2.5) + 0.10(0.0) = 6.025$
$EU(\text{don't market}) = EU(\$0) = 5.0$

Market the new product.

e.   Yes - Both EV and EU recommend marketing the product.

10. a. $EV(\text{Western}) = 0.30(30) + 0.60(25) + 0.10(20) = 26\%$
$EV(\text{Musical}) = 0.30(40) + 0.40(20) + 0.30(15) = 24.5\%$

∴ Western

b.   Lottery

$$p = \text{probability of a 40\% audience show}$$
$$(1 - p) = \text{probability of a 15\% audience show}$$

c. $EU(\text{Western}) = 0.30(4.0) + 0.60(3.0) + 0.10(1.0) = 3.1$
$EU(\text{Musical}) = 0.30(10.0) + 0.40(1.0) + 0.30(0.0) = 3.4$

∴ Musical

Risk Taker.

Chapter 6
Forecasting

Learning Objectives

1. Understand that the long-run success of an organization is often closely related to how well management is able to predict future aspects of the operation.

2. Know the various components of a time series.

3. Be able to use smoothing techniques such as moving averages and exponential smoothing.

4. Be able to use the least squares method to identify the trend component of a time series.

5. Understand how the classical time series model can be used to explain the pattern or behavior of the data in a time series and to develop a forecast for the time series.

6. Be able to determine and use seasonal indexes for a time series.

7. Know how regression models can be used in forecasting.

8. Know the definition of the following terms:

time series	mean squared error
forecast	moving averages
trend component	weighted moving averages
cyclical component	smoothing constant
seasonal component	seasonal constant
irregular component	

Solutions

1. a.

Month	Time-Series Value	3-Month Moving Average Forecast	(Error)^2	4-Month Moving Average Forecast	(Error)^2
1	9.5				
2	9.3				
3	9.4				
4	9.6	9.40	0.04		
5	9.8	9.43	0.14	9.45	0.12
6	9.7	9.60	0.01	9.53	0.03
7	9.8	9.70	0.01	9.63	0.03
8	10.5	9.77	0.53	9.73	0.59
9	9.9	10.00	0.01	9.95	0.00
10	9.7	10.07	0.14	9.98	0.08
11	9.6	10.03	0.18	9.97	0.14
12	9.6	9.73	0.02	9.92	0.10
			1.08		1.09

MSE(3-Month) = 1.08 / 9 = .12

MSE(4-Month) = 1.09 / 8 = .14

Use 3-Month moving averages.

b. forecast = (9.7 + 9.6 + 9.6) / 3 = 9.63

c. For the limited data provided, the 5-week moving average provides the smallest MSE.

2. a.

Week	Time-Series Value	4-Week Moving Average Forecast	(Error)^2	5-Week Moving Average Forecast	(Error)^2
1	17				
2	21				
3	19				
4	23				
5	18	20.00	4.00		
6	16	20.25	18.06	19.60	12.96
7	20	19.00	1.00	19.40	0.36
8	18	19.25	1.56	19.20	1.44
9	22	18.00	16.00	19.00	9.00
10	20	19.00	1.00	18.80	1.44
11	15	20.00	25.00	19.20	17.64
12	22	18.75	10.56	19.00	9.00
			77.18		51.84

b. MSE(4-Week) = 77.18 / 8 = 9.65

MSE(5-Week) = 51.84 / 7 = 7.41

c. For the limited data provided, the 5-week moving average provides the smallest MSE.

3. a.

Week	Time-Series Value	Weighted Moving Average Forecast	Forecast Error	(Error)^2
1	17			
2	21			
3	19			
4	23	19.33	3.67	13.47
5	18	21.33	-3.33	11.09
6	16	19.83	-3.83	14.67
7	20	17.83	2.17	4.71
8	18	18.33	-0.33	0.11
9	22	18.33	3.67	13.47
10	20	20.33	-0.33	0.11
11	15	20.33	-5.33	28.41
12	22	17.83	4.17	17.39
				103.43

b. MSE = 103.43 / 9 = 11.49

Prefer the unweighted moving average here.

c. You could always find a weighted moving average at least as good as the unweighted one. Actually the unweighted moving average is a special case of the weighted ones where the weights are equal.

4.

Week	Time-Series Value	Forecast	Error	(Error)^2
1	17			
2	21	17.00	4.00	16.00
3	19	17.40	1.60	2.56
4	23	17.56	5.44	29.59
5	18	18.10	-0.10	0.01
6	16	18.09	-2.09	4.37
7	20	17.88	2.12	4.49
8	18	18.10	-0.10	0.01
9	22	18.09	3.91	15.29
10	20	18.48	1.52	2.31
11	15	18.63	-3.63	13.18
12	22	18.27	3.73	13.91
				101.72

MSE = 101.72 / 11 = 9.25

α = .2 provided a lower MSE; therefore α = .2 is better than α = .1.

5. a.

Month	Y_t	3-Month Moving Averages Forecast	(Error)^2	$\alpha = 2$ Forecast	(Error)^2
1	80				
2	82			80.00	4.00
3	84			80.40	12.96
4	83	82.00	1.00	81.12	3.53
5	83	83.00	0.00	81.50	2.25
6	84	83.33	0.45	81.80	4.84
7	85	83.33	2.79	82.24	7.62
8	84	84.00	0.00	82.79	1.46
9	82	84.33	5.43	83.03	1.06
10	83	83.67	0.45	82.83	0.03
11	84	83.00	1.00	82.86	1.30
12	83	83.00	0.00	83.09	0.01
			11.12		39.06

$$\text{MSE(3-Month)} = 11.12 \,/\, 9 = 1.24$$

$$\text{MSE}(\alpha = .2) = 39.06 \,/\, 11 = 3.55$$

Use 3-month moving averages.

b. $(83 + 84 + 83) \,/\, 3 = 83.3$

6. a. $F_{13} = .2Y_{12} + .16Y_{11} + .64(.2Y_{10} + .8F_{10})$

$\qquad = .2Y_{12} + .16Y_{11} + .128Y_{10} + .512F_{10}$

$F_{13} = .2Y_{12} + .16Y_{11} + .128Y_{10} + .512(.2Y_9 + .8F_9)$

$\qquad = .2Y_{12} + .16Y_{11} + .128Y_{10} + .1024Y_9 + .4096F_9$

$F_{13} = .2Y_{12} + .16Y_{11} + .128Y_{10} + .1024Y_9 + .4096(.2Y_8 + .8F_8)$

$\qquad = .2Y_{12} + .16Y_{11} + .128Y_{10} + .1024Y_9 + .08192Y_8 + .32768F_8$

b. The more recent data receives the greater weight or importance in determining the forecast. The moving averages method weights the last n data values equally in determining the forecast.

7. a.

Month	Time-Series Value	3-Month Moving Average Forecast	$(\text{Error})^2$	$\alpha = .2$ Forecast	$(\text{Error})^2$
1	240				
2	350			240.00	12100.00
3	230			262.00	1024.00
4	260	273.33	177.69	255.60	19.36
5	280	280.00	0.00	256.48	553.19
6	320	256.67	4010.69	261.18	3459.79
7	220	286.67	4444.89	272.95	2803.70
8	310	273.33	1344.69	262.36	2269.57
9	240	283.33	1877.49	271.89	1016.97
10	310	256.67	2844.09	265.51	1979.36
11	240	286.67	2178.09	274.41	1184.05
12	230	263.33	1110.89	267.53	1408.50
			17,988.52		27,818.49

$$\text{MSE(3-Month)} = 17,988.52 / 9 = 1998.72$$

$$\text{MSE}(\alpha = .2) = 27,818.49 / 11 = 2528.95$$

Based on the above MSE values, the 3-month moving averages appears better. However, exponential smoothing was penalized by including month 2 which was difficult for any method to forecast. Using only the errors for months 4 to 12, the MSE for exponential smoothing is revised to

$$\text{MSE}(\alpha = .2) = 14,694.49 / 9 = 1632.72$$

Thus, exponential smoothing was better considering months 4 to 12.

b. Using exponential smoothing,

$$F_{13} = \alpha Y_{12} + (1 - \alpha)F_{12}$$

$$= .20(230) + .80(267.53) = 260$$

8. a.   Smoothing constant = .3.

Month t	Time-Series Value Y_t	Forecast F_t	Forecast Error $Y_t - F_t$	Squared Error $(Y_t - F_t)^2$
1	105.0			
2	135.0	105.00	30.00	900.00
3	120.0	114.00	6.00	36.00
4	105.0	115.80	-10.80	116.64
5	90.0	112.56	-22.56	508.95
6	120.0	105.79	14.21	201.92
7	145.0	110.05	34.95	1221.50
8	140.0	120.54	19.46	378.69
9	100.0	126.38	-26.38	395.90
10	80.0	118.46	-38.46	1479.17
11	100.0	106.92	-6.92	47.89
12	110.0	104.85	5.15	26.52
			Total	5613.18

$$\text{MSE} = 5613.18 \: / \: 11 = 510.29$$

Forecast for month 13:

$$F_{13} = .3(110) + .7(104.85) = 106.4$$

b.   Smoothing constant = .5

Month t	Time-Series Value Y_t	Forecast F_t	Forecast Error $Y_t - F_t$	Squared Error $(Y_t - F_t)^2$
1	105			
2	135	105	30.00	900.00
3	120	.5(135) + .5(105) = 120	0.00	0.00
4	105	.5(120) + .5(120) = 120	-15.00	225.00
5	90	.5(105) + .5(120) = 112.50	-22.50	506.25
6	120	.5(90) + .5(112.5) = 101.25	18.75	351.56
7	145	.5(120) + .5(101.25) = 110.63	34.37	1181.30
8	140	.5(145) + .5(110.63) = 127.81	12.19	148.60
9	100	.5(140) + .5(127.81) = 133.91	-33.91	1149.89
10	80	.5(100) + .5(133.91) = 116.95	-36.95	1365.30
11	100	.5(80) + .5(116.95) = 98.48	1.52	2.31
12	110	.5(100) + .5(98.48) = 99.24	10.76	115.78
				5945.99

$$\text{MSE} = 5945.99 \: / \: 11 = 540.55$$

Forecast for month 13:

$$F_{13} = .5(110) + .5(99.24) = 104.62$$

Conclusion: a smoothing constant of .3 is better than a smoothing constant of .5 since the MSE is less for 0.3.

9. a & b.

Week	Time-Series Value	$\alpha = .2$ Forecasts	$\alpha = .3$ Forecasts
1	2480		
2	2470	2480.00	2480.00
3	2475	2478.00	2477.00
4	2510	2477.40	2476.40
5	2500	2483.92	2486.48
6	2480	2487.14	2490.54
7	2520	2485.71	2487.38
8	2470	2492.57	2497.16
9	2440	2488.05	2489.01
10	2480	2478.44	2474.31
11	2530	2478.75	2476.02
12	2550	2489.00	2492.21

$$\text{MSE}(\alpha = .2) = 11{,}825.31 \,/\, 11 = 1075$$

$$\text{MSE}(\alpha = .3) = 12{,}016.45 \,/\, 11 = 1092$$

Consider $\alpha = .2$ the better smoothing constant.

$$F_{13} = .2(2550) + .8(2489) = 2501.2$$

10.

Week t	Time-Series Value Y_t	Forecast F_t	Forecast Error $Y_t - F_t$	Squared Error $(Y_t - F_t)^2$
1	200			
2	350	200.00	150.00	22,500.00
3	250	237.50	12.50	156.25
4	360	240.63	119.37	14,249.20
5	250	270.47	-20.47	419.02
6	210	265.35	-55.35	3,063.62
7	280	251.51	28.49	811.68
8	350	258.64	91.36	8,346.65
9	290	281.48	8.52	72.59
10	320	283.61	36.39	1,324.23
			Total	50,943.24

$$\text{MSE} = 50{,}943.24 \,/\, 9 = 5{,}660.36$$

Forecast for week 11:

$$F_{11} = 0.25(320) + 0.75(283.61) = 292.71$$

11.

Week t	Time-Series Value Y_t	Forecast F_t	Forecast Error $Y_t - F_t$	Squared Error $(Y_t - F_t)^2$
1	22			
2	18	22.00	-4.00	16.00
3	23	21.20	1.80	3.24
4	21	21.56	-0.56	0.31
5	17	21.45	-4.45	19.80
6	24	20.56	3.44	11.83
7	20	21.25	-1.25	1.56
8	19	21.00	-2.00	4.00
9	18	20.60	-2.60	6.76
10	21	20.08	0.92	0.85
			Total	64.35

MSE = 64.35 / 9 = 7.15

Forecast for week 11:

$$F_{11} = 0.2(21) + 0.8(20.08) = 20.26$$

12.

t	Y_t	F_t	$Y_t - F_t$	$(Y_t - F_t)^2$
1	2,750			
2	3,100	2,750.00	350.00	122,500.00
3	3,250	2,890.00	360.00	129,600.00
4	2,800	3,034.00	-234.00	54,756.00
5	2,900	2,940.40	-40.40	1,632.16
6	3,050	2,924.24	125.76	15,815.58
7	3,300	2,974.54	325.46	105,924.21
8	3,100	3,104.73	-4.73	22.37
9	2,950	3,102.84	-152.84	23,260.07
10	3,000	3,041.70	-41.70	1,738.89
11	3,200	3,025.02	174.98	30,618.00
12	3,150	3,095.01	54.99	3,023.90
			Total	488,991.18

MSE = 488,991.18 / 11 = 44,453.74

Forecast for week 13:

$$F_{13} = 0.4(3,150) + 0.6(3,095.01) = 3,117.01$$

13.a & b.

Week	Time-Series Value	$\alpha = .2$ Forecast	(Error)^2	$\alpha = .3$ Forecast	(Error)^2
1	7.35				
2	7.40	7.35	.0025	7.35	.0025
3	7.55	7.36	.0361	7.36	.0361
4	7.56	7.40	.0256	7.42	.0196
5	7.60	7.43	.0289	7.46	.0196
6	7.52	7.46	.0036	7.50	.0004
7	7.52	7.48	.0016	7.51	.0001
8	7.70	7.48	.0484	7.51	.0361
9	7.62	7.53	.0081	7.57	.0025
10	7.55	7.55	<u>.0000</u>	7.58	<u>.0009</u>
			.1548		.1178

c. $MSE(\alpha = .2) = .1548 / 9 = .0172$

$MSE(\alpha = .3) = .1178 / 9 = .0131$

Use $\alpha = .3$.

$$F_{11} = .3Y_{10} + .7F_{10}$$

$$= .3(7.55) + .7(7.58) = 7.57$$

14. $\sum t = 21, \ \sum t^2 = 91, \ \sum Y_t = 117,100, \ \sum tY_t = 403,700, \ n = 6$

$$b_1 = \frac{\sum tY_t - (\sum t \sum Y_t) / n}{\sum t^2 - (\sum t)^2 / n}$$

$$= \frac{403,700 - (21)(117,100) / 6}{91 - (21)^2 / 6}$$

$$= \frac{-6,150}{17.5} = -351.429$$

$$b_0 = \bar{Y} - b_1\bar{t} = 19,516.667 - (-351.429)(3.5) = 20,746.67$$

$$T_t = 20,746.67 - 351.429t$$

Conclusion: enrollment appears to be decreasing by an average of approximately 351 students per year.

15. $\qquad \sum t = 45, \quad \sum t^2 = 285, \quad \sum Y_t = 798.3, \quad \sum tY_t = 4275.6$

$$b_1 = \frac{4275.6 - (45)(798.3) / 9}{285 - (45)^2 / 9} = 4.735$$

$$b_0 = \bar{Y} - b_1\bar{t} = (798.3/9) - 4.735(45/9)$$

$$= 65.025$$

$$T_t = 65.025 + 4.735t$$

$$T_{10} = 65.025 + 4.735(10) = 112.4$$

$$T_{11} = 65.025 + 4.735(11) = 117.1$$

16. $\qquad \sum t = 28, \quad \sum t^2 = 140, \quad \sum Y_t = 213,400, \quad \sum tY_t = 865,400, \quad n = 7$

$$b_1 = \frac{\sum tY_t - (\sum t \sum Y_t) / n}{\sum t^2 - (\sum t)^2 / n}$$

$$b_1 = \frac{865,400 - (28)(213,400) / 7}{140 - (28)^2 / 7}$$

$$= \frac{11,800}{28} = 421.429$$

$$b_0 = \bar{Y} - b_1\bar{t} = 30,485.714 - 421.429(4) = 28,800$$

$$T_t = 28,800 + 421.429t$$

17. A linear trend model is not appropriate. A nonlinear model would provide a better approximation.

18.a. A linear trend appears to be reasonable.

b. $\qquad \sum t = 36, \quad \sum t^2 = 204, \quad \sum Y_t = 223.8, \quad \sum tY_t = 1081.6, \quad n = 8$

$$b_1 = \frac{\sum tY_t - (\sum t \sum Y_t) / n}{\sum t^2 - (\sum t)^2 / n}$$

$$= \frac{1081.6 - (36)(223.8) / 8}{204 - (36)^2 / 8}$$

$$= \frac{74.5}{42} = 1.7738$$

$$b_0 = \bar{Y} - b_1\bar{t} = 27.975 - 1.7738(4.5) = 19.993$$

$$T_t = 19.993 + 1.774t$$

Conclusion: The firm has been realizing an average cost increase of $1.77 per unit per year.

19.a.　　$\sum t = 55$, $\sum t^2 = 385$, $\sum Y_t = 14.26$, $\sum tY_t = 94.34$, $n = 10$

$$b_1 = \frac{94.35 - (55)(14.26) / 10}{385 - (55)^2 / 10} = .19297$$

$$b_0 = \bar{y} - b_1\bar{t}$$

$$= 14.26/10 - (.19297)(55/10) = .365$$

$$T_t = .365 + .193t$$

$$T_t = .365 + .193(11) = \$2.49$$

b.　　Over the past ten years the earnings per share have been increasing at the average rate of $.193 per year. This is a positive indicator of Walgreen's performance although more information would be necessary to conclude "good investment".

20.a.　　$\sum t = 55$, $\sum t^2 = 385$, $\sum Y_t = 41841$, $\sum tY_t = 262923$

$$b_1 = \frac{262923 - (55)(41841) / 10}{385 - (55)^2 / 10} = 397.545$$

$$b_0 = \bar{y} - b_1\bar{t}$$

$$= 4184.1 - (397.545)(5.5) = 1997.6$$

$$T_t = 1997.6 + 397.545t$$

b.　　$T_{11} = 1997.6 + 397.545(11) = 6371$

$$T_{12} = 1997.6 + 397.545(12) = 6768$$

21.a. $\sum t = 36, \quad \sum t^2 = 204, \quad \sum Y_t = 66.9, \quad \sum tY_t = 338.9, \quad n = 8$

$$b_1 = \frac{\sum tY_t - (\sum t \sum Y_t) / n}{\sum t^2 - (\sum t)^2 / n}$$

$$b_1 = \frac{338.9 - (36)(66.9) / 8}{204 - (36)^2 / 8} = .9012$$

$$b_0 = \bar{Y} - b_1 \bar{t}$$

$$= (66.9/8) - .9012(36/8) = 4.3071$$

$$T_t = 4.3071 + .9012t$$

b. $T_9 = 4.3071 + .9012(9) = 12.4$

$T_{10} = 4.3071 + .9012(10) = 13.3$

$T_{11} = 4.3071 + .9012(11) = 14.2$

c. Yes; the forecasts show an increase in office vacancy.

22. $\sum t = 28, \quad \sum t^2 = 140, \quad \sum Y_t = 1575, \quad \sum tY_t = 6491, \quad n = 7$

$$b_1 = \frac{\sum tY_t - (\sum t \sum Y_t) / n}{\sum t^2 - (\sum t)^2 / n}$$

$$b_1 = \frac{6491 - (28)(1575) / 7}{140 - (28)^2 / 7} = \frac{191}{28} = 6.8214$$

$$b_0 = \bar{Y} - b_1 \bar{t} = 225 - 6.8214(4) = 197.714$$

$$T_t = 197.714 + 6.821t$$

$$T_8 = 197.714 + 6.821(8) = 252.28$$

$$T_9 = 197.714 + 6.821(9) = 259.10$$

23.a. $\sum t = 78,\ \sum t^2 = 650,\ \sum Y_t = 343,\ \sum tY_t = 2441,\ n = 12$

$$b_1 = \frac{\sum tY_t - (\sum t \sum Y_t)\,/\,n}{\sum t^2 - (\sum t)^2\,/\,n}$$

$$b_1 = \frac{2441 - (78)(343)\,/\,12}{650 - (78)^2\,/\,12} = 1.479$$

$$b_0 = \bar{Y} - b_1\bar{t}$$

$$= (343/12) - 1.479(78/12) = 18.97$$

$$T_t = 18.97 + 1.479t$$

b.   Figure will be inserted.

c.   Capital expenditures are increasing. One year or four quarters $t = 16$.

$$T_{16} = 18.97 + 1.479(16) = 42.63$$

24.a.   Figure will be inserted

A linear trend appears to exist.

b. $\sum t = 15,\ \sum t^2 = 55,\ \sum Y_t = 200,\ \sum tY_t = 750,\ n = 5$

$$b_1 = \frac{\sum tY_t - (\sum t \sum Y_t)\,/\,n}{\sum t^2 - (\sum t)^2\,/\,n}$$

$$= \frac{750 - (15)(200)\,/\,5}{55 - (15)^2\,/\,5} = \frac{150}{10} = 15$$

$$b_0 = \bar{Y} - b_1\bar{t} = 40 - 15(3) = -5$$

$$T_t = -5 + 15t$$

Conclusion: average increase in sales is 15 units per year.

25.a.   Yes; a linear trend appears to exist.

b. $\sum t = 28$, $\sum t^2 = 140$, $\sum Y_t = 595$, $\sum tY_t = 2815$, $n = 7$

$$b_1 = \frac{\sum tY_t - (\sum t \sum Y_t) / n}{\sum t^2 - (\sum t)^2 / n}$$

$$= \frac{2815 - (28)(595) / 7}{140 - (28)^2 / 7} = \frac{435}{28} = 15.5357$$

$$b_0 = \bar{Y} - b_1\bar{t} = 85 - 15.5357(4) = 22.857$$

$$T_t = 22.857 + 15.536t$$

c. $T_8 = 22.857 + 15.536(8) = 147.15$

26.a. $\sum t = 78$, $\sum t^2 = 650$, $\sum Y_t = 48.7$, $\sum tY_t = 319.93$, $n = 12$

$$b_1 = \frac{319.93 - (78)(48.7) / 12}{650 - (78)^2 / 12} = .0236$$

$$b_0 = \bar{Y} - b_1\bar{t}$$

$$= (48.7/12) - .0236(78/12) = 3.9049$$

$$T_t = 3.9041 + .0236t$$

Personal income increasing at an average of .0236 per month.

b.   Using $t = 13, 14, 15, 16, 17$, and 18, the forecasts T_t are as follows:

Jan.   4.21
Feb.   4.23
March   4.26
April   4.28
May   4.31
June   4.33

c.   Actual 4.41 is above the forecast 4.33. Personal income continues to increase and even exceeds the forecasted increase.

27.a. Four quarter moving averages beginning with

$$(1690 + 940 + 2625 + 2500) / 4 = 1938.75$$

Other moving averages are

1966.25	2002.50
1956.25	2052.50
2025.00	2060.00
1990.00	2123.75

b.

Quarter	Seasonal-Irregular Component Values		Seasonal Index	Adjusted Seasonal Index
1	0.904	0.900	0.9020	0.900
2	0.448	0.526	0.4970	0.486
3	1.344	1.453	1.3985	1.396
4	1.275	1.164	1.2195	1.217
		Total	4.0070	

Note: Adjustment for seasonal index = 4.000 / 4.007 = 0.9983

c. The largest seasonal effect is in the third quarter which corresponds to the back-to-school demand during July, August, and September of each year.

28.

Month	Seasonal-Irregular Component Values		Seasonal Index	Adjusted Seasonal Index
1	0.72	0.70	0.71	0.707
2	0.80	0.75	0.78	0.777
3	0.83	0.82	0.83	0.827
4	0.94	0.99	0.97	0.966
5	1.01	1.02	1.02	1.016
6	1.25	1.36	1.31	1.305
7	1.49	1.51	1.50	1.494
8	1.19	1.26	1.23	1.225
9	0.98	0.97	0.98	0.976
10	0.98	1.00	0.99	0.986
11	0.93	0.94	0.94	0.936
12	0.78	0.80	0.79	0.787
		Total	12.05	

Notes: 1. Adjustment for seasonal index = 12 / 12.05 = 0.996

2. The adjustment is really not necessary in this problem since it imples more accuracy than is warranted. That is, the seasonal component values and the seasonal index were rounded to two decimal places.

29.a. Use a twelve period moving averages. After centering the moving averages, you should obtain the following seasonal indexes:

Hour	Seasonal Index	Hour	Seasonal Index
1	0.771	7	1.207
2	0.864	8	0.994
3	0.954	9	0.850
4	1.392	10	0.647
5	1.571	11	0.579
6	1.667	12	0.504

b. The hours of July 18 are number 37 to 48 in the time series. Thus the trend component for 7:00 a.m. on July 18 (period 37) would be

$$T_{37} = 32.983 + .3922(37) = 47.49$$

A summary of the trend components for the twelve hours on July 18 is as follows:

Hour	Trend Component	Hour	Trend Component
1	47.49	7	49.85
2	47.89	8	50.24
3	48.28	9	50.63
4	48.67	10	51.02
5	49.06	11	51.42
6	49.46	12	51.81

c. Multiply the trend component in part b by the seasonal indexes in part a to obtain the twelve hourly forecasts for July 18. For example,

$$47.49 \times (.771) = 36.6$$

or rounded to 37, would be the forecast for 7:00 a.m. on July 18th.

The seasonally adjusted hourly forecasts for July 18 are as follows:

Hour	Forecast	Hour	Forecast
1	37	7	60
2	41	8	50
3	46	9	43
4	68	10	33
5	77	11	30
6	82	12	26

30.a.

t	Sales	Centered Moving Average	Seasonal-Irregular Component
1	6		
2	15		
3	10	9.250	1.081
4	4	10.125	0.395
5	10	11.125	0.899
6	18	12.125	1.485
7	15	13.000	1.154
8	7	14.500	0.483
9	14	16.500	0.848
10	26	18.125	1.434
11	23	19.375	1.187
12	12	20.250	0.593
13	19	20.750	0.916
14	28	21.750	1.287
15	25	22.875	1.093
16	18	24.000	0.750
17	22	25.125	0.876
18	34	25.875	1.314
19	28	26.500	1.057
20	21	27.000	0.778
21	24	27.500	0.873
22	36	27.625	1.303
23	30	28.000	1.071
24	20	29.000	0.690
25	28	30.125	0.929
26	40	31.625	1.265
27	35		
28	27		

b.

Quarter	Seasonal-Irregular Component Values	Seasonal Index
1	0.899, 0.848, 0.916, 0.876, 0.873, 0.929	0.890
2	1.485, 1.434, 1.287, 1.314, 1.303, 1.265	1.348
3	1.081, 1.154, 1.187, 1.093, 1.057, 1.071	1.107
4	0.395, 0.483, 0.593, 0.750, 0.778, 0.690	0.615
	Total	3.960

Quarter	Adjusted Seasonal Index
1	0.899
2	1.362
3	1.118
4	0.621

Note: Adjustment for seasonal index = 4.00 / 3.96 = 1.0101

c.   Hudson Marine experiences the largest seasonal increase in quarter 2. Since this quarter occurs prior to the peak summer boating season, this result seems reasonable.

31.a.

t	Sales	Centered Moving Average	Seasonal-Irregular Component
1	4		
2	2		
3	1	3.250	0.308
4	5	3.750	1.333
5	6	4.375	1.371
6	4	5.875	0.681
7	4	7.500	0.533
8	14	7.875	1.778
9	10	7.875	1.270
10	3	8.250	0.364
11	5	8.750	0.571
12	16	9.750	1.641
13	12	10.750	1.116
14	9	11.750	0.766
15	7	13.250	0.528
16	22	14.125	1.558
17	18	15.000	1.200
18	10	17.375	0.576
19	13		
20	35		

Quarter	Seasonal-Irregular Component Values		Seasonal Index
1	1.371, 1.270, 1.116, 1.200		1.239
2	0.681, 0.364, 0.776, 0.576		0.597
3	0.308, 0.533, 0.571, 0.528		0.485
4	1.333, 1.778, 1.641, 1.558		1.578
		Total	3.899

Quarter	Adjusted Seasonal Index
1	1.271
2	0.613
3	0.498
4	1.619

Note: Adjustment for seasonal index = 4 / 3.899 = 1.026

b. The largest effect is in quarter 4; this seems reasonable since retail sales are generally higher during October, November, and December.

32.a. Note: To simplify the calculations the seasonal indexes calculated in problem 19 have been rounded to two decimal places.

Year	Quarter	Sales Y_t	Seasonal Factor S_t	Deseasonalized Sales $Y_t / S_t = T_t I_t$
1	1	6	0.90	6.67
	2	15	1.36	11.03
	3	10	1.12	8.93
	4	4	0.62	6.45
2	1	10	0.90	11.11
	2	18	1.36	13.24
	3	15	1.12	13.39
	4	7	0.62	11.29
3	1	14	0.90	15.56
	2	26	1.36	19.12
	3	23	1.12	20.54
	4	12	0.62	19.35
4	1	19	0.90	21.11
	2	28	1.36	20.59
	3	25	1.12	22.32
	4	18	0.62	29.03
5	1	22	0.90	24.44
	2	34	1.36	25.00
	3	28	1.12	25.00
	4	21	0.62	33.87
6	1	24	0.90	26.67
	2	36	1.36	26.47
	3	30	1.12	26.79
	4	20	0.62	32.26
7	1	28	0.90	31.11
	2	40	1.36	29.41
	3	35	1.12	31.25
	4	27	0.62	43.55

t	Y_t (deseasonalized)	tY_t	t^2
1	6.67	6.67	1
2	11.03	22.06	4
3	8.93	26.79	9
4	6.45	25.80	16
5	11.11	55.55	25
6	13.24	79.44	36
7	13.39	93.73	49
8	11.29	90.32	64
9	15.56	140.04	81
10	19.12	191.20	100
11	20.54	225.94	121
12	19.35	232.20	144
13	21.11	274.43	169
14	20.59	288.26	196
15	22.32	334.80	225
16	29.03	464.48	256
17	24.44	415.48	289
18	25.00	450.00	324
19	25.00	475.00	361
20	33.87	677.40	400
21	26.67	560.07	441
22	26.47	582.34	484
23	26.79	616.17	529
24	32.26	774.24	576
25	31.11	777.75	625
26	29.41	764.66	676
27	31.25	843.75	729
28	43.55	1,219.40	784
406	605.55	10,707.34	7,714

$$\bar{t} = \frac{406}{28} = 14.5$$

$$\bar{Y} = \frac{605.55}{28} = 21.627$$

$$b_1 = \frac{\Sigma t Y_t - (\Sigma t \Sigma Y_t)/n}{\Sigma t^2 - (\Sigma t)^2/n}$$

$$= \frac{10,707.34 - (406)(605.55)/28}{7,714 - (406)^2/28}$$

$$= \frac{1,926.865}{1,827} = 1.055$$

$$b_0 = \bar{Y} - b_1\,\bar{t} = 21.6268 - 1.055(14.5) = 6.329$$

$$T_t = 6.329 + 1.055t$$

b.

t	Trend Forecast
29	36.92
30	37.98
31	39.03
32	40.09

c.

Year	Quarter	Trend Forecast	Seasonal Index	Quarterly Forecast
8	1	36.92	0.90	33.23
	2	37.98	1.36	51.65
	3	29.03	1.12	43.71
	4	40.09	0.62	24.86

33.a. Note: To simplify the calculations the seasonal indexes in problem 20 have been rounded to two decimal places.

Year	Quarter	Sales Y_t	Seasonal Factor S_t	Deseasonalized Sales $Y_t / S_t = T_tJ_t$
1	1	4	1.27	3.15
	2	2	0.61	3.28
	3	1	0.50	2.00
	4	5	1.62	3.09
2	1	6	1.27	4.72
	2	4	0.61	6.56
	3	4	0.50	8.00
	4	14	1.62	8.64
3	1	10	1.27	7.87
	2	3	0.61	4.92
	3	5	0.50	10.00
	4	16	1.62	9.88
4	1	12	1.27	9.45
	2	9	0.61	14.75
	3	7	0.50	14.00
	4	22	1.62	13.58
5	1	18	1.27	14.17
	2	10	0.61	16.39
	3	13	0.50	26.00
	4	35	1.62	21.60

t	Y_t (deseasonalized)	tY_t	t^2
1	3.15	3.15	1
2	3.28	6.56	4
3	2.00	6.00	9
4	3.09	12.36	16
5	4.72	23.60	25
6	6.56	39.36	36
7	8.00	56.00	49
8	8.64	69.12	64
9	7.87	70.83	81
10	4.92	49.20	100
11	10.00	110.00	121
12	9.88	118.56	144
13	9.45	122.85	169
14	14.75	206.50	196
15	14.00	210.00	225
16	13.58	217.28	256
17	14.17	240.89	289
18	16.39	295.02	324
19	26.00	494.00	361
20	21.60	432.00	400
210	202.05	2783.28	2870

$$\bar{t} = \frac{210}{20} = 10.5$$

$$\bar{Y} = \frac{202.05}{20} = 10.1025$$

$$b_1 = \frac{\Sigma tY_t - (\Sigma t \Sigma Y_t)/n}{\Sigma t^2 - (\Sigma t)^2/n}$$

$$= \frac{2783.28 - (210)(202.05)/20}{2870 - (210)^2/20} = \frac{661.755}{665} = 0.995$$

$$b_0 = \bar{Y} - b_1 \bar{t} = 10.1025 - 0.995(10.5) = -0.345$$

$$T_t = -0.345 + 0.995t$$

b.

y	Trend Forecast
21	20.55
22	21.55
23	22.54
24	23.54

c.

Year	Quarter	Trend Forecast	Seasonal Index	Quarterly Forecast
6	1	20.55	1.27	26.10
	2	21.55	0.61	13.15
	3	22.54	0.50	11.27
	4	23.54	1.62	38.13

34.

Restaurant (i)	x_i	y_i	x_iy_i	x_i^2
1	1	19	19	1
2	4	44	176	16
3	6	40	240	36
4	10	52	520	100
5	14	53	742	196
Totals	35	208	1,697	349

$$\bar{x} = \frac{35}{5} = 7$$

$$\bar{y} = \frac{208}{5} = 41.6$$

$$b_1 = \frac{\sum x_i y_i - (\sum x_i \sum y_i)/n}{\sum x_i^2 - (\sum x_i)^2/n}$$

$$= \frac{1697 - (35)(208)/5}{349 - (35)^2/5}$$

$$= \frac{241}{104} = 2.317$$

$b_0 = \bar{y} - b_1\bar{x} = 41.6 - 2.317(7) = 25.381$

$\hat{y} = 25.381 + 2.317x$

b.　　$\hat{y} = 25.381 + 2.317(8) = 43.917$ or \$43,917

35.　　Note: To simplify the calculations let y = sales (\$100s)

x_i	y_i	x_iy_i	x_i^2
1	36	36	1
1	33	33	1
2	31	62	4
3	29	87	9
3	27	81	9
4	25	100	16
5	23	115	25
5	20	100	25
Totals 24	224	614	90

$\bar{x} = \dfrac{24}{8} = 3$

$\bar{y} = \dfrac{224}{8} = 28$

$b_1 = \dfrac{\sum x_iy_i - (\sum x_i \sum y_i)/n}{\sum x_i^2 - (\sum x_i)^2/n}$

$\quad = \dfrac{614 - (24)(224)/8}{90 - (24)^2/8}$

$\quad = \dfrac{-58}{18} = -3.222$

$b_0 = \bar{y} - b_1\bar{x} = 28 - (-3.222)(3) = 37.666$

$\hat{y} = 37.666 + 3.222x$

b.　　$\hat{y} = 37.666 - 3.222(1) = 34.44$ or \$3444

36.

	x_i	y_i	$x_i y_i$	x_i^2
	20	21	420	400
	20	19	380	400
	40	15	600	1600
	30	16	480	900
	60	14	840	3600
	40	17	680	1600
Totals	210	102	3400	8500

$$\bar{x} = \frac{210}{6} = 35$$

$$\bar{y} = \frac{102}{6} = 17$$

$$b_1 = \frac{\sum x_i y_i - (\sum x_i \sum y_i)/n}{\sum x_i^2 - (\sum x_i)^2/n}$$

$$= \frac{3400 - (210)(102)/6}{8500 - (210)^2/6}$$

$$= \frac{-170}{1150} = -0.1478$$

$$b_0 = \bar{y} - b_1\bar{x} = 17 - (-0.1478)35 = 22.173$$

$$\hat{y} = 22.173 + 0.1478x$$

b. $\hat{y} = 22.173 - 0.1478(50) = 14.783$ or approximately 15 defective parts

Case Problem

1. Graph of the time series:

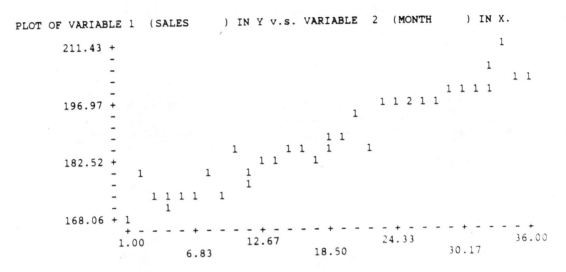

PLOT OF VARIABLE 1 (SALES) IN Y v.s. VARIABLE 2 (MONTH) IN X.

2. Analysis of seasonality

    Note: Detailed computations appear on the following pages.

Month	Seasonal-Irregular Component Values		Seasonal Index
January	1.445	1.441	1.44
February	1.301	1.297	1.30
March	1.344	1.343	1.34
April	1.047	1.034	1.04
May	1.044	1.054	1.05
June	.799	.801	0.80
July	.822	.834	0.83
August	.857	.848	0.85
September	.618	.638	0.63
October	.725	.675	0.70
November	.843	.862	0.85
December	1.137	1.180	1.16

Year	Month	Sales (1000s)	12-Month Moving Average	Centered Moving Average
1	January	242		
	February	235		
	March	232		
	April	178		
	May	184		
	June	140		
			175.5	
	July	145		176.375
			177.25	
	August	152		177.375
			177.5	
	September	110		178.125
			178.75	
	October	130		179.375
			180.0	
	November	152		180.375
			180.75	
	December	206		181.125
			181.5	
2	January	263		182.0
			182.5	
	February	238		182.875
			183.25	
	March	247		183.75
			184.25	
	April	193		184.25
			184.25	
	May	193		184.875
			185.5	
	June	149		186.5
			187.5	
	July	157		188.2917
			189.0833	
	August	161		189.7917
			190.5	
	September	122		191.25
			192.0	

Year	Month	Sales (1000s)	12-Month Moving Average	Centered Moving Average
	October	130		192.5
			193.0	
	November	167		193.7083
			194.4167	
	December	230		194.875
			195.3333	
3	January	282		195.7083
			196.0833	
	February	255		196.625
			197.1667	
	March	265		197.3333
			197.5	
	April	205		198.25
			199.0	
	May	210		199.25
			199.5	
	June	160		199.7083
			199.9167	
	July	166		
	August	174		
	September	126		
	October	148		
	November	173		
	December	235		

Year	Month	Sales (1000s)	Centered Moving Average	Seasonal-Irregular Component
1	January	242		
	February	235		
	March	232		
	April	178		
	May	184		
	June	140		
	July	145	176.375	.822
	August	152	177.375	.857
	September	110	178.125	.618
	October	130	179.375	.725
	November	152	180.375	.843
	December	206	181.125	1.137
2	January	263	182.0	1.445
	February	238	182.875	1.301
	March	247	183.75	1.344
	April	193	184.25	1.047
	May	193	184.875	1.044
	June	149	186.5	.799
	July	157	188.2917	.834
	August	161	189.7917	.848
	September	122	191.25	.638
	October	130	192.5	.675
	November	167	193.7083	.862
	December	230	194.875	1.180
3	January	282	195.7083	1.441
	February	255	196.625	1.297
	March	265	197.3333	1.343
	April	205	198.25	1.034
	May	210	199.25	1.054
	June	160	199.7083	.801
	July	166		
	August	174		
	September	126		
	October	148		
	November	173		
	December	235		

The deseasonalized time series is shown below:

t	Deseasonalized Sales	t	Deseasonalized Sales
1	168.06	19	189.16
2	180.77	20	189.41
3	173.13	21	193.65
4	171.15	22	185.71
5	175.24	23	196.47
6	175.00	24	198.28
7	174.70	25	195.83
8	178.82	26	196.15
9	174.60	27	197.76
10	185.71	28	197.12
11	178.82	29	200.00
12	177.59	30	200.00
13	182.64	31	200.00
14	183.08	32	204.71
15	184.33	33	200.00
16	185.58	34	211.43
17	183.81	35	203.53
18	186.25	36	202.59

The trend line fitted to the deseasonalized time series is

$$T_t = 169.499 + 1.02t$$

3.   Sales forecasts

Forecast for Year 4

Using $T_t = 169.499 + 1.02t$

Month	Trend Forecast	Seasonal Index	Monthly Forecast
January	207.239	1.44	298.424
February	208.259	1.30	270.737
March	209.279	1.34	280.434
April	210.299	1.04	218.711
May	211.319	1.05	221.885
June	212.339	0.80	169.871
July	213.359	0.83	177.088
August	214.379	0.85	182.222
September	215.399	0.63	135.701
October	216.419	0.70	151.493
November	217.439	0.85	184.823
December	218.459	1.16	253.194

4. Forecast error = $295,000 − $298,424 = −$3,424

    The forecast we developed overpredicted by $3,424; this represents a very small error.

5. The analysis can be easily updated each month, especially if a computer software package like The Management Scientist is used to perform the analysis.

Answers to Questions for Quantitative Methods in Practice

1. Since there are no finished-goods or in-process inventories of electricity, this product must be generated to meet the instantaneous requirements of the customers. Electrical shortages are not just lost sales, but "brownouts" or "blackouts". On the positive side, the demand and sale of energy are more predictable than for many other products. Also, unlike the situation in a multiproduct firm, a great amount of forecasting effort and expertise can be concentrated on the two products: gas and electricity.

2. In the mid 1970's a variety of actions by the government, the off-and-on energy shortages, and price signals to the consumer began to affect the consumption of electric energy. As a result, the behavior of the peak load and electric energy time series became more and more unpredictable. Hence a simple trend projection forecasting model was no longer adequate.

3. A special forecasting model - referred to as an econometric model - was developed by CG&E to better account for the behavior of these time series. The purpose of the econometric model is to forecast the annual energy consumption by residential, commercial, and industrial classes of service. These forecasts are then used to develop forecasts of summer and winter peak loads.

Chapter 7
Linear Programming:
The Graphical Method

Learning Objectives

1.   Obtain an overview of the kinds of problems linear programming has been used to solve.

2.   Learn how to develop linear programming models for simple problems.

3.   Be able to identify the special features of a model that make it a linear programming model.

4.   Learn how to solve two variable linear programming models by the graphical solution procedure.

5.   Understand the importance of extreme points in obtaining the optimal solution.

6.   Know the use and interpretation of slack and surplus variables.

7.   Understand how alternate optimal solutions, infeasibility and unboundedness can occur in linear programming problems.

8.   Understand the following terms:

objective function	redundant constraint
constraint function	simultaneous linear equations
solution	standard form
feasible solution	slack variable
optimal solution	surplus variable
nonnegativity constraints	alternate optimal solutions
linear equations or functions	infeasibility
feasible region	unboundedness
extreme point	

Solutions

1.   a, b, and e, are acceptable linear programming relationships.

c is not acceptable because of $-2x_2^2$

d is not acceptable because of $3\sqrt{x_1}$

f is not acceptable because of $1x_1x_2$

c, d, and f could not be found in a linear programming model because they have the above nonlinear terms.

2.

a.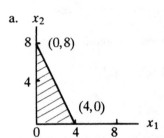

b.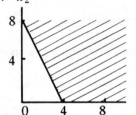

c.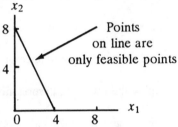

3.

a.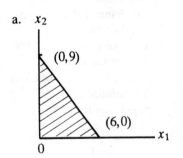

b.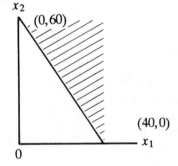

c.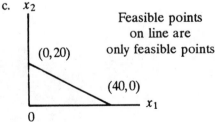

4.

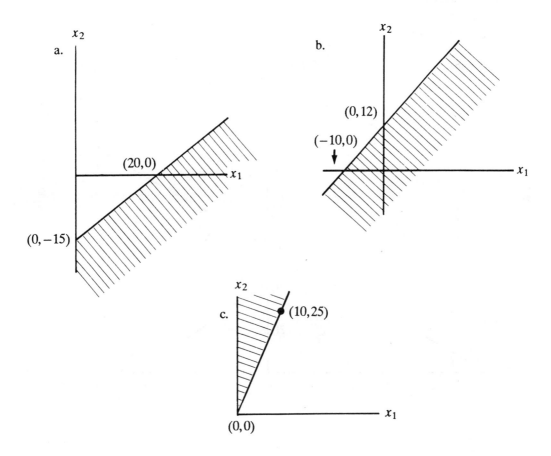

5.

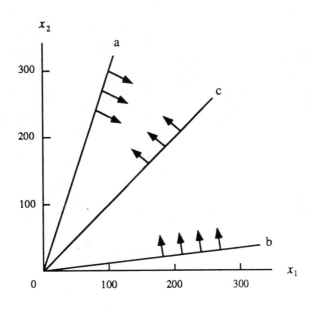

6.   Slope of objective function: $-c_1/c_2$

For $z = 7x_1 + 10x_2$,   slope $= -7/10$

For $z = 6x_1 + 4x_2$,   slope $= -6/4 = -3/2$

For $z = -4x_1 + 7x_2$,   slope $= 4/7$

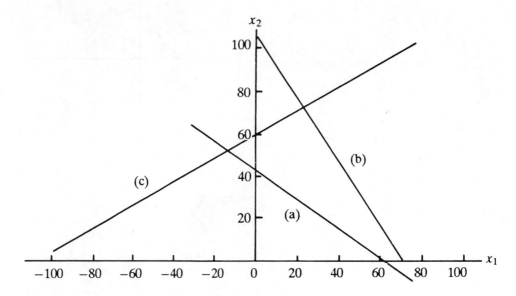

7.

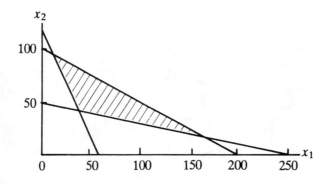

8.

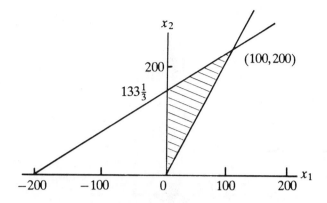

9.

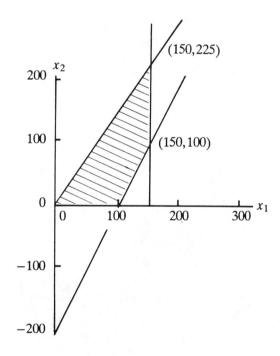

10.

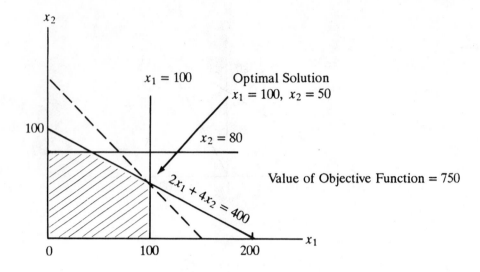

11.

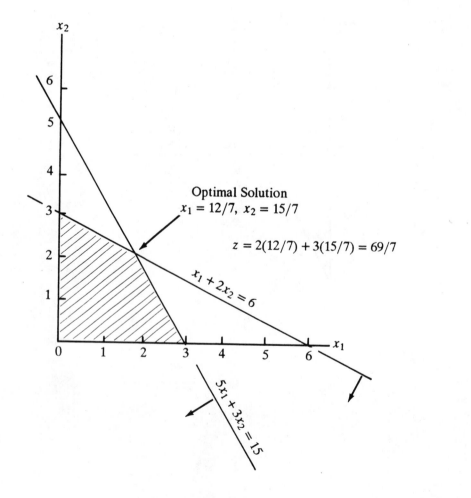

$$
\begin{array}{rrrrrl}
& x_1 & + & 2x_2 & = & 6 & (1) \\
& 5x_1 & + & 3x_2 & = & 15 & (2) \\
(1) \times 5 \quad & 5x_1 & + & 10x_2 & = & 30 & (3) \\
(2) - (3) \quad & & - & 7x_2 & = & -15 & \\
& & & x_2 & = & 15/7 &
\end{array}
$$

From (1)
$$x_1 = 6 - 2(15/7)$$
$$= 6 - 30/7 = 12/7$$

12.a.

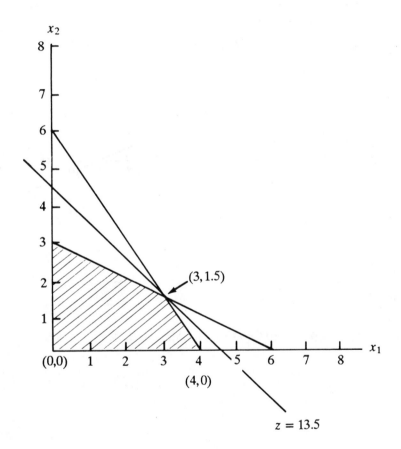

Solution:

$x_1 = 3$, $x_2 = 1.5$

Profit $= 13.5$

b.

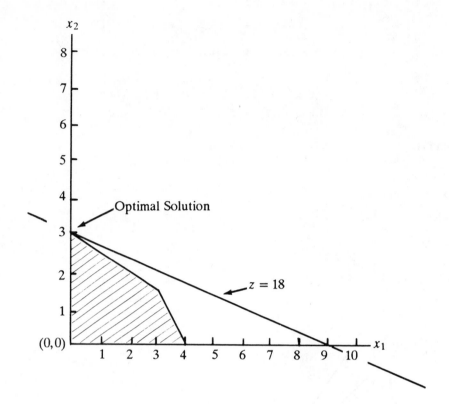

Solution:

$x_1 = 0, x_2 = 3$

Profit $= 18$

c.   There are four extreme points: (0,0), (4,0), (3,1.5), and (0,3).

13.a.

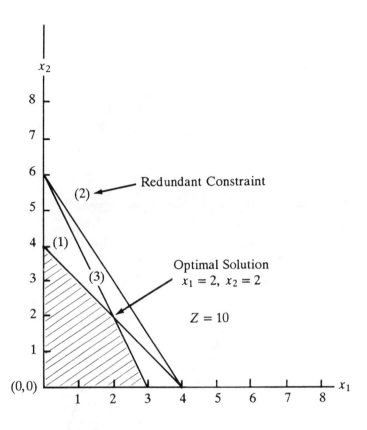

b. Yes, constraint 2.

The solution remains $x_1 = 2$, $x_2 = 2$ if constraint 2 is removed.

14.a.

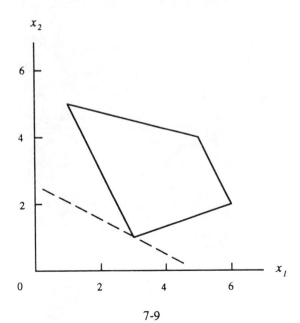

Optimal Solution: $x_1 = 3$, $x_2 = 1$, value $= 5$

b.

(1)	$3\ \ +4(1)$	$= 7$	Slack $= 21$	$-\ 7$	$= 14$
(2)	$2(3) +1$	$= 7$	Surplus $= 7$	$-\ 7$	$= 0$
(3)	$3(3) +1.5$	$= 10.5$	Slack $= 21$	$-\ 10.5$	$= 10.5$
(4)	$2(3) +6(1)$	$= 12$	Surplus $= 12$	$-\ 0$	$= 12$

c.

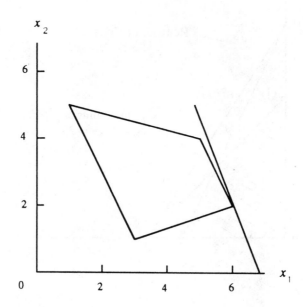

Optimal Solution: $x_1 = 6$, $x_2 = 2$, value $= 34$

15.a.

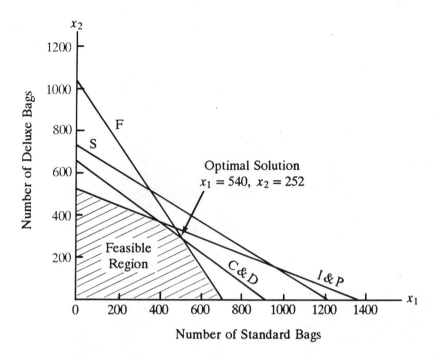

b.   Profit = $7668

c. & d.

Operation	Production Time	Slack
Cutting and Dyeing	630	0
Sewing	480	120
Finishing	708	0
Inspection and Packaging	117	18

16.a. $x_1 = 0$, $x_2 = 540$ Profit = 4860

b.   Inspection and Pacakaging and the nonnegativity constraint on x_1.

17.a.

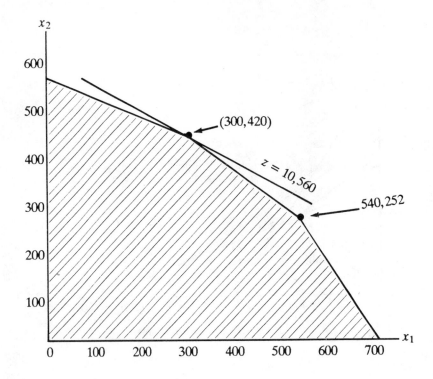

Optimal Solution: $x_1 = 300$, $x_2 = 420$, $z = 10,560$

b. Similar to part (a): the same feasible region with a different objective function. The optimal solution occurs at (708, 0) with a profit of $z = 20(708) + 9(0) = 14,160$.

c. The sewing constraint is redundant. Such a change would not change the optimal solution to the original problem.

18.a. & b.
    With the coefficient of x_2 equal to 30, any coefficient for x_1 greater-than-or-equal to 60 will make extreme point 2 optimal. Shown below is an objective function of $90x_1 + 30x_2$.

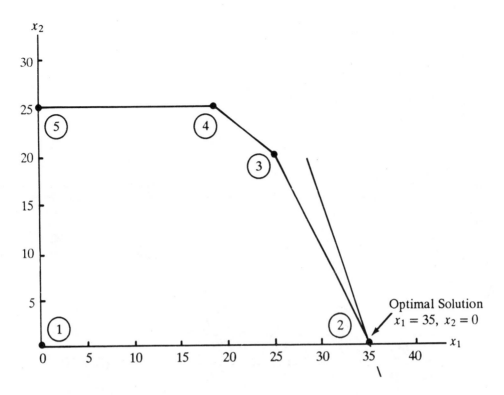

c.   Material 1: $s_1 = 6$

            Material 2: $s_2 = 5$

            Material 3: $s_3 = 0$

19.a.   Let x_1 = number of units of regular model.
                  x_2 = number of units of regular model.

$$\max \quad 5x_1 \quad + \quad 8x_2$$

s.t.

$1x_1$	+	$^3/_2\, x_2$	$\leq$	900	cutting and sewing
$^1/_2\, x_1$	+	$^1/_3\, x_2$	$\leq$	300	finishing
$^1/_8\, x_1$	+	$^1/_4\, x_2$	$\leq$	100	packing and shipping

$$x_1,\ x_2 \geq 0$$

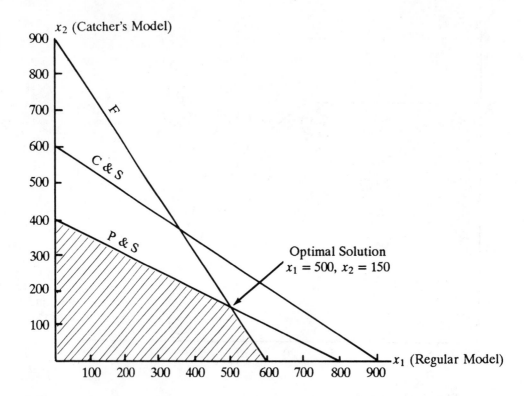

b. $5(500) + 8(150) = \$3,700$

c.   C & S $1(500) + {}^3/_2(150) = 725$

F ${}^1/_2(500) + {}^1/_3(150) = 300$

P & S ${}^1/_8(500) + {}^1/_4(150) = 100$

d.

Department	Capacity	Usage	Slack
C & S	900	725	175 hours
F	300	300	0 hours
P & S	100	100	0 hours

20.a. Let x_1 = units of product 1
x_2 = units of product 2

$$\max \quad 25x_1 \quad + \quad 30x_2$$

s.t.

$$1.5x_1 \quad + \quad 3x_2 \quad \leq \quad 450 \quad \text{Dept. A}$$

$$2x_1 \quad + \quad 1x_2 \quad \leq \quad 350 \quad \text{Dept. B}$$

$$.25x_1 \quad + \quad .25x_2 \quad \leq \quad 50 \quad \text{Dept. C}$$

$$x_1, \ x_2, \ \geq 0$$

b.

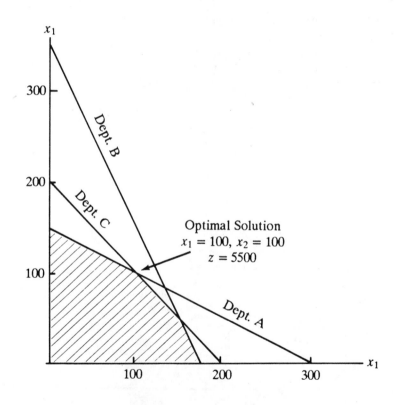

Optimal Solution
$x_1 = 100$, $x_2 = 100$
$z = 5500$

c.

Department	Capacity	Usage	Slack
Dept. A	450	450	0 hours
Dept. B	350	300	50 hours
Dept. C	50	50	0 hours

21.   Let x_1 = number of Mount Everest Parkas
                x_2 = number of Rocky Mountain Parkas

$$\max \quad 100x_1 \; + \; 150x_2$$

s.t.

$30x_1$	+	$20x_2$	$\leq$	7200	Cutting time
$45x_1$	+	$15x_2$	$\leq$	7200	Sewing time
$0.8x_1$	-	$0.2x_2$	$\geq$	0	% requirement

Note: Students often have difficulty formulating constraints such as the % requirement constraint. We encourage our students to proceed in a systematic step-by-step fashion when formulating these types of constraints. For example:

x_1 must be at least 20% of total production
$x_1 \geq 0.2$ (total production)
$x_1 \geq 0.2 \, (x_1 + x_2)$
$x_1 \geq 0.2x_1 + 0.2x_2$
$0.8x_1 - 0.2x_2 \geq 0$

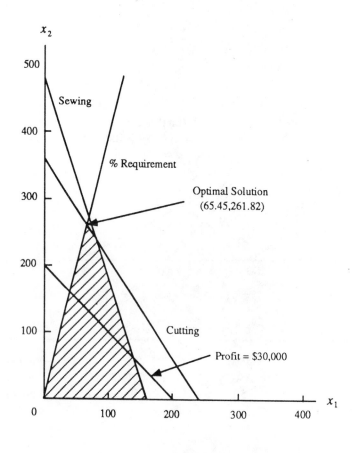

The optimal solution is $x_1 = 65.45$ and $x_2 = 261.82$; the value of this solution is $z = 100(65.45) + 150(261.82) = \$45,818$. If we think of this situation as an on-going continuous production process, the fractional values simply represent partially completed products. If this is not the case, we can approximate the optimal solution by rounding down; this yields the solution $x_1 = 65$ and $x_2 = 261$ with a corresponding profit of \$45,650.

22.a. Let x_1 = pounds of Greenlawn
              x_2 = pounds of Lawn Care

$$\text{max} \quad 3x_1 \quad + \quad 3x_2$$

s.t.

$$\tfrac{3}{5}x_1 \quad + \quad \tfrac{3}{4}x_2 \quad \leq \quad 900 \quad \text{K-40}$$

$$\tfrac{2}{5}x_1 \quad + \quad \tfrac{1}{4}x_2 \quad \leq \quad 400 \quad \text{K-50}$$

$$1x_2 \quad \leq \quad 500$$

$$x_1, \quad x_2, \quad \geq 0$$

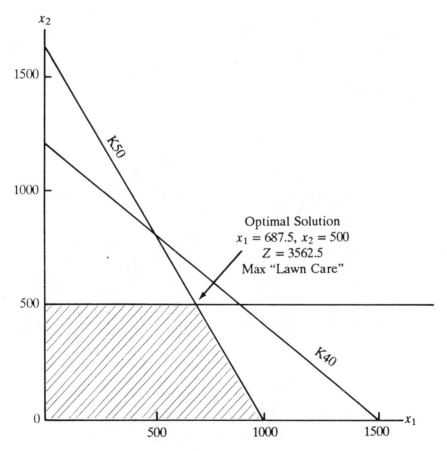

b. Yes. $x_1 = 500$, $x_2 = 800$, $z = 3900$ if "Lawn Care" restriction is removed.

23.   Let x_1 = shares of U.S. Oil
              x_2 = shares of Hub Properties

$$\max \quad 3x_1 \quad + \quad 5x_2$$

s.t.

$25x_1$	+	$50x_2$	$\leq$	80,000	Funds available
$.50x_1$	+	$.25x_2$	$\leq$	700	Risk max
$1x_1$			$\leq$	1,000	U.S. Oil max
		$x_1,\ x_2,\ \geq 0$			

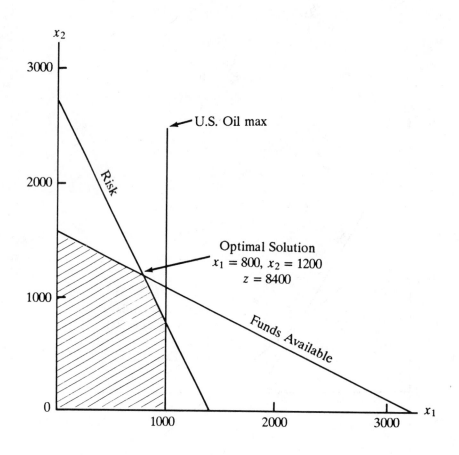

24.   Let x_1 = number of NOW-100 computers
              x_2 = number of NOW-200 computers

       max $500x_1$ + $750x_2$

       s.t.

                    x_1 + x_2 ≤   3400 # 68040 microprocessors

                    $1.5x_1$ + $3x_2$ ≤   6000 assembly time

                    $-0.25x_1$ + $0.75x_2$ ≥   0 % requirement
                                $x_1, x_2 ≥ 0$

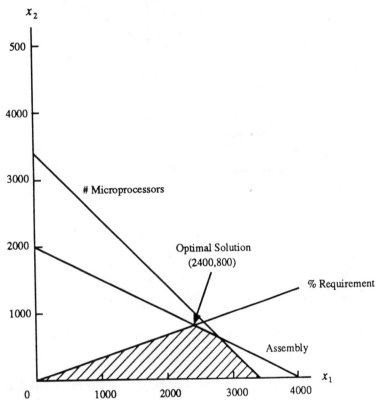

25.   Let x_1 = number of sq. ft. for national brands
              x_2 = number of sq. ft. for generic brands
       Problem Constraints:

                    x_1 + x_2 ≤   200   Space available

                    x_1 ≥   120   National brands

                              x_2 ≥   20   Generic

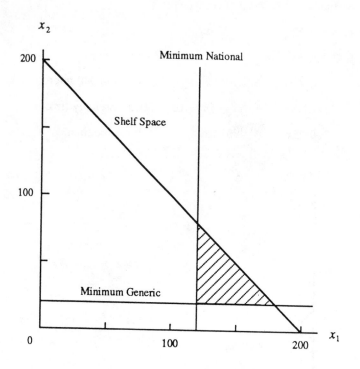

Extreme Point	x_1	x_2
1	120	20
2	180	20
3	120	80

a. Optimal solution is extreme point 2; 180 sq. ft. for the national brand and 20 sq. ft. for the generic brand.

b. Alternate optima. Any point on the line segment joining extreme point 2 and extreme point 3 is optimal.

c. Optimal solution is extreme point 3; 120 sq. ft. for the national brand and 80 sq. ft. for the generic brand.

26.

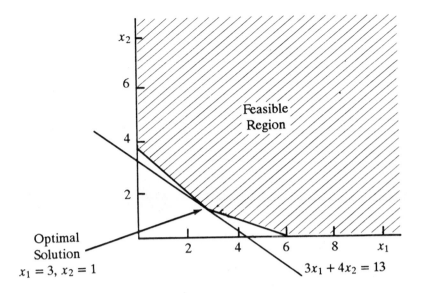

Optimal
Solution
$x_1 = 3, x_2 = 1$

$3x_1 + 4x_2 = 13$

Objective Function Value = 13

27.a.　Let　x_1 = gallons of Product 1
　　　　　x_2 = gallons of Product 2

$$\min \quad 2x_1 \quad + \quad 3x_2$$

s.t.

x_1			$\geq$	125	Product 1 Demand
x_1	+	x_2	$\geq$	350	Total Production
$2x_1$	+	x_2	$\leq$	600	Processing Time

$$x_1, x_2 \geq 0$$

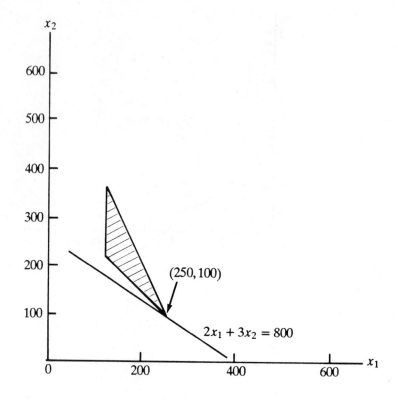

Optimal Solution: $x_1 = 250$, $x_2 = 100$.

b. Total production cost = \$800

c. There is a surplus production of 125 gallons of Product 1.

28.a. Only the objective function coefficient for x_2 is changed from the formulation in Problem 27.

$$\min \quad 2x_1 \quad + \quad 1.5x_2$$

s.t.

x_1			$\geq$	125	Product 1 Demand
x_1	$+$	x_2	$\geq$	350	Total Production
$2x_1$	$+$	x_2	$\leq$	600	Processing Time
		$x_1, x_2 \geq 0$			

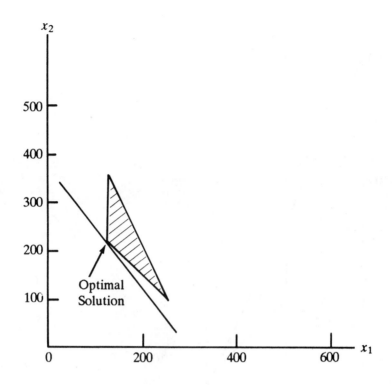

Optimal production quantities: $x_1 = 125$, $x_2 = 225$

b.   The first and second constraints combine to form the optimal extreme point.

29.

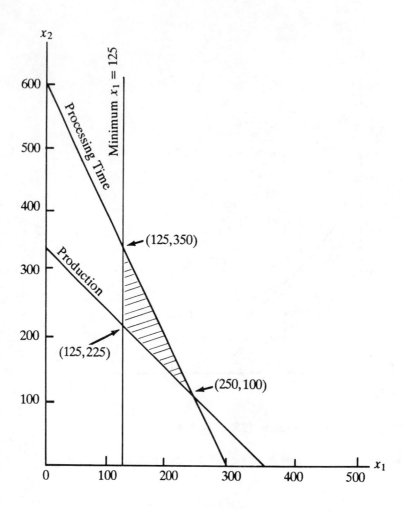

Extreme Points	Objective Function Value	Surplus Demand x_1	Surplus Total Production	Slack Processing Time
($x_1 = 250$, $x_2 = 100$)	800	125	-	-
($x_1 = 125$, $x_2 = 225$)	925	-	-	125
($x_1 = 125$, $x_2 = 350$)	1300	-	125	-

30.   Let x_1 = ounces of Bark Bits in feed mix
              x_2 = ounces of Canine Chow in feed mix

The problem can be formulated and solved as follows:

$$\max \quad .06x_1 \quad + \quad .05x_2$$

s.t.

$$.30x_1 \quad + \quad .20x_2 \quad \geq \quad 5 \quad \text{Protein}$$

$$.15x_1 \quad + \quad .30x_2 \quad \geq \quad 3 \quad \text{Fat}$$
$$x_1, \ x_2, \ \geq 0$$

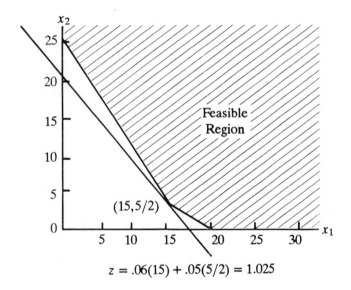

$$z = .06(15) + .05(5/2) = 1.025$$

31.   The mathematical formulation is:

$$\min \quad 4x_1 \quad + \quad 5x_2$$

s.t.

$$\tfrac{1}{5}(20)x_1 \quad + \quad \tfrac{1}{10}(40)x_2 \quad \geq \quad 60 \quad \text{Nitrogen}$$

$$\tfrac{1}{20}(20)x_1 \quad + \quad \tfrac{1}{10}(40)x_2 \quad \geq \quad 24 \quad \text{Phosphorus}$$

$$\tfrac{1}{5}(20)x_1 \quad + \quad \tfrac{1}{20}(40)x_2 \quad \geq \quad 40 \quad \text{Potassium}$$
$$x_1, \ x_2, \ \geq 0$$

where x_1 =   number of bags of 20-5-20 (20 lb. bags)

          x_2 =   number of bags of 10-10-5 (40 lb. bags)

Optimal Solution: $x_1 = 12$, $x_2 = 3$, and $s_3 = 14$; Cost = \$63.00

The surplus variables indicate the optimal solution will supply exactly the minimum requirements of nitrogen and phosphorous, but that 14 pounds more potassium will be provided than necessary.

32.

Let x_1 =   units of Model X

        x_2 =   units of Model Y

max $40x_1$ + $50x_2$

s.t.

$$3x_1 + 5x_2 \leq 600 \quad \text{Sales time}$$

$$1x_1 \quad\quad\quad \geq 25 \quad \text{Model X}$$

$$1x_2 \geq 25 \quad \text{Model Y}$$

$$x_1, \ x_2, \ \geq 0$$

a.

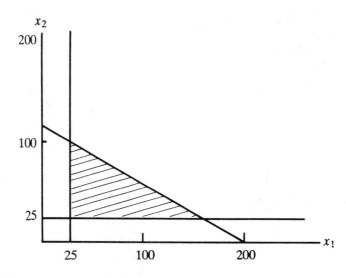

b.   Optimal Solution: $x_1 = 158^1/_3$, $x_2 = 25$, profit = 7583

c.

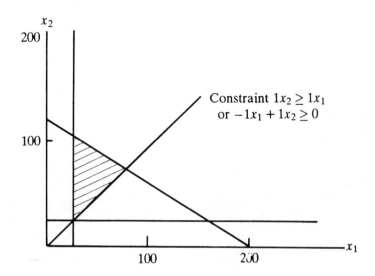

d. Optimal Solution: $x_1 = 75$, $x_2 = 75$, profit = 6750

33. Let x_1 = ounces of A
     Let x_2 = ounces of B

$$\min \quad 0.04x_1 \quad + \quad 0.03x_2$$

$\frac{1}{2}x_1$	$+$	$\frac{1}{10}x_2$	$\geq$	4	Protein
$\frac{1}{8}x_1$	$+$	$\frac{1}{3}x_2$	$\geq$	2.5	Fat
x_1	$+$	x_2	$=$	16	16 ounce can

$$x_1, \ x_2, \ \geq 0$$

34.

$$\min \quad 1x_1 \quad + \quad 1x_2$$

s.t.

$1x_1$	$+$		$\geq$	30 Product 1 minimum
		$1x_2$	$\geq$	20 Product 2 minimum
$1x_1$	$+$	$2x_2$	$\geq$	80 Raw material

$$x_1, x_2 \geq 0$$

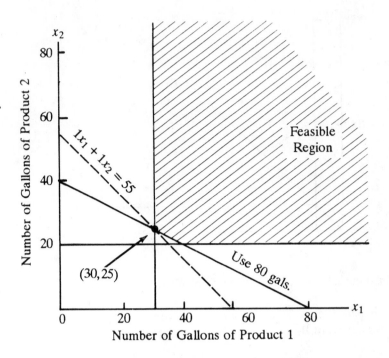

Optimal Solution: $x_1 = 30$, $x_2 = 25$ Cost $= \$55$

35.a.   Let x_1 = number of regular pizzas
              x_2 = number of deluxe pizzas

$$\begin{array}{ll}
\max & 1x_1 \quad + 1.5x_2 + 0s_1 + 0s_2 + 0s_3 + 0s_4 \\
\text{s.t.} & \\
\end{array}$$

$1x_1$	$+ \ 1x_2$	$+ 1s_1$		$= 150$	Dough
$\frac{1}{4}x_1$	$+ \frac{1}{2}x_2$	$+ 1s_2$		$= \ 50$	Topping
$1x_1$			$- 1s_3$	$= \ 50$	Regular
	$1x_2$		$- 1s_4$	$= \ 25$	Deluxe

$$x_1,\ x_2,\ s_1,\ s_2,\ s_3,\ s_4,\ \geq 0$$

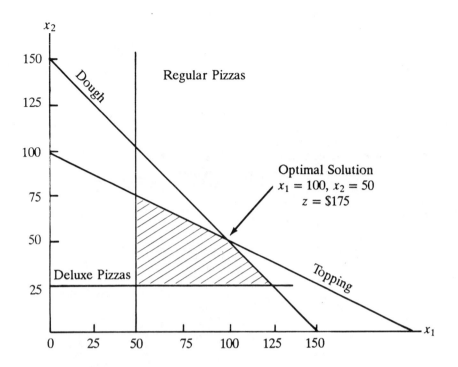

b. $s_1 = 0$ and is the amount of dough not used.

$s_2 = 0$ and is the amount of topping not used.

$s_3 = 50$ and is the number of regular pizzas produced over the minimum demand.

$s_4 = 25$ and is the number of deluxe pizzas produced over the minimum demand.

c. Binding constraints: dough ($s_1 = 0$) and topping ($s_2 = 0$) constraints.

36.a.   Let x_1 = number of automobiles
             x_2 = number of station wagons

$$\max \quad 400x_1 \quad + \quad 500x_2$$

s.t.

x_1			$\leq$	300	Auto limit
		x_2	$\leq$	150	Wagon limit
$2x_1$	$+$	$3x_2$	$\leq$	900	Dealer prep. time
		$x_1, \ x_2,$	$\geq$	0	

b.

$$\max \quad 400x_1 + 500x_2 + 0s_1 + 0s_2 + 0s_3$$
$$\text{s.t.}$$
$$x_1 \qquad\qquad + s_1 \qquad\qquad\qquad = 300$$
$$x_2 \qquad\qquad + s_2 \qquad\qquad = 150$$
$$2x_1 + 3x_2 \qquad\qquad\qquad + s_3 = 900$$
$$x_1, \ x_2, \ s_1, \ s_2, \ s_3, \ \geq 0.$$

where

s_1 = number of automobiles below the limit of 300
s_2 = number of station wagons below the limit of 150
s_3 = amount of unused dealer preparation time

c.

$$x_1 = 0, \qquad x_2 = 0$$
$$x_1 = 300, \qquad x_2 = 0$$
$$x_1 = 300, \qquad x_2 = 100 \qquad \text{(See graph in (d)}$$
$$\text{below)}$$
$$x_1 = 225, \qquad x_2 = 150$$
$$x_1 = 0, \qquad x_2 = 150$$

d.

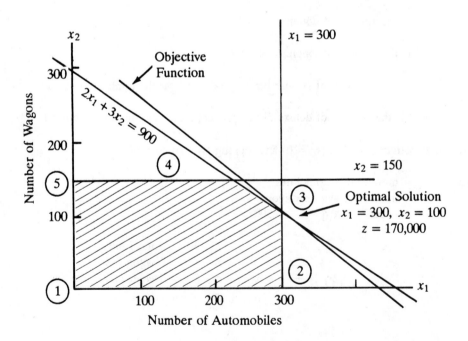

e.   Binding constraints: auto limit and dealer preparation time.

37.a.   Let x_1 = acres of soybean
x_2 = acres of corn

$$\max \quad 100x_1 + 200x_2$$

s.t.

$$
\begin{aligned}
x_1 + x_2 &\leq 500 \quad \text{Land} \\
x_1 &\leq 200 \quad \text{Soybean limit} \\
2x_1 + 6x_2 &\leq 1200 \quad \text{Labor hours} \\
x_1, \ x_2 &\geq 0
\end{aligned}
$$

b.

$$\max \quad 100x_1 + 200x_2 + 0s_1 + 0s_2 + 0s_3$$

s.t.

$$
\begin{aligned}
x_1 + x_2 + s_1 &= 500 \\
x_1 \qquad\qquad + s_2 &= 200 \\
2x_1 + 6x_2 \qquad\qquad + s_3 &= 1200 \\
x_1, \ x_2, \ s_1, \ s_2, \ s_3 &\geq 0
\end{aligned}
$$

where

s_1 = unused land
s_2 = amount below the soybean limit of 200 acres
s_3 = unused planting time

c.

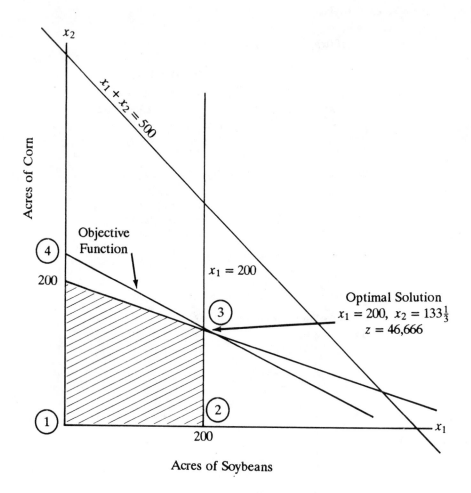

d.

$$x_1 = \;\;\; 0, \qquad x_2 = \;\;\; 0$$
$$x_1 = 200, \qquad x_2 = \;\;\; 0$$
$$x_1 = 200, \qquad x_2 = 133\;^1/_3$$
$$x_1 = \;\;\; 0, \qquad x_2 = 200$$

e. Labor-hours. Labor-hours is a binding constraint, while the land constraint is redundant; currently not all available 500 acres are being used.

38.a.

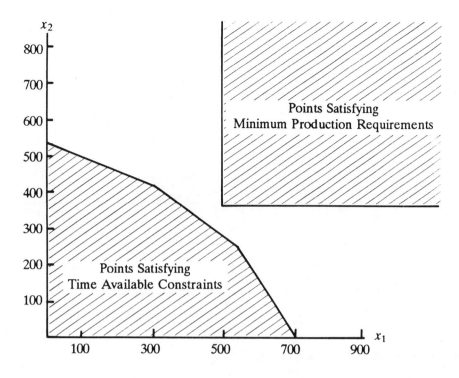

There is no feasible region. None of the points satisfying the labor availability constraints allow satisfying the newly imposed minimum production requirements.

b.

Resources Needed to Manufacture 500 Standard Bags and 360 Deluxe Bags

Operation	Minimum Requires Resources (hours)	Available Resources (hours)	Additional Resources Needed (hours)
Cutting and Dyeing	$\frac{7}{10}(500) + 1(360) = 710$	630	80
Sewing	$\frac{1}{2}(500) + \frac{5}{6}(360) = 550$	600	none
Finishing	$1(500) + \frac{2}{3}(360) = 740$	708	32
Inspection and Packaging	$\frac{1}{10}(500) + \frac{1}{4}(360) = 140$	135	5

39.a.

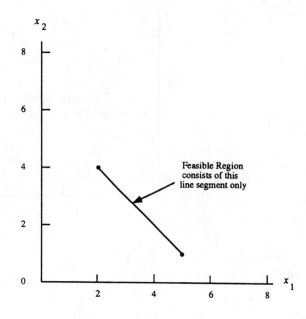

b.   The extreme points are (5, 1) and (2, 4).

c.

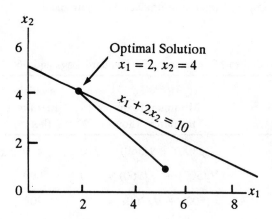

40.a.

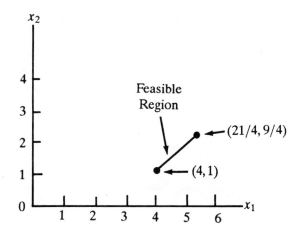

b.   There are two extreme points.

$x_1 = 4$ $x_1 = 21/4$
$x_2 = 1$ $x_2 = 9/4$

c.   The optimal solution (see (a)) is $x_1 = 4$, $x_2 = 1$

41.

$$
\begin{aligned}
\max \quad & 5x_1 && + 2x_2 && + && 8x_3 + 0s_1 + 0s_2 + 0s_3 \\
\text{s.t.} \quad & && && && \\
& 1x_1 && - 2x_2 && + \tfrac{1}{2}x_3 + 1s_1 && = 420 \\
& 2x_1 && + 3x_2 && - \quad 1x_3 \quad + 1s_2 && = 610 \\
& 6x_1 && - 1x_2 && + \quad 3x_3 \quad\quad\quad + 1s_3 && = 125 \\
& && x_1, \ x_2, \ x_3, \ s_1, \ s_2, \ s_3 \ \geq 0 &&
\end{aligned}
$$

42.a.

$$
\begin{aligned}
\max \quad & 4x_1 && + 1x_2 && + 0s_1 + 0s_2 + 0s_3 \\
\text{s.t.} \quad & && && \\
& 10x_1 && + 2x_2 && + 1s_1 && = 30 \\
& 3x_1 && + 2x_2 && + 1s_2 && = 12 \\
& 2x_1 && + 2x_2 && + 1s_3 && = 10 \\
& && x_1, \ x_2, \ s_1, \ s_2, \ s_3 \ \geq 0 &&
\end{aligned}
$$

b.

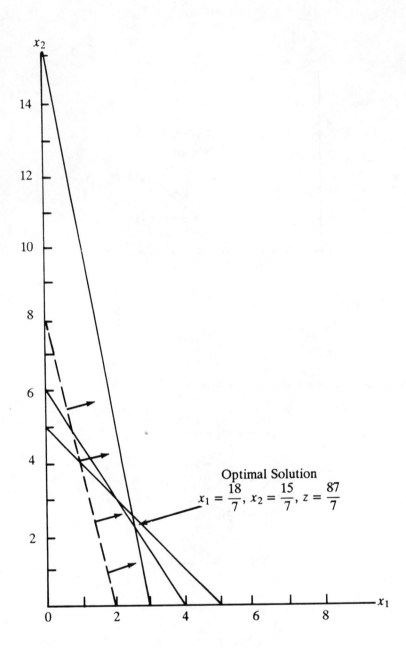

Optimal Solution
$x_1 = \dfrac{18}{7}, \; x_2 = \dfrac{15}{7}, \; z = \dfrac{87}{7}$

c. $s_1 = 0, \; s_2 = 0, \; s_3 = 4/7$

43.a.

$$\begin{aligned}
\max \quad & 3x_1 \; + 4x_2 \; + 0s_1 + 0s_2 + 0s_3 \\
\text{s.t.} \quad & \\
& -1x_1 \; + 2x_2 \; + 1s_1 \qquad\qquad\quad = 8 \\
& 1x_1 \; + 2x_2 \qquad\quad + 1s_2 \qquad\quad = 12 \\
& 2x_1 \; + 1x_2 \qquad\qquad\qquad + 1s_3 = 16 \\
& x_1, \; x_2, \; s_1, \; s_2, \; s_3 \; \geq 0
\end{aligned}$$

b.

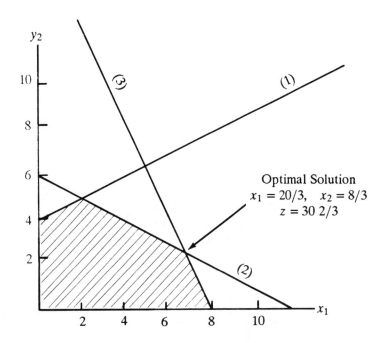

Optimal Solution
$x_1 = 20/3, \quad x_2 = 8/3$
$z = 30\ 2/3$

c. $s_1 = 8 + x_1 - 2x_2$

       $= 8 + 20/3 - 16/3$

       $= 28/3$

   $s_2 = 12 - x_1 - 2x_2$

       $= 12 - 20/3 - 16/3$

       $= 0$

   $s_3 = 16 - 2x_1 - x_2$

       $= 16 - 40/3 - 8/3$

       $= 0$

44.a.

$$
\begin{array}{llllll}
\min & 6x_1 & + 4x_2 & + 0s_1 + 0s_2 + 0s_3 \\
\text{s.t.} \\
& 2x_1 & + 1x_2 & - s_1 & & = 12 \\
& 1x_1 & + 1x_2 & & - s_2 & = 10 \\
& & 1x_2 & & + s_3 & = 4 \\
& x_1, & x_2, & s_1, & s_2, & s_3 \geq 0
\end{array}
$$

b. The optimal solution is $x_1 = 6$, $x_2 = 4$.

c. $s_1 = 4$, $s_2 = 0$, $s_3 = 0$.

45.

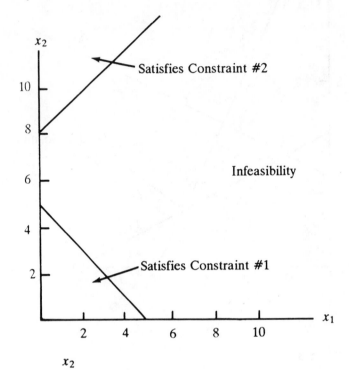

46.

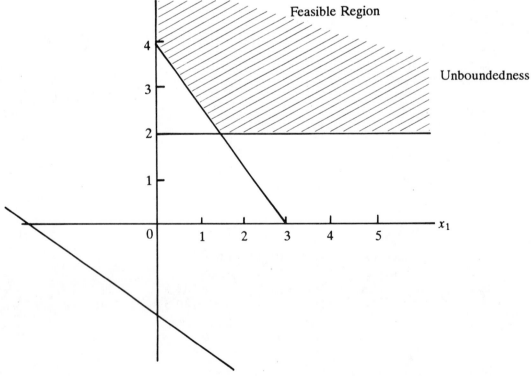

47.a.

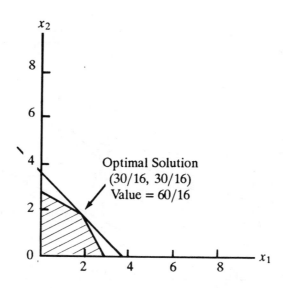

b. New optimal solution is $x_1 = 0$, $x_2 = 3$, value $= 6$.

c. Slope intercept form of constraint 2: $x_2 = -^3/_5 x_1 + 3$

Slope intercept form of objective function: $\dfrac{-1}{c_2} x_1 + \dfrac{3}{c_2}$ with $c_1 = 1$

Set slopes equal: $-1/c_2 = -3/5$

$$-5 = -3c_2$$

$$c_2 = 5/3$$

Objective function needed: max $x_1 + ^5/_3 x_2$

48.a.

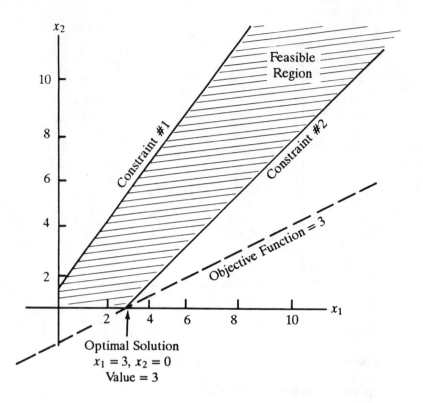

b.   Feasible region is unbounded.

c.   Optimal Solution: $x_1 = 3$, $x_2 = 0$, $z = 3$.

d.   An unbounded feasible region does not imply the problem is unbounded. This will only be the case when it is unbounded in the direction of improvement for the objective function.

49.   The only change in the formulation is the coefficient of x_2 in the objective function.

$$\min \quad 8x_1 \quad + \quad 6.4x_2$$

s.t.

$$50x_1 \quad + \quad 100x_2 \quad \leq \quad 1{,}200{,}000$$

$$5x_1 \quad + \quad 4x_2 \quad \geq \quad 60{,}000$$

$$x_2 \quad \geq \quad 3{,}000$$

$$x_1, x_2 \geq 0$$

There are now alternate optimal solutions. The objective function is parallel to the annual income constraint.

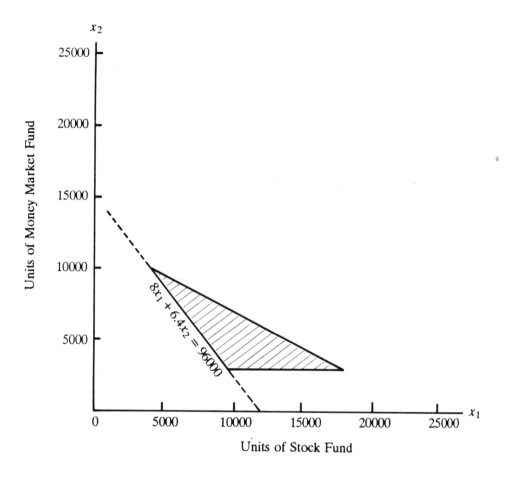

50.

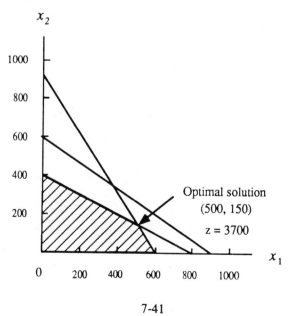

a.   Infeasibility. Kelson cannot produce 750 gloves.

b.   Objective Function $4x_1 + 8x_2$.

Alternate optimal solutions along the line segment joining extreme points ($x_1 = 500$, $x_2 = 150$) and ($x_1 = 0$, $x_2 = 400$).

c.   For unboundedness all three constraints would have to be removed.

51.   Let x_1 = number of standard size rackets
            x_2 = number of oversize size rackets

$$\text{max} \quad 10x_1 \quad + \quad 15x_2$$

s.t.

$0.8x_1$	$-$	$0.2x_2$	$\geq$	0	% standard
$10x_1$	$+$	$12x_2$	$\leq$	4800	Time
$0.125x_1$	$+$	$0.4x_2$	$\leq$	80	Alloy
		$x_1, \ x_2, \ \geq 0$		

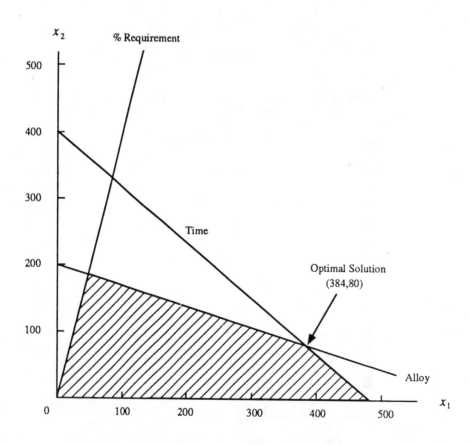

52.a. Let x_1 = time allocated to regular customer service
               x_2 = time allocated to new customer service

$$\text{max} \quad 1.2x_1 \quad + \quad x_2$$

s.t.

$$x_1 \quad + \quad x_2 \quad \leq \quad 80$$

$$25x_1 \quad + \quad 8x_2 \quad \geq \quad 800$$

$$-0.6x_1 \quad + \quad x_2 \quad \geq \quad 0$$

$$x_1, \ x_2, \ \geq 0$$

b.

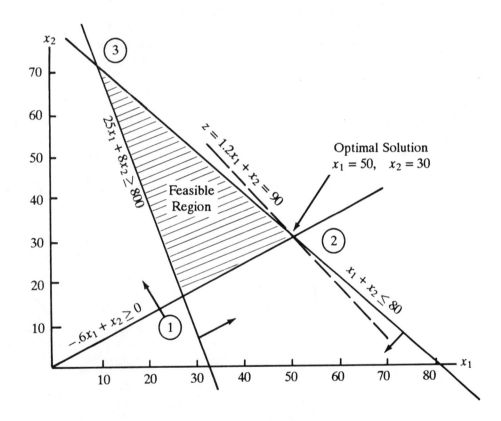

c.   Solving for extreme point 1

$$25x_1 + 8x_2 = 800$$

$$-0.6x_1 + x_2 = 0 \qquad \therefore x_2 = .6x_1$$

Substituting this value for x_2 we obtain:

$$25(x_1) + 8(.6x_1) = 800$$

$$29.8x_1 = 800$$

$$x_1 = 26.85 \text{ (rounded)}$$

Substituting 26.85 into the first equation yields $x_2 = 16.09$, whereas substituting $x_1 = 26.85$ into the second equation yields $x_2 = 16.11$. This difference is simply due to rounding.

Solving for extreme point 2

Solve $x_1 + x_2 = 80$ and $-0.6x_1 + x_2 = 0$ simultaneously to obtain $x_1 = 50$, $x_2 = 30$.

Solving for extreme point 3

Solve $25x_1 + 8x_2 = 800$ and $x_1 + x_2 = 80$ simultaneously to obtain $x_1 = 9.41$, $x_2 = 70.59$.

d.   Optimal solution: $x_1 = 50$, $x_2 = 30$, value = 90

HTS should allocate 50 hours to service for regular customers and 30 hours to calling on new customers.

Case Problem

Let x_1 = number of television advertisements
        x_2 = number of radio advertisements

$$\text{max} \quad 600x_1 + 200x_2$$
$$\text{s.t.}$$

$1x_1 +$	$1x_2$	$\geq$	30	Min announcements
	$1x_2$	$\leq$	25	Max radio announcements
$-1x_1 +$	$1x_2$	$\geq$	0	Radio/T.V. balance
$1200x_1 +$	$300x_2$	$\leq$	$25,500$	Budget
	$x_1, \; x_2$	≥ 0		

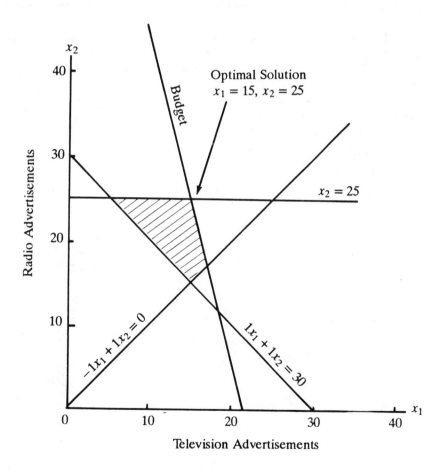

a.   Optimal Solution: $x_1 = 15$, $x_2 = 25$, $z = 14,000$

b.   To evaluate the relative merits of the media, consider the rating per dollar expenditure.

$$\text{Television} = 600/1200 = 0.5/\text{dollar}$$
$$\text{Radio} = 200/300 = 0.67/\text{dollar}$$

On a per dollar basis, radio provides the higher rated advertising exposure.

c.   The television rating would need to increase until the objective function coincides with the budget constraint line. In this case the television rating would have to be 800. Alternative optimal solutions would exist. Television spots could be increased by 2 to 17 until $x_1 = 17$, $x_2 = 17$, the new optimal solution. Note also that at 800, the television rating per dollar ($800/1200 = 0.67$) is the same as radio.

d.   Based on part (c), the television spots should be increased from 15 to 17, but no more.

e.   The budget of $25,500 and the restriction of no more than 25 radio announcements are the binding constraints to the original formulation. Thus Midtown could consider increasing the advertising budget and/or allowing additional radio advertisements. Either of these changes will improve the overall rating of the advertising strategy.

f.   If the constraint for a maximum of 25 radio announcements remains, the increase in advertising budget should be allocated to television.

Chapter 8
Linear Programming:Sensitivity Analysis and Computer Solution

Learning Objectives

1. Be able to conduct graphical sensitivity analysis for two variable linear programming problems.

2. Be able to compute and interpret the range of optimality for objective function coefficients.

3. Be able to compute and interpret the range of feasibility for constraint right-hand sides.

4. Be able to interpret the shadow and/or dual price and relate it to the value of a resource.

5. Be able to interpret the computer solution of a linear programming problem involving any number of variables and constraints.

6. Understand how the 100 percent rule can be used to assist in sensitivity analysis when simultaneous changes are made.

Solutions

1.

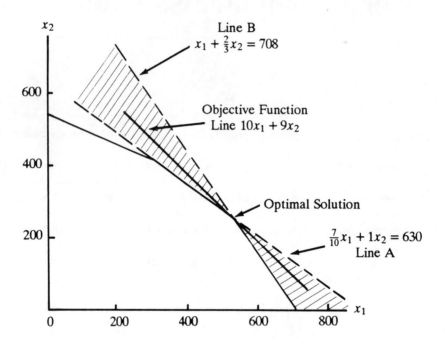

The slope of Line B = -3/2.
The slope of Line A = - 7/10.

Current solution is optimal for

$$-\frac{3}{2} \le -\frac{c_1}{9} \le -\frac{7}{10}$$

or

$$6.3 \le c_1 \le 13.5$$

Current solution is optimal for

$$-\frac{3}{2} \le -\frac{10}{c_2} \le -\frac{7}{10}$$

or

$$6\frac{2}{3} \le c_2 \le 14\frac{2}{7}$$

2.

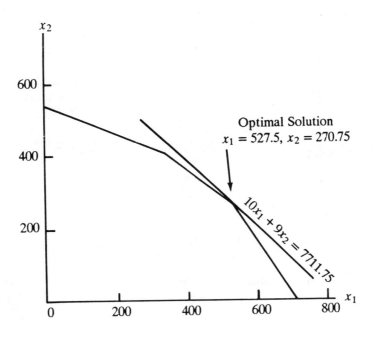

Computation of dual price:

Value of optimal solution	7711.75
Value of optimal solution	7668.00
Increase due to 10 extra hours of C & D time	43.75

$$\text{Per hour increase} = \frac{43.75}{10} = 4.375$$

Therefore, the dual price = 4.375

3. a.

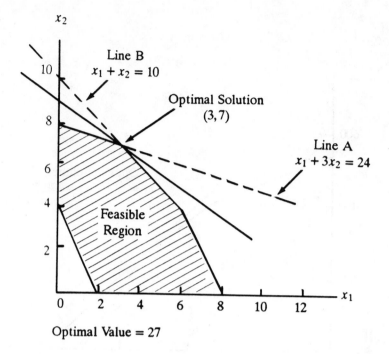

Optimal Value = 27

b. Slope of Line B = -1
    Slope of Line A = -1/3

$$-1 \leq -c_1/3 \leq -1/3$$

$$1 \geq c_1/3 \quad c_1/3 \geq 1/3$$

$$c_1 \leq 3 \quad c_1 \geq 1$$

Range: $1 \leq c_1 \leq 3$

c. $$-1 \leq -2/c_2 \leq -1/3$$

$$1 \geq 2/c_2 \quad 2/c_2 \geq 1/3$$

$$c_2 \geq 2 \quad c_2 \leq 6$$

Range : $2 \leq c_2 \leq 6$

d. Since this change leaves c_1 in its range of optimality, the same solution ($x_1 = 3$, $x_2 = 7$) is optimal.

e. This change moves c_2 outside its range of optimality. The new optimal solution is shown below.

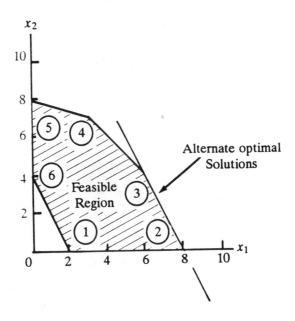

Alternate optimal solutions exist. Extreme points 2 and 3 and all points on the line segment between them are optimal.

4. a. By making a small increase in the right-hand side of constraint one and resolving we find a shadow price of 1.5 for the constraint. Thus the objective function will increase at the rate of 1.5 per unit increase in the right-hand side.

Since constraint two is not binding, its shadow price is zero.

To determine the range over which these shadow prices are applicable, one must obtain the range of feasibility.

b. Since this is a maximization problem, the dual prices are the same as the shadow prices.

5. a.

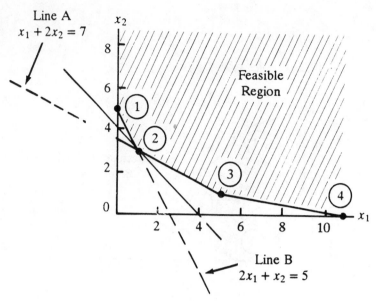

Line A
$x_1 + 2x_2 = 7$

Feasible
Region

Line B
$2x_1 + x_2 = 5$

Optimal Solution: $x_1 = 1$, $x_2 = 3$, $z = 4$

Optimal Solution: $x_1 = 1$, $x_2 = 3$, $z = 4$

b. Slope of Line B $= -2$
Slope of Line A $= -1/2$

$$-2 \leq -c_1/1 \leq -1/2$$

$$2 \geq c_1 \quad c_1 \geq 1/2$$

Range: $1/2 \leq c_1 \leq 2$

c. $$-2 \leq -1/c_2 \leq -1/2$$

$$2 \geq 1/c_2 \quad 1/c_2 \geq 1/2$$

$$c_2 \geq 1/2 \quad 2 \leq c_2$$

Range: $1/2 \leq c_2 \leq 2$

d. Since this change leaves c_1 in its range of optimality, the same solution is optimal.

e. This change moves c_2 outside of its range of optimality. The new optimal solution is found at
extreme point 1; $x_1 = 0$, $x_2 = 5$.

6. a.　Constraint 1:　　Shadow price = 0.333

Constraint 2:　　Shadow price = 0.333

Constraint 3:　　Shadow price = 0

The shadow prices for constraints one and two indicate that increasing the right-hand side will cause the optimal value of the objective function to increase (get worse) by 0.333 per unit increase. The shadow price for constraint three indicates that increasing the right hand side a small amount will not affect the optimal solution.

b.　The dual prices for a minimization problem are the negative of the shadow prices. Thus the dual prices for constraints one and two are - 0.333. This indicates that an increase in the right-hand side will not *improve* the optimal value; it will cause an increase of 0.333 per unit increase in either right-hand side.

The dual price for constraint three indicates that a small increase in the right-hand side will not affect the optimal solution.

7. a.

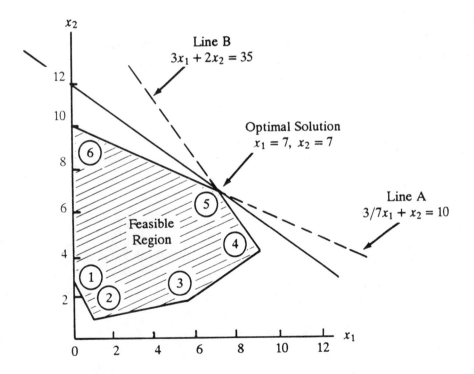

b.   Slope of Line B = -3/2
      Slope of Line A = -3/7

$$-3/2 \leq -c_1/7 \leq -3/7$$

$$3/2 \geq c_1/7 \quad c_1/7 \geq 3/7$$

$$c_1 \leq 21/2 \quad c_1 \geq 3$$

Range: $3 \leq c_1 \leq 10.5$

c. $$-3/2 \leq -5/c_2 \leq -3/7$$

$$3/2 \geq 5/c_2 \quad 5/c_2 \geq 3/7$$

$$c_2 \geq 10/3 \quad c_2 \leq 35/3$$

Range: $10/3 \leq c_2 \leq 35/3$

d.   This change moves c_1 outside its range of optimality. The new optimal solution is found at extreme point 6. It is $x_1 = 0$, $x_2 = 10$. The value is 70.

e.   Since this change leaves c_2 in its range of optimality, the same solution , with a value of 105, is optimal. Its value = 105.

8. a.

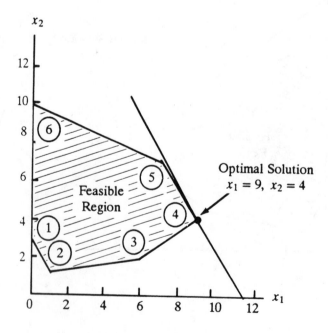

b.   Constraint 2:   Dual price = 0

Constraint 3:   Dual price = 0.0769

9.   From the solution to Problem 3, we see that the optimal solution will not change as long as the slope of the objective function stays in the following interval:

$$-1 \leq -c_1/c_2 \leq -1/3$$

a.   The slope of the new objective function is

$$-c_1/c_2 = -3/4$$

Since this is in the above interval, these simultaneous changes do not cause a change in the optimal solution.

b.   The slope of the new objective function is

$$-c_1/c_2 = -3/2.$$

This is outside the above interval; therefore, the optimal solution will change. Extreme point 3 is now optimal; the optimal solution is $x_1 = 6$, $x_2 = 4$, and $z = 26$.

10.   From the Solution to problem 7, we see that the optimal solution will not change as long as the slope of the objective function stays in the following interval:

$$-3/2 \leq -c_1/c_2 \leq -3/7$$

a.   The slope of the new objective function is

$$-c_1/c_2 = -4/10 = -0.40$$

Since $-0.40 > -3/7$, we conclude that the optimal solution will change. Extreme point 6 is now optimal. The values are $x_1 = 0$, $x_2 = 10$, $z = 100$.

b.   The slope of the new objective function is

$$-c_1/c_2 = -4/8 = -0.50$$
Since
$$-3/2 \leq -0.50 \leq -3/7$$

these simultaneous changes do not cause a change in the optimal solution; it remains $x_1 = 7$, $x_2 = 7$.

11.a.

$$x_1 = 500$$
$$x_2 = 150$$
$$\text{Value} = 3700$$

b. The finishing, packaging, and shipping constraints are binding. There is no slack.

c.

Cutting and Sewing $= 0$
Finishing $= 3$
Packaging and Shipping $= 28$

Additional finishing time is worth $3 per unit and additional packaging and shipping time is worth $28 per unit.

d. In the packaging and shipping department. Each additional hour is worth $28.

12.a.

$$4 \leq c_1 \leq 12$$

$$3.33 \leq c_2 \leq 10$$

b. As long as the profit contribution for the regular glove is between $4.00 and $12.00, the current solution is optimal.

As long as the profit contribution for the catcher's mitt stays between $3.33 and $10.00, the current solution is optimal.

The optimal solution is not sensitive to small changes in the profit contributions for the gloves.

c. The dual prices for the resources are applicable over the following ranges:

Constraint	Min RHS	Max RHS
Cutting and Sewing	725	No Upper Limit
Finishing	133.33	400
Packaging	75	135

d. Amount of increase $= (28)(20) = \$560$

13.a.

$$x_1 = 800$$
$$x_2 = 1200$$
$$\text{Estimated Annual Return} = \$8400$$

b. Constraints 1 and 2. All funds available are being utilized and the maximum permissible risk is being incurred.

c.

Constraint	Dual Prices
Funds Avail.	0.09
Risk Max	1.33
U.S. Oil Max	0

d.   No, the optimal solution does not call for investing the maximum amount in U.S. Oil.

14.a.   By more than $7.00 per share.

b.   By more than $3.50 per share.

c.   None. This is only a reduction of 100 shares and there is slack of 200 in the U.S. Oil Max constraint.

15.a.

Automobiles:	300
Station Wagons:	100
Maximum Profit Contribution:	$170,000

b.   Approximately $66.67

c.   No, the optimal solution only calls for 100 station wagons.

d.   Apply the 100% rule

$$\frac{30}{66.67} + \frac{50}{100} = 0.95$$

The accumulated percentage change is 95%. Thus, the 100% rule is satisfied and the optimal solution will not change.

16.a.
$$x_1 = 30$$
$$x_2 = 25$$
Minimum production cost = $55

b. $0.5 \leq c_1 < \infty$
$0.0 \leq c_2 \leq 2$

c.

Constraint	Dual Price
raw material	-0.50
prod. 1 minimum	-0.50
prod. 2 minimum	0.00

d.

Constraint	Shadow Price
raw material	0.50
prod. 1 minimum	0.50
prod. 2 minimum	0.00

e.　It would increase by $(0.50)(5) = 2.50$

f.

Constraint	Min RHS	Max RHS
raw material	70.0	∞
prod. 1 minimum	0.0	40.0
prod. 2 minimum	$-\infty$	25.0

17.a.　Optimal Solution: $x_1 = 250$, $x_2 = 100$, $z = 800$.

b.　$-\infty < c_1 \le 3$
$2 \le c_2 < \infty$

c.

Constraint	Dual Price
Prod. 1 demand	0
Total production	-4
Processing time	1

d.

Constraint	Shadow Price
Prod. 1 demand	0
Total production	4
Processing time	-1

e.　It would increase by $400 = 4(100)$

Constraint	Min RHS	Max RHS
Prod. 1 demand	-∞	250
Total production	300	475
Processing time	475	700

18.a.
$$x_1 = 0$$
$$x_2 = 25$$
$$x_3 = 125$$
$$x_4 = 0$$

Value of Solution: 525.0

b.   The constraints on machine A and machine C hours are binding.

c.   Machine B has 425 hours of excess capacity.

d.   Yes, the allowable increase is only 0.05.

19.a.
$$\text{No Lower Limit} \leq c_1 \leq 4.05$$
$$5.923 \leq c_2 \leq 9$$
$$2 \leq c_3 \leq 12$$
$$\text{No Lower Limit} \leq c_4 \leq 4.5$$

b.   The allowable decrease for c_1 is ∞, thus the percentage decrease is 0%.

$$\frac{1.5}{3.0} + \frac{1}{3.5} = 0.79$$

The accumulated percentage of allowable increases and decreases is 79%. Since this is less than 100%, the optimal solution will not change.

c.

Constraint	Min RHS	Max RHS
Machine A hours	133.33	800
Machine B hours	275	No Upper Limit
Machine C hours	137.5	825

d.   Yes, because that is outside the range of feasibility.

20.a.
$$x_1 = 7.30$$
$$x_2 = 0$$
$$x_3 = 1.89$$

Optimal value: 139.73

b. Constraints two and three.

c.

Constraint	Dual Price
1	0
2	-3.41
3	-4.43

The dual price is the improvement in the value of the objective function per unit increase in value of the RHS (right-hand side). In this problem no improvement can be made by increasing RHS's.

d.

Constraint	Shadow Price
1	0
2	3.41
3	4.43

Note: The shadow price gives the *increase* in value per unit increase in the RHS.

e. I would decrease the right-hand side of constraint three from 20 to 19.

21.a. $1.33 \leq c_1 \leq 15.54$

$14.32 \leq c_2 <$ No Upper Limit

$13.50 \leq c_3 \leq 180$

A change in one of the coefficients will not cause a change in the optimal solution as long as the change does not move the coefficient outside of its range of optimality.

b. Same as before.

c. Apply the 100% rule.

$$\frac{0.25}{0.543} + \frac{0.25}{0.676} = 0.83$$

The accumulated percentage change is 83%. Since the 100% rule is satisfied, the optimal solution will not change.

22.a.

All Pro:	1000
College:	200
High School:	0

b. The sewing constraint and the minimum production requirement for the All Pro model.

c.   Constraint 1: There are 4000 minutes of unused cutting and dyeing time.

       Constraint 2: All the sewing time is being utilized at the optimal solution.

       Constraint 3: There are 5200 minutes of unused inspection and packaging time.

       Constraint 4: Only the minimum number of All-Pro models is being produced.

d.   No Lower Limit $< c_1 \leq 5$
                     $5 \leq c_2 <$ No Upper Limit
       No Lower Limit $< c_3 \leq 4$

       No amount of decrease in the profit contribution for the All Pro and High School models will cause the optimal solution to change. A small decrease in the profit contribution for the College model will cause the optimal solution to change. A small increase in the profit contribution for the High School model will cause a change in the optimal solution.

23.a. $12.00 per hour is $.20 per minute. Since the dual price for the sewing constraint is 0.33, I would recommend using overtime.

    b.   Shadow price: -2.0 This indicates that an increase of one unit in the All Pro requirement will cause a $2.00 decrease in profit contribution.

    c.   Alternate optimal solutions exist. Another solution with $x_2 > 0$ may be found which yields the same value for the objective function.

    d.   No change in the optimal solution since there is no upper limit for c_2 in the range of optimality.

24.a.   Let $x_1 =$ units of component 1 manufactured
                  $x_2 =$ units of component 2 manufactured
                  $x_3 =$ units of component 3 manufactured

$$\max \quad 8x_1 + 6x_2 + 9x_3$$

$$\text{s.t.}$$

$$
\begin{array}{rcrcrcl}
6x_1 &+& 4x_2 &+& 4x_3 &\leq& 7200 \\
4x_1 &+& 5x_2 &+& 2x_3 &\leq& 6600 \\
     & &   & &   &\leq& 200 \\
x_1 & &   & &   &\leq& 1000 \\
     & & x_2 & &   &\leq& 1000 \\
x_1 & &   & &   &\geq& 600 \\
\end{array}
$$

$$x_1, \ x_2, \ x_3 \geq 0$$

The optimal solution is

       $x_1 = 600$
       $x_2 = 700$
       $x_3 = 200$

b. No Lower Limit $< c_1 \leq 9.0$
$5.33 \leq c_2 \leq 9.0$
$6.00 \leq c_3 <$ No Upper Limit

Individual changes in the profit coefficients within these ranges will not cause a change in the optimal number of components to produce.

Constraint	Min RHS	Max RHS
1	4400	7440
2	6300	No Upper Limit
3	100	900
4	600	No Upper Limit
5	700	No Upper Limit
6	514.29	1000

These are the ranges over which the dual and shadow prices for the associated constraints are applicable.

d. Nothing, since there are 300 minutes of slack time on the grinder at the optimal solution.

e. No, since at that price it would not be profitable to produce any of component 3.

25.a. Let x_1 = amount invested in growth stock fund
x_2 = amount invested in income stock fund
x_3 = amount invested in money market fund

max $0.20x_1 + 0.10x_2 + 0.06x_3$
s.t.

$0.10x_1 + 0.05x_2 + 0.01x_3 \leq (0.05)(300,000)$	Hartmann's max risk
$x_1 \geq (0.10)(300,000)$	Growth fund min.
$x_2 \geq (0.10)(300,000)$	Income fund min.
$x_3 \geq (0.20)(300,000)$	Money market min,
$x_1 + x_2 + x_3 \leq 300,000$	Funds available
$x_1, x_2, x_3 \geq 0$	

b. The solution to Hartmann's portfolio mix problem is given.

OPTIMAL SOLUTION

Objective Function Value =   36000.000000

Variable	Value	Reduced Costs
X1	120000.000000	0.000000
X2	30000.000000	0.000000
X3	150000.000000	0.000000

Constraint	Slack/Surplus	Dual Prices
1	0.000000	1.555555
2	89999.984000	0.000000
3	0.000000	-0.022222
4	90000.000000	0.000000
5	0.000000	0.044444

OBJECTIVE COEFFICIENT RANGES

Variable	Lower Limit	Current Value	Upper Limit
X1	0.150000	0.200000	0.600000
X2	No Lower Limit	0.100000	0.122222
X3	0.020000	0.060000	0.200000

RIGHT HAND SIDE RANGES

Constraint	Lower Limit	Current Value	Upper Limit
1	6900.001000	15000.000000	23100.000000
2	No Lower Limit	30000.000000	119999.984000
3	0.000000	30000.000000	192000.000000
4	No Lower Limit	60000.000000	150000.000000
5	219000.000000	300000.000000	1109999.880000

c. These are given by the ranges of optimality on the objective function coefficients. The portfolio above will be optimal as long as the yields remain in the following intervals:

Growth stock	$0.15 \leq c_1 \leq 0.60$
Income stock	No Lower Limit $< c_2 \leq 0.1222$
Money Market	$0.02 \leq c_3 \leq 0.20$

d. The dual price for the first constraint provides this information. A change in the risk index from 0.05 to 0.06 would increase the constraint RHS by 3000 (from 15,000 to 18,000). This is within the range of feasibility, so the dual price of 1.55555 is applicable. The value of the optimal solution would increase by (3000)(1,55555) = 4,666.67.

Hartmann's yield with a risk index of 0.05 is

$$\frac{36000}{300,000} = 0.12$$

His yield with a risk index of 0.06 would be

$$\frac{40,000.67}{300,000} = 0.1355.$$

e. This change is outside the range of optimality so we must resolve the problem. The solution is shown below.

LINEAR PROGRAMMING PROBLEM

max .1X1 + .1X2 + .06X3

    S.T.

        1)   .1X1 + .05X2 + .01X3 < 15000
        2)   X1 > 30000
        3)   X2 > 30000
        4)   X3 > 60000
        5)   X1 + X2 + X3 < 300000

OPTIMAL SOLUTION

Objective Function Value =   27600.000000

Variable	Value	Reduced Costs
X1	48000.000000	0.000000
X2	192000.000000	0.000000
X3	60000.000000	0.000000

Constraint	Slack/Surplus	Dual Prices
1	0.000000	0.000000
2	18000.000000	0.000000
3	162000.000000	0.000000
4	0.000000	-0.040000
5	0.000000	0.100000

OBJECTIVE COEFFICIENT RANGES

Variable	Lower Limit	Current Value	Upper Limit
X1	0.100000	0.100000	0.150000
X2	0.077778	0.100000	0.100000
X3	No Lower Limit	0.060000	0.100000

RIGHT HAND SIDE RANGES

Constraint	Lower Limit	Current Value	Upper Limit
1	14100.000000	15000.000000	23100.000000
2	No Lower Limit	30000.000000	48000.000000
3	No Lower Limit	30000.000000	192000.000000
4	37500.000000	60000.000000	150000.000000
5	219000.000000	300000.000000	318000.000000

f.   The client's risk index and the amount of funds available.

g.   With the new yield estimates, Pfeiffer would solve a new linear program to find the optimal portfolio mix for each client. Then by summing across all 50 clients he would determine the total amount that should be placed in a growth fund, an increase fund, and a money market fund. Pfeiffer then would make the necessary switches to have the correct total amount in each account. There would be no actual switching of funds for individual clients.

26.a.   Relevant cost since LaJolla Beverage Products can purchase wine and fruit juice on an as - needed basis.

b.   Let x_1 = gallons of white wine
  x_2 = gallons of rose wine
  x_3 = gallons of fruit wine

max $1 x_1 + 1.5x_2 + 2x_3$

s.t.

$0.5x_1$	$- 0.5x_2$	$- 0.5x_3$	$\geq$	0	% white
$0.2x_1$	$+ 0.8x_2$	$+ 0.2x_3$	$\geq$	0	% rose minimum
$-0.3x_1$	$+ 0.7x_2$	$- 0.3x_3$	$\leq$	0	% rose maximum
$-0.2x_1$	$- 0.2x_2$	$+ 0.8x_3$	$=$	0	% fruit juice
x_1			$\leq$	10000	Available white
	x_2		$\leq$	8000	Available rose

$$x_1, \ x_2, \ x_3 \geq 0$$

Optimal Solution: $x_1 = 10,000$, $x_2 = 6000$, $x_3 = 4000$
profit contribution = $27,000.

c. Since the cost of the wine is a relevant cost, the dual price of $2.90 is the maximum premium (over the normal price of $1.00) that LaJolla Beverage Products should be willing to pay to obtain one additional gallon of white wine. In other words, at a price of $3.90 = $2.90 + $1.00, the additional cost is exactly equal to the additional revenue.

d. No; only 6000 gallons of the rose are currently being used.

e. Requiring 50% plus one gallon of white wine would reduce profit by $2.40. Note to instructor: Although this explanation is technically correct, it does not provide an explanation that is especially useful in the context of the problem. Alternatively, we find it useful to explore the question of what would happen if the white wine requirement were changed to at least 51%. Note that in this case, the first constraint would change to $0.49x_1 - 0.51x_2 - 0.51x_3 \geq 0$. This shows the student that the coefficients on the left-hand side are changing; note that this is beyond the scope of sensitivity analysis discussed in this chapter. Resolving the problem with this revised constraint will show the effect on profit of a 1% change.

f. Allowing the amount of fruit juice to exceed 20% by one gallon will increase profit by $1.00.

27.a. Let x_1 = minutes devoted to local news
x_2 = minutes devoted to national news
x_3 = minutes devoted to weather
x_4 = minutes devoted to sports

min $300x_1 + 200x_2 + 100x_3 + 150x_4$

s.t.

x_1	+	x_2	+	x_3	+	x_4	= 20	time available
x_1							$\geq$ 3	15% local
x_1	+	x_2					$\geq$ 10	50% requirement
				x_3	-	x_4	$\leq$ 0	weather - sports
$-x_1$	-	x_2			+	x_4	$\leq$ 0	sports requirement
				x_3			$\geq$ 4	20% weather

$$x_1, \; x_2, \; x_3, \; x_4 \geq 0$$

Optimal Solution: $x_1 = 3$, $x_2 = 7$, $x_3 = 5$, $x_4 = 5$
Total cost = $3,300

b. Each additional minute of broadcast time increases cost by $100; conversely, each minute reduced will decrease cost by $100. These interpretations are valid for increase up to 10 minutes and decreases up to 2 minutes from the current level of 20 minutes.

c. If local coverage is increased by 1 minute, total cost will increase by $100.

d. If the time devoted to local and national news is increased by 1 minute, total cost will increase by $100.

e. Increasing the sports by one minute will have no effect for this constraint since the dual price is 0.

28.a. Let x_i = number of Classic 21 boats produced in Quarter i; i = 1,2,3,4
s_i = ending inventory of Classic 21 boats in Quarter i; i = 1,2,3,4

min $10,000x_1 + 11,000x_2 + 12,100x_3 + 13,310x_4 + 250s_1 + 250s_2 + 300s_3 + 300s_4$
s.t.

$x_1 - s_1 = 1900$	Quarter 1 demand
$s_1 + x_2 - s_2 = 4000$	Quarter 2 demand
$s_2 + x_3 - s_3 = 3000$	Quarter 3 demand
$s_3 + x_4 - s_4 = 1500$	Quarter 4 demand
$s_4 \geq 500$	Ending Inventory
$x_1 \leq 4000$	Quarter 1 capacity
$x_2 \leq 3000$	Quarter 2 capacity
$x_3 \leq 2000$	Quarter 3 capacity
$x_4 \leq 4000$	Quarter 4 capacity

b.

Quarter	Production	Ending Inventory	Cost
1	4000	2100	40,525,000
2	3000	1100	33,275,000
3	2000	100	24,230,000
4	1900	500	25,439,000
			$123,469,000

c. The dual prices tell us how much it would cost if demand were to increase by one additional unit. For example, in Quarter 2 the dual price is -12,760; thus, demand for one more boat in Quarter 2 will increase costs by $12,760.

d. The dual price of 0 for Quarter 4 tells us we have excess capacity in Quarter 4. The positive dual prices in Quarters 1-3 tell us how much increasing the production capacity will improve the objective function. For example, the dual price of $2510 for Quarter 1 tells us that if capacity is increased by 1 unit for this quarter, costs will go down $2510.

29.a.　Let　　x_1 = number of copies done by Benson Printing
　　　　　　x_2 = number of copies done by Johnson Printing
　　　　　　x_3 = number of copies done by Lakeside Litho

min　　$2.45x_1$　+　$2.5x_2$　+　$2.75x_3$

s.t.

x_1			$\leq$	30,000	Benson
	x_2		$\leq$	50,000	Johnson
		x_3	$\leq$	50,000	Lakeside
$0.9x_1$ +	$0.99x_2$ +	$0.995x_3$	=	75,000	# useful reports
x_1 -	$0.1x_2$		$\geq$	0	Benson - Johnson %
		x_3	$\geq$	30,000	Minimum Lakeside

$$x_1,\ _2,\ x_3 \geq 0$$

Optimal Solution: $x_1 = 4,181$, $x_2 = 41,806$, $x_3 = 30,000$

b.　Suppose that Benson printing has a defective rate of 2% instead of 10%. The new optimal solution would increase the copies assigned to Benson printing to 30,000. In this case, the additional copies assigned to Benson Printing would reduce on a one-for-one basis the number assigned to Johnson Printing.

c.　If the Lakeside Litho requirement is reduced by 1 unit, total cost will decrease by $0.2210.

Case Problem

Note to Instructor: The difference between relevant and sunk costs is critical. The cost of the shipment of nuts is a sunk cost. Practice in applying sensitivity analysis to a business decision is obtained. You may want to suggest that sensitivity analyses other than the ones we have suggested be undertaken.

1. Cost per pound of ingredients

Almonds	$7500/6000 = $1.25
Brazil	$7125/7500 = $.95
Filberts	$6750/7500 = $.90
Pecans	$7200/6000 = $1.20
Walnuts	$7875/7500 = $1.05

Cost of nuts in three mixes:

Regular mix: .15($1.25) + .25($.95) + .25($90) + .10($1.20) + .25($1.05)
= $1.0325

Deluxe mix   .20($1.25) + .20($.95) + .20($.90) + .20($1.20) + .20($1.05)
= $1.07

Holiday mix: .25($1.25) + .15($.95) + .15($.90) + .25($1.20) + .20($1.05)
= $1.10

2. Let x_1 = pounds of Regular Mix produced
x_2 = pounds of Deluxe Mix produced
x_3 = pounds of Holiday Mix produced

Note that the cost of the five shipments of nuts is a sunk (not a relevant) cost and should not affect the decision. However, this information may be useful to management in future pricing and purchasing decisions. A linear programming model for the optimal product mix is given.

The following linear programming model can be solved to maximize profit contribution for the nuts already purchased.

$$\max \quad 1.65x_1 + 2.00x_2 + 2.25x_3$$

s.t.

$0.15x_1$	$+0.20x_2$	$+0.25x_3$	≤ 6000	Almonds
$0.25x_1$	$+0.20x_2$	$+0.15x_3$	≤ 7500	Brazil
$0.25x_1$	$+0.20x_2$	$+0.15x_3$	≤ 7500	Filberts
$0.10x_1$	$+0.20x_2$	$+0.25x_3$	≤ 6000	Pecans
$0.25x_1$	$+0.20x_2$	$+0.20x_3$	≤ 7500	Walnuts
x_1			≥ 10000	Regular
	x_2		≥ 3000	Deluxe
		x_3	≥ 5000	Holiday

$$x_1, \ x_2, \ x_3 \ \geq 0$$

The solution found using The Management Scientist is shown below.

LINEAR PROGRAMMING PROBLEM

max 1.65x1 + 2x2 + 2.25x3

    S.T.

        1) .15x1 + .2x2 + .25x3 < 6000
        2) .25x1 + .2x2 + .15x3 < 7500
        3) .25x1 + .2x2 + .15x3 < 7500
        4) .1x1 + .2x2 + .25x3 < 6000
        5) .25x1 + .2x2 + .2x3 < 7500
        6) x1 > 10000
        7) x2 > 3000
        8) x3 > 5000

OPTIMAL SOLUTION

Objective Function Value =   61374.992000

Variable	Value	Reduced Costs
X1	17500.000000	0.000000
X2	10624.996100	0.000000
X3	4999.999500	0.000000

Constraint	Slack/Surplus	Dual Prices
1	0.000000	8.500000
2	249.999527	0.000000
3	249.999527	0.000000
4	875.000490	0.000000
5	0.000000	1.499999
6	7499.999500	0.000000
7	7624.996600	0.000000
8	0.000000	-0.175000

OBJECTIVE COEFFICIENT RANGES

Variable	Lower Limit	Current Value	Upper Limit
X1	1.500000	1.650000	2.000001
X2	1.892308	2.000000	2.200000
X3	No Lower Limit	2.250000	2.425000

RIGHT HAND SIDE RANGES

Constraint	Lower Limit	Current Value	Upper Limit
1	5390.000000	6000.000000	6583.333500
2	7250.000500	7500.000000	No Upper Limit
3	7250.000500	7500.000000	No Upper Limit
4	5124.999500	6000.000000	No Upper Limit
5	6750.000000	7500.000000	7749.999500
6	No Lower Limit	10000.000000	17500.000000
7	No Lower Limit	3000.000000	10624.996100
8	0.009766	5000.000000	9692.306600

3. From the dual prices it can be seen that additional almonds are worth $8.50 per pound to TJ. Additional walnuts are worth $1.50 per pound. From the slack variables, we see that additional Brazil nuts, Filberts, and Pecans are of no value since they are already in excess supply.

4. Yes, purchase the almonds. The dual price shows that each pound is worth $8.50; the dual price is applicable for increases up to 583.33 pounds.

Resolving the problem by changing the right-hand side of constraint 1 from 6000 to 7000 yields the following optimal solution,. The optimal solution has increased in value by $4958.34. Note that only 583.33 pounds of the additional almonds were used, but that the increase in profit contribution more than justifies the $1000 cost of the shipment.

OPTIMAL SOLUTION

Objective Function Value =   66333.328000

Variable	Value	Reduced Costs
X1	11666.669900	0.000000
X2	17916.664100	0.000000
X3	5000.000000	0.000000

Constraint	Slack/Surplus	Dual Prices
1	416.666690	0.000000
2	249.998550	0.000000
3	249.998550	0.000000
4	0.000000	5.666666
5	0.000000	4.333333
6	1666.670290	0.000000
7	14916.665000	0.000000
8	0.000000	-0.033333

OBJECTIVE COEFFICIENT RANGES

Variable	Lower Limit	Current Value	Upper Limit
X1	1.000000	1.650000	1.750000
X2	1.976471	2.000000	3.300000
X3	No Lower Limit	2.250000	2.283333

RIGHT HAND SIDE RANGES

Constraint	Lower Limit	Current Value	Upper Limit
1	6583.333500	7000.000000	No Upper Limit
2	7250.001500	7500.000000	No Upper Limit
3	7250.001500	7500.000000	No Upper Limit
4	4210.000000	6000.000000	6250.000500
5	7249.999500	7500.000000	7749.998500
6	No Lower Limit	10000.000000	11666.669900
7	No Lower Limit	3000.000000	17916.664100
8	0.029297	5000.000000	15529.411100

5. From the dual prices it is clear that there is no advantage to not satisfying the orders for the Regular and Deluxe mixes. However, it would be advantageous to negotiate a decrease in the Holiday mix requirement.

Chapter 9
Linear Programming Applications

Learning Objectives

1. Learn about applications of linear programming that have been encountered in practice.

2. Develop an appreciation for the diversity of problems that can be modeled as linear programs.

3. Obtain practice and experience in formulating realistic linear programming models.

4. Understand linear programming applications such as:

   media selection   production scheduling
   portfolio selection   labor planning
   financial mix strategy   blending problems

Note to Instructor

The application problems of Chapter 9 have been designed to give the student an understanding and appreciation of the broad range of problems that can be approached by linear programming. While the problems are indicative of the many linear programming applications, they have been kept relatively small in order to ease the student's formulation and solution effort. Each problem will give the student an opportunity to practice formulating an approximate linear programming model. However, the solution and the interpretation of the solution will require the use of a software package such as The Management Scientist.

Solutions

1. **Product Mix**

   a. Let x_1 = units of product 1
   x_2 = units of product 2
   x_3 = units of product 3

$$\begin{array}{lllllll}
\max & 30x_1 & + 50x_2 & + 20x_3 \\
\text{s.t.} \\
& 0.5x_1 & + 2x_2 & + 0.75x_3 & \leq & 40 & \text{Machine 1} \\
& x_1 & + x_2 & + 0.5x_3 & \leq & 40 & \text{Machine 2} \\
& 2x_1 & + 5x_2 & + 2x_3 & \leq & 100 & \text{Labor} \\
& 0.5x_1 & - 0.5x_2 & - 0.5x_3 & \leq & 0 & \text{Max } x_1 \\
& -0.2x_1 & - 0.2x_2 & + 0.8x_3 & \geq & 0 & \text{Min } x_3 \\
& & x_1, x_2, x_3 \geq 0
\end{array}$$

The optimal solution obtained using The Management Scientist is shown.

```
OPTIMAL SOLUTION

Objective Function Value =        1250.000000
```

Variable	Value	Reduced Costs
X1	25.000000	0.000000
X2	0.000000	7.500000
X3	25.000000	0.000000

Constraint	Slack/Surplus	Dual Prices
1	8.750000	0.000000
2	2.500000	0.000000
3	0.000000	12.500000
4	0.000000	10.000000
5	15.000001	0.000000

Optimal Solution: $x_1 = 25$, $x_2 = 0$, $x_3 = 25$ Profit $1250

b.

$$\underline{\text{Machine Hours Schedule}}$$

Machine 1	31.25 Hours
Machine 2	37.50 Hours

c. $12.50

d.   Increase Labor Hours to → 120 Machines and Labor Fully Utilized

$x_1 = 24$
$x_2 = 8$
$x_3 = 16$
Profit = $1440

2.   **Media Selection**

a.   Let x_1 = number of television spot advertisements
          x_2 = number of radio advertisements
          x_3 = number of newspaper advertisements

max $100,000x_1 + 18,000x_2 + 40,000x_3$
s.t.

$2,000x_1 +$	$300x_2 +$	$600x_3 \le$	18,200	Budget
x_1		$\le$	10	Max TV
	x_2	$\le$	20	Max Radio
		$x_3 \le$	10	Max News
$-0.5x_1 +$	$0.5x_2 -$	$0.5x_3 \le$	0	Max 50% Radio
$0.9x_1 -$	$0.1x_2 -$	$0.1x_3 \le$	0	Min 10% TV
		$x_1, x_2, x_3, \ge 0$		

Solution:

		Budget $
	$x_1 = 4$	$8,000
	$x_2 = 14$	4,200
	$x_3 = 10$	6,000
		$18,200 Audience = 1,052,000.

This information can be obtained from The Management Scientist as follows.

OPTIMAL SOLUTION

Objective Function Value =   1052000.000000

Variable	Value	Reduced Costs
X1	4.000000	0.000977
X2	14.000000	0.000977
X3	10.000000	0.006836

Constraint	Slack/Surplus	Dual Prices
1	0.000000	51.304348
2	6.000000	0.000000
3	6.000000	0.000000
4	0.000000	11826.093800
5	0.000000	5217.392600
6	1.199999	0.000000

OBJECTIVE COEFFICIENT RANGES

Variable	Lower Limit	Current Value	Upper Limit
X1	-18000.007800	100000.000000	120000.008000
X2	14999.999000	18000.000000	No Upper Limit
X3	28173.906200	40000.000000	No Upper Limit

RIGHT HAND SIDE RANGES

Constraint	Lower Limit	Current Value	Upper Limit
1	14750.002000	18200.000000	32000.000000
2	4.000000	10.000000	No Upper Limit
3	14.000000	20.000000	No Upper Limit
4	0.000000	10.000000	12.338982
5	-8.049999	0.000000	2.936169
6	No Lower Limit	0.000000	1.199999

b. A $1.00 budget increase shows a value (shadow price or dual price) of 51.30. Thus, a $100 increase in budget should provide an increase in audience coverage of approximately 5,130. The range of feasibility for the right-hand side of the budget constraint will show this interpretation is correct.

3.   **Diet Problem**

a. & b.

x_1 = pounds of standard feed
x_2 = pounds of enriched oats
x_3 = pounds of additive

$$\max \quad 0.25x_1 + 0.50x_2 + 3x_3$$

s.t.					Ingredient
$0.8x_1$	$+ \ 0.2x_2$		$\geq$	3	(A)
$1.0x_1$	$+ \ 1.5x_2$	$+ \ 3.0x_3$	$\geq$	6	(B)
$0.1x_1$	$+ \ 0.6x_2$	$+ \ 2.0x_3$	$\geq$	4	(C)
x_1	$+ \ x_2$	$+ \ x_3$	$\leq$	6	Diet Max. Pounds

$$x_1, x_2, x_3 \geq 0$$

		Cost
Optimal diet mix	x_1 = 3.51 pounds @ 0.25	$0.88
	x_2 = 0.95 pounds @ 0.50	0.47
	x_3 = <u>1.54</u> pounds @ 3.00	<u>4.62</u>
	6.00 pounds	$5.97

This information can be obtained from The Management Scientist as follows.

```
OPTIMAL SOLUTION

Objective Function Value =          5.972973

        Variable              Value              Reduced Costs
   -------------------   -------------------   ----------------------
          X1                 3.513513               0.000000
          X2                 0.945947               0.000000
          X3                 1.540540               0.000000



       Constraint         Slack/Surplus            Dual Prices
   -------------------   -------------------   ----------------------
           1                 0.000000              -1.216216
           2                 3.554054               0.000000
           3                 0.000000              -1.959460
           4                 0.000000               0.918919
```

OBJECTIVE COEFFICIENT RANGES

Variable	Lower Limit	Current Value	Upper Limit
X1	-0.392857	0.250000	No Upper Limit
X2	No Lower Limit	0.500000	0.925000
X3	1.521739	3.000000	No Upper Limit

RIGHT HAND SIDE RANGES

Constraint	Lower Limit	Current Value	Upper Limit
1	1.142857	3.000000	3.368421
2	No Lower Limit	6.000000	9.554054
3	2.100001	4.000000	4.875001
4	5.562500	6.000000	8.478260

c. Dual price for constraint 4 is approximately $0.92. Thus increasing diet to seven pounds will decrease the cost by $0.92 per day to $5.05. Even though there are more pounds, the diet ingredient requirement can be met with the less expensive standard feed and oats. Reducing the expensive additive will reduce the overall cost.

4. **Overtime Planning**

a. Let x_1 = units of product 1 produced
x_2 = units of product 2 produced

$$\max \quad 30x_1 + 15x_2$$
$$\text{s.t.}$$
$$x_1 + 0.35x_2 \leq 100 \quad \text{Dept. A}$$
$$0.30x_1 + 0.20x_2 \leq 36 \quad \text{Dept. B}$$
$$0.20x_1 + 0.50x_2 \leq 50 \quad \text{Dept. C}$$
$$x_1, \ x_2 \geq 0$$

Solution: $x_1 = 77.89$, $x_2 = 63.16$ Profit = 3284.21

b. The shadow price for Dept. A is $15.79, for Dept. B it is $47.37, and for Dept. C it is $0.00. Therefore we would attempt to schedule overtime in Departments A and B. Assuming the current labor available is a sunk cost, we should be willing to pay up to $15.79 per hour in Department A and up to $47.37 in Department B.

c.   Let x_A = hours of overtime in Dept. A
x_B = hours of overtime in Dept. B
x_C = hours of overtime in Dept. C

$$\max \quad 30x_1 + 15x_2 - 18x_A - 22.5x_B - 12x_C$$

s.t.

$$
\begin{array}{rrrrrl}
x_1 + 0.35x_2 - x_A & & & \leq & 100 \\
0.30x_1 + 0.20x_2 & - x_B & & \leq & 36 \\
0.20x_1 + 0.50x_2 & & - x_C & \leq & 50 \\
x_A & & & \leq & 10 \\
& x_B & & \leq & 6 \\
& & x_C & \leq & 8
\end{array}
$$

$$x_1, x_2, x_A, x_B, x_C \geq 0$$

$x_1 = 87.21$
$x_2 = 65.12$
Profit = \$3341.34

	Overtime
Dept. A	10 hrs.
Dept. B	3.186 hrs
Dept. C	0 hours

Increase in Profit from overtime = \$3341.34 - 3284.21 = \$57.13

5.   **Investment and Loan Planning**

x_1 = \$ automobile loans
x_2 = \$ furniture loans
x_3 = \$ other secured loans
x_4 = \$ signature loans
x_5 = \$ "risk free" securities

$$\max \quad 0.08x_1 + 0.10x_2 + 0.11x_3 + 0.12x_4 + 0.09x_5$$

s.t.

$$
\begin{array}{ll}
x_5 \leq 600,000 & [1] \\
x_4 \leq 0.10(x_1 + x_2 + x_3 + x_4) \\
\text{or} \quad -0.10x_1 - 0.10x_2 - 0.10x_3 + 90x_4 \leq 0 & [2] \\
x_2 + x_3 \leq x_1 \\
\text{or} \quad -x_1 + x_2 + x_3 \leq 0 & [3] \\
x_3 + x_4 \leq x_5 \\
\text{or} \quad x_3 + x_4 - x_5 \leq 0 & [4] \\
x_1 + x_2 + x_3 + x_4 + x_5 = 2,000,000 & [5]
\end{array}
$$

$$x_1, x_2, x_3, x_4, x_5 \geq 0$$

Solution: Automobile Loans (x_1) = \$630,000
Furniture Loans (x_2) = \$170,000
Other Secured Loans (x_3) = \$460,000
Signature Loans (x_4) = \$140,000
Risk Free Loans (x_5) = \$600,000

Annual Return \$188,800 (9.44%)

6.   **Quality Assurance**

a. x_1 = pounds of bean 1
x_2 = pounds of bean 2
x_3 = pounds of bean 3

$$\max \; 0.50x_1 \; + 0.70x_2 \; + 0.45x_3$$
s.t.

$$\frac{75x_1 \; + \; 85x_2 \; + \; 60x_3}{x_1 \; + \; x_2 \; + \; x_3} \; \geq \; 75$$

or $10x_2 - 15x_3 \; \geq \quad 0$ Aroma

$$\frac{86x_1 \; + \; 88x_2 \; + \; 75x_3}{x_1 \; + \; x_2 \; + \; x_3} \; \geq \; 80$$

or $6x_1$ + $8x_2$ - $5x_3$	$\geq$	0	Taste
x_1	$\leq$	500	Bean 1
x_2	$\leq$	600	Bean 2
x_3	$\leq$	400	Bean 3
x_1 + x_2 + x_3	=	1000	1000 pounds

$$x_1, \; x_2, \; x_3 \; \geq 0$$

Optimal Solution: x_1 = 500, x_2 = 300, x_3 = 200 Cost: \$550

b.   Cost per pound = \$550/1000 = \$0.55

c.   Surplus for aroma: x_1 = 0; thus aroma rating = 75
Surplus for taste: s_2 = 4400; thus taste rating = 80 + 4400/1000 lbs. = 84.4

d.   Dual price = -\$0.60. Extra coffee can be produced at a cost of \$0.60 per pound.

7.   **Blending Problem**

Let x_1 = amount of ingredient A
       x_2 = amount of ingredient B
       x_3 = amount of ingredient C

$$\max \quad 0.10x_1 \quad + 0.03x_2 \quad + 0.09x_3$$

s.t.

	$1x_1$	+	$1x_2$	+	$1x_3$	$\geq$	10	[1]
	$1x_1$	+	$1x_2$	+	$1x_3$	$\leq$	15	[2]
	$1x_1$					$\geq$	$1x_2$	
or	$1x_1$	-	$1x_2$			$\geq$	0	[3]
					$1x_3$	$\geq$	$1/2x_1$	
or	$-1/2x_1$			+	$1x_3$	$\geq$	0	[4]

$$x_1, \ x_2, \ x_3, \ x_4 \geq 0$$

Solution: $x_i = 4$, $x_2 = 4$, $x_3 = 2$ Cost = \$0.70 per gallon.

8.   **Labor Planning**

Let x_1 = units of product 1
       x_2 = units of product 2
       b_1 = labor-hours Dept. A
       b_2 = labor-hours Dept. B

$$\max \quad 25x_1 \quad + 20x_2 \quad + 0b_1 \quad + 0b_2$$

s.t.

$6x_1$	+ $8x_2$	- $1b_1$		=	0
$12x_1$	+ $10x_2$		- $1b_2$	=	0
		$1b_1$	+ $1b_2$	$\leq$	900

$$x_1, \ x_2, \ b_1, \ b_2 \geq 0$$

Solution: $x_1 = 50$, $x_2 = 0$, $b_1 = 300$, $b_2 = 600$ Profit: \$1,250

9.   **Transportation**

a.   Let x_{11} = units shipped from Kansas City to Region 1
x_{12} = units shipped from Kansas City to Region 2
x_{13} = units shipped from Kansas City to Region 3
x_{21} = units shipped from Louisville to Region 1
x_{22} = units shipped from Louisville to Region 2
x_{23} = units shipped from Louisville to Region 3

$$\min\ 2.10x_{11} + 2.25x_{12} + 3.00x_{13} + 2.00x_{21} + 2.40x_{22} + 2.80x_{23}$$

s.t.

x_{11} +	x_{12} +	x_{13}				$\leq$	500
			x_{21} +	x_{22} +	x_{23}	$\leq$	400
x_{11}		+	x_{21}			=	200
	x_{12}		+	x_{22}		=	250
		x_{13}		+	x_{23}	=	300

$$x_{11},\ x_{12},\ x_{13},\ x_{21},\ x_{22},\ x_{23} \geq 0$$

Transportation Schedule:

	Region 1	Region 2	Region 3
Kansas City	100	250	
Louisville	100		300

Total Cost = $1,812.50

b.   Transportation Schedule:

	Region 1	Region 2	Region 3
Kansas City	200	250	50
Louisville			250

Total Cost = $3,395.00

10.   **Staff Scheduling**

Let x_1 = the number of officers scheduled to begin at 8:00 a.m.
x_2 = the number of officers scheduled to begin at noon
x_3 = the number of officers scheduled to begin at 4:00 p.m.
x_4 = the number of officers scheduled to begin at 8:00 p.m.
x_5 = the number of officers scheduled to begin at midnight
x_6 = the number of officers scheduled to begin at 4:00 a.m.

The objective function to minimize the number of officers required is as follows:

$$\min\quad x_1 + x_2 + x_3 + x_4 + x_5 + x_6$$

The constraints require the total number of officers of duty each of the six four-hour periods to be at least equal to the minimum officer requirements. The constraints for the six four-hour periods are as follows:

Time of Day

8:00 a.m. - noon	x_1					$+ x_6$	$\geq$ 5
noon to 4:00 p.m.	x_1	$+ x_2$					$\geq$ 6
4:00 p.m. - 8:00 p.m.		x_2	$+ x_3$				$\geq$ 10
8:00 p.m. - midnight			x_3	$+ x_4$			$\geq$ 7
midnight - 4:00 a.m.				x_4	$+ x_5$		$\geq$ 4
4:00 a.m. - 8:00 a.m.					x_5	$+ x_6$	$\geq$ 6

$$x_1, \ x_2, \ x_3, \ x_4, \ x_5, \ x_6 \geq 0$$

Schedule 19 officers as follows:

$x_1 = 3$ begin at 8:00 a.m.
$x_2 = 3$ begin at noon
$x_3 = 7$ begin at 4:00 p.m.
$x_4 = 0$ begin at 8:00 p.m.
$x_5 = 4$ begin at midnight
$x_6 = 2$ begin at 4:00 a.m.

11. **Portfolio Selection**

Let x_1 = number of shares of stock A
x_2 = number of shares of stock B
x_3 = number of shares of stock C
x_4 = number of shares of stock D

a. To get data on a per share basis multiply price by rate of return or risk measure value.

$$\min \ 10x_1 + 3.5x_2 + 4x_3 + 3.2x_4$$

s.t.

$100x_1$	$+ 50x_2$	$+ 80x_3$	$+ 40x_4$	$=$	$200,000$
$12x_1$	$+ 4x_2$	$+ 4.8x_3$	$+ 4x_4$	$\geq$	$18,000$ (9% of 200,00)
$100x_1$				$\leq$	$100,000$
	$50x_2$			$\leq$	$100,000$
		$80x_3$		$\leq$	$100,000$
			$40x_4$	$\leq$	$100,000$

$$x_1, \ x_2, \ x_3, \ x_4 \geq 0$$

Solution: $x_1 = 333.3$, $x_2 = 0$, $x_3 = 833.3$, $x_4 = 2500$
Risk: 14,666.7
Return: 18,000 (9%) from constraint 2

b.

$$\max \quad 12x_1 \quad + \quad 4x_2 \quad + 4.8x_3 \quad + \quad 4x_4$$

s.t.

$$
\begin{array}{lllll}
100x_1 & + 50x_2 & + 80x_3 & + 40x_4 & = 200{,}000 \\
100x_1 & & & & \le 100{,}000 \\
& 50x_2 & & & \le 100{,}000 \\
& & 80x_3 & & \le 100{,}000 \\
& & & 40x_4 & \le 100{,}000
\end{array}
$$

$$x_1, \ x_2, \ x_3, \ x_4 \ge 0$$

Solution: $x_1 = 1000$, $x_2 = 0$, $x_3 = 0$, $x_4 = 2500$
Risk: $10x_1 + 3.5x_2 + 4x_3 + 3.2x_4 = 18{,}000$
Return: 22,000 (11%)

c. The return in part (b) is $4,000 or 2% greater, but the risk index has increased by 3,333.

Obtaining a reasonable return with a lower risk is a preferred strategy in many financial firms. The more speculative, higher return investments are not always preferred because of their associated higher risk.

12. **Production Routing**

Let x_{11} = Units of product 1 produced on Line 1
x_{12} = Units of product 1 produced on Line 2
x_{21} = Units of product 2 produced on Line 1
x_{22} = Units of product 2 produced on Line 2

$$\min \quad 3.00x_{11} + 5.00x_{12} + 2.50x_{21} + 4.00x_{22}$$

s.t.

$$
\begin{array}{llllll}
x_{11} & + & x_{12} & & & \ge 500 \\
& & & x_{21} & + \quad x_{22} & \ge 700 \\
x_{11} & & & + \quad x_{21} & & \le 800 \\
& & x_{12} & & + \quad x_{22} & \le 600
\end{array}
$$

$$x_{11}, \ x_{12}, \ x_{21}, \ x_{22} \ge 0$$

Solution:

	Modern Line	Old Line
Product 1	500	0
Product 2	300	400

Total Cost $3,850

13. **Purchasing**

Let x_{ij} = units of component i purchased from supplier j

$$\min \quad 12x_{11} + 13x_{12} + 14x_{13} + 10x_{21} + 11x_{22} + 10x_{23}$$

s.t.

$$
\begin{array}{llllllll}
x_{11} + & x_{12} + & x_{13} & & & & = & 1000 \\
& & & x_{21} + & x_{22} + & x_{23} & = & 800 \\
x_{11} & & & + \quad x_{21} & & & \leq & 600 \\
& x_{12} & & & + \quad x_{22} & & \leq & 1000 \\
& & x_{13} & & & + \quad x_{23} & \leq & 800 \\
\end{array}
$$

$$x_{11}, \ x_{12}, \ x_{13}, \ x_{21}, \ x_{22}, \ x_{23} \geq 0$$

Solution:

	Supplier		
	1	2	3
Component 1	600	400	0
Component 2	0	0	800

Purchase Cost = $20,400

14. **Make or Buy**

Let x_1 = number of units of the base manufactured
x_2 = number of units of the cartridge manufactured
x_3 = number of units of the handle manufactured
x_4 = number of units of the base purchased
x_5 = number of units of the cartridge purchased
x_6 = number of units of the handle purchased

$$\min \quad 0.75x_1 + 0.40x_2 + 1.10x_3 + 0.95x_4 + 0.55x_5 + 1.40x_6$$

s.t.

$$
\begin{array}{lllllll}
0.03x_1 + & 0.02x_2 + & 0.05x_3 & & & \leq 400 & \text{Dept. A} \\
0.04x_1 + & 0.02x_2 + & 0.04x_3 & & & \leq 400 & \text{Dept. B} \\
0.02x_1 + & 0.03x_2 + & 0.01x_3 & & & \leq 400 & \text{Dept. C} \\
x_1 & & + \quad x_4 & & & = 5000 \\
& x_2 & & + \quad x_5 & & = 5000 \\
& & x_3 & & + \quad x_6 & = 5000 \\
\end{array}
$$

$$x_1, \ x_2, \ x_3, \ x_4, \ x_5, \ x_6 \geq 0$$

a.
$x_1 = 3,750$
$x_2 = 5,000$
$x_3 = 3,750$
$x_4 = 1,250$ purchase
$x_5 = 0$
$x_6 = 1,250$ purchase   Cost = $11,875

b. Departments A and B are at capacity. The dual prices show additional hours in A are worth $5 and additional hours in B are worth $1.25. Based on the added $3 per hour cost, we should only consider adding hours in Department A (Net Value $5 - $3 = $2 per hour).

c. All 80 hours cannot be used in Department A. In fact only 25 hours can be added before a change in solution occurs. New solution:

$$x_1 = 2500$$
$$x_2 = 5000$$
$$x_3 = 5000 \quad \text{Total Cost} \qquad\qquad \$11,750$$
$$x_4 = 2500 \quad \text{plus 25 hrs. @ \$3/hr.} \qquad \underline{\quad 75}$$
$$x_5 = 0 \qquad\qquad\qquad\qquad\qquad\qquad \$11,825$$
$$x_6 = 0$$

At this point, only Department B is at capacity. Overtime hours in this department now have a potential value of $5 per hour.

15. **Blending Problem**

Let x_{11} = gallons of crude 1 used to produce regular
        x_{12} = gallons of crude 1 used to produce high-octane
        x_{21} = gallons of crude 2 used to produce regular
        x_{22} = gallons of crude 2 used to produce high-octane

min $0.10x_{11} + 0.10x_{12} + 0.15x_{21} + 0.15x_{22}$
s.t.

Each gallon of regular must have at least 40% A.

$$x_{11} + x_{21} = \text{amount of regular produced}$$
$$0.4(x_{11} + x_{21}) = \text{amount of A required for regular}$$
$$0.2x_{11} + 0.50x_{21} = \text{amount of A in } (x_{11} + x_{21}) \text{ gallons of regular gas}$$

$$\therefore \ 0.2x_{11} + 0.50x_{21} \geq 0.4x_{11} + 0.40x_{21} \qquad\qquad [1]$$
$$\therefore \ -0.2x_{11} + 0.10x_{21} \geq 0$$

Each gallon of high octane can have at most 50% B.

$$x_{12} + x_{22} = \text{amount high-octane}$$
$$0.5(x_{12} + x_{22}) = \text{amount of B required for high octane}$$
$$0.60x_{12} + 0.30x_{22} = \text{amount of B in } (x_{12} + x_{22}) \text{ gallons of high octane.}$$

$$\therefore \ 0.60x_{12} + 0.30x_{22} \leq 0.5x_{12} + 0.5x_{22}$$
$$\therefore \ 0.1x_{12} - 0.2x_{22} \leq 0. \qquad\qquad\qquad\qquad [2]$$
$$x_{11} + x_{21} \geq 800,000 \qquad\qquad [3]$$
$$x_{12} + x_{22} \geq 500,000 \qquad\qquad [4]$$
$$x_{11}, \ x_{12}, \ x_{21}, \ x_{22} \geq 0$$

Optimal Solution: $x_{11} = 266,667$, $x_{12} = 333,333$, $x_{21} = 533,333$, $x_{22} = 166,667$
Cost = \$165,000

16.   **Cutting Stock Problem**

Let x_i = number of 10-inch rolls of paper processed by cutting alternative i; $i = 1,2...,7$

$$\min \quad x_1 + x_2 + x_3 + x_4 + x_5 + x_6 + x_7$$
s.t.

$$
\begin{array}{llllll}
6x_1 & + 2x_3 & + x_5 + x_6 + 4x_7 & \geq 1000 & 1\ 1/2" \text{ production} \\
& 4x_2 & + x_4 + 3x_5 + 2x_6 & \geq 2000 & 2\ 1/2" \text{ production} \\
& 2x_3 + 2x_4 & + x_6 + x_7 & \geq 4000 & 3\ 1/2" \text{ production}
\end{array}
$$

$$x_1, \ x_2, \ x_3, \ x_4, \ x_5, \ x_6, \ x_7 \geq 0$$

$x_1 = 0$
$x_2 = 125$
$x_3 = 500$ 2125 Rolls
$x_4 = 1500$
$x_5 = 0$ Production:
$x_6 = 0$ 1 1/2" 1000
$x_7 = 0$ 2 1/2" 2000
            3 1/2" 4000

Waste: Cut alternative #4 (1/2" per roll)
∴ 750 inches.

b.   Only the objective function needs to be changed. An objective function minimizing waste production and the new optimal solution are given.

$$\min \quad x_1 + 0x_2 + 0x_3 + 0.5x_4 + x_5 + 0x_6 + 0.5x_7$$

$x_1 = 0$
$x_2 = 500$
$x_3 = 2000$ 2500 Rolls
$x_4 = 0$
$x_5 = 0$ Production:
$x_6 = 0$ 1 1/2" 4000
$x_7 = 0$ 2 2/1" 2000
            3 1/2" 4000

Waste:
0 But we have over-produced the 1 1/2" size by 300 units. Perhaps these can be inventoried for future use.

c.   Minimizing waste may cause you to over-produce. In this case, we used 375 more rolls to generate a 3000 surplus of the 1 1/2" product. Alternative b might be preferred on the basis that the 3000 surplus could be held in inventory for later demand. However, in some trim problems, excess production cannot be used and must be scrapped. If this were the case, the 3000 unit 1 1/2" size would result in 4500 inches of waste, and thus alternative a would be the preferred solution.

17. **Inspection**

Let x_1 = hours per day for inspector Davis
x_2 = hours per day for inspector Wilson
x_3 = hours per day for inspector Lawson

min $5.90x_1 + 5.20x_2 + 5.50x_3$
s.t.

$300x_1 + 200x_2 + 350x_3 \geq 2000$ Inspection Volume
$300(.02)x_1 + 200(.01)x_2 + 350(.04)x_3 \leq .02(300x_1 + 200x_2 + 350x_3)$

or

$-2x_2 + 7x_3 \leq 0$ Accuracy Requirement

$x_1 \leq 4$

$x_2 \leq 4$ Maximum Daily Hours per
     Inspection

$x_3 \leq 4$

$x_1 + x_2 + x_3 = 8$ Must have 8 hours of
     inspection

$$x_1, x_2, x_3 \geq 0$$

The minimum cost solution is given.

$$x_1 = 2.86 \text{ hours}$$
$$x_2 = 4 \text{ hours}$$
$$x_3 = 1.14 \text{ hours}$$
Daily Cost = \$43.94
Inspection Volume = 2057

18.a. **Equipment Acquisition**

Let x_1 = number of Super Tankers purchased
x_2 = number of Regular Line Tankers purchased
x_3 = number of Econo-Tankers purchased

min $550x_1 + 425x_2 + 350x_3$
s.t.

$6700x_1 + 55000x_2 + 4600x_3 \leq 600,000$ Budget
$15(5000)x_1 + 20(2500)x_2 + 25(1000)x_3 \geq 550,000$

or

$75000x_1 + 50000x_2 + 25000x_3 \geq 550,000$ Meet Demand
$x_1 + x_2 + x_3 \leq 15$ Max. Total Vehicles
$x_3 \geq 3$ Min. Econo-Tankers

$x_1 \leq 1/2(x_1 + x_2 + x_3)$
or
$1/2x_1 - 1/2x_2 - 1/2x_3 \leq 0$ No more than 50% Super Tankers

$x_1, x_2, x_3 \geq 0$

Solution:

     5 Super Tankers
     2 Regular Tankers
     3 Econo-Tankers

Total Cost: $583,000
Monthly Operating Cost: $4,650

b.   The last two constraints in the formulation above must be deleted and the problem resolved.

The optimal solution calls for 7 1/3 Super Tankers at an annual operating cost of $4033. However, since a partial Super Tanker can't be purchased we must round up to find a feasible solution of 8 Super Tankers with a monthly operating cost of $4,400.

Actually this is an integer programming problem, since partial tankers can't be purchased. (See Chapter 12). We were fortunate in part (a) that the optimal solution turned out integer.

The true optimal integer solution to part (b) is $x_1 = 6$ and $x_2 = 2$ with a monthly operating cost of $4150. This is 6 Super Tankers and 2 Regular Line Tankers.

19.   **Multiple-Period Planning**

a.   Let x_{11} = amount of men's model in month 1
                x_{21} = amount of women's model in month 1
                x_{12} = amount of men's model in month 2
                x_{22} = amount of women's model in month 2
                s_{11} = inventory of men's model at end of month 1
                s_{21} = inventory of women's model at end of month 1
                s_{12} = inventory of men's model at end of month 2
                s_{22} = inventory of women's model at end of month 2

The model formulation for part (a) is given.

min $\quad 40x_{11} + 30x_{21} + 40x_{12} + 30x_{22} + 0.8s_{11} + 0.6s_{21} + 0.8s_{12} + 0.6s_{22}$

s.t.

$\quad 20 + x_{11} - s_{11} = 150$

or

$\qquad + x_{11} - s_{11} = 130$ $\hspace{6cm}$ [1]

$\quad 30 + x_{21} - s_{21} = 125$

or

$\qquad + x_{21} - s_{21} = 95 \qquad$ Satisfy Demand $\hspace{2.5cm}$ [2]

$\quad s_{11} + x_{12} - s_{12} = 200$ $\hspace{6cm}$ [3]

$\quad s_{21} + x_{22} - x_{22} = 150$ $\hspace{6cm}$ [4]

$\qquad\qquad\qquad s_{12} \geq 25 \qquad$ Ending Inventory Requirement $\hspace{1cm}$ [5]

$\qquad\qquad\qquad s_{22} \geq 25$ $\hspace{6.5cm}$ [6]

$4000 - 10x_{11} - 3x_{11} - \quad 8x_{21} - 2x_{21}$	≤ 500	
and $\quad 4000 - 10x_{11} - 3x_{11} - \quad 8x_{21} - 2x_{21}$	≥ -500	Labor Force
or $\qquad\qquad 13x_{11} + \qquad 10x_{21}$	≥ 3500	Smoothing [7]
and $\qquad\qquad 13x_{11} + \qquad 10x_{21}$	≤ 4500	Month 1 [8]
$\qquad\qquad 13x_{11} + \qquad 10x_{21} - 13x_{12} - 10x_{22}$	≤ 500	Labor Force [9]
and $\qquad\qquad 13x_{11} + 10x_{21} - 13x_{12} - 10x_{22}$	≥ -500	Smoothing
or $\qquad\qquad -13x_{11} - 10x_{21} + 13x_{12} + 10x_{22}$	≤ 500	Month 2 [10]

$$x_{11}, \ x_{12}, \ x_{21}, \ x_{22}, \ s_{11}, \ s_{21}, \ s_{22} \geq 0$$

The optimal solution is given. It calls for production of 130 of the men's model in month 1 and 225 in month 2. The optimal production schedule calls for 181 units of the women's model 1 and 89 in month 2.

$\quad x_{11} = 130$
$\quad x_{21} = 181$
$\quad x_{12} = 225$
$\quad x_{22} = 89 \qquad$ Total Cost = \$22,386.60

Inventory Schedule

Month 1	0 Men's	86 Women's
Month 2	25 Men's	25 Women's

Labor Levels

Previous month	4000 labor-levels
Month 1	3500 labor-levels
Month 2	3815 labor-hours

b. To accommodate this new policy the right-hand sides of constraints [7] to [10] must be changed to 3750, 4250, 250, and 250 respectively. The revised optimal solution is given.

$$x_{11} = 130$$
$$x_{21} = 206$$
$$x_{12} = 225$$
$$x_{22} = 64 \qquad \text{Total Cost} = \$22,401.60$$

We produce more women's models in the first month and carry a larger women's model inventory; the added cost however is only $15. This seems to be a small expense to have less drastic labor force fluctuations. The new labor levels are 4000, 3750, and 3565 hours each month. Since the added cost is only $15, management might want to experiment with the labor force smoothing restrictions to enforce even less fluctuations. You may want to experiment yourself to see what happens.

20. **Labor Balancing**

Let x_1 = number of TW100's per day
         x_2 = number of TW200's per day

max $2.50x_1 + 3.50x_2$

$$\left. \begin{array}{l} 4x_1 + 3x_2 \leq 480 \\ 4x_1 + 3x_2 \geq 450 \end{array} \right\} \text{Assembler 1}$$

$$\left. \begin{array}{l} 2x_1 + 4x_2 \leq 480 \\ 2x_1 + 4x_2 \geq 450 \end{array} \right\} \text{Assembler 2}$$

$$\left. \begin{array}{l} 3.5x_1 + 3x_2 \leq 480 \\ 3.5x_1 + 3x_2 \geq 450 \end{array} \right\} \text{Assembler 3}$$

Production: x_1 = 48 units, x_2 = 96 units

Profit = $456

Assembler Time	
Assembler 1	480 minutes
Assembler 2	480 minutes
Assembler 3	456 minutes

21.   **Multi-Period Production and Inventory Planning**

Let d_1 = demand in period 1
       d_2 = demand in period 2
       d_3 = demand in period 3
       x_1 = regular production in period 1
       x_2 = regular production in period 2
       x_3 = regular production in period 3
       y_1 = overtime production in period 1
       y_2 = overtime production in period 2
       y_3 = overtime production in period 3
       I_0 = beginning inventory
       I_1 = ending inventory for period 1
       I_2 = ending inventory for period 2
       I_3 = ending inventory for period 3
       z_1 = sales in period 1
       z_2 = sales in period 2
       z_3 = sales in period 3
       L_1 = lost sales in period 1
       L_2 = lost sales in period 2
       L_3 = lost sales in period 3

Objective Function:

max	$5z_1$	+	$5z_2$	+ $5.5z_3$	Sales Revenue
	$-2.8x_1$	-	$2.9x_2$	$-3x_3$	Regular Production Cost
	$-3.36y_1$	-	$3.48y_2$	$-3.6y_3$	Overtime Production Cost
	$-0.5I_1$	-	$0.55I_2$	$-0.5I_3$	Inventory Cost
	$-4L_1$	-	$4L_2$	$-4L_3$	Lost Sales Cost

Constraints:

$d_1 = 500$
$d_2 = 300$ Demand
$d_3 = 400$

$x_1 \leq 250$
$x_2 \leq 300$ Regular Production Capacity
$x_3 \leq 300$

$y_1 \leq 100$
$y_2 \leq 100$ Overtime Production Capacity
$y_3 \leq 125$

$I_0 = 100$ Beginning Inventory
$I_3 \geq 50$ Ending Inventory

$$z_1 - d_1 + L_1 = 0$$
$$z_2 - d_2 + L_2 = 0$$
$$z_3 - d_3 - L_3 = 0$$

Lost Sales Balance Constraints

$$I_1 - I_0 - x_1 - y_1 + z_1 = 0$$
$$I_2 - I_1 - x_2 - y_2 + z_2 = 0$$
$$I_3 - I_2 - x_3 - y_3 + z_3 = 0$$

Inventory Balance Constraints

Optimal Solution:

	Period 1	Period 2	Period 3
Regular Production	250	300	300
Overtime Production	100	25	125
Sales	450	300	400
Ending Inventory	—	25	50
Lost Sales	50	—	—

Profit = $2367

22. Multi-Period Financial Planning

Let x_1 = proportion of investment A undertaken
x_2 = proportion of investment B undertaken
s_1 = funds placed in savings for period 1
s_2 = funds placed in savings for period 2
s_3 = funds placed in savings for period 3
s_4 = funds placed in savings for period 4
L_1 = funds received from loan in period 1
L_2 = funds received from loan in period 2
L_3 = funds received from loan in period 3
L_4 = funds received from loan in period 4

Objective Function:

In order to maximize the cash value at the end of the four periods, we must consider the value of investment A, the value of investment B, savings income from period 4, and loan expenses for period 4.

max $3200x_1 + 2500x_2 + 1.1s_4 - 1.18L_4$

Constraints require the *use* of funds to equal the *source* of funds for each period.

Period 1:
$$1000x_1 + 800x_2 + s_1 = 1500 + L_1$$
or
$$1000x_1 + 800x_2 + s_1 - L_1 = 1500$$

Period 2:
$$800x_1 + 500x_2 + s_2 + 1.18L_1 = 400 + 1.1s_1 + L_2$$
or
$$800x_1 + 500x_2 - 1.1s_1 + s_2 + 1.18L_1 - L_2 = 400$$

Period 3
$$200x_1 + 300x_2 + s_3 + 1.18L_2 = 500 + 1.1s_1 + L_3$$
or
$$200x_1 + 300x_2 - 1.1s_2 + s_3 + 1.18L_2 - L_3 = 500$$

Period 4
$$s_4 + 1.18L_3 = 100 + 200x_1 + 500x_2 + 1.1s_3 + L_4$$
or
$$-200x_1 - 300x_2 - 1.1s_3 + s_4 + 1.18L_3 - L_4 = 100$$

Limits on Loan Funds Available

$$L_1 \leq 200$$
$$L_2 \leq 200$$
$$L_3 \leq 200$$
$$L_4 \leq 200$$

Proportion of Investment Undertaken

$$x_1 \leq 1$$
$$x_2 \leq 1$$

Optimal Solution $4340.40

Investment A $x_1 = 0.457895$ or   45.8%
Investment B $x_2 = 1.0$ or   100.0%

Savings/Loan Schedule:

	Period 1	Period 2	Period 3	Period 4
Savings	242.11	—	—	341.04
Loan	—	200.00	127.58	—

23.   **Staff Scheduling**

Let x_1 = number of part-time employees beginning at 11:00 a.m.
x_2 = number of part-time employees beginning at 12:00 p.m.
x_3 = number of part-time employees beginning at 1:00 p.m.
x_4 = number of part-time employees beginning at 2:00 p.m.
x_5 = number of part-time employees beginning at 3:00 p.m.
x_6 = number of part-time employees beginning at 4:00 p.m.
x_7 = number of part-time employees beginning at 5:00 p.m.
x_8 = number of part-time employees beginning at 6:00 p.m.

$$\min \ 14.4x_1 + 14.4x_2 + 14.4x_3 + 14.4x_4 + 14.4x_5 + 14.4x_6 + 14.4x_7 + 14.4x_8$$

s.t.

								Part-Time Employees Needed[*]	
x_1								≥ 8	11:00 a.m.
$x_1 +$	x_2							≥ 8	12:00 p.m.
$x_1 +$	$x_2 +$	x_3						≥ 7	1:00 p.m.
$x_1 +$	$x_2 +$	$x_3 +$	x_4					≥ 1	2:00 p.m.
	$x_2 +$	$x_3 +$	$x_4 +$	x_5				≥ 2	3:00 p.m.
		$x_3 +$	$x_4 +$	$x_5 +$	x_6			≥ 1	4:00 p.m.
			$x_4 +$	$x_5 +$	$x_6 +$	x_7		≥ 5	5:00 p.m.
				$x_5 +$	$x_6 +$	$x_7 +$	x_8	≥ 10	6:00 p.m.
					$x_6 +$	$x_7 +$	x_8	≥ 10	7:00 p.m.
						$x_7 +$	x_8	≥ 6	8:00 p.m.
							x_8	≥ 6	9:00 p.m.

$$x_j \geq 0 \quad j = 1,2,...8$$

[*]Full-time employees reduce the number of part-time employees needed.
A portion of The Management Scientist solution to the model is shown.

OPTIMAL SOLUTION

Objective Function Value =   288.000000

Variable	Value	Reduced Costs
X1	8.000000	0.000000
X2	0.000000	0.000000
X3	1.000000	0.000000
X4	1.000000	0.000000
X5	0.000000	0.000000
X6	4.000000	0.000000
X7	0.000000	0.000000
X8	6.000000	0.000000

Constraint	Slack/Surplus	Dual Prices
1	0.000000	-14.400000
2	0.000000	0.000000
3	2.000000	0.000000
4	9.000000	0.000000
5	0.000000	-14.400000
6	5.000000	0.000000
7	0.000000	0.000000
8	0.000000	0.000000
9	0.000000	-14.400000
10	0.000000	0.000000
11	0.000000	0.000000

The optimal schedule calls for

8 starting at 11:00 a.m.
1 starting at 1:00 p.m.
1 starting at 2:00 p.m.
4 starting at 4:00 p.m.
6 starting at 6:00 p.m.

b.   Total daily salary cost = $288

There are 9 surplus employees scheduled from 2:00 - 3:00 p.m. and 5 from 4:00 - 5:00 p.m. suggesting the desirability of rotating employees off sooner.

c.   Considering 3-hour shifts
Let x denote 4-hour shifts and y denote 3-hour shifts where

y_1 = number of part-time employees beginning at 11:00 a.m.
y_2 = number of part-time employees beginning at 12:00 p.m.
y_3 = number of part-time employees beginning at 1:00 p.m.
y_4 = number of part-time employees beginning at 2:00 p.m.
y_5 = number of part-time employees beginning at 3:00 p.m.
y_6 = number of part-time employees beginning at 4:00 p.m.
y_7 = number of part-time employees beginning at 5:00 p.m.
y_8 = number of part-time employees beginning at 6:00 p.m.
y_9 = number of part-time employees beginning at 7:00 p.m.

New objective function:

$$\min \sum_{j=1}^{8} 14.40x_j + \sum_{i=1}^{9} 10.80y_i$$

Each constraint must be modified with the addition of the y_i variables. For instance, the first constraint becomes

$$x_1 + y_1 \geq 8$$

and so on. Each y_i appears in three constraints because each refers to a three hour shift. The optimal solution is given.

$x_8 = 6$ $y_1 = 8$
            $y_3 = 1$
            $y_5 = 1$
            $y_7 = 4$ $237.60

Optimal schedule for part-time employees:

4-Hour Shifts	3-Hour Shifts
$x_8 = 6$	$y_1 = 8$
	$y_3 = 1$
	$y_5 = 1$
	$y_7 = 4$

Total cost reduced to $237.60. Still have 20 part-time shifts, but 14 are 3-hour shifts. The surplus has been reduced by a total of 14 hours.

24. Computer Solution

a. The dual price for constraint 6 is 0.06. Therefore we would expect an increase of 0.06 exposure units per dollar.

$$\text{Ave. Exposure/dollar} = \frac{total\ exposure}{total\ budget} = \frac{2370}{30000} = 0.079$$

Diminishing marginal returns have set in. The marginal return is 0.06, the average return is 0.079. It may not yet make sense to invest more now.

b. Requiring 10 television commercials is reducing the value of the optimal solution. The dual price shows that relaxing this requirement would improve the solution. The exposure per dollar is not as great for T.V. as it is for the other media.

Case Problem: Environmental Protection

Note to instructor. Unlike the case problem at the end of chapter three, the cost of raw materials is viewed as a relevant cost here. Therefore, the raw material costs should be deducted in computing objective function coefficients. The dual prices must be interpreted as the premium (over the usual cost) that would be paid per unit.

1.   The profit contribution per pound is given by the sales prices minus the variable cost per pound.

Primary Product:	$5.70 - 1.50 - 1.60 - 0.50	= $ 2.10
Product K:	$0.85 - 0.75 - 0.20	= $-0.10
Product M:	$0.65 - 0.40 - 0.10	= $ 0.15

2.   Let P = pounds of Primary Product
K = pounds of Product K
M = pounds of Product M
SW = pounds of specially treated waste

A linear programming model is given.

$$\max \quad 2.10P - 0.10K + 0.15M - 0.25SW$$

s.t.

$$
\begin{array}{rcll}
P + 0.5K & \leq & 5000 & \text{Raw Mat A} \\
2P + 0.5M & \leq & 7000 & \text{Raw Mat B} \\
-P + 0.5K + 0.5M + SW & = & 0 & \text{Material Balance} \\
P, K, M, SW & \geq & 0 &
\end{array}
$$

Note that the third constraint enforces the balance among all outputs in the proper proportions.

The Management Scientist solution to this linear program is shown below.

```
OPTIMAL SOLUTION

Objective Function Value =        6550.000000
```

Variable	Value	Reduced Costs
P	3500.000000	0.000000
K	3000.000000	0.000000
M	0.000000	0.175000
SW	2000.000000	0.000000

Constraint	Slack/Surplus	Dual Prices
1	0.000000	0.050000
2	0.000000	0.900000
3	0.000000	-0.250000

OBJECTIVE COEFFICIENT RANGES

Variable	Lower Limit	Current Value	Upper Limit
P	1.400000	2.100000	No Upper Limit
K	-0.125000	-0.100000	0.250000
M	No Lower Limit	0.150000	0.325000
SW	-0.425000	-0.250000	-0.200000

RIGHT HAND SIDE RANGES

Constraint	Lower Limit	Current Value	Upper Limit
1	3500.000000	5000.000000	7000.000000
2	5000.000000	7000.000000	10000.000000
3	-2000.000000	0.000000	No Upper Limit

3.   From the dual prices we see that additional raw material A would be worth a premium of $0.05 per pound and additional raw material B would be worth a premium of $0.90 per pound.

4.   The ranges on the objective function coefficients indicate that the optimal solution is not very sensitive to changes in the profit contributions. The only exception is for a decrease in the profit contribution of product K. A decrease from -0.10 to less than -0.125 for product K would necessitate resolving to find a new optimal solution.

5.   Product K is clearly optimal given its existing profit contribution and the qualities of raw materials available. Eliminating product K from the model and resolving shows a $75 decrease in profit contribution and a reduction in the usage of raw material A.

Case Problem: Textile Mill Scheduling

Let   X3R = Yards of fabric 3 on regular looms
X4R = Yards of fabric 4 on regular looms
X5R = Yards of fabric 5 on regular looms
X1D = Yards of fabric 1 on dobbie looms
X2D = Yards of fabric 2 on dobbie looms
X3D = Yards of fabric 3 on dobbie looms
X4D = Yards of fabric 4 on dobbie looms
X5D = Yards of fabric 5 on dobbie looms
Y1   = Yards of fabric 1 purchased
Y2   = Yards of fabric 2 purchased
Y3   = Yards of fabric 3 purchased
Y4   = Yards of fabric 4 purchased
Y5   = Yards of fabric 5 purchased

Profit Contribution per Yard

		Manufactured	Purchased
	1	0.33	0.19
	2	0.31	0.16
Fabric	3	0.61	0.50
	4	0.73	0.54
	5	0.20	0.00

Production Times in Hours per Yard

		Regular	Dobbie
	1	—	0.21598
	2	—	0.21598
Fabric	3	0.1912	0.1912
	4	0.1912	0.1912
	5	0.2398	0.2398

Model may use a Max Profit or Min Cost objective function.

max   0.61X3R + 0.73X4R + 0.20X5R
+ 0.33X1D + 0.31X2D + 0.61X3D + 0.73X4D + 0.20X5D
+ 0.19Y1 + 0.16Y2 + 0.50Y3 + 0.54Y4
or
min   0.49X3R + 0.51X4R + 0.50X5R
+ 0.66X1D + 0.55X2D + 0.49X3D + 0.51X4D + 0.50X5D
+ 0.80Y1 + 0.70Y2 + 0.60Y3 + 0.70Y4 + 0.70Y5

Regular Hours Available

    30 Looms × 30 days × 24 hours/day = 21600

Dobbie Hours Available

8 Looms × 30 days × 24 hours/day = 5760

Constraints

Regular Looms:

$$0.192X3R + 0.1912\ X4R + 0.2398X5R \le 21600$$

Dobbie Looms:

$$0.21598X1D + 0.21598X2D + 0.1912X3D + 0.1912X4D + 0.2398X5D \le 5760$$

Demand Constraints

$$\begin{aligned}
X1D + Y1 &= 16500\\
X2D + Y2 &= 22000\\
X3R + X3D + Y3 &= 62000\\
X4R + X4D + Y4 &= 7500\\
X5R + X5D + Y5 &= 62000
\end{aligned}$$

OPTIMAL SOLUTION

Objective Function Value =   62531.922000

Variable	Value	Reduced Costs
X3R	27711.296900	0.000000
X4R	7500.000000	0.000000
X5R	62000.000000	0.000000
X1D	4669.136700	0.000000
X2D	22000.000000	0.000000
X3D	0.000000	0.013937
X4D	0.000000	0.013937
X5D	0.000000	0.017480
Y1	11830.863300	0.000000
Y2	0.000000	0.010000
Y3	34288.703000	0.000000
Y4	0.000000	0.080000
Y5	0.000000	0.062040

Constraint	Slack/Surplus	Dual Prices
1	0.000000	0.575314
2	0.000000	0.648208
3	0.000000	0.190000
4	0.000000	0.170000
5	0.000000	0.500000
6	0.000000	0.620000
7	0.000000	0.062040

OBJECTIVE COEFFICIENT RANGES

Variable	Lower Limit	Current Value	Upper Limit
X3R	0.500000	0.610000	0.623937
X4R	0.716063	0.730000	No Upper Limit
X5R	0.182520	0.200000	167772.203000
X1D	0.314256	0.330000	0.340000
X2D	0.300000	0.310000	No Upper Limit
X3D	No Lower Limit	0.610000	0.623937
X4D	No Lower Limit	0.730000	0.743937
X5D	No Lower Limit	0.200000	0.217480
Y1	0.180000	0.190000	0.205744
Y2	No Lower Limit	0.160000	0.170000
Y3	0.486063	0.500000	0.610000
Y4	No Lower Limit	0.540000	0.620000
Y5	No Lower Limit	0.000000	0.062040

RIGHT HAND SIDE RANGES

Constraint	Lower Limit	Current Value	Upper Limit
1	16301.599600	21600.000000	28156.000000
2	4751.559600	5760.000000	8315.230500
3	4669.136700	16500.000000	No Upper Limit
4	10169.136700	22000.000000	26669.136700
5	27711.296900	62000.000000	No Upper Limit
6	0.000000	7500.000000	35211.297000
7	34660.551000	62000.000000	84095.078000

Production/Purchase Schedule (Yards)

		Regular Looms	Dobbie Looms	Purchased
	1		4669	118321
	2		22000	
Fabric	3	27711		34289
	4	7500		
	5	63000		

Projected Profit: $62,531.92

Value of 9th Dobbie Loom

Dual Price (Constraint 2) = 0.648208 per hour dobbie

Monthly Value of 1 Dobbie Loom

(30 days)(24 hours/day)($0.648208) = $466.71

Note: This change is within the Right-Hand Side Ranges for Constraint 2.

Discussion of Objective Coefficient Ranges

For example, fabric one on the dobbie loom shares ranges of 0.314256 to 0.34 for the profit maximization model or 0.644256 to 0.67 for the cost minimization model.

Note here that since demand for the fabrics is fixed, both the profit maximization and cost minimization models will provide the same optimal solution. However, the interpretation of the ranges for the objective function coefficients differ for the two models. In the profit maximization case, the coefficients are profit contributions. Thus, the range information indicates how price per unit and cost per unit may vary simultaneously. That is, as long as the net changes in price per unit and cost per unit keep the profit contributions within the ranges., the solution will remain optimal. In the cost minimization model, the coefficients are costs per unit. Thus, the range information indicates that assuming price per unit remains *fixed* how much the cost per unit may vary and still maintain the same optimal solution.

Answers to Questions for Quantitative Methods in Practice

1.   The objective is to minimize the cost of meeting a given demand structure, taking into action account sales price, pipeline tariffs, exchange contract costs, product demand, terminal operating costs, refining costs, and product purchases.

2. a.   Evaluation of additional product demand locations, pipelines, refinery units, and exchange contracts.

   b.   Profitability of shifting sales from one product demand location to another.

   c.   Effects on refinery gasoline blending when octane requirements are increased, blendstock availabilities are decreased, or there is a major shift in the demand patten.

   d.   The effects on supply and distribution when a pipeline increases its tariff.

   e.   Optimize production of the three grades of gasoline at the four refineries.

3. $10,000

Chapter 10
Linear Programming: The Simplex Method

Learning Objectives

1. Know how to use elementary row operations to solve systems of linear equations.

2. Learn how to use the simplex method for solving linear programming problems.

3. Obtain an understanding of why and how the simplex calculations are made.

4. Understand the following terms:

simplex method	net evaluation row
basic solution	basis
basic feasible solution	iteration
tableau form	pivot element
simplex tableau	artificial variable

5. Know how to recognize the following special situations when using the simplex method to solve linear programs.

   infeasibility
   unboundedness
   alternate optimal solutions
   degeneracy

Solutions

1. Elementary row operations:
   a. Multiply any row by a nonzero number.
   b. Replace any row by the result of adding or subtracting a multiple of another row to it.

	Equation Number
$6x_1 + 3x_2 = 33$	[1]
$10x_1 - 2x_2 = 6$	[2]

Multiply [1] by 1/6

$1x_1 + \frac{1}{2}x_2 = 11/2$	[1']

Multiply [1'] by -10 and add to [2]

$0x_1 - 7x_2 = -49$	[2']

Multiply [2'] by -1/7

$0x_1 + 1x_2 = 7$	[2'']

Multiply [2''] by -1/2 and add to [1']

$1x_1 + 0x_2 = 2$	[1'']

The above elementary row operations provide

$1x_1 + 0x_2 = 2$	[1'']
$0x_1 + 1x_2 = 7$	[2'']

Thus the solution to the equations is

$x_1 = 2$ and $x_2 = 7$.

2. Using the elementary row operations used in the solution to problem 1, we have

	Equation Number
$1x_1 + 3x_2 - 1x_3 = 4$	[1]
$2x_1 + 4x_2 + 2x_3 = 22$	[2]
$5x_1 - 2x_2 + 1x_3 = 27$	[3]

Multiply [1] by -2 and add to [2]

$0x_1 - 2x_2 + 4x_3 = 14$	[2']

Multiply [1] by -5 and add to [3]

$0x_1 - 17x_2 + 6x_3 = 7$	[3']

Multiply [2'] by -1/2

$$0x_1 + 1x_2 - 2x_3 = -7 \qquad\qquad [2'']$$

Multiply [2''] by -3 and add to [1]

$$1x_1 + 0x_2 + 5x_3 = 25 \qquad\qquad [1']$$

Multiply [2''] by +17 and add to [3']

$$0x_1 + 0x_2 - 28x_3 = -112 \qquad\qquad [3'']$$

Multiply [3''] by -1/28

$$0x_1 + 0x_2 + 1x_3 = 4 \qquad\qquad [3''']$$

Multiply [3'''] by 2 and add to [2'']

$$0x_1 + 1x_2 + 0x_3 = 1 \qquad\qquad [2''']$$

Multiply [3'''] by -5 and add to [1']

$$1x_1 + 0x_2 + 0x_3 = 5 \qquad\qquad [1'']$$

At this point we have the revised equations

$$1x_1 + 0x_2 + 0x_3 = 5 \qquad\qquad [1'']$$

$$0x_1 + 1x_2 + 0x_3 = 1 \qquad\qquad [2''']$$

$$0x_1 + 0x_2 + 1x_3 = 4 \qquad\qquad [3''']$$

Thus the solution to the equations is

$$x_1 = 5, x_2 = 1, x_3 = 4.$$

3. a.

$$
\begin{aligned}
\max \quad & 5x_1 + 9x_2 + 0s_1 + 0s_2 + 0s_3 \\
\text{s.t.} \quad & \\
& \tfrac{1}{2}x_1 + 1x_2 + 1s_1 \qquad\qquad = 8 \\
& 1x_1 + 1x_2 \qquad - 1s_2 \qquad = 10 \\
& \tfrac{1}{4}x_1 + \tfrac{3}{2}x_2 \qquad\qquad - 1s_3 = 6 \\
& x_1,\ x_2,\ s_1,\ s_2,\ s_3,\ \geq 0
\end{aligned}
$$

b. 2

c. $x_1 = 4$, $x_2 = 6$, and $s_3 = 4$.

d. $x_2 = 4$, $s_1 = 4$, and $s_2 = -6$.

e. The answer to part c is a basic feasible solution and an extreme point solution. The answer to part d is not a basic feasible solution because s_2 is negative.

f.

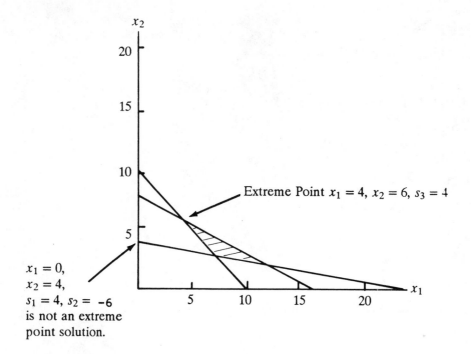

x_2

20

15

10

5

Extreme Point $x_1 = 4$, $x_2 = 6$, $s_3 = 4$

$x_1 = 0$,
$x_2 = 4$,
$s_1 = 4$, $s_2 = -6$
is not an extreme
point solution.

5   10   15   20 x_1

4. a.

Basis	C_B	x_1	x_2	x_3	s_1	s_2	s_3	
		5	20	25	0	0	0	
s_1	0	2	1	0	1	0	0	40
s_2	0	0	2	1	0	1	0	30
s_3	0	3	0	-1/2	0	0	1	15
z_j		0	0	0	0	0	0	0
$c_j - z_j$		5	20	25	0	0	0	

b.

$$\max \; 5x_1 + 20x_2 + 25x_3 + 0s_1 + 0s_2 + 0s_3$$
$$\text{s.t.}$$
$$2x_1 + 1x_2 + \quad + 1s_1 \quad\quad = 40$$
$$2x_2 + 1x_3 \quad + 1s_2 \quad = 30$$
$$3x_1 \quad - \tfrac{1}{2}x_3 \quad\quad + 1s_3 = 15$$
$$x_1, \; x_2, \; x_3, \; s_1, \; s_2, \; s_3, \; \geq 0.$$

c.   The original basis consists of s_1, s_2, and s_3. It is the origin since the nonbasic variables are x_1, x_2, and x_3 and are all zero.

d.   0.

e. x_3 enters because it has the largest $c_j - z_j$ and s_2 will leave because row 2 has the only positive cooefficient.

f.   30; objective function value is 30 times 25 or 750.

g.   Optimal Solution:

$x_1 = 10$ $s_1 = 20$

$x_2 = 0$ $s_2 = 0$

$x_3 = 30$ $s_3 = 0$

$z = 800$.

5.

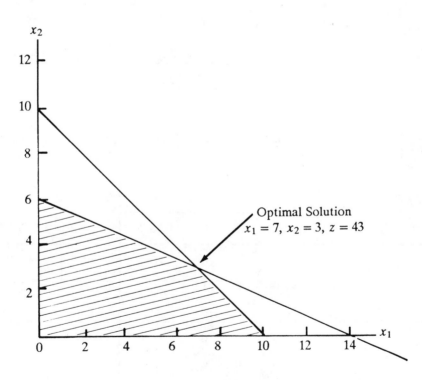

Optimal Solution
$x_1 = 7$, $x_2 = 3$, $z = 43$

Sequence of extreme points generated by the simplex method:

$$(x_1 = 0, x_2 = 0)$$

$$(x_1 = 0, x_2 = 6)$$

$$(x_1 = 7, x_2 = 3)$$

6. There are two requirements for tableau form: (1) m of the variables must have both a coefficient of one and appear in only one equation each and (2) the right-hand side of the constraint equations must be non-negative. For a problem with less-than-or-equal-to constraints and non-negative b_i's, we form standard form by adding slack variables. This process will satisfy requirements (1) for the tableau form. Since the problem is assumed to have non-negative b_i's, our second property of tableau form, we see that the standard form representation of the problem is equivalent to tableau form.

7.

Basis	C_B	x_1 100	x_2 200	s_1 0	s_2 0	s_3 0		$\bar{b}_i / \bar{a}_{il}$
s_1	0	1	1	1	0	0	500	500/1
s_2	0	1	0	0	1	0	200	200
s_3	0	2	⑥	0	0	1	1200	1200/6
	c_j	0	0	0	0	0	0	
	$c_j - z_j$	100	200	0	0	0		

Note: This tableau corresponds to extreme point 1 in the solution to the Ryland Farms problem from Chapter 7, No. 37.

Basis	C_B	x_1 100	x_2 200	s_1 0	s_2 0	s_3 0		$\bar{b}_i / \bar{a}_l$
s_1	0	2/3	0	1	0	-1/6	300	300/(2/3)
s_2	0	①	0	0	1	0	200	200/1
s_3	200	1/3	1	0	0	1/6	200	200/(1/3)
	z_j	200/3	200	0	0	200/6	40,000	
	$c_j - z_j$	100/3	0	0	0	-200/6		

Note: This tableau corresponds to extreme point 4 .

Basis	C_B	x_1 100	x_2 200	s_1 0	s_2 0	s_3 0	
s_1	0	0	0	1	-2/3	-1/6	500 / 3
x_1	100	1	0	0	1	0	200
x_2	200	0	1	0	-1/3	1/6	400 / 3
z_j		100	200	0	100/3	200/6	46,666 $^2/_3$
$c_j - z_j$		0	0	0	-100/3	-200/6	

Optimal Solution:

$s_1 = 500/3, \ x_1 = 200, \ x_2 = 400/3$

Note: The optimal tableau corresponds to extreme point 3 .

8. a.   Initial simplex tableau

Basis	C_B	x_1 10	x_2 9	s_1 0	s_2 0	s_3 0	s_4 0	
s_1	0	7/10	1	1	0	0	0	630
s_2	0	1/2	5/6	0	1	0	0	600
s_3	0	1	2/3	0	0	1	0	708
s_4	0	1/10	1/4	0	0	0	1	135
z_j		0	0	0	0	0	0	0
$c_j - z_j$		10	9	0	0	0	0	

Final simplex tableau

		x_1	x_2	s_1	s_2	s_3	s_4	
Basis	C_B	10	9	0	0	0	0	
x_2	9	0	1	30/16	0	-21/16	0	252
s_2	0	0	0	-15/16	1	5/32	0	120
x_1	10	1	0	-20/16	0	30/16	0	540
s_4	0	0	0	-11/32	0	9/64	1	18
z_j		10	9	70/16	0	111/16	0	7668
$c_j - z_j$		0	0	-70/16	0	-111/16	0	

x_1 = 540 standard bags

x_2 = 252 deluxe bags

b. $7668

c. & d.

Slack	Production Time
$s_1 = 0$	Cutting and dyeing time = 630 hours
$s_2 = 120$	Sewing time = 600 - 120 = 480 hours
$s_3 = 0$	Finishing time = 708 hours
$s_4 = 18$	Inspecting and Packaging time = 135 - 18 = 117 hours

9.   Final tableau

		x_1	x_2	x_3	x_4	s_1	s_2	s_3	
Basis	C_B	2.5	5	1	1	0	0	0	
s_1	0	-.4	0	-.92	.1	1	-.7	0	690
x_2	5	1.0	1	.80	.5	0	.5	0	650
s_3	0	.2	0	.20	.7	0	-.5	1	310
z_j		5	5	4	2.5	0	2.5	0	3250
$c_j - z_j$		-2.5	0	-3	-1.5	0	-2.5	0	

Optimal Solution:

$x_1 = 0$ $s_1 = 690$

$x_2 = 650$ $s_2 = 0$

$x_3 = 0$ $s_3 = 310$

$x_4 = 0$

$z = 3250$

10.

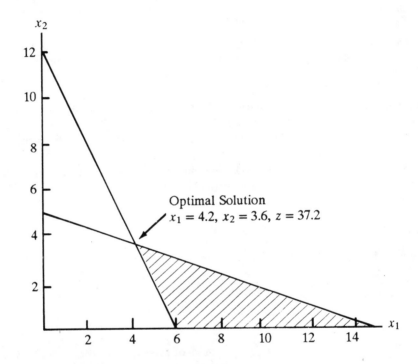

Optimal Solution
$x_1 = 4.2$, $x_2 = 3.6$, $z = 37.2$

Extreme Points:
$(x_1 = 6, x_2 = 0)$, $(x_1 = 4.2, x_2 = 3.6)$,

$(x_1 = 15, x_2 = 0)$

Simplex Solution Sequence:
$(x_1 = 0, x_2 = 0)$

$(x_1 = 6, x_2 = 0)$

$(x_1 = 4.2, x_2 = 3.6)$

11.   The number of combinations of 7 things (variables) taken 4 at a time.

$$\frac{7!}{4! \ 3!} = 35$$

12.   The $\bar{a}_{ij}$'s tell us how many additional units of resource i have to be "given up" in order to introduce one unit of x_j into solution. Negative or zero $\bar{a}_{ij}$ can never limit the amount of x_j that can be introduced into solution, since a negative value implies additional units of the resource are made available when x_j is made basic. Thus, we need only consider $\bar{a}_{ij}$'s which are strictly greater than zero.

13.a.   The same optimal solution is obtained, but with one more iteration.

  b.   No, any $c_j - z_j > 0$ will work.

  c.   Choosing the variable with the largest $c_j - z_j$ value provides the largest per unit increase in the objective function and is a good criterion in terms of minimizing the number of iterations necessary to reach the optimal solution.

        But choosing another variable that permits more units to be introduced could cause a larger total change from one iteration to the next. Experiments have shown, however, that the extra work necessary to select the variable causing the largest total change for introduction is not worth it.

        Many of the large-scale computer codes introduce several variable at an iteration and do not examine all the $c_j - z_j$'s before selecting which variable to introduce.

14.   We select the basic variables with the smallest ratio of $\bar{b}_i / \bar{a}_{ij}$ to ensure the feasibility of the new solution. That is, on the next iteration, if we do not select the basic variable with the smallest ratio, a $\bar{b}_i$ value may be driven negative - hence, an infeasible solution.

15.

$$\text{Let} \quad x_1 \ = \ \text{units of product A.}$$
$$x_2 \ = \ \text{units of product B.}$$
$$x_3 \ = \ \text{units of product C.}$$

$$\begin{array}{llll}
\max \ 20x_1 & + \ 20x_2 & + \ 15x_3 & \\
\text{s.t.} & & & \\
7x_1 & + \ 6x_2 & + \ 3x_3 & \leq \ 100 \\
5x_1 & + \ 4x_2 & + \ 2x_3 & \leq \ 200
\end{array}$$

$$x_1, \ x_2, \ x_3 \geq 0$$

Optimal Solution: $x_1 = 0$, $x_2 = 0$, $x_3 = 33 \ 1/3$

Profit = 500.

16.

$$\text{Let} \quad x_1 \quad = \quad \text{units of Deskpro}$$

$$x_2 \quad = \quad \text{units of Portable}$$

$$\max 50x_1 + 40x_2$$

s.t.

$$3x_1 + 5x_2 \leq 150 \quad \text{Assembly time}$$
$$x_2 \leq 20 \quad \text{Display units}$$
$$8x_1 + 5x_2 \leq 300 \quad \text{Warehouse space}$$

$$x_1, \; x_2 \geq 0$$

Initial tableau

Basis	c_B	x_1 50	x_2 40	s_1 0	s_2 0	s_3 0		b_i / a_{i1}
s_1	0	3	5	1	0	0	150	$150/3 = 50$
s_2	0	0	1	0	1	0	20	–
s_3	0	⑧	5	0	0	1	300	$300/8 = 37.5$
	z_j	0	0	0	0	0	0	
	$c_j - z_j$	50	40	0	0	0		

Result of first iteration

Basis	c_B	x_1 50	x_2 40	s_1 0	s_2 0	s_3 0		$\bar{b}_i / \bar{a}_{i2}$
s_1	0	0	㉕/8	1	0	-3/8	75/2	12
s_2	0	0	1	0	1	0	20	20
x_1	50	1	5/8	0	0	1/8	75/2	60
	z_j	50	250/8	0	0	50/8	1875	
	$c_j - z_j$.	0	70/8	0	0	-50/8		

Result of second iteration

Basis	c_B	x_1 50	x_2 40	s_1 0	s_2 0	s_3 0	
x_2	40	0	1	8/25	0	-3/25	12
s_2	0	0	0	-8/25	1	3/25	8
x_1	50	1	0	-5/25	0	5/25	30
	z_j	50	40	14/5	0	26/5	1980
	$c_j - z_j$	0	0	-14/5	0	-26/5	

Optimal Solution: Produce 30 Deskpros and 12 Portables

Profit contribution = $1980

17.

Let x_1 = number of units of Grade A Plywood produced

x_2 = number of units of Grade B Plywood produced

x_3 = number of units of Grade X Plywood produced

$$\max \ 40x_1 + 30x_2 + 20x_3$$
s.t.
$$2x_1 + 5x_2 + 10x_3 \leq 900$$
$$2x_1 + 5x_2 + 3x_3 \leq 400$$
$$4x_1 + 2x_2 - 2x_3 \leq 600$$
$$x_1, \ x_2, \ x_3 \geq 0$$

Optimal Solution:

$x_1 = 137.5, \ x_2 = 25, \ x_3 = 0$

Profit = 6250.

18.

Let x_1 = gallons of Heidelberg Sweet produced

x_2 = gallons of Heidelberg Regular produced

x_3 = gallons of Deutschland Extra Dry produced

max $1.00x_1 + 1.20x_2 + 2.00x_3$
s.t.

$$
\begin{array}{llllll}
1x_1 & + & 2x_2 & & \leq & 150 \text{ Grapes Grade A} \\
1x_1 & + & & + \; 2x_3 & \leq & 150 \text{ Grapes Grade B} \\
2x_1 & + & 1x_2 & & \leq & 80 \text{ Sugar} \\
2x_1 & + & 3x_2 & + \; 1x_3 & \leq & 225 \text{ Labor-hours}
\end{array}
$$

$$x_1, \; x_2, \; x_3, \; x_4, \; \geq 0$$

a.

$$
\begin{array}{ll}
x_1 = 0 & s_1 = 50 \\
x_2 = 50 & s_2 = 0 \\
x_3 = 75 & s_3 = 30 \\
& s_4 = 0
\end{array}
$$

Profit = $210

b. s_1 = unused bushels of grapes (Grade A)

s_2 = unused bushels of grapes (Grade B)

s_3 = unused pounds of sugar

s_4 = unused labor-hours

c. $s_2 = 0$ and $s_4 = 0$. Therefore the Grade B grapes and the labor-hours are the binding resources. Increasing the amounts of these resources will improve profit.

19.

max $4x_1 + 2x_2 - 3x_3 + 5x_4 + 0s_1 - Ma_1 + 0s_2 - Ma_3$
s.t.

$$
\begin{array}{llllllll}
2x_1 & - 1x_2 & + 1x_3 & + 2x_4 & - 1s_1 & + 1a_1 & & = 50 \\
3x_1 & & - 1x_3 & + 2x_4 & & & + 1s_2 & = 80 \\
1x_1 & + 1x_2 & & + 1x_4 & & & + 1a_3 & = 60
\end{array}
$$

$$x_1, \; x_2, \; x_3, \; x_4, \; s_1, \; s_2, \; a_1, \; a_3, \; \geq 0$$

20.

$$\max -4x_1 - 5x_2 - 3x_3 + 0s_1 + 0s_2 + 0s_4 - Ma_1 - Ma_2 - Ma_3$$

s.t.

$$
\begin{aligned}
4x_1 \quad\quad + 2x_3 - 1s_1 \quad\quad\quad\quad\quad\quad + 1a_1 \quad\quad\quad\quad &= 20 \\
- 1x_2 + 1x_3 \quad\quad - 1s_2 \quad\quad\quad + 1a_2 \quad\quad &= 8 \\
-1x_1 + 2x_2 \quad\quad\quad\quad\quad\quad\quad\quad\quad + 1a_3 &= 5 \\
2x_1 + 1x_2 + 1x_3 \quad\quad\quad + 1s_4 \quad\quad\quad\quad\quad &= 12
\end{aligned}
$$

$$x_1, \ x_2, \ x_3, \ s_1, \ s_2, \ s_4, \ a_1, \ a_2, \ a_3 \geq 0$$

21. $x_1 = 1, x_2 = 4, z = 19$

Converting to a max problem and solving using the simplex method, the final simplex tableau is:

Basis	C_B	x_1 -3	x_2 -4	x_3 -8	s_1 0	s_2 0	
x_1	-3	1	0	-1	-1/4	1/8	1
x_2	-4	0	1	2	0	-1/4	4
z_j		-3	-4	-5	3/4	5/8	-19
$c_j - z_j$		0	0	-3	-3/4	-5/8	

22. Converting to a max problem and solving using the simplex method, the final simplex tableau is:

Basis	C_B	x_1 -4	x_2 -2	x_3 -3	s_1 0	s_2 0	s_3 0	
x_2	-2	0	1	0	-2/5	0	1/5	2
x_3	-3	0	0	1	-1/10	-1/2	3/10	1/2
x_1	-4	1	0	0	1/5	0	-3/5	9
z_j		-4	-2	-3	3/10	3/2	11/10	-41.5
$c_j - z_j$		0	0	0	-3/10	-3/2	-11/10	

$x_1 = 9, x_2 = 2, x_3 = 1/2, z = 41.5$

23.a.   Initial tableau

Basis	c_B	x_1 -1	x_2 -1	s_1 0	s_2 0	s_3 0	a_1 -M	a_2 -M	a_3 -M	
a_1	-M	1	2	-1	0	0	1	0	0	80
a_2	-M	1	0	0	-1	0	0	1	0	30
a_3	-M	0	(1)	0	0	-1	0	0	1	20
	z_j	-2M	-3M	M	M	M	-M	-M	-M	-130M
	$c_j - z_j$	-1 + 2M	-1 + 3M	-M	-M	-M	0	0	0	

Result of iteration 1

Basis	c_B	x_1 -1	x_2 -1	s_1 0	s_2 0	s_3 0	a_1 -M	a_2 -M	
a_1	-M	1	0	-1	0	2	1	0	40
a_2	-M	(1)	0	0	-1	0	0	1	30
x_2	-1	0	1	0	0	-1	0	0	20
	z_j	-2M	-1	M	M	1 - 2M	-M	-M	-20 - 70M
	$c_j - z_j$	-1 + 2M	0	-M	-M	-1 + 2M	0	0	

Result of iteration 2

Basis	c_B	x_1 -1	x_2 -1	s_1 0	s_2 0	s_3 0	a_1 -M	
a_1	-M	0	0	-1	1	(2)	1	10
x_1	-1	1	0	0	-1	0	0	30
x_2	-1	0	1	0	0	-1	0	20
	z_j	-1	-1	M	1 - M	1 - 2M	-M	-50 - 10M
	$c_j - z_j$	0	0	-M	1 + M	-1 + 2M	0	

Result of iteration 3

Basis	c_B	x_1 -1	x_2 -1	s_1 0	s_2 0	s_3 0	
s_3	0	0	0	-1/2	1/2	1	5
x_1	-1	1	0	0	-1	0	30
x_2	-1	0	1	-1/2	1/2	0	25
z_j		-1	-1	1/2	1/2	0	-55
$c_j - z_j$		0	0	-1/2	-1/2	0	

Optimal Solution: $x_1 = 30$, $x_2 = 25$ Cost = \$55

b.

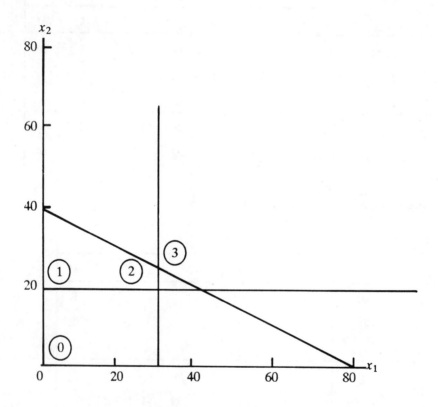

Solution 0 corresponds to the initial solution. The solutions at successive iterations are numbered.

c.   Three iterations are required for Phase I before all the artificial variables are eliminated.

d.   None. The solution obtained at the end of Phase I is optimal.

24.a. Initial tableau

Basis	c_B	x_1 -2	x_2 -3	s_1 0	s_2 0	s_3 0	a_1 $-M$	a_2 $-M$	
a_1	$-M$	①	0	-1	0	0	1	0	125
a_2	$-M$	1	1	0	-1	0	0	1	350
s_3	0	2	1	0	0	1	0	0	600
	z_j	$-2M$	$-M$	M	M	0	$-M$	$-M$	$-475M$
	$c_j - z_j$	$-2 + 2M$	$-3 + M$	$-M$	$-M$	0	0	0	

Result of first iteration

Basis	c_B	x_1 -2	x_2 -3	s_1 0	s_2 0	s_3 0	a_2 $-M$	
x_1	-2	1	0	-1	0	0	0	125
a_2	$-M$	0	①	1	-1	0	1	225
s_3	0	0	1	2	0	1	0	350
	z_j	-2	$-M$	$2 - M$	M	0	$-M$	$-250 - 225M$
	$c_j - z_j$	0	$-3 + M$	$-2 + M$	$-M$	0	0	

Result of second iteration

Basis	c_B	x_1 -2	x_2 -3	s_1 0	s_2 0	s_3 0	
x_1	-2	1	0	-1	0	0	125
x_2	-3	0	1	1	-1	0	225
s_3	0	0	0	①	1	1	125
	z_j	-2	-3	-1	3	0	-925
	$c_j - z_j$	0	0	1	-3	0	

Result of third iteration

Basis	c_B	x_1 -2	x_2 -3	s_1 0	s_2 0	s_3 0	
x_1	-2	1	0	0	1	1	250
x_2	-3	0	1	0	-2	-1	100
s_1	0	0	0	1	1	1	125
	z_j	-2	-3	0	4	1	-800
	$c_j - z_j$	0	0	0	-4	-1	

Optimal Solution: $x_1 = 250$, $x_2 = 100$ Cost = 800

b.

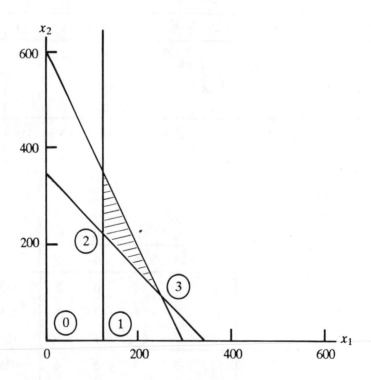

Solution 0 corresponds to the initial solution. The solutions and successive iterations are numbered accordingly.

c. Two iterations are required to drive all the artificial variables out of solution and complete Phase I.

d. One iteration is required for Phase II to reach the optimal solution.

25.

Let x_1 = no. of gallons of Chocolate produced

x_2 = no. of gallons of Vanilla produced

x_3 = no. of gallons of Banana produced

$$\max 1.00x_1 + .90x_2 + .95x_3$$

s.t.

$$.45x_1 + .50x_2 + .40x_3 \le 200 \quad \text{Milk}$$
$$.50x_1 + .40x_2 + .40x_3 \le 150 \quad \text{Sugar}$$
$$.10x_1 + .15x_2 + .20x_3 \le 60 \quad \text{Cream}$$

$$x_1, \ x_2, \ x_3, \ \ge 0$$

Optimal Solution

$x_1 = 0, x_2 = 300, x_3 = 75$

Profit = \$341.25. Additional resources: Sugar and Cream.

26.

Let x_1 = number of cases of Incentive sold by John

x_2 = number of cases of Temptation sold by John

x_3 = number of cases of Incentive sold by Brenda

x_4 = number of cases of Temptation sold by Brenda

x_5 = number of cases of Incentive sold by Red

x_6 = number of cases of Temptation sold by Red

$$\max \ 30x_1 + 25x_2 + 30x_3 + 25x_4 + 30x_5 + 25x_6$$

s.t.

$$10x_1 + 15x_2 \qquad\qquad\qquad \le 4800$$
$$15x_3 + 10x_4 \qquad\qquad \le 4800$$
$$12x_5 + 6x_6 \le 4800$$

$$x_1, \ x_2, \ x_3, \ x_4, \ x_5, \ x_6, \ \ge 0$$

Optimal Solution:

$x_1 = 480 \qquad x_4 = 480$

$x_2 = 0 \qquad x_5 = 0$

$x_3 = 0 \qquad x_6 = 800$

Objective Function maximized at 46400.

Time Allocation:

	Incentive	Temptation
John	4800 min.	no time
Brenda	no time	4800 min.
Red	no time	4800 min.

27.   Final simplex tableau

Basis	C_B	x_1 4	x_2 8	s_1 0	s_2 0	a_2 -M	
x_2	8	1	1	1/2	0	0	5
a_2	-M	-2	0	-1/2	-1	1	3
	z_j	8+2M	8	4+M/2	+M	-M	40 - 3M
	$c_j - z_j$	-4-2M	0	-4-M/2	-M	0	

Infeasible; optimal solution condition is reached with the artificial variable a_2 still in the solution.

28.   Alternate Optimal Solution

Basis	C_B	x_1 -3	x_2 -3	s_1 0	s_2 0	s_3 0	
s_2	0	0	0	-4/3	1	1/6	4
x_1	-3	1	0	-2/3	0	1/12	4
x_2	-3	0	1	2/3	0	-1/3	4
	z_j	-3	-3	0	0	3/4	-24
	$c_j - z_j$	0	0	0	0	-3/4	

↑

indicates alternate optimal solutions exist.

$$x_1 = 4, x_2 = 4, z = 24$$

$$x_1 = 8, x_2 = 0, z = 24$$

29.   Unbounded Solution

Basis	C_B	x_1	x_2	s_1	s_2	s_3	
		1	1	0	0	0	
s_3	0	8/3	0	-1/3	0	1	4
s_2	0	4	0	-1	1	0	36
x_2	1	4/3	1	-1/6	0	0	4
z_j		4/3	1	-1/6	0	0	4
$c_j - z_j$		-1/3	0	1/6	0	0	

$\uparrow$

30.   Alternate Optimal Solutions

Basis	C_B	x_1	x_2	x_3	s_1	s_2	s_3	
		2	1	1	0	0	0	
x_1	2	1	2	1/2	0	0	1/4	4
s_2	0	0	0	-1	0	1	-1/2	12
s_1	0	0	6	0	1	0	1	12
z_j		2	4	1	0	0	1/4	8
$c_j - z_j$		0	-3	0	0	0	-1/4	

Two possible solutions:

$x_1 = 4, x_2 = 0, x_3 = 0$

or

$x_1 = 0, x_2 = 0, x_3 = 8$

31.   The final simplex tableau is given by:

Basis	C_B	x_1 2	x_2 4	s_1 0	s_3 0	
s_1	0	1/2	0	1	0	4
x_2	4	1	1	0	0	12
s_3	0	-1/2	0	0	1	0
	z_j	4	4	0	0	48
	$c_j - z_j$	-2	0	0	0	

This solution is degenerate since the basic variable s_3 is in solution at a zero value.

32.   The final simplex tableau is:

Basis	C_B	x_1 +4	x_2 -5	x_3 -5	s_1 0	s_2 0	s_3 0	a_1 -M	a_3 -M	
a_1	-M	1	-2	0	-1	1	0	1	0	1
x_3	-5	-1	1	1	0	-1	0	0	0	1
a_3	-M	-1	1	0	0	-1	-1	0	1	2
	z_j	+5	-5+M	-5	+M	+5	+M	-M	-M	-5 - 3M
	$c_j - z_j$	-1	-M	0	-M	-5	-M	0	0	

Since both artificial variables a_1 and a_3 are contained in this solution, we can conclude that we have an infeasible problem.

33.a.   The mathematical formulation of this problem is:

$$\max 3x_1 \quad + 5x_2 \quad + 4x_3$$

s.t.

$$12x_1 \quad + 10x_2 \quad + 8x_3 \quad \leq \quad 18{,}000 \, C \,\&\, D$$
$$15x_1 \quad + 15x_2 \quad + 12x_3 \quad \leq \quad 12{,}000 \, S$$
$$3x_1 \quad + 4x_2 \quad + 2x_3 \quad \leq \quad 6{,}000 \, I \text{ and } P$$
$$x_1 \qquad\qquad\qquad\qquad \geq \quad 1{,}000$$
$$x_1, \; x_2, \; x_3, \; \geq 0$$

There is no feasible solution. Not enough sewing time is available to make 1000 All-Pro footballs.

b.   The mathematical formulation of this problem is now

$$\max 3x_1 \quad + 5x_2 \quad + 4x_3$$

s.t.

$$
\begin{array}{rlll}
12x_1 & + 10x_2 & + 8x_3 & \le 18{,}000 \text{ C \& D} \\
15x_1 & + 15x_2 & + 12x_3 & \le 18{,}000 \text{ S} \\
3x_1 & + 4x_2 & + 2x_3 & \le 9{,}000 \text{ I \& P} \\
x_1 & & & \ge 1{,}000
\end{array}
$$

$$x_1, \; x_2, \; x_3, \; \ge 0$$

Optimal Solution

$x_1 = 1000, \; x_2 = \quad 0, \; x_3 = 250$

Profit = \$4000

There is an alternate optimal solution with $x_1 = 1000$, $x_2 = 200$, and $x_3 = 0$.

Note that the additional Inspection and Packaging time is not needed.

34.a.

Basis	c_B	x_1 10	x_2 18	s_1 0	s_2 0	s_3 0	s_4 0	
x_2	18	0	1	30/16	0	-21/16	0	252
s_2	0	0	0	-15/16	1	25/160	0	120
x_1	10	1	0	-20/16	0	300/160	0	540
s_4	0	0	0	-11/32	0	45/320	1	18
z_j		10	18	340/16	0	-78/16	0	9936
$c_j - z_j$		0	0	-340/16	0	78/16	0	

↑

Positive, therefore not
optimal

b.   Optimal: $x_1 = 300$, $x_2 = 420$, $s_2 = 100$, $s_3 = 128$ Profit = \$10,560

s_3 enters the basis and s_4 leaves.

c.   The new optimal solution is at the extreme point formed by the intersection of the Cutting and Dyeing and Inspection and Packaging constraints. The Cutting and Dyeing and Inspection and Packaging constraints are binding.

35. New formulation has one additional constraint.

$$\max 50x_1 + 40x_2$$
$$\text{s.t.}$$
$$3x_1 + 5x_2 \leq 150$$
$$x_2 \leq 20$$
$$8x_1 + 5x_2 \leq 300$$
$$x_1 + x_2 \geq 25$$

$$x_1,\ x_2 \geq 0$$

Initial tableau

Basis	c_B	x_1 50	x_2 40	s_1 0	s_2 0	s_3 0	s_4 0	a_1 -M	
s_1	0	3	5	1	0	0	0	0	150
s_2	0	0	1	0	1	0	0	0	20
s_3	0	8	5	0	0	1	0	0	300
a_1	-M	①	1	0	0	0	-1	1	25
	z_j	-M	-M	0	0	0	M	-M	-25M
	$c_j - z_j$	50 + M	40 + M	0	0	0	-M	0	

Basis	c_B	x_1 50	x_2 40	s_1 0	s_2 0	s_3 0	s_4 0	
s_1	0	0	2	1	0	0	3	75
s_2	0	0	1	0	1	0	0	20
s_3	0	0	-3	0	0	1	⑧	100
x_1	50	1	1	0	0	0	-1	25
	z_j	50	50	0	0	0	-50	1250
	$c_j - z_j$	0	-10	0	0	0	50	

Basis	c_B	x_1 50	x_2 40	s_1 0	s_2 0	s_3 0	s_4 0	
s_1	0	0	(25/8)	1	0	-3/8	0	75/2
s_2	0	0	1	0	1	0	0	20
s_4	0	0	-3/8	0	0	1/8	1	25/2
x_1	50	1	5/8	0	0	1/8	0	75/2
z_j		50	250/8	0	0	50/8	0	1875
$c_j - z_j$		0	70/8	0	0	-50/8	0	

Basis	c_B	x_1 50	x_2 40	s_1 0	s_2 0	s_3 0	s_4 0	
x_1	40	0	1	8/25	0	-3/25	0	12
s_2	0	0	0	-8/25	1	3/25	0	8
s_4	0	0	0	3/25	0	2/25	1	17
x_1	50	1	0	-5/25	0	5/25	0	30
z_j		50	40	14/5	0	26/5	0	1980
$c_j - z_j$		0	0	-14/5	0	-26/5	0	

b.   Sequence of Simplex Solutions for the Modified HighTech Industries Problem

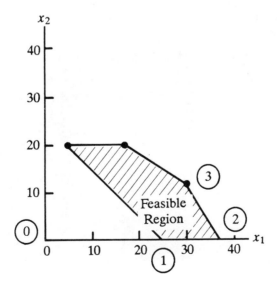

36. The final simplex tableau is shown

Basis	c_B	x_1 50	x_2 40	s_1 0	s_2 0	s_3 0	s_4 0	a_4 -M	
x_2	40	0	1	8/25	0	-3/25	0	0	12
s_2	0	0	0	-8/25	1	3/25	0	0	8
x_1	50	1	0	-5/25	0	5/25	0	0	30
a_4	-M	0	0	-3/25	0	-2/25	-1	1	8
z_j		50	40	$(70 + 3M)/25$	0	$(130 + 2M)/25$	M	-M	1980 -8M
$c_j - z_j$		0	0	$(-70 - 3M)/25$	0	$(-130 - 2M)/25$	-M	0	

The artificial variable a_4 is in solution at a positive value and all $c_j - z_j \geq 0$. Therefore Phase I cannot be completed and there is no feasible solution.

37.a.

Basis	C_B	x_1 7.5	x_2 15	x_3 10	s_1 0	s_2 0	s_3 0	
x_1	7.5	1	0	1	1/2	0	0	4
x_2	15	0	1	1/4	-1/8	1/2	0	0.5
s_3	0	0	0	3/4	-3/8	-1/2	1	1.5
z_j		7.5	15	11 ¼	1 ⅞	7 ½	0	37.5
$c_j - z_j$		0	0	-1 ¼	-1 ⅞	-7 ½	0	

$x_1 = 4$, $x_2 = 0.5$, $s_3 = 1.5$

$z = 37.5$

b. Final tableau with c_1 as coefficient of x_1 in objective function.

Basis	C_B	x_1 c_1	x_2 15	x_3 10	s_1 0	s_2 0	s_3 0	
x_1	c_1	1	0	1	1/2	0	0	4
x_2	15	0	1	1/4	-1/8	1/2	0	1/2
s_3	0	0	0	3/4	-3/8	-1/2	1	3/2
	z_j	c_1	15	$c_1 + 15/4$	$(4c_1 - 15)/8$	7 ½	0	$4c_1 + 15/2$
	$c_j - z_j$	0	0	$(25/4)-c_1$	$(15 - 4c_1)/8$	-7 ½	0	

$25/4 - c_1 \leq 0$ $\qquad$ $c_1 \geq 25/4 = 6.25$

$(15 - 4c_1)/8 \leq 0$ $\qquad$ $c_1 \geq 15/4 = 3.75$

Range: $6.25 \leq c_1 < \infty$

c. The optimal solution would not change because $c_1 = 10$ is in the range of optimality. The value of the solution would increase to $10 (4) + 15 (.5) = 47.5$.

d. Since x_3 is a nonbasic variable only the $c_j - z_j$ entry in the x_3 column is affected.

$\qquad$ $c_3 - 11.25 \leq 0$
Range: $c_3 \leq 11.25$

e. Increasing c_3 to 15 moves it out of the range of optimality. The new final simplex tableau and optimal solution are shown below. There are alternate optimal solutions.

Basis	C_B	x_1 7.5	x_2 15	x_3 15	s_1 0	s_2 0	s_3 0	
x_1	7.5	1	0	0	1	2/3	-4/3	2
x_2	15	0	1	0	0	2/3	-1/3	0
s_3	15	0	0	1	-1/2	-2/3	4/3	2
	z_j	7.5	15	15	0	5	5	45
	$c_j - z_j$	0	0	0	0	-5	-5	

$x_1 = 2$, $x_3 = 2$, value $= 45$ or

$x_3 = 3$, value $= 45$

38.a.

For b_1

$$4 \quad + \quad \Delta b_1 \, (1/2) \quad \geq \quad 0 \quad \rightarrow \quad \Delta b_1 \quad \geq \quad -8$$

$$1/2 \quad + \quad \Delta b_1 \, (-1/8) \quad \geq \quad 0 \quad \rightarrow \quad \Delta b_1 \quad \leq \quad 4$$

$$3/2 \quad + \quad \Delta b_1 \, (-3/8) \quad \geq \quad 0 \quad \rightarrow \quad \Delta b_1 \quad \leq \quad 4$$

therefore $-8 \leq \Delta b_1 \leq 4$

Range: $0 \leq b_1 \leq 12$

For b_2

$$4 \quad + \quad \Delta b_2 \, (0) \quad \geq \quad 0 \quad \rightarrow \quad \text{no restriction on } \Delta b_2$$

$$1/2 \quad + \quad \Delta b_2 \, (1/2) \quad \geq \quad 0 \quad \rightarrow \quad \Delta b_2 \quad \geq \quad -1$$

$$3/2 \quad + \quad \Delta b_2 \, (-1/2) \quad \geq \quad 0 \quad \rightarrow \quad \Delta b_2 \quad \leq \quad 3$$

therefore $-1 \leq \Delta b_2 \leq 3$

Range: $2 \leq b_2 \leq 6$

For b_3

$$4 \quad + \quad \Delta b_3 \, (0) \quad \geq \quad 0 \quad \rightarrow \quad \text{no restriction}$$

$$1/2 \quad + \quad \Delta b_3 \, (0) \quad \geq \quad 0 \quad \rightarrow \quad \text{no restriction}$$

$$3/2 \quad + \quad \Delta b_3 \, (1) \quad \geq \quad 0 \quad \rightarrow \quad \Delta b_3 \quad \geq \quad -3/2$$

therefore $-3/2 \leq \Delta b_3$

Range: $4.5 \leq b_3 < \infty$

b. The proposed increase is within the range of feasibility so the change is given by multiplying the shadow price by the amount of change.

Change in Value: $(1 \, ^7/_8) \, (1) = 1 \, ^7/_8$

c. The change is within the range of feasibility .

Change in Value: $(7 \, ^1/_2) \, (1) = 7 \, ^1/_2$

d.   The change is within the range of feasibility.

Change in Value: (0) (1) = 0

39.a.   The final simplex tableau with c_1 shown as the coefficient of x_1 is

Basis	C_B	x_1 c_1	x_2 9	s_1 0	s_2 0	s_3 0	s_4 0	
x_2	9	0	1	30/16	0	-21/16	0	252
s_2	0	0	0	-15/16	1	5/32	0	120
x_1	c_1	1	0	-20/16	0	30/16	0	540
s_4	0	0	0	-11/32	0	9/64	1	18
z_j		c_1	9	$(270-20c_1)/16$	0	$(30c_1-189)/16$	0	$2268+540c_1$
$c_j - z_j$		0	0	$(20c_1-270)/16$	0	$(189-30c_1)/16$	0	

$(20c_1 - 270) / 16 \le 0$ $\rightarrow$ $c_1 \le 13.5$

$(189 - 30c_1) / 16 \le 0$ $\rightarrow$ $c_1 \ge 6.3$

Range: $6.3 \le c_1 \le 13.5$

b.   Following a similar procedure for c_2 leads to

$(200 - 30c_2) / 16 \le 0$ $\rightarrow$ $c_2 \ge 6\,^2/_3$

$(21c_2 - 300) / 16 \le 0$ $\rightarrow$ $c_2 \le 14\,^2/_7$

Range : $6\,^2/_3 \le c_2 \le 14\,^2/_7$

c.   There would be no change in product mix, but profit will drop to 540 (10) + 252 (7) = 7164.

d.   It would have to drop below $6\,^2/_3$ or increase above $14\,^2/_7$.

e.   We should expect more production of deluxe bags since its profit contribution has increased. The new optimal solution is given by

$x_1 = 300, x_2 = 420$

Optimal Value: $9300

40.a.

$$252 \ + \ \Delta b_1 \,(30/16) \ \geq \ 0 \ \rightarrow \ \Delta b_1 \ \geq \ -134.4$$
$$120 \ + \ \Delta b_1 \,(-15/16) \ \geq \ 0 \ \rightarrow \ \Delta b_1 \ \leq \ 128$$
$$540 \ + \ \Delta b_1 \,(-20/16) \ \geq \ 0 \ \rightarrow \ \Delta b_1 \ \leq \ 432$$
$$18 \ + \ \Delta b_1 \,(-11/32) \ \geq \ 0 \ \rightarrow \ \Delta b_1 \ \leq \ 52.36$$

therefore $-134.4 \leq \Delta b_1 \leq 52.36$

Range: $495.6 \leq b_1 \leq 682.36$

b. $480 \leq b_2 < \infty$

c. $580 \leq b_3 \leq 900$

d. $117 \leq b_4 < \infty$

e. The cutting and dyeing and finishing since the shadow prices and the allowable increase are positive for both.

41.a.

Basis	C_B	x_1 10	x_2 9	s_1 0	s_2 0	s_3 0	s_4 0	
x_2	9	0	1	30/16	0	-21/16	0	3852/11
s_2	0	0	0	-15/16	1	5/32	0	780/11
x_1	10	1	0	-20/16	0	(30/16)	0	5220/11
s_4	0	0	0	-11/32	0	9/64	1	0
z_j		10	9	70/16	0	111/16	0	86,868/11 = 7897 $^1/_{11}$
$c_j - z_j$		0	0	-70/16	0	-111/16	0	

b. No, s_4 would become nonbasic and s_1 would become a basic variable.

42.a. Since this is within the range of feasibility for b_1, the increase in profit is given by

$$\left(\frac{70}{16}\right) 30 = \frac{2100}{16}.$$

b. It would not decrease since there is already idle time in this department and $600 - 40 = 560$ is still within the range of feasibility for b_2.

c. Since 570 is within the range of feasibility for b_1, the lost profit would be equal to

$$\left(\frac{70}{16}\right) 60 = \frac{4200}{16}.$$

43.a. The value of the objective function would go up since the first constraint is binding. When there is no idle time, increased efficiency results in increased profits.

b. No. This would just increase the number of idle hours in the sewing department.

44.a. The final simplex tableau is given by

Basis	C_B	x_1	x_2	x_3	x_4	s_2	s_3	
		3	1	5	3	0	0	
s_2	0	5/2	7/6	0	0	1	1/3	115/3
x_3	5	3/2	1/2	1	0	0	0	15
x_4	3	0	2/3	0	1	0	1/3	25/3
	z_j	15/2	9/2	5	3	0	1	100
	$c_j - z_j$	-9/2	-7/2	0	0	0	-1	

b. Range: $2 \leq c_3 < \infty$

c. Since 1 is not contained in the range of optimality, a new basis will become optimal.

   The new optimal solution and its value is

   $x_1 = 10$

   $x_4 = 25/3$

   $s_2 = 40/3$ (Surplus associated with constraint 2)

d. Since x_2 is a nonbasic variable we simply require

   $c_2 - 9/2 \leq 0.$

   Range: $-\infty < c_2 \leq 4 \frac{1}{2}$

e. Since 4 is contained in the range, a three unit increase in c_2 would have no effect on the optimal solution or on the value of that solution.

45.a. $400/3 \leq b_1 \leq 800$

   b. $275 \leq b_2 < \infty$

   c. $275/2 \leq b_3 \leq 625$

46.a.   The final simplex tableau is restated below with c_1 replacing 50.

		x_1	x_2	s_1	s_2	s_3	
Basis	c_B	c_1	40	0	0	0	
x_2	40	0	1	8/25	0	-3/25	12
s_2	0	0	0	-8/25	1	3/25	8
x_1	c_1	1	0	-5/25	0	5/25	30
z_j		c_1	40	$(64 - c_1)/5$	0	$(c_1 - 24)/5$	$480 + 30c_1$
$c_j - z_j$		0	0	$(c_1 - 64)/5$	0	$(24 - c_1)/5$	

Therefore,
$$(c_1 - 64)/5 \geq 0 \rightarrow c_1 \geq 64$$
$$(24 - c_1)/5 \geq 0 \rightarrow c_1 \leq 24$$
$$24 \leq c_1 \leq 64$$

   b. $31.25 \leq c_2 \leq 83.33$

   c.   The same solution will be optimal. Its value is reduced to $30(30) + 40(12) = 1380$.

   d.   A new optimal solution will be obtained, since this change is outside the range of optimality.

         The new solution is $x_1 = 16\frac{2}{3}$, $x_2 = 20$, value $= 1133.33$

47.a.   From the final tableau (see problem 16) we can obtain

$$12 + (8/25)\Delta b_1 \geq 0 \rightarrow \Delta b_1 \geq -37.5$$
$$8 + (-8/25)\Delta b_1 \geq 0 \rightarrow \Delta b_1 \leq 25$$
$$30 + (-5/25)\Delta b_1 \geq 0 \rightarrow \Delta b_1 \leq 150$$
$$-37.5 \leq \Delta b_1 \leq 25$$
$$112.5 \leq \Delta b_1 \leq 175$$

   b. $233.33 \leq b_1 \leq 400$

c.   Assembly time: Dual price = 2.80
      Warehouse space: Dual price = 5.20

d.   For decreases up to 37.5 in b_1 or increases of up to 25 in b_1.

Chapter 11
Transportation, Assignment, and Transshipment Problems

Learning Objectives

1. Be able to identify the special features of the transportation problem.

2. Become familiar with the types of problems that can be solved by applying a transportation model.

3. Be able to develop network and linear programming models of the transportation problem.

4. Be able to utilize the minimum-cost method to find an initial feasible solution to a transportation problem.

5. Be able to utilize the transportation simplex method to find the optimal solution to a transportation problem.

6. Know how to handle the cases of (1) unequal supply and demand, (2) unacceptable routes, and (3) maximization objective for a transportation problem.

7. Be able to identify the special features of the assignment problem.

8. Become familiar with the types of problems that can be solved by applying an assignment model.

9. Be able to develop network and linear programming models of the assignment problem.

10. Be able to utilize the Hungarian algorithm to solve an assignment problem.

11. Be familiar with the special features of the transshipment problem.

12. Become familiar with the types of problems that can be solved by applying a transshipment model.

13. Be able to develop network and linear programming models of the transshipment problem.

14. Understand the following terms.

transportation problem	modified distribution (MODI) method
origin	assignment problem
destination	Hungarian method
network flow problem	opportunity loss
transportation tableau	transshipment problem
minimum cost method	capacitated transshipment problem
stepping-stone path	

Solutions

1. a.

Let x_{11} :   Amount shipped from Jefferson City to Des Moines

        x_{12} :   Amount shipped from Jefferson City to Kansas City

        •

        •

        •

        x_{23} :   Amount shipped from Omaha to St. Louis

$$\min \; 14x_{11} + 9x_{12} + 7x_{13} + 8x_{21} + 10x_{22} + 5x_{23}$$

$$\text{s.t.}$$

$$
\begin{aligned}
x_{11} + x_{12} + x_{13} &\leq 30 \\
x_{21} + x_{22} + x_{23} &\leq 20 \\
x_{11} + x_{21} &= 25 \\
x_{12} + x_{22} &= 15 \\
x_{13} + x_{23} &= 10
\end{aligned}
$$

$$x_{11}, \; x_{12}, \; x_{13}, \; x_{21}, \; x_{22}, \; x_{23}, \; \geq 0$$

b.

Optimal Solution

	Amount	Cost
Jefferson City - Des Moines	5	70
Jefferson City - Kansas City	15	135
Jefferson City - St. Louis	10	70
Omaha - Des Moines	20	160
Total		435

2. a.

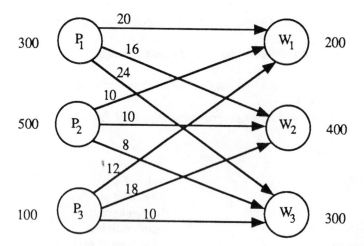

b.

Let $\quad x_{ij} \quad =$ Amount shipped from plant i to warehouse j

$\min \quad 20x_{11} + 16x_{12} + 24x_{13} + 10x_{21} + 10x_{22} + 8x_{23} + 12x_{31} + 18x_{32} + 10x_{33}$

s.t.

$$
\begin{array}{ll}
x_{11} + x_{12} + x_{13} & \leq 300 \\
x_{21} + x_{22} + x_{23} & \leq 500 \\
x_{31} + x_{32} + x_{33} & \leq 100 \\
x_{11} \quad + \quad x_{21} \quad + \quad x_{31} & = 200 \\
x_{12} \quad + \quad x_{22} \quad + \quad x_{32} & = 400 \\
x_{13} \quad + \quad x_{23} \quad + \quad x_{33} & = 300
\end{array}
$$

$x_{ij} \geq 0 \quad i = 1, 2, 3; \quad j = 1, 2, 3$

Optimal Solution

	Amount	Cost
P_1 - W_2	300	4800
P_2 - W_1	100	1000
P_2 - W_2	100	1000
P_2 - W_3	300	2400
P_3 - W_1	100	1200
		10,400

c. The only change necessary, if the data are profit values, is to change the objective to one of maximization.

3. a.

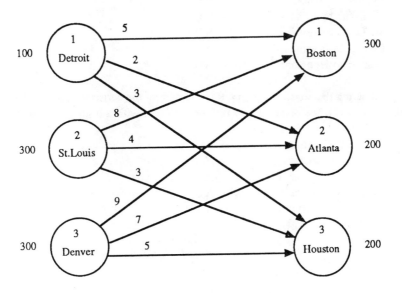

b.

$$\text{min} \quad 5x_{11} + 2x_{12} + 3x_{13} + 8x_{21} + 4x_{22} + 3x_{23} + 9x_{31} + 7x_{32} + 5x_{33}$$

s.t.

$$
\begin{array}{rcl}
x_{11} + x_{12} + x_{13} & \leq & 100 \\
x_{21} + x_{22} + x_{23} & \leq & 300 \\
x_{31} + x_{32} + x_{33} & \leq & 300 \\
x_{11} \quad\quad + x_{21} \quad\quad + x_{31} & = & 300 \\
x_{12} \quad\quad + x_{22} \quad\quad + x_{32} & = & 200 \\
x_{13} \quad\quad + x_{23} \quad\quad + x_{33} & = & 200
\end{array}
$$

$$x_{ij} \geq 0 \quad i = 1, 2, 3; \quad j = 1, 2, 3$$

c.   Optimal Solution

Detroit to Atlanta:	$x_{12} = 100$
St. Louis to Atlanta:	$x_{22} = 100$
St. Louis to Houston:	$x_{23} = 200$
Denver to Boston:	$x_{31} = 300$
Total Cost: $3900	

d.   Add the constraint: $x_{11} = 100$

e.   Delete variables x_{31} and x_{22} everywhere they appear in the model (i.e., from the objective function and constraints). Alternately one may add 2 constraints to the model in part a: $x_{31} = 0$ and $x_{22} = 0$.

f.   (1) After adding the constraint $x_{11} = 100$, the value of the solution remains at 3900 since the problem has alternate optimal solutions. The shipping pattern changes, however.

Detroit to Boston:	$x_{11} = 100$
St. Louis to Atlanta:	$x_{22} = 200$
St. Louis to Houston:	$x_{23} = 100$
Denver to Boston:	$x_{31} = 200$
Denver to Houston:	$x_{33} = 100$

(2) After deleting the constraint $x_{11} = 100$ and adding the constraints $x_{31} = 0$ and $x_{22} = 0$ from the formulation in f (1), we obtain a new optimal solution with a higher shipping cost.

Detroit to Boston:	$x_{11} = 100$
St Louis to Boston:	$x_{21} = 200$
St. Louis to Houston:	$x_{23} = 100$
Denver to Atlanta:	$x_{32} = 200$
Denver to Houston:	$x_{33} = 100$
Total Cost: $4300	

4. a.

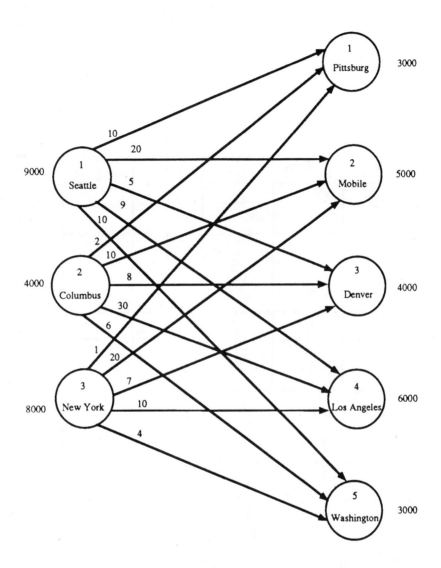

b. The initial feasible solution found using the minimum cost method is optimal. The optimal solution results in total shipping cost of $150,000. The solution (with u_i and v_j values) is shown in the tableau below.

u_i		v_j				
		0	19	5	9	3	
0		10 ⑩	20 ①	5 / 4000	9 / 5000	10 ⑦	9000
-9		2 ⑪	10 / 4000	8 ⑫	30 ㉚	6 ⑫	4000
1		1 / 3000	20 / 1000	7 ①	10 / 1000	4 / 3000	8000
		3000	5000	4000	6000	3000	21000

c. The new optimal solution is shown below. It results in a total shipping cost of $141,000.

u_i		0	19	5	9	3	
		10	20	5	9	10	
0		⑩	①	4000	5000	⑦	9000
		2	10	8	30	6	
-9		⑪	5000	⑫	㉚	⑫	5000
		1	20	7	10	4	
1		4000	0	①	1000	3000	8000
		4000	5000	4000	6000	3000	22000

It may seem surprising that with more total units to be shipped the total cost has been decreased. The increased production at Columbus permits satisfying all of the Mobile demand at a cost of $10 per unit. The additional demand at Pittsburgh is satisfied very economically by the New York plant.

5. a.

	Des Moines	Kansas City	St. Louis	
Jefferson City	14	9	7	30
Omaha	8	10	5	20
	25	15	10	

b.

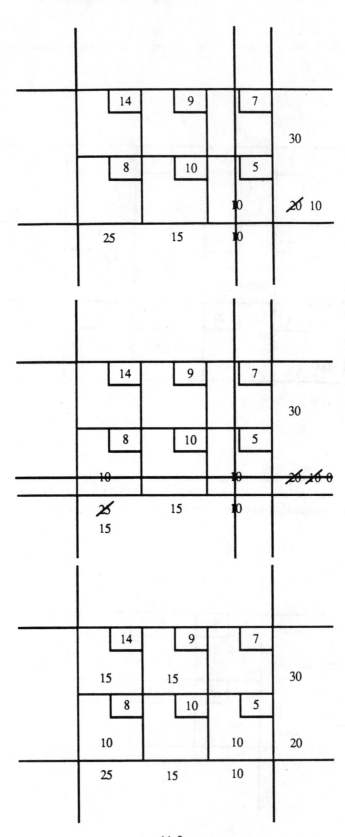

This is an initial feasible solution with a total cost of $475.

6.   An initial feasible solution found by the minimum cost method is given below.

	W_1	W_2	W_3
P_1	20 — 100	16 — 200	24
P_2	10	10 — 200	8 — 300
P_3	12 — 100	18	10

Computing row and column indexes and evaluating the unoccupied cells and identifies the cell in row 2 and column 1 as the incoming cell.

u_i	v_j = 20	16	14
0	$-$ 20 — 100	$+$ 16 — 200	24 — (10)
-6	10 — (-4)	$-$ 10 — 200	8 — 300
-8	12 — 100	18 — (10)	10 — (4)

The +'s and -'s above show the cycle of adjustments necessary on the stepping-stone path as flow is allocated to the cell in row 2 and column 1. The cell in row 1 and column 1 is identified as corresponding to the outgoing arc. The new solution is shown below.

u_i	v_j 16	16	14
0	20 ④	16 300	24 ⑩
-6	10 100	10 100	8 300
-4	12 100	18 ⑥	10 ⓪

Since all per-unit costs are ≥ 0, this solution is optimal. However, an alternate optimal solution can be found by shipping 100 units over the P_3 - W_3 route.

7. a. An initial solution is given below.

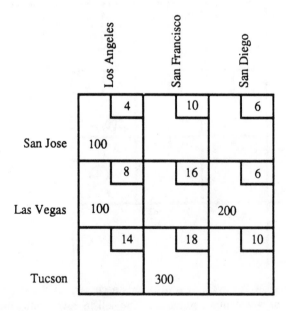

	Los Angeles	San Francisco	San Diego
San Jose	4 100	10	6
Las Vegas	8 100	16	6 200
Tucson	14	18 300	10

Total Cost: $7800

b. Note that the initial solution is degenerate. A zero is assigned to the cell in row 3 and column 1 so that the row and column indices can be computed.

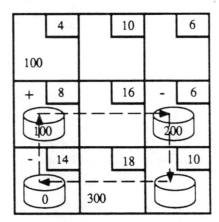

Cell in row 3 and column 3 is identified as an incoming cell.

Stepping-stone path shows cycle of adjustments. Outgoing cell is in row 3 and column 1.

u_i v_j

u_i		4	10	2
0	100	4	10 ⓪	6 ④
4	100	8	16 ②	6 200
8	②	14	18 300	10 0

Solution is recognized as optimal. It is degenerate.

Thus, the initial solution turns out to be the optimal solution; total cost = $7800.

c.   To begin with we reduce the supply at Tucson by 100 and the demand at San Diego by 100; the new solution is shown below:

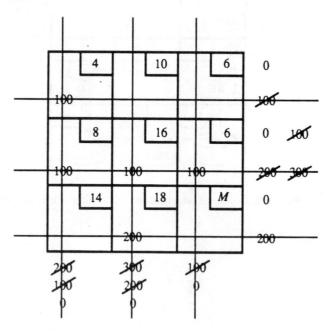

u_i v_j

	4	12	2
0	− 4 100	10 (−2)	6 (4)
4	+ 8 100	− 16 100	6 100
6	14 (4)	18 200	M (M − 8)

u_i v_j

	2	10	0
0	4 (2)	10 100	6 (6)
6	8 200	16 0	6 100
8	14 (4)	18 200	M (M − 8)

Optimal Solution: recall, however, that the 100 units shipped from Tucson to San Diego must be added to obtain the total cost.

San Jose to San Francisco:	100
Las Vegas to Los Angeles:	200
Las Vegas to San Diego:	100
Tucson to San Francisco:	200
Tucson to San Diego:	100
Total Cost: $7800	

Note that this total cost is the same as for part (a); thus, we have alternate optima.

d. The final transportation tableau is shown below. The total transportation cost is $8,000, an increase of $200 over the solution to part (a).

u_i	v_j = 2	v_j = 10	v_j = 2	
0	4 ②	10 100	6 ④	100
6	8 200	16 100	M Ⓜ-8	300
8	14 ④	18 100	10 200	300
	200	300	200	700

8. a. Initial Solution:

	D_1	D_2	D_3
O_1	6 150	8 100	8
O_2	18	12 100	14 50
O_3	8	12	10 100

Total Cost: $4600

b.

u_i	v_j		
	6	8	10
	6	− 8	8
			Ⓜ(-2)
0	150	100	
	18	+ 12	− 14
	Ⓜ(8)		
4		100	50
	8	12	10
	Ⓜ(2)	Ⓜ(4)	
0			100

Incoming arc: $O_1 - D_3$

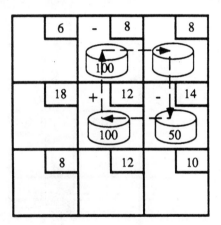

Outgoing arc: $O_2 - D_3$

u_i v_j

	6	8	8
0	6 150	8 50	8 50
4	18 (8)	12 150	14 (2)
2	8 (0)	12 (2)	10 100

Since all cell evaluations are non-negative, the solution is optimal; Total Cost: $4500.

c.   At the optimal solution found in part (b), the cell evaluation for O_3 - D_1 = 0. Thus, additional units can be shipped over the O_3 - D_1 route with no increase in total cost.

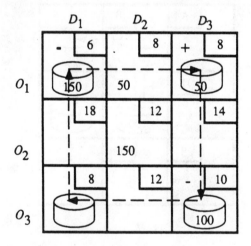

Thus, an alternate optimal solution is

	D_1	D_2	D_3
O_1	6 50	8 50	8 150
O_2	18	12 150	14
O_3	8 100	12	10

9.   Initial Solution:

	D_1	D_2	D_3	Dummy
O_1	1	3	4	0 200
O_2	2 200	6	8 200	0 100
O_3	2	5 100	7 200	0

Note: a different initial solution is obtained if the first allocation is made to another cell in the dummy column.

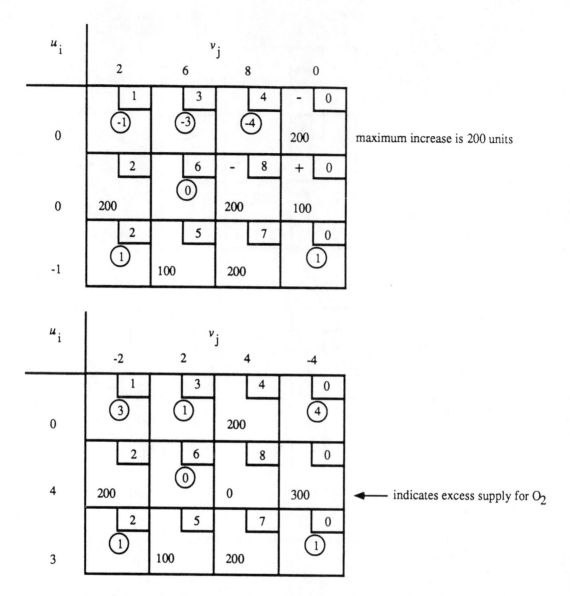

maximum increase is 200 units

◄── indicates excess supply for O_2

Since the cell evaluations for all unoccupied cells are non-negative, the solution is optimal; the total cost of the optimal solution is $3100. Note also that origin 2 has 300 units of excess supply for which it may consider alternate uses.

10.   Initial Solution:

	D_1	D_2	D_3	D_4	
Clifton Springs	32	34 3000	32 0	40 2000	5000
Danville	34	30	28 3000	38	3000
Dummy	0 2000	0 2000	0	0	4000
	2000	5000	3000	2000	

The final transportation tableau is shown below; the total profit is $282,000.

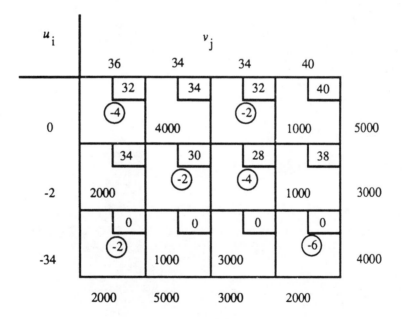

Customer 2 demand is   Customer 3 demand is
not satisfied (1000 short) not satisfied (3000 short)

Note: we recognize that this solution is optimal because the cell evaluations for all unoccupied cells are negative and this is a maximization problem.

11. We show a linear programming formulation. The cost of shipping from Martinsville is incremented by \$29.50 to every destination, the cost of shipping from Plymouth is incremented by \$31.20, and the cost of shipping from Franklin is incremented by \$30.35.

Let c_{ij} = cost of producing at plant i and shipping to distributor j

x_{ij} = amount produced at plant i and shipped to distributor j

Note that no variable is included for the unacceptable Plymouth to Dallas route.

$$\min 30.95x_{11} + 31.10x_{12} + 30.90x_{13} + 32.30x_{21} + 31.80x_{23} + 31.55x_{31} + 31.55x_{32} + 32.15x_{33}$$

s.t.

$x_{11} +$	$x_{12} +$	x_{13}						≤ 400
			$x_{21} +$	x_{23}				≤ 600
					$x_{31} +$	$x_{32} + x_{33}$		≤ 300
x_{11}		$+$	x_{21}	$+$	x_{31}			$= 400$
	x_{12}					$+$	x_{32}	$= 400$
		x_{13}	$+$	x_{23}			$+ x_{33}$	$= 400$

$x_{ij} \geq 0$ for all i, j

Optimal Plan:

Martinsville to Chicago:	300
Martinsville to Dallas:	100
Plymouth to Chicago:	100
Plymouth to New York:	400
Franklin to Dallas:	300
Total Cost: \$37,810	

Note: Plymouth has excess supply of 100.

12.a. The final transportation tableau is shown below; the total cost is $3990.

u_i		v_j 1.00	0.90	0.90	Dummy -0.30	
0		1.00	1.20 (0.30)	0.90	0 (0.30)	1500
		300		1200		
0.30		1.30	1.40 (0.20)	1.20 (0)	0	1500
		1200			300	
0.10		1.10	1.00	1.20 (0.20)	0 (0.20)	1000
		500	500			
		2000	500	1200	300	

b. An alternate optimal solution is indicated since the cell evaluation for II-C = 0. After entering a maximum flow of 1200 units in the II-C cell, we obtain the following alternate optimal solution.

	A	B	C	Dummy	Capacity
I	1500				1500
II			1200	300	1500
III	500	500			1000
Order Size	2000	500	1200	300	

Total Cost: $3990

13.a.

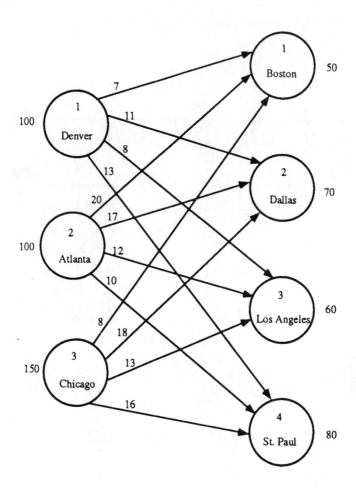

b.   There are alternate optimal solutions.

Solution #1	Solution # 2
Denver to St. Paul:10	Denver to St. Paul:10
Atlanta to Boston:50	Atlanta to Boston:50
Atlanta to Dallas:50	Atlanta to Los Angeles:50
Chicago to Dallas:20	Chicago to Dallas:70
Chicago to Los Angeles:60	Chicago to Los Angeles:10
Chicago to St. Paul:70	Chicago to St. Paul:70

Total Profit: $4240

If solution #1 is used, Forbelt should produce 10 motors at Denver, 100 motors at Atlanta, and 150 motors at Chicago. There will be idle capacity for 90 motors at Denver.

If solution #2 is used, Forbelt should adopt the same production schedule.

14.a.

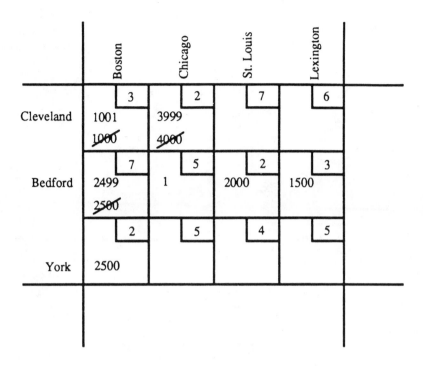

	Boston	Chicago	St. Louis	Lexington
Cleveland	3 ⟋ 1001 1000	2 ⟋ 3999 4000	7	6
Bedford	7 2499 2500	5 1	2 2000	3 1500
York	2 2500	5	4	5

	Changes	Effect on Cost
Add 1 unit	York to Lexington	+ 5
Reduce 1 unit	Bedford to Lexington	− 3
Add 1 unit	Bedford to Boston	+ 7
Reduce 1 unit	York to Boston	− 2
	Net Effect	+ 7

We note that the net effect is the same as the per-unit cost change obtained using the MODI method.

b.

	Changes	Effect on Cost
Add 1 unit	York to Lexington	+ 5
Reduce 1 unit	Bedford to Lexington	− 3
Add 1 unit	Bedford to Boston	+ 7
Reduce 1 unit	York to Boston	− 2
	Net Effect	+ 7

Again the net effect is the same as $e_{34} = +7$ computed using the MODI method

15.a. Modify Figure 7.9 by adding two nodes and two arcs. Let node 0 be a beginning inventory node with a supply of 50 and an arc connecting it to node 5 (period 1 demand). Let node 9 be an ending inventory node with a demand of 100 and an arc connecting node 8 (period 4 demand to it).

b.

$$\min \quad +2x_{15} +5x_{26} +3x_{37} +3x_{48} +0.25x_{56} +0.25x_{67} +0.25x_{78} +0.25x_{89}$$

s.t.

$$
\begin{aligned}
x_{05} & && && && && && && && && && &= 50 \\
& x_{15} && && && && && && && && && &\leq 600 \\
&& x_{26} && && && && && && && && &\leq 300 \\
&&& x_{37} && && && && && && && &\leq 500 \\
&&&& x_{48} && && && && && && &\leq 400 \\
x_{05} + x_{15} &&&& && -\, x_{56} && && && && &= 400 \\
&& x_{26} && && +\, x_{56} && -\, x_{67} && && && &= 500 \\
&&& x_{37} && && && +\, x_{67} && -\, x_{78} && && &= 400 \\
&&&& x_{48} && && && +\, x_{78} && -\, x_{89} &= 400 \\
&&&& && && && && x_{89} &= 100
\end{aligned}
$$

$x_{ij} \geq 0$ for all i and j

Optimal Solution:

$x_{05} = 50$ $x_{56} = 250$
$x_{15} = 600$ $x_{67} = 0$
$x_{26} = 250$ $x_{78} = 100$
$x_{37} = 500$ $x_{89} = 100$
$x_{48} = 400$

Total Cost = $5262.50

16.a.

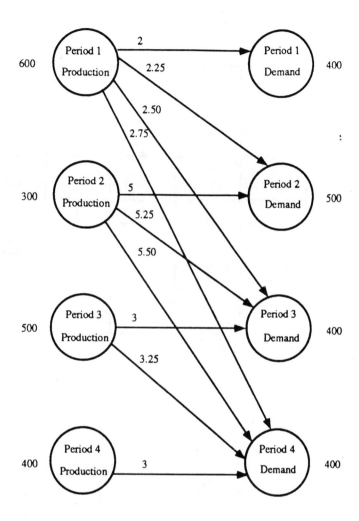

b. All of the cells corresponding to production in one period being used to satisify demand in a previous period are assigned a "big M" cost.

The initial solution found using the minimum cost method is optimal.

	2		2.25		2.50		2.75	
400		200						600
	M		5		5.25		5.50	
		300						300
	M		M		3		3.25	
				400				500
	M		M		M		3	
						400		400
400		500		400		400		

17.a.

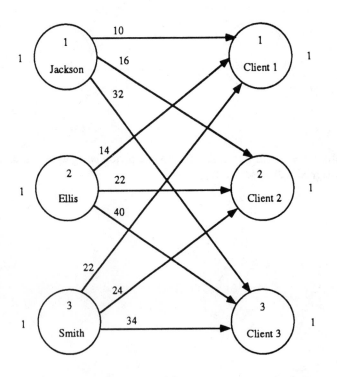

b.

$$\min \quad 10x_{11} + 16x_{12} + 32x_{13} + 14x_{21} + 22x_{22} + 40x_{23} + 22x_{31} + 24x_{32} + 34x_{33}$$

s.t.

$$
\begin{array}{llllll}
x_{11} + x_{12} + x_{13} & & & \le 1 \\
& x_{21} + x_{22} + x_{23} & & \le 1 \\
& & x_{31} + x_{32} + x_{33} & \le 1 \\
x_{11} & + x_{21} & + x_{31} & = 1 \\
x_{12} & + x_{22} & + x_{32} & = 1 \\
x_{13} & + x_{23} & + x_{33} & = 1 \\
\end{array}
$$

$x_{ij} \ge 0$ for all i, j

Solution $x_{12} = 1$, $x_{21} = 1$, $x_{33} = 1$ Total completion time $= 64$

18.   Subtract 10 from row 1, 14 from row 2, and 22 from row 3 to obtain:

	1	2	3
Jackson	0	6	22
Ellis	0	8	26
Smith	0	2	12

Subtract 0 from column 1, 2 from column 2, and 12 from column 3 to obtain:

	1	2	3
Jackson	0	④	10
Ellis	0	6	14
Smith	0	0	0

Two lines cover the zeros. The minimum unlined element is 4. Step 3 yields:

	1	2	3
Jackson	0	[0]	6
Ellis	[0]	2	10
Smith	0	0	[0]

Optimal Solution:

Jackson - 2
Ellis   - 1
Smith   - 3

Time requirement is 64 days.

19.a.   Optimal assignment: Jackson to 1, Smith to 3, and Burton to 2. Time requirement is 62 days.

   b.   Considering Burton has saved 2 days.

   c.   Ellis.

20.a.

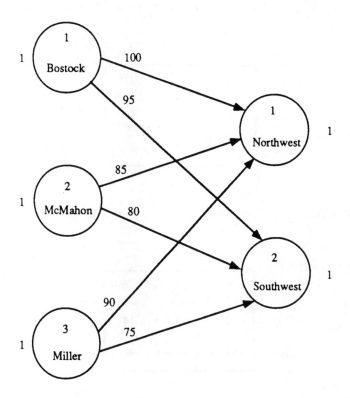

   b.

$$\max \ 100x_{11} + 95x_{12} + 85x_{21} + 80x_{22} + 90x_{31} + 75x_{32}$$

s.t.

x_{11}	$+ \ x_{12}$				$\leq$	1
		$x_{21} \ + \ x_{22}$			$\leq$	1
			$x_{31} \ + \ x_{32}$		$\leq$	1
x_{11}		$+ \ x_{21}$	$+ \ x_{31}$		$=$	1
	x_{12}	$+ \ x_{22}$		$+ \ x_{32}$	$=$	1

$x_{ij} \geq 0, \ i = 1,2; \ j = 1,2,3$

Optimal Solution: $x_{12} = 1, x_{31} = 1$ Value: 185

Assign Bostock to the Southwest territory and Miller to the Northwest territory.

21. We first add a dummy sales region with sales projections of 0.

100	95	0
85	80	0
90	75	0

Subtracting each element from the largest element in its column leads to the following opportunity loss matrix.

0	0	0
15	15	0
⑩	20	0

0	0	10
5	5	0
0	10	0

Optimal Solution:

   Bostock to Southwest
   McMahon to Dummy
   Miller to Northwest

22.   After adding a dummy column, we get an initial assignment matrix.

10	15	9	0
9	18	5	0
6	14	3	0
8	16	6	0

Applying Steps 1 and 2 we obtain:

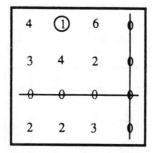

4	①	6	0
3	4	2	0
0	0	0	0
2	2	3	0

Applying Step 3 followed by Step 2 results in:

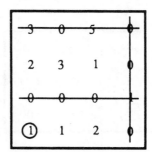

3	0	5	0
2	3	1	0
0	0	0	1
①	1	2	0

Finally, application of Step's 3 and 2 lead to the optimal solution shown below.

3	[0]	5	1
1	2	[0]	0
[0]	0	0	2
0	0	1	[0]

Terry: Client 2 (15 days)
Carle: Client 3 (5 days)
McClymonds: Client 1 (6 days)
Higley: Not accepted

Total time = 26 days

Note: An alternate optimal solution is Terry: Client 2, Carle: unassigned, McClymonds: Client 3, and Higley: Client 1.

23.a.

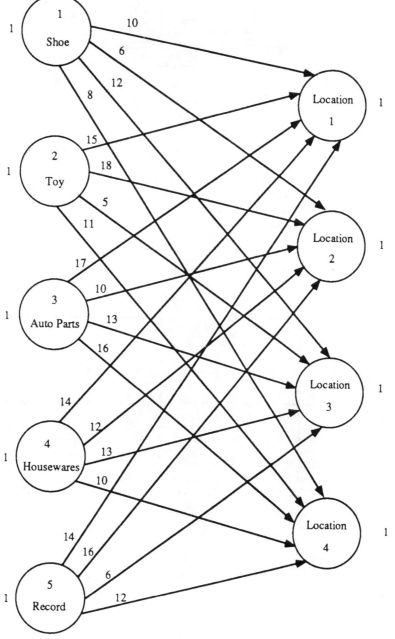

b. $\quad$ *Let* $x_{ij} = \begin{cases} 1 \ \ \textit{if department i is assigned location j} \\ 0 \ \ \textit{otherwise} \end{cases}$

max $\quad 10x_{11} + 6x_{12} + 12x_{13} + 8x_{14} + 15x_{21} + 18x_{22} + 5x_{23} + 11x_{24}$
$\quad\quad + 17x_{31} + 10x_{32} + 13x_{33} + 16x_{34} + 14x_{41} + 12x_{42} + 13x_{43} + 10x_{44}$
$\quad\quad + 14x_{51} + 16x_{52} + 6x_{53} + 12x_{54}$

s.t.

$$
\begin{array}{llllllllllll}
x_{11} & + & x_{12} & + & x_{13} & + & x_{14} & & & & & & & & \leq & 1 \\
 & & & & & & & x_{21} & + & x_{22} & + & x_{23} & + & x_{24} & \leq & 1 \\
x_{31} & + & x_{32} & + & x_{33} & + & x_{34} & & & & & & & & \leq & 1 \\
 & & & & & & & x_{41} & + & x_{42} & + & x_{43} & + & x_{44} & \leq & 1 \\
x_{51} & + & x_{52} & + & x_{53} & + & x_{54} & & & & & & & & \leq & 1 \\
\end{array}
$$

$$
\begin{array}{llllllll}
x_{11} & +x_{21} & +x_{31} & +x_{41} & +x_{51} & & = & 1 \\
x_{12} & +x_{22} & +x_{32} & +x_{42} & +x_{52} & & = & 1 \\
x_{13} & +x_{23} & +x_{33} & +x_{43} & +x_{53} & & = & 1 \\
x_{14} & +x_{24} & +x_{34} & +x_{44} & +x_{54} & & = & 1 \\
\end{array}
$$

$x_{ij} \geq 0$

Optimal Solution:

Toy:	Location 2
Auto Parts:	Location 4
Housewares:	Location 3
Record:	Location 1
Profit: 61	

24.   We start with the opportunity loss matrix (Table 7.36).

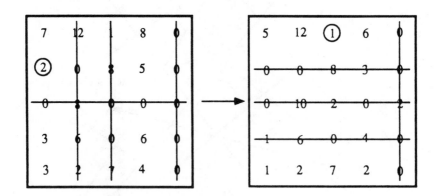

	1	2	3	4	Dummy
Shoe	4	11	0	5	0
Toy	0	0	8	3	1
Auto	0	10	2	0	3
Houseware	1	6	0	4	1
Record	0	1	6	1	0

Optimal Solution		Profit
Toy :	2	18
Auto :	4	16
Houseware:	3	13
Record :	1	14
		61

25.a. Simply delete 2 arcs from the network representation in the solution to 23 part (a): the arc from Toy to location 2 and the arc from Auto Parts to location 4.

b. Simply add two constraints to the linear programming model in the solution to problem 23 part (b).

$$x_{22} = 0 \text{ and } x_{34} = 0$$

Revised optimal solution:

Toy:	Location 4
Auto Parts:	Location 1
Housewares:	Location 3
Record:	Location 2
Profit: 57	

26. Starting with the matrix in Table 7.37 and subtracting each element from the largest element in its column leads to the opportunity loss matrix.

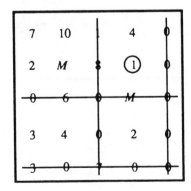

	1	2	3	4	Dummy
Shoe	6	9	1	3	[0]
Toy	1	M	8	[0]	0
Auto	[0]	6	1	M	1
Houseware	2	3	[0]	1	0
Record	3	[0]	8	0	1

Optimal Solution		Profit
Toy :	4	11
Auto :	1	17
Houseware :	3	13
Record :	2	16
		57

27. Shown are the steps of the solution using the Hungarian method. Row reduction is all that's necessary.

32	18	32	26
22	24	12	16
24	30	26	24
32	30	28	20

Row → Reduction

14	[0]	14	8
10	12	[0]	4
[0]	6	2	0
6	10	8	[0]

Optimal Solution	Hours
1 to B	18
2 to C	12
3 to A	24
4 to D	20
Total	74

28. Original problem:

44	80	52	60
60	56	40	72
36	60	48	48
52	76	36	40

Opportunity loss matrix;

14	0	0	12
0	24	12	0
24	20	4	24
8	4	16	32

Step 1 (row reduction) and lining out zeros.

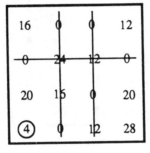

Step 3 followed by Step 2 results in the optimal solution

12	[0]	0	8
0	28	16	[0]
16	16	[0]	16
[0]	0	12	24

Optimal Solution:

Washington to B:	80
Benson to D:	72
Fredricks to C:	48
Hodson to A:	52
Total Sales	252

29. Original problem with a dummy report

24	12	10	0
19	11	11	0
25	16	16	0
25	14	13	0

Step 1 (column reduction) and Step 2

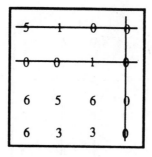

Step 3 and Step 2 lead to the optimal solution

5	1	[0]	3
[0]	0	1	3
3	2	3	[0]
3	[0]	0	0

Optimal Solution:

Phyllis to C:	10
Linda to A:	19
Dave unassigned	—
Marlene to B:	<u>14</u>
	43 hours

30.   Step 1 (row reduction)

10	5	0	15
20	10	0	20
5	0	M	20
10	10	0	M

Step 1 (column reduction) and Step 2

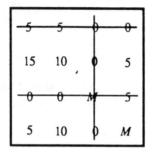

Step 3 and Step 2 result in the optimal solution

5	5	5	[0]
10	5	[0]	0
0	[0]	M	5
[0]	5	0	M

Optimal Solution:

1 to D	135
2 to C	100
3 to B	120
4 to A	150
	505 miles

31.a.

$$\min 150x_{11} + 210x_{12} + 270x_{13}$$
$$+ 170x_{21} + 230x_{22} + 220x_{23}$$
$$+ 180x_{31} + 230x_{32} + 225x_{33}$$
$$+ 160x_{41} + 240x_{42} + 230x_{43}$$

s.t.

$x_{11} +$	$x_{12} +$	x_{13}			≤ 1
	$x_{21} +$	$x_{22} +$	x_{23}		≤ 1
		$x_{31} +$	$x_{32} +$	x_{33}	≤ 1
			$x_{41} +$	$x_{42} + x_{43}$	≤ 1
x_{11}	$+x_{21}$	$+x_{31}$	$+x_{41}$		$= 1$
x_{12}	$+x_{22}$	$+x_{32}$	$+x_{42}$		$= 1$
x_{13}	$+x_{23}$	$+x_{33}$	$+x_{43}$		$= 1$

$x_{ij} \geq$ for all i, j

Optimal Solution: $x_{12} = 1$, $x_{23} = 1$, $x_{41} = 1$

Total hours required: 590

Note: statistician 3 is not assigned.

b. The solution will not change, but the total hours required will increase by 5. This is the extra time required for statistician 4 to complete the job for client A.

c. The solution will not change, but the total time required will decrease by 20 hours.

d. The solution will not change; statistician 3 will not be assigned. Note that this occurs because increasing the time for statistician 3 makes statistician 3 an even less attractive candidate for assignment.

32.a. The total cost is the sum of the purchase cost and the transportation cost. We show the calculation for Division 1 - Supplier 1 and present the result for the other Division-Supplier combinations.

Division 1 - Supplier 1	
Purchase cost (40,000 × $12.60)	$504,000
Transportation Cost (40,000 × $2.75)	110,000
Total Cost	$614,000

Cost Matrix ($1,000s)

		Supplier					
		1	2	3	4	5	6
	1	614	660	534	680	590	630
	2	603	639	702	693	693	630
Division	3	865	830	775	850	900	930
	4	532	553	511	581	595	553
	5	720	648	684	693	657	747

b. Optimal Solution:

Supplier 1 - Division 2	$603
Supplier 2 - Division 5	648
Supplier 3 - Division 3	775
Supplier 5 - Division 1	590
Supplier 5 - Division 4	553
Total	$3,169

33.a.

$$\min \ 4x_{13} + 10x_{14} + 8x_{15} + 4x_{23} + 9x_{24} + 6x_{25} + 4x_{34} + 3x_{35}$$

s.t.

$$
\begin{aligned}
x_{13} + x_{14} + x_{15} &\leq 400 \\
x_{23} + x_{24} + x_{25} &\leq 600 \\
-x_{13} - x_{23} + x_{34} + x_{35} &= 0 \\
x_{14} + x_{24} + x_{34} &= 750 \\
x_{15} + x_{25} + x_{35} &= 250
\end{aligned}
$$

$x_{ij} \geq$ for all i and j

b. Optimal Solution:

Variable	Value
x_{13}	400
x_{14}	0
x_{15}	0
x_{23}	350
x_{24}	0
x_{25}	250
x_{34}	750
x_{35}	0

Value of optimal solution: 7500

c. Add the constraint $x_{34} \leq 500$.
    New optimal solution:

Variable	Value
x_{13}	400
x_{14}	0
x_{15}	0
x_{23}	100
x_{24}	250
x_{25}	250
x_{34}	500
x_{35}	0

Value of optimal solution: 7750

34.a.

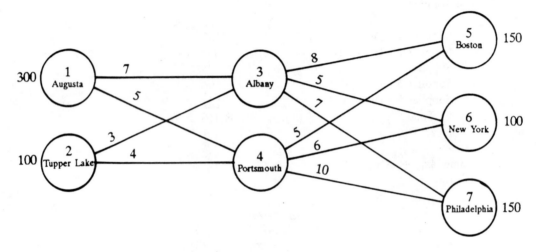

b.

$$\min \; 7x_{13} + 5x_{14} + 3x_{23} + 4x_{24} + 8x_{35} + 5x_{36} + 7x_{37} + 5x_{45} + 6x_{46} + 10x_{47}$$

s.t.

$$
\begin{aligned}
x_{13} + x_{14} && \leq && 300 \\
x_{23} + x_{24} && \leq && 100 \\
-x_{13} \quad\quad - x_{23} \quad\quad + x_{35} + x_{36} + x_{37} && = && 0 \\
- x_{14} \quad\quad - x_{24} \quad\quad\quad\quad\quad\quad\quad + x_{45} + x_{46} + x_{47} && = && 0 \\
x_{35} \quad\quad\quad\quad + x_{45} && = && 150 \\
+ x_{36} \quad\quad\quad\quad + x_{46} && = && 100 \\
x_{37} \quad\quad\quad\quad + x_{47} && = && 150
\end{aligned}
$$

$x_{ij} \geq 0$ for all i and j

c.   Optimal Solution:

Variable	Value
x_{13}	50
x_{14}	250
x_{23}	100
x_{24}	0
x_{35}	0
x_{36}	0
x_{37}	150
x_{45}	150
x_{46}	100
x_{47}	0

Objective Function: 4300

35.a.

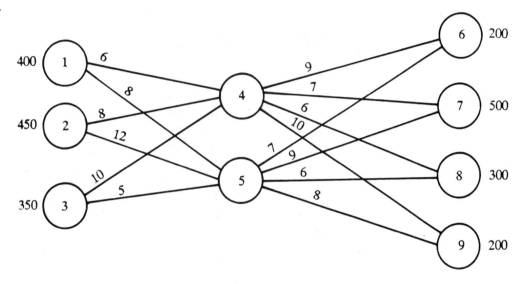

b.

min

$$6x_{14} + 8x_{15} + 8x_{24} + 12x_{25} + 10x_{34} + 5x_{35} + 9x_{46} + 7x_{47} + 6x_{48} + 10x_{49} + 7x_{56} + 9x_{57} + 6x_{58} + 8x_{59}$$

s.t.

$$
\begin{array}{llllllll}
x_{14} + x_{15} & & & & & & & \leq 400 \\
x_{24} + x_{25} & & & & & & \leq 450 \\
x_{34} + x_{35} & & & & & \leq 350 \\
-x_{14} \quad - x_{24} \quad - x_{34} \quad + x_{46} + x_{47} + x_{48} + x_{49} & & = 0 \\
- x_{15} \quad - x_{25} \quad - x_{35} \quad + x_{56} + x_{57} + x_{58} + x_{59} = 0 \\
x_{46} \quad + x_{56} & = 200 \\
x_{47} \quad + x_{57} & = 500 \\
x_{48} \quad + x_{58} & = 300 \\
x_{49} \quad + x_{59} = 200
\end{array}
$$

$x_{ij} \leq 0$ for all ij

c.   Optimal Solution

Variable	Value
x_{14}	400
x_{15}	0
x_{24}	450
x_{25}	0
x_{34}	0
x_{35}	350
x_{46}	0
x_{47}	500
x_{48}	300
x_{49}	50
x_{56}	200
x_{57}	0
x_{58}	0
x_{59}	150

Value of optimal solution: 16150

36.   A network representation of this problem is shown below.

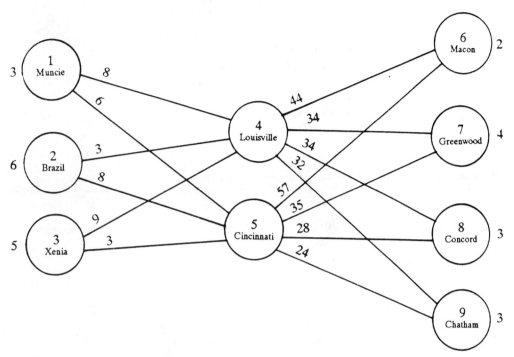

A linear programming model is

$$\min 8x_{14} + 6x_{15} + 3x_{24} + 8x_{25} + 9x_{34} + 3x_{35}$$
$$+ 44x_{46} + 34x_{47} + 34x_{48} + 32x_{49}$$
$$+ 57x_{56} + 35x_{57} + 28x_{58} + 24x_{59}$$

s.t.

$$
\begin{aligned}
x_{14} + x_{15} &\le 3 \\
x_{24} + x_{25} &\le 6 \\
x_{34} + x_{35} &\le 5 \\
-x_{14} \quad - x_{24} + x_{34} + x_{46} + x_{47} + x_{48} + x_{49} &= 0 \\
- x_{15} - x_{25} - x_{35} + x_{56} + x_{57} + x_{58} + x_{59} &= 0 \\
x_{46} + x_{56} &= 2 \\
x_{47} + x_{57} &= 4 \\
x_{48} + x_{58} &= 3 \\
x_{49} + x_{59} &= 3
\end{aligned}
$$

$x_{ij} \ge 0$ for all i,j

Optimal Solution	Units Shipped	Cost
Muncie to Cincinnati	1	6
Cincinnati to Concord	3	84
Brazil to Louisville	6	18
Louisville to Macon	2	88
Louisville to Greenwood	4	136
Xenia to Cincinnati	5	15
Cincinnati to Chatham	3	72
		419

Two rail cars must be held at Muncie until a buyer is found.

37.a.

$$\min \quad 20x_{12} + 25x_{15} + 30x_{25} + 45x_{27} + 20x_{31} + 35x_{36}$$
$$+ \; 30x_{42} + 25x_{53} + 15x_{54} + 28x_{56} + 12x_{67} + 27x_{74}$$

s.t.

$$
\begin{array}{rcr}
x_{31} - x_{12} - x_{15} & = & 8 \\
x_{25} + x_{27} - x_{12} - x_{42} & = & 5 \\
x_{31} + x_{36} - x_{53} & = & 3 \\
x_{54} + x_{74} - x_{42} & = & 3 \\
x_{53} + x_{54} + x_{56} - x_{15} - x_{25} & = & 2 \\
x_{36} + x_{56} - x_{67} & = & 5 \\
x_{74} - x_{27} - x_{67} & = & 6 \\
\end{array}
$$

$x_{ij} \geq 0$ for all i, j

b.

$x_{12} = 0$	$x_{53} = 5$
$x_{15} = 0$	$x_{54} = 0$
$x_{25} = 8$	$x_{56} = 5$
$x_{27} = 0$	$x_{67} = 0$
$x_{31} = 8$	$x_{74} = 6$
$x_{36} = 0$	$x_{35} = 5$
$x_{42} = 3$	

Total cost of redistributing cars = $917

38.

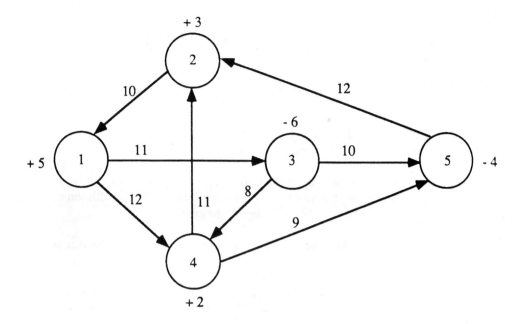

The positive numbers by nodes indicate the amount of supply at that node. The negative numbers by nodes indicate the amount of demand at the node.

Case Problem

A first step is to identify which assignments do not satisfy the requirements stated in 1 through 5 of the case description.

1. All of the first games in series 5 are night games so no crew assignments call for a crew to be assigned to an afternoon game following a night game in another city.

2. The crews at Seattle, Oakland, and California cannot be assigned to Chicago for series 5 because of the second requirement. The fifth series starts on Tuesday in the Eastern Division cities.

3. The fourth series finishes on Monday night in Toronto. So that crew cannot be assigned Kansas City, Minnesota, Chicago, or Milwaukee. Traveling into Toronto for the fifth series, beginning on Tuesday night, does not cause a problem for any of the crews.

4. The crew in Seattle for series 4 cannot be assigned to series 5 in Kansas City because series 4 finishes with a night game.

5. The crew at Texas for series 4 cannot be assigned to the Texas - Kansas City series because it has umpired two straight series involving Texas. The crew at Toronto for series 4 may not stay at Toronto for a third series.

Solution

1. An assignment matrix that will minimize distance travelled by the crews while not allowing assignments that violate the above restrictions is shown below.

Crew From	KC	MIN	CHI	To MKE	DET	TOR	NY
SEA (7)	M	1399	M	1694	1939	[2124]	2421
OAK (3)	1498	1589	M	[1845]	2079	2286	2586
CAL (7)	[1363]	1536	M	1756	1979	2175	2475
TEX (6)	M	853	798	843	[982]	1186	1383
MIN (5)	394	[0]	334	297	528	780	1028
CHI (4)	403	334	[0]	74	235	430	740
TOR (1)	M	M	M	M	206	M	[366]

The optimal solution is shown by the boxed-in elements in the above matrix. The total distance traveled is 6680 miles.

2.   Crew 4 is assigned to the Cleveland - Chicago series in Chicago and need not travel.

3.   Crew 5 is assigned to the Boston - Minnesota series in Minnesota and need not travel. The discussion suggests that we might want to consider assigning crew 5 to New York, Toronto, or Detroit. To evaluate the impact of making this a requirement we could eliminate the first four possibilities in the fifth row of the matrix above.

Note: The instructor might want to consider the effect of dropping or adding restrictions. This can be accomplished by placing big "M"s appropriately in the above matrix. Alternately, if a linear programming model is being used, one can add and delete variables as appropriate.

Answers to Questions for Quantitative Methods in Practice

1.

Origin Nodes	Transshipment Nodes	Destination Nodes
Location of each driver with tractor and trailer	Demand locations which require a truck be available for a load pickup	Delivery locations where the load will be dropped off

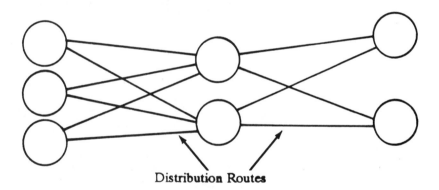

Distribution Routes

2.   The supply at the origin nodes is 1 driver with tractor and trailer at each origin node. The demand is also expressed in terms of the need for a driver with tractor and trailer to carry the load or shipment. A driver with tractor and trailer is the unit of flow over the arcs or shipping routes in the network.

Chapter 12
Integer Linear Programming

Learning Objectives

1. Understand the types of situations where integer linear programming problem formulations are desirable.

2. Know the difference between all-integer and mixed integer linear programming problems.

3. Be able to solve small integer linear programs with a graphical solution procedure.

4. Learn how capital budgeting and distribution system design problems can be formulated and solved as integer linear programs.

5. See how zero-one integer linear variables can be used to handle special situations such as multiple choice, k out of n alternatives, and conditional constraints.

6. Be familiar with the computer solution of MILPs.

7. Understand the following terms:

    all-integer   mutually exclusive constraint
    mixed integer k out of n alternatives constraint
    zero-one variables   conditional constraint
    LP relaxation   co-requisite constraint
    multiple choice constraint

Solutions

1. a.   This is a mixed integer linear program. Its LP Relaxation is

$$\begin{array}{lrcrcr}
\max & 30x_1 & + & 25x_2 & & \\
\text{s.t.} & & & & & \\
& 3x_1 & + & 2x_2 & \leq & 400 \\
& 1.5x_1 & + & 2x_2 & \leq & 250 \\
& x_1 & + & x_2 & \leq & 150 \\
\end{array}$$

$$x_1, \; x_2 \geq 0$$

   b.   This is an all-integer linear program. Its LP Relaxation just requires dropping the words "and integer" from the last line.

   c.   This is a mixed-integer linear program. Its LP Relaxation is obtained by dropping the integer requirement on x_1.

   d.   This is an all-integer linear program. Its LP Relaxation is obtained by dropping the integer requirement on all the variables.

   e.   This is a linear program. No variables are required to be integer.

2. a.

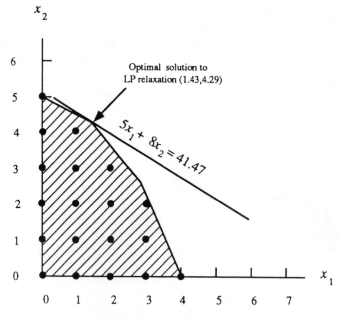

   b.   The optimal solution to the LP Relaxation is given by $x_1 = 1.43$, $x_2 = 4.29$ with an objective function value of 41.47.

   Rounding down gives the feasible integer solution $x_1 = 1$, $x_2 = 4$. Its value is 37.

c.

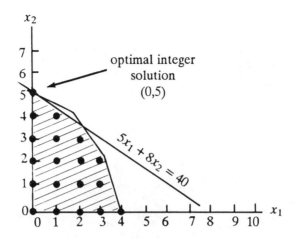

The optimal solution is given by $x_1 = 0$, $x_2 = 5$. Its value is 40. This is not the same solution as that found by rounding down. It provides a 3 unit increase in the value of the objective function.

3. a.

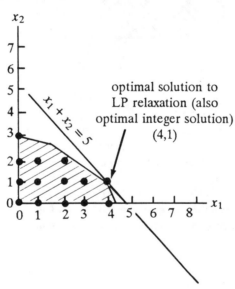

b.   The optimal solution to the LP Relaxation is shown on the above graph to be $x_1 = 4$, $x_2 = 1$. Its value is 5.

c.   The optimal integer solution is the same as the optimal solution to the LP Relaxation. This is always the case whenever all the variables take on integer values in the optimal solution to the LP Relaxation.

4. a.

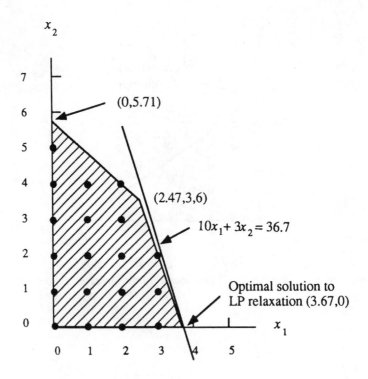

The value of the optimal solution to the LP Relaxation is 36.7 and it is given by $x_1 = 3.67$, $x_2 = 0.0$. Since we have all less-than-or-equal-to constraints with positive coefficients, the solution obtained by "rounding down" the values of the variables in the optimal solution to the LP Relaxation is feasible. The solution obtained by rounding down is $x_1 = 3$, $x_2 = 0$ with value 30.

Thus a lower bound on the value of the optimal solution is given by this feasible integer solution with value 30. An upper bound is given by the value of the LP Relaxation, 36.7. (Actually an upper bound of 36 could be established since no integer solution could have a value between 36 and 37.)

b.

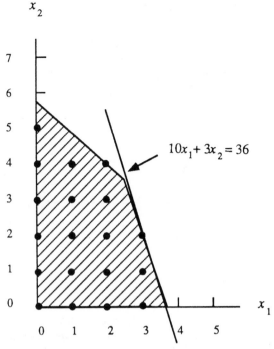

The optimal solution to the ILP is given by $x_1 = 3$, $x_2 = 2$. Its value is 36. The solution found by "rounding down" the solution to the LP relaxation had a value of 30. A 20% increase in this value was obtained by finding the optimal integer solution - a substantial difference if the objective function is being measured in thousands of dollars.

c.

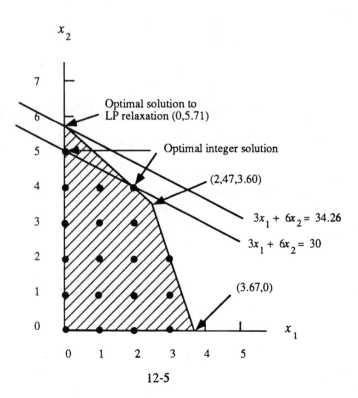

The optimal solution to the LP Relaxation is $x_1 = 0$, $x_2 = 5.71$ with value = 34.26. The solution obtained by "rounding down" is $x_1 = 0$, $x_2 = 5$ with value 30. These two values provide an upper bound of 34.26 and a lower bound of 30 on the value of the optimal integer solution.

There are alternate optimal integer solutions given by $x_1 = 0$, $x_2 = 5$ and $x_1 = 2$, $x_2 = 4$; value is 30. In this case rounding the LP solution down does provide the optimal integer solution.

5. a.

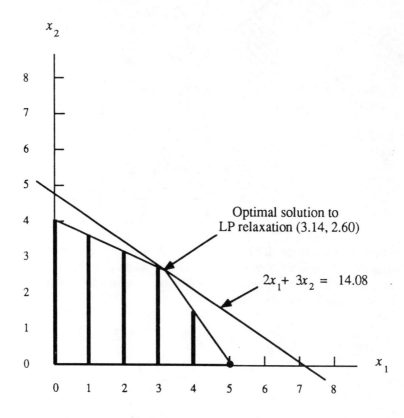

The feasible mixed integer solutions are indicated by the boldface vertical lines in the graph above.

b.   The optimal solution to the LP relaxation is given by $x_1 = 3.14$, $x_2 = 2.60$. Its value is 14.08.

Rounding the value of x_1 down to find a feasible mixed integer solution yields $x_1 = 3$, $x_2 = 2.60$ with a value of 13.8. This solution is clearly not optimal. With $x_1 = 3$ we can see from the graph that x_2 can be made larger without violating the constraints.

c.

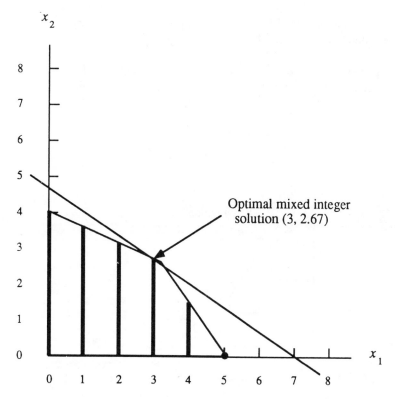

Optimal mixed integer solution (3, 2.67)

The optimal solution to the MILP is given by $x_1 = 3$, $x_2 = 2.67$. Its value is 14.

6. a.

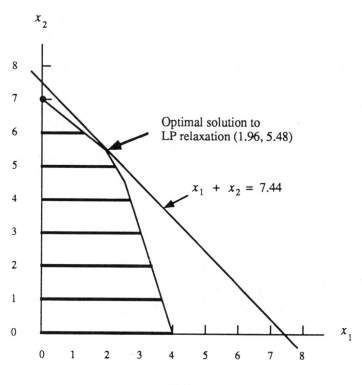

Optimal solution to LP relaxation (1.96, 5.48)

$x_1 + x_2 = 7.44$

b.   The optimal solution to the LP Relaxation is given by $x_1 = 1.96$, $x_2 = 5.48$. Its value is 7.44. Thus an upper bound on the value of the optimal is given by 7.44.

Rounding the value of x_2 down yields a feasible solution of $x_1 = 1.96$, $x_2 = 5$ with value 6.96. Thus a lower bound on the value of the optimal solution is given by 6.96.

c.

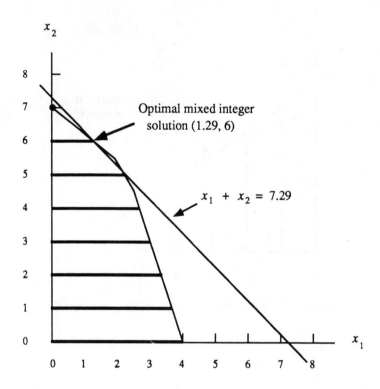

The optimal solution to the MILP is $x_1 = 1.29$, $x_2 = 6$. Its value is 7.29.

The solution $x_1 = 2.22$, $x_2 = 5$ is almost as good. Its value is 7.22.

7. a. $x_1 = x_2 = x_3 = 1, x_4 = 0; z = 140$

   b. Using the Management Scientist, the optimal solution given in (a) is obtained.

8. a.

$$\text{Let} \quad x_1 \quad = \quad 1 \text{ if PPB is Lorain, 0 otherwise}$$

$$x_2 \quad = \quad 1 \text{ if PPB is Huron, 0 otherwise}$$

$$x_3 \quad = \quad 1 \text{ if PPB is Richland, 0 otherwise}$$

$$x_4 \quad = \quad 1 \text{ if PPB is Ashland, 0 otherwise}$$

$$x_5 \quad = \quad 1 \text{ if PPB is Wayne, 0 otherwise}$$

$$x_6 \quad = \quad 1 \text{ if PPB is Medina, 0 otherwise}$$

$$x_7 \quad = \quad 1 \text{ if PPB is Knox, 0 otherwise}$$

max $x_1 + x_2 + x_3 + x_4 + x_5 + x_6 + x_7$
s.t.

$$
\begin{array}{llllllllll}
x_1 & + x_2 & & + x_4 & & + x_6 & & \geq & 1 & \text{(Lorain)} \\
x_1 & + x_2 & + x_3 & + x_4 & & & & \geq & 1 & \text{(Huron)} \\
& x_2 & + x_3 & + x_4 & & & + x_7 & \geq & 1 & \text{(Richland)} \\
x_1 & + x_2 & + x_3 & + x_4 & + x_5 & + x_6 & + x_7 & \geq & 1 & \text{(Ashland)} \\
& & & x_4 & + x_5 & + x_6 & & \geq & 1 & \text{(Wayne)} \\
x_1 & & & + x_4 & + x_5 & + x_6 & & \geq & 1 & \text{(Medina)} \\
& & x_3 & + x_4 & & & + x_7 & \geq & 1 & \text{(Knox)}
\end{array}
$$

   b. Locating a principal place of business in Ashland county will permit Ohio Trust to do business in all 7 counties.

9. a. Let $x_i = 1$ if a substation is located at site i, 0 otherwise

min $x_A + x_B + x_C + x_D + x_E + x_F + x_G$
s.t.

$$
\begin{array}{llllllllll}
x_A & + x_B & + x_C & & & & + x_G & \geq & 1 & \text{(area 1 covered)} \\
& x_B & & + x_D & & & & \geq & 1 & \text{(area 2 covered)} \\
& & x_C & & + x_E & & & \geq & 1 & \text{(area 3 covered)} \\
& & & x_D & + x_E & + x_F & & \geq & 1 & \text{(area 4 covered)} \\
x_A & + x_B & + x_C & + x_D & & + x_F & + x_G & \geq & 1 & \text{(area 5 covered)} \\
& & & & x_E & + x_F & + x_G & \geq & 1 & \text{(area 6 covered)} \\
x_A & + x_B & & & & & + x_G & \geq & 1 & \text{(area 7 covered)}
\end{array}
$$

   b. Choose locations B and E.

10.a. Let $y_1 = \begin{cases} 1 \text{ if a plant is located at Detroit} \\ 0 \text{ otherwise} \end{cases}$

$y_2 = \begin{cases} 1 \text{ if a plant is located at Toledo} \\ 0 \text{ otherwise} \end{cases}$

$y_3 = \begin{cases} 1 \text{ if a plant is located at Denver} \\ 0 \text{ otherwise} \end{cases}$

$y_4 = \begin{cases} 1 \text{ if a plant is located at Kansas City} \\ 0 \text{ otherwise} \end{cases}$

x_{ij} = units shipped from plant i to destination j
$$i = 1, 2, 3, 4, 5; \quad j = 1, 2, 3$$

$$\min \quad 5x_{11} + 2x_{12} + 3x_{13} + 4x_{21} + 3x_{22} + 4x_{23} + 9x_{31} + 7x_{32} + 5x_{33}$$
$$+ 10x_{41} + 4x_{42} + 2x_{43} + 8x_{51} + 4x_{52} + 3x_{53}$$
$$+ 175{,}000y_1 + 300{,}000y_2 + 375{,}000y_3 + 500{,}000y_4$$

s.t.

$$
\begin{array}{llllll}
x_{11} + x_{12} + x_{13} & & & & & \le & 10{,}000y_1 \\
 & x_{21} + x_{22} + x_{23} & & & & \le & 20{,}000y_2 \\
 & & x_{31} + x_{32} + x_{33} & & & \le & 30{,}000y_3 \\
 & & & x_{41} + x_{42} + x_{43} & & \le & 40{,}000y_4 \\
 & & & & x_{51} + x_{52} + x_{53} & \le & 30{,}000 \\
x_{11} & + x_{21} & + x_{31} & + x_{41} & + x_{51} & = & 30{,}000 \\
 + x_{21} & + x_{22} & + x_{32} & + x_{42} & + x_{52} & = & 20{,}000 \\
 + x_{13} & + x_{23} & + x_{33} & + x_{43} & + x_{53} & = & 20{,}000 \\
\end{array}
$$

$$x_{ij} \ge 0 \quad i = 1, 2, 3, 4, 5$$
$$j = 1, 2, 3$$

$$y_i = 0, 1 \quad i = 1, 2, 3, 4$$

b. One just needs to add the following mutually exclusive constraint to the problem.

$$y_1 + y_2 = 1$$

c. Since one plant is already located at St. Louis it is only necessary to add the following constraint to the model in a.

$$y_3 + y_4 \le 1$$

d. An additional 0, 1 variable and 3 additional x_{ij} variables must be added to the problem.

$$\text{Let} \quad y_5 = \begin{cases} 1 & \text{if a plant with capacity of 60,000 is at Denver} \\ 0 & \text{otherwise} \end{cases}$$

Additional terms of the form $550{,}000y_5 + 9x_{61} + 7x_{62} + 5x_{63}$ must be added to the objective function. The additional supply constraint given below must be added.

$$x_{61} + x_{62} + x_{63} \le 60{,}000y_5$$

The following mutually exclusive constraint must be added.

$$y_3 + y_5 \le 1.$$

11.a. $\text{Let} \quad x_i = \begin{cases} 1 & \text{if investment alternative } i \text{ is selected} \\ 0 & \text{otherwise} \end{cases}$

$$\max \; 4000x_1 + 6000x_2 + 10500x_3 + 4000x_4 + 8000x_5 + 3000x_6$$

s.t.

$$3000x_1 + 2500x_2 + 6000x_3 + 2000x_4 + 5000x_5 + 1000x_6 \le 10{,}500$$
$$1000x_1 + 3500x_2 + 4000x_3 + 1500x_4 + 1000x_5 + 500x_6 \le 7{,}000$$
$$4000x_1 + 3500x_2 + 5000x_3 + 1800x_4 + 4000x_5 + 900x_6 \le 8{,}750$$

$$x_1, \; x_2, \; x_3, \; x_4, \; x_5, \; x_6 = 0, 1$$

b. The following multiple choice constraint must be added to the model.

$$x_1 + x_2 \le 1$$

c. The following co-requisite constraint must be added to the model in b.

$$x_3 - x_4 \le 0.$$

12.a. $x_1 + x_3 + x_5 + x_6 = 2$

b. $x_3 - x_5 = 0$

c. $x_1 + x_4 = 1$

d. $x_4 \le x_1$

$x_4 \le x_3$

e. $x_4 \le x_1$

$x_4 \le x_3$

$x_4 \ge x_1 + x_3 - 1$

13.a.

min $52.50x_9 + 52.50x_{10} + 52.50x_{11} + 16y_9 + 16y_{10} + 16y_{11} + 16y_{12} + 16y_1 + 16y_2 + 16y_3$

x_9			$+$ y_9							$\ge$	6
$x_9 +$	x_{10}		$+$ $y_9 +$	y_{10}						$\ge$	4
$x_9 +$	$x_{10} +$	$x_{11} +$	$y_9 +$	$y_{10} +$	y_{11}					$\ge$	8
$x_9 +$	$x_{10} +$	$x_{11} +$	$y_9 +$	$y_{10} +$	$y_{11} +$	y_{12}				$\ge$	10
	$x_{10} +$	x_{11}	$+$ $y_{10} +$	$y_{11} +$	$y_{12} +$	y_1				$\ge$	9
x_9		x_{11}	$+$	$y_{11} +$	$y_{12} +$	$y_1 +$	y_2			$\ge$	6
$x_9 +$	x_{10}		$+$		$y_{12} +$	$y_1 +$	$y_2 +$	y_3		$\ge$	4
$x_9 +$	$x_{10} +$	x_{11}			$+$	$y_1 +$	$y_2 +$	y_3		$\ge$	7
	$x_{10} +$	x_{11}				$+$	$y_2 +$	y_3		$\ge$	6
		x_{11}					$+$	y_3		$\ge$	6

$x_i, \ y_j \ge 0$ and integer for $i = 9, \ 10, \ 11$ and $j = 9, \ 10, \ 11, \ 12, \ 1, \ 2, \ 3$

b. Solution to LP Relaxation obtained using LINDO/PC:

$y_9 = 6$ $y_{12} = 6$ $y_3 = 6$ All other variables $= 0$.

$y_{10} = 2$ $y_1 = 6$ Cost: $336.

c. The solution to the LP Relaxation is integral therefore it is the optimal solution to the integer program.

A difficulty with this solution is that only part-time employees are used; this may cause problems with supervision, etc. The large surpluses from 10-11 (4 employees), 12-1 (4 employees), and 3-4 (9 employees) indicate times when the tellers not needed for customer services may be reassigned to other tasks.

d. Add the following constraints to the formulation in part (a).

$$x_9 \ge 1$$
$$x_{11} \ge 1$$
$$x_9 + x_{10} + x_{11} \ge 5$$

The new optimal solution, which has a daily cost of $454.50 is

$x_9 = 1$ $y_9 = 5$

$x_{11} = 4$ $y_{12} = 5$

$y_3 = 2$

There is now much less reliance on part-time employees. The new solution uses 5 full-time employees and 12 part-time employees; the previous solution used no full-time employees and 21 part-time employees.

14.a. Let $x_i = \begin{cases} 1 & \text{if a principal place of business is in county } i \\ 0 & \text{otherwise} \end{cases}$

$y_i = \begin{cases} 1 & \text{if county } i \text{ is not served} \\ 0 & \text{if county } i \text{ is served} \end{cases}$

The objective function for an integer programming model calls for minimizing the population not served.

min $195y_1 + 96y_2 + \bullet \bullet \bullet + 175\, y_{13}$

There are 13 constraints needed; each is written so that y_i will be forced to equal one whenever it is not possible to do business in county i.

$$\begin{array}{llllllllll}
\text{Constraint 1:} & x_1 & + x_2 + & x_3 & & & & + & y_1 & \geq 1 \\
\text{Constraint 2:} & x_1 & + x_2 + & x_3 & + x_4 & + x_6 & + x_7 & + & y_2 & \geq 1 \\
& \bullet & & & & \bullet & & & & \bullet \\
& \bullet & & & & \bullet & & & & \bullet \\
& \bullet & & & & \bullet & & & & \bullet \\
\text{Constraint 13:} & & x_{11} + x_{12} & + x_{13} & & & & + & y_{13} & \geq 1
\end{array}$$

One more constraint must be added to reflect the requirement that only one principal place of business may be established.

$$x_1 + x_2 + \bullet \bullet \bullet + x_{13} = 1$$

The optimal solution has a principal place of business in County 11 with an optimal value of 739,000. A population of 739,000 cannot be served by this solution. Counties 1-5 and 10 will not be served.

b. The only change necessary in the integer programming model for part a is that the right-hand side of the last constraint is increased from 1 to 2.

$$x_1 + x_2 + \bullet \bullet \bullet + x_{13} = 2.$$

The optimal solution has principal places of business in counties 3 and 11 with an optimal value of 76,000. Only County 10 with a population of 76,000 is not served.

c. It is not the best location if only one principal place of business can be established; 1,058,000 customers in the region cannot be served. However, 642,000 can be served and if there is no opportunity to obtain a principal place of business in County 11, this may be a good start. Perhaps later there will be an opportunity in County 11.

15.a. Let 1 denote the Michigan plant
2 denote the first New York plant
3 denote the second New York plant
4 denote the Ohio plant
5 denote the California plant

The following table shows the options which involve modernizing two plants.

Plant					Transmission Capacity	Engine Block Capacity	Feasible ?	Cost
1	2	3	4	5				
✓	✓				700	1300	No	
✓		✓			1100	900	Yes	60
✓			✓		900	1400	Yes	65
✓				✓	600	700	No	
	✓	✓			1200	1200	Yes	70
	✓		✓		1000	1700	Yes	75
	✓			✓	700	1000	No	
		✓	✓		1400	1300	Yes	75
		✓		✓	1100	600	No	
			✓	✓	900	1100	Yes	60

b. Modernize plants 1 and 3 or plants 4 and 5.

c. Let $x_i = \begin{cases} 1 & \text{if plant } i \text{ is modernized} \\ 0 & \text{if plant } i \text{ is not modernized} \end{cases}$

$$\min \quad 25x_1 + 35x_2 + 35x_3 + 40x_4 + 25x_5$$
s.t.
$$300x_1 + 400x_2 + 800x_3 + 600x_4 + 300x_5 \geq 900 \quad \text{Transmissions}$$
$$500x_1 + 800x_2 + 400x_3 + 900x_4 + 200x_5 \geq 900 \quad \text{Engine Blocks}$$

d. Optimal Solution: $x_1 = x_3 = 1$.

16.a. Objective function changes to
$$\min \; 25x_1 + 40x_2 + 40x_3 + 40x_4 + 25x_5$$

b. $x_4 = x_5 = 1$; modernize the Ohio and California plants.

c. Add the constraint $x_2 + x_3 = 1$

d. $x_1 = x_3 = 1$; modernize the Michigan plant and the first New York plant.

17.a.   Let $x_i = \begin{cases} 1 & \text{if a camera is located at opening } i \\ 0 & \text{if not} \end{cases}$

$\min x_1 + x_2 + x_3 + x_4 + x_5 + x_6 + x_7 + x_8 + x_9 + x_{10} + x_{11} + x_{12} + x_{13}$
s.t.

$x_1 + x_4 + x_6 \geq 1$	Room 1
$x_6 + x_8 + x_{12} \geq 1$	Room 2
$x_1 + x_2 + x_3 \geq 1$	Room 3
$x_3 + x_4 + x_5 + x_7 \geq 1$	Room 4
$x_7 + x_8 + x_9 + x_{10} \geq 1$	Room 5
$x_{10} + x_{12} + x_{13} \geq 1$	Room 6
$x_2 + x_5 + x_9 + x_{11} \geq 1$	Room 7
$x_{11} + x_{13} \geq 1$	Room 8

b. $x_1 = x_5 = x_8 = x_{13} = 1$. Thus, cameras should be located at openings 1, 5, 8, and 13.

c.   Add the constraint $x_2 + x_5 + x_9 + x_{11} = 2$

d. $x_3 = x_6 = x_9 = x_{11} = x_{12}$. Thus, cameras should be located at openings 3, 6, 9, 11, and 12.

Case Problem

An integer programming model can be used advantageously to assist in developing recommendations.

Let $x_i = \begin{cases} 1 \ \textit{if book i is scheduled for publication} \\ 0 \ \textit{otherwise} \end{cases}$

The subscripts correspond to the books as follows:

i	Book
1	Business Calculus
2	Finite Math
3	General Statistics
4	Mathematical Statistics
5	Business Statistics
6	Finance
7	Financial Accounting
8	Managerial Accounting
9	English Literature
10	German

An integer programming model for maximizing projected sales (thousands of units) subject to the restrictions mentioned is given.

$$\max \ 20x_1 + 30x_2 + 15x_3 + 10x_4 + 25x_5 + 18x_6 + 25x_7 + 50x_8 + 20x_9 + 30x_{10}$$

s.t.

$$
\begin{array}{ll}
30x_1 + 16x_2 + 24x_3 + 20x_4 + 10x_5 \qquad\qquad\qquad\quad + 40x_9 \quad\quad\quad\quad \le 60 & \text{John} \\
40x_1 + 24x_2 \qquad\qquad\qquad\qquad\qquad + 24x_7 + 28x_8 + 34x_9 + 50x_{10} \le 40 & \text{Susan} \\
\qquad\quad 30x_3 + 24x_4 + 16x_5 + 14x_6 + 26x_7 + 30x_8 + 30x_9 + 36x_{10} \le 40 & \text{Monica} \\
\qquad\quad\ x_3 + x_4 + x_5 \qquad\qquad\qquad\qquad\qquad\qquad\qquad \le 2 & \text{No. of Stat Books} \\
\qquad\qquad\qquad\qquad\qquad\qquad x_7 + x_8 \qquad\qquad\qquad\qquad \le 1 & \text{Account Book} \\
x_1 + x_2 \qquad\qquad\qquad\qquad\qquad\qquad\qquad\qquad\qquad\qquad = 1 & \text{Math Book}
\end{array}
$$

$$x_i = 0, 1 \text{ for all } i, j$$

The optimal solution ($x_2 = x_5 = x_6 = 1$) calls for publishing the finite math, the business statistics and the finance books. Projected sales are 73,000 copies.

(1) If Susan can be made available for another 12 days, the optimal solution is $x_2 = x_8 = 1$. This calls for publishing the finite math and managerial accounting texts for projected sales of 80,000 copies.

(2) If Monica is also available for 10 more days, a big improvement can be made. The new optimal solution calls for producing the finite math book, the business statistics book, and the managerial accounting book. Projected sales are 105,000 copies.

(3)   The solution in (2) above does not include any new books. In the long run this would appear to be a bad strategy for the company. A variety of modifications can be made to the model to examine the short run impact of postponing a revision. For instance, a constraint could be added to require publication of at least one new book.

Answers to Questions for Quantitative Methods in Practice

1.   The guaranteed orders must be satisfies by the company and are thus handled by the constraints in the model. The secondary orders (approximately 20% of all orders) are to be satisfied if at all possible. However, because of raw material capacity and manufacturing capacity constraints, the company realizes that it may not be possible to satisfy all secondary orders. Thus, the secondary orders become goals rather than constraints in the model. Deviations for the secondary order goals incur a penalty cost. Thus deviations will tend to be minimized and the company will do the best it can to satisfy the secondary orders.

2.   Since secondary orders are handled with a penalty cost, the minimum cost solution includes a combination of actual costs and penalty costs. For this reason, as well as for the size and complexity of the model, it is doubtful the solution of the model achieves an "optimum" minimum cost solution. The model will provide a "good" feasible solution in that it will satisfy the guaranteed orders and attempt to satisfy as many of the secondary orders as possible considering manufacturing and penalty costs. Thus the model is looking for a "good" feasible solution and not just any feasible solution.

Chapter 13
Project Management: PERT/CPM

Learning Objectives

1. Understand the role and application of PERT/CPM for project management.

2. Learn how to define a project in terms of activities such that a network can be used to describe the project.

3. Know how to compute the critical path and the project completion time.

4. Know how to convert optimistic, most probable, and pessimistic time estimates into expected activity time estimates.

5. With uncertain activity times, be able to compute the probability of the project being completed by a specific time.

6. Understand the concept and need for crashing.

7. Be able to formulate the crashing problem as a linear programming model.

8. Learn how to schedule and control project costs with PERT/Cost.

9. Understand the following terms:

network	beta distribution
PERT/CPM	path
activities	critical path
event	critical activities
dummy activity	slack
optimistic time	crashing
most probable time	PERT/Cost
pessimistic time	

Solutions

1.

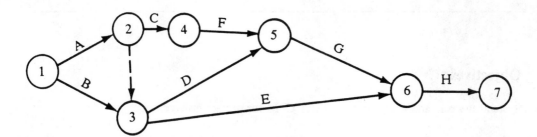

2.

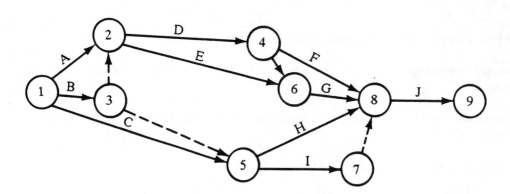

3.

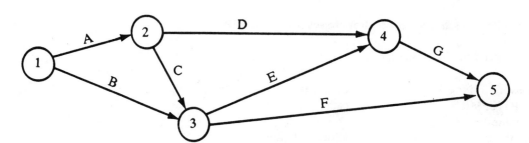

4. a.

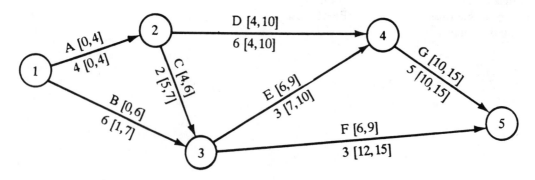

Critical Path: A-D-G   Time = 15 months

b. The critical path activities require 15 months to complete. Thus the project should be completed in 1 1/2 years.

5.

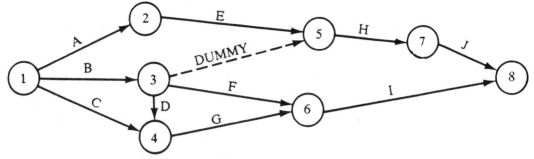

6.

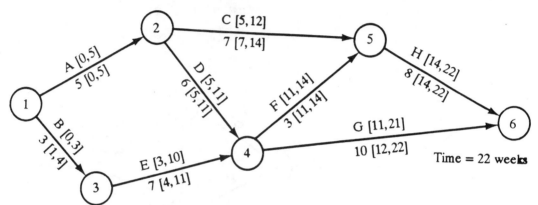

Time = 22 weeks

a. Critical path: A-D-F-H

b. 22 weeks

c. No, it is a critical activity

d. Yes, 2 weeks

e. Schedule for activity E:

Earliest Start	3
Latest Start	4
Earliest Finish	10
Latest Finish	11

7. a.

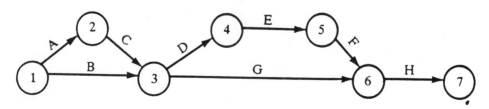

b. B-D-E-F-H

c.   21 weeks

Activity	Earliest Start	Latest Start	Earliest Finish	Latest Finish	Slack	Critical Activity
A	0	1	3	4	1	
B	0	0	6	6	0	Yes
C	3	4	5	6	1	
D	6	6	11	11	0	Yes
E	11	11	15	15	0	Yes
F	15	15	18	18	0	Yes
G	6	9	15	18	3	
H	18	18	21	21	0	Yes

8. a.

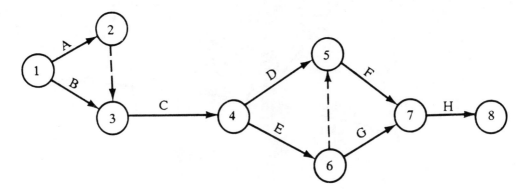

b.   B-C-E-F-H

c.

Activity	Earliest Start	Latest Start	Earliest Finish	Latest Finish	Slack	Critical Activity
A	0	2	6	8	2	
B	0	0	8	8	0	Yes
C	8	8	20	20	0	Yes
D	20	22	24	26	2	
E	20	20	26	26	0	Yes
F	26	26	41	41	0	Yes
G	26	29	38	41	3	
H	41	41	49	49	0	Yes

d.   Yes. Project Completion Time 49 weeks.

9. a.   A-C-E-H-I

b.

Activity	Earliest Start	Latest Start	Earliest Finish	Latest Finish	Slack	Critical Activity
A	0	0	9	9	0	Yes
B	0	9	6	15	9	
C	9	9	15	15	0	Yes
D	9	12	12	15	3	
E	15	15	15	15	0	Yes
F	15	16	18	19	1	
G	18	19	20	21	1	
H	15	15	21	21	0	Yes
I	21	21	24	24	0	Yes

c. Project completion 24 weeks. The park can open within the 6 months (26 weeks) after the project is started.

10.a.

Activity	Optimistic	Most Probable	Pessimistic	Expected Times	Variance
A	4	5	6	5.00	0.11
B	8	9	10	9.00	0.11
C	7	7.5	11	8.00	0.44
D	6	9	10	8.83	0.25
E	6	7	9	7.17	0.25
F	5	6	7	6.00	0.11

b. Critical activities: B-D-F
Expected project completion time: 9.00 + 8.83 + 6.00 = 23.83.
Variance of projection completion time: 0.11 + 0.25 + 0.11 = 0.47

11.

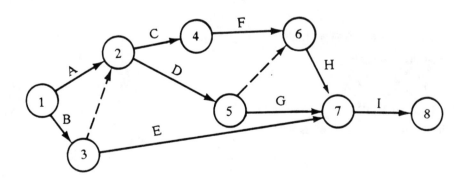

12.a.

Activity	Expected Time	Variance
A	4.83	0.25
B	4.00	0.44
C	6.00	0.11
D	8.83	0.25
E	4.00	0.44
F	2.00	0.11
G	7.83	0.69
H	8.00	0.44
I	4.00	0.11

Activity	Earliest Start	Latest Start	Earliest Finish	Latest Finish	Slack	Critical Activity
A	0.00	0.00	4.83	4.83	0.00	Yes
B	0.00	0.83	4.00	4.83	0.83	
C	4.83	5.67	10.83	11.67	0.83	
D	4.83	4.83	13.67	13.67	0.00	Yes
E	4.00	17.67	8.00	21.67	13.67	
F	10.83	11.67	12.83	13.67	0.83	
G	13.67	13.83	21.50	21.67	0.17	
H	13.67	13.67	21.67	21.67	0.00	Yes
I	21.67	21.67	25.67	25.67	0.00	Yes

Critical Path: A-D-H-I

b. $E(T) = t_A + t_D + t_H + t_I$
    $= 4.83 + 8.83 + 8 + 4 = 25.66$ days

c.

$$\sigma^2 = \sigma_A^2 + \sigma_D^2 + \sigma_H^2 + \sigma_I^2$$
$$= 0.25 + 0.25 + 0.44 + 0.11 = 1.05$$

Using the normal distribution,

$$z = \frac{25 - E(T)}{\sigma} = \frac{25 - 25.66}{\sqrt{1.05}} = -0.65$$

From Appendix C, area for $z = -0.65$ is 0.2422.

Probability of 25 days or less = 0.5000 - 0.2422 = 0.2578

13.

Activity	Expected Time	Variance
A	5	0.11
B	3	0.03
C	7	0.11
D	6	0.44
E	7	0.44
F	3	0.11
G	10	0.44
H	8	1.78

From problem 6, A-D-F-H is the critical path.

$$E(T) = 5 + 6 + 3 + 8 = 22$$
$$\sigma^2 = 0.11 + 0.44 + 0.11 + 1.78 = 2.44$$
$$z = \frac{Time - E(T)}{\sigma} = \frac{Time - 22}{\sqrt{2.44}}$$

a.

From Appendix C

		Area
Time = 21	$z = -0.64$	0.2389

$$P(21 \text{ weeks}) = 0.5000 - 0.2389 = 0.2611$$

b.

		Area
Time = 22	$z = 0$	0.0000

$$P(22 \text{ weeks}) = 0.5000$$

c.

		Area
Time = 25	$z = +1.92$	0.4726

$$P(22 \text{ weeks}) = 0.5000 + 0.4726 = 0.9726$$

14.a.

Activity	Expected Time	Variance
A	6.0	0.11
B	11.0	1.78
C	8.0	0.44
D	9.0	1.00
E	7.0	1.78
F	7.5	0.25
G	7.0	1.00

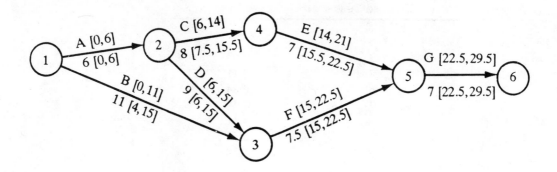

Critical Path: A-D-F-G

b. Activity C:
   $$\text{Slack} = \text{LS} - \text{ES} = 7.5 - 6 = 1.5 \text{ days}$$

c. $E(T) = t_A + t_D + t_F + t_G$
   $$= 6 + 9 + 7.5 + 7 = 29.5 \text{ days}$$

   $\sigma^2 = \sigma_A^2 + \sigma_D^2 + \sigma_F^2 + \sigma_G^2$
   $$= 0.11 + 1.00 + 0.25 + 1.00 = 2.36$$

d.

<u>Area</u>

$$z = \frac{30 - E(T)}{\sigma} = \frac{30 - 29.5}{\sqrt{2.36}} = 0.33 \qquad 0.1293$$

$$P(30 \text{ days}) = 0.5000 + 0.1293 = 0.6293$$

15.a.

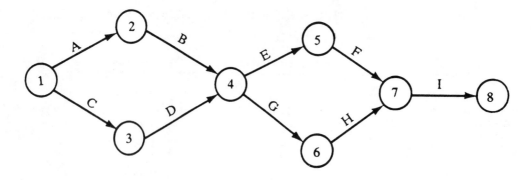

b.

Activity	Expected Time	Variance
A	2	0.03
B	3	0.44
C	2	0.11
D	2	0.03
E	1	0.03
F	2	0.11
G	4	0.44
H	4	0.11
I	2	0.03

Activity	Earliest Start	Latest Start	Earliest Finish	Latest Finish	Slack	Critical Activity
A	0	0	2	2	0	Yes
B	2	2	5	5	0	Yes
C	0	1	2	3	1	
D	2	3	4	5	1	
E	5	10	6	11	5	
F	6	11	8	13	5	
G	5	5	9	9	0	Yes
H	9	9	13	13	0	Yes
I	13	13	15	15	0	Yes

c. Critical Path: A-B-G-H-I
Expected Project Completion Time = 2 + 3 + 4 + 4 + 2 = 15 weeks

d. Variance on critical path

$\sigma^2 = 0.03 + 0.44 + 0.44 + 0.11 + 0.03 = 1.05$

From Appendix C, we find 0.99 probability occurs at $z = +2.33$. Thus

$$z = \frac{T - E(T)}{\sigma} = \frac{T - 15}{\sqrt{1.05}} = 2.33$$

or

$$T = 15 + 2.33\sqrt{1.05} = 17.4 \ weeks$$

16.a. A-D-G-J

$$E(T) = 6 + 5 + 3 + 2 = 16$$
$$\sigma^2 = 1.78 + 1.78 + 0.25 + 0.11 = 3.92$$

A-C-F-J

$$E(T) = 6 + 3 + 2 + 2 = 13$$
$$\sigma^2 = 1.78 + 0.11 + 0.03 + 0.11 = 2.03$$

B-H-I-J

$$E(T) = 2 + 4 + 2 + 2 = 10$$
$$\sigma^2 = 0.44 + 0.69 + 0.03 + 0.11 = 1.27$$

b.   A-D-G-J

$$z = \frac{20 - 16}{\sqrt{3.92}} = 2.02 \quad \text{Area} = 0.4783 + 0.5000 = 0.9783$$

A-C-F-J

$$z = \frac{20 - 13}{\sqrt{2.03}} = 4.91 \quad \text{Area is approximately } 1.0000$$

B-H-I-J

$$z = \frac{20 - 10}{\sqrt{1.27}} = 8.87 \quad \text{Area is approximately } 1.0000$$

c.   Critical path is the longest path and generally will have the lowest probability of being completed by the desired time. The noncritical paths should have a higher probability of being completed on time.

It may be desirable to consider the probability calculation for a noncritical path if the path activities have little slack, if the path completion time is almost equal to the critical path completion time, or if the path activity times have relatively high variances. When all of these situations occur, the noncritical path may have a probability of completion on time that is less than the critical path.

17.a.

Activity	Expected Time	Variance
A	7	1.78
B	3	0.44
C	3	0.11
D	8	1.78
E	3	0.11
F	3	0.03
G	4	0.25
H	6	0.69
I	2	0.11
J	2	0.11

b.

Activity	Earliest Start	Latest Start	Earliest Finish	Latest Finish	Slack	Critical Activity
A	0	0	7	7	0	Yes
B	0	8	3	11	8	
C	7	13	10	16	6	
D	7	7	15	15	0	Yes
E	7	8	10	11	1	
F	10	16	13	19	6	
G	15	15	19	19	0	Yes
H	10	11	16	17	1	
I	16	17	18	19	1	
J	19	19	21	21	0	Yes

c.   Critical Path: A-D-G-J

d.   Expected Project Completion Time = 7 + 8 + 4 + 2 = 21 weeks

e.

$$\sigma^2 = \sigma_A^2 + \sigma_D^2 + \sigma_G^2 + \sigma_J^2$$
$$= 1.78 + 1.78 + 0.25 + 0.11 = 3.92$$
$$z = \frac{T - E(T)}{\sigma} = \frac{20 - 21}{\sqrt{3.92}} = -0.51$$

Area
0.1950

$$P(20 \text{ weeks}) = 0.5000 - 0.1950 = 0.3050$$

18.a.

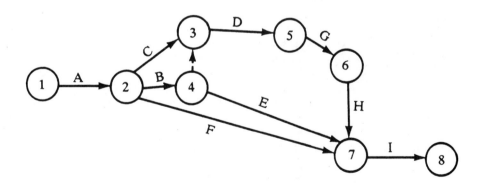

b.

Activity	Expected Time	Variance
A	1.17	0.03
B	6.00	0.44
C	4.00	0.44
D	2.00	0.11
E	3.00	0.11
F	2.00	0.11
G	2.00	0.11
H	2.00	0.11
I	1.00	0.00

Activity	Earliest Start	Latest Start	Earliest Finish	Latest Finish	Slack	Critical Activity
A	0.00	0.00	1.17	1.17	0.00	Yes
B	1.17	1.17	7.17	7.17	0.00	Yes
C	1.17	3.17	5.17	7.17	2.00	
D	7.17	7.17	9.17	9.17	0.00	Yes
E	7.17	10.17	10.17	13.17	3.00	
F	1.17	11.17	3.17	13.17	10.00	
G	9.17	9.17	11.17	11.17	0.00	Yes
H	11.17	11.17	13.17	13.17	0.00	Yes
I	13.17	13.17	14.17	14.17	0.00	Yes

c. Critical Path: A-B-G-H-I
    Expected Project Completion Time = 1.17 + 6 + 2 + 2 + 2 + 1 = 14.17 weeks

d. Compute the probability of project completion in 13 weeks or less.

$$\sigma^2 = \sigma_A^2 + \sigma_B^2 + \sigma_D^2 + \sigma_G^2 + \sigma_H^2 + \sigma_I^2$$
$$= 0.03 + 0.44 + 0.11 + 0.11 + 0.11 + 0.00 = 0.80$$

$$z = \frac{13 - E(T)}{\sigma} = \frac{13 - 14.17}{\sqrt{0.80}} = -1.31$$

Area
0.4049

$$P(13 \text{ weeks}) = 0.5000 - 0.4049 = 0.0951$$

With this low probability, the manager should start prior to February 1.

19.a.

Activity	Expected Time	Variance
A	4	0.11
B	4	0.44
C	5	0.11
D	3	0.11
E	10	1.78
F	9	0.69
G	6	0.25
H	7	1.78
I	3	0.44
J	5	0.11

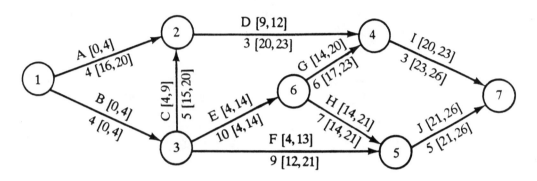

Activity	Earliest Start	Latest Start	Earliest Finish	Latest Finish	Slack	Critical Activity
A	0	16	4	20	16	
B	0	0	4	4	0	Yes
C	4	15	9	20	11	
D	9	20	12	23	11	
E	4	4	14	14	0	Yes
F	4	12	13	21	8	
G	14	17	20	23	3	
H	14	14	21	21	0	Yes
I	20	23	23	26	3	
J	21	21	26	26	0	Yes

Critical Path: B-E-H-J

$$E(T) = t_B + t_E + t_H + t_J = 4 + 10 + 7 + 5 = 26$$

$$\sigma^2 = \sigma_B^2 + \sigma_E^2 + \sigma_H^2 + \sigma_J^2 = 0.44 + 1.78 + 1.78 + 0.11 = 4.11$$

$$z = \frac{T - E(T)}{\sigma}$$

$$z = \frac{25 - 26}{\sqrt{4.11}} = -0.49 \qquad P(25 \ weeks) = 0.5000 - 0.1879 = 0.3121$$

$$z = \frac{30 - 26}{\sqrt{4.11}} = 1.97 \qquad P(30 \ weeks) = 0.5000 + 0.4756 = 0.9756$$

20.a.

Activity	Maximum Crash	Crash Cost/Week
A	2	400
B	3	667
C	1	500
D	2	300
E	1	350
F	2	450
G	5	360
H	1	1000

Min $400Y_A + 667Y_B + 500Y_C + 300Y_D + 350Y_E + 450Y_F + 360Y_G + 1000Y_H$

s.t.

Network Constraints

$$X_2 \geq 3 - Y_A \qquad\qquad X_2 + Y_A \geq 3$$
$$X_3 \geq 2 - Y_C + X_2 \qquad -X_2 + X_3 + Y_C \geq 2$$
$$X_3 \geq 6 - Y_B \qquad\qquad X_3 + Y_B \geq 6$$
$$X_4 \geq 5 - Y_D + X_3 \qquad -X_3 + X_4 + Y_D \geq 5$$
$$X_5 \geq 4 - Y_E + X_4 \qquad -X_4 + X_5 + Y_E \geq 4$$
$$X_6 \geq 3 - Y_F + X_5 \qquad -X_5 + X_6 + Y_F \geq 3$$
$$X_6 \geq 9 - Y_G + X_3 \qquad -X_3 + X_6 + Y_G \geq 9$$
$$X_7 \geq 3 - Y_H + X_6 \qquad -X_6 + X_7 + Y_H \geq 3$$

Project Completion: $X_7 \leq 16$

Maximum Crashing:

$$Y_A \leq 2$$
$$Y_B \leq 3$$
$$Y_C \leq 1$$
$$Y_D \leq 2$$
$$Y_E \leq 1$$
$$Y_F \leq 2$$
$$Y_G \leq 5$$
$$Y_H \leq 1$$

b.   Linear Programming Solution

Activity	Crash Time	New Time	Crash Cost
A	0	3	—
B	1	5	667
C	0	2	—
D	2	3	600
E	1	3	350
F	1	2	450
G	1	8	360
H	0	3	—
		Total Crashing Cost	$2,427

c.

Activity	Earliest Start	Latest Start	Earliest Finish	Latest Finish	Slack	Critical Activity
A	0	0	3	3	0	Yes
B	0	0	5	5	0	Yes
C	3	3	5	5	0	Yes
D	5	5	8	8	0	Yes
E	8	8	11	11	0	Yes
F	11	11	13	13	0	Yes
G	5	5	13	13	0	Yes
H	13	13	16	16	0	Yes

All activities are critical.

21.a.

Activity	Earliest Start	Latest Start	Earliest Finish	Latest Finish	Slack	Critical Activity
A	0	0	3	3	0	Yes
B	0	1	2	3	1	
C	3	3	8	8	0	Yes
D	2	3	7	8	1	
E	8	8	14	14	0	Yes
F	8	10	10	12	2	
G	10	12	12	14	2	

Critical Path: A-C-E

Project Completion Time $= t_A + t_C + t_E = 3 + 5 + 6 = 14$ days

b.   Total Cost = $8,400

22.a.

Activity	Max Crash Days	Crash Cost/Day
A	1	$600
B	1	$700
C	2	$400
D	2	$400
E	2	$500
F	1	$400
G	1	$500

$$\text{Min } 600Y_A + 700Y_B + 400Y_C + 400Y_D + 500Y_E + 400Y_F + 400Y_G$$

s.t.

(event 2)	$X_2 \geq 3 - Y_A$	[1]
(event 3)	$X_3 \geq 2 - Y_B$	[2]
(event 4)	$X_4 \geq X_2 + 5 - Y_C$	[3]
	$X_4 \geq X_3 + 5 - Y_D$	[4]
(event 5)	$X_5 \geq X_4 + 2 - Y_F$	[5]
(event 6)	$X_6 \geq X_4 + 6 - Y_E$	[6]
	$X_6 \geq X_5 + 2 - Y_G$	[7]

or

$X_2 + Y_A \geq 3$	[1]
$X_3 + Y_B \geq 2$	[2]
$-X_2 + X_4 + Y_C \geq 5$	[3]
$-X_3 + X_4 + Y_D \geq 5$	[4]
$-X_4 + X_5 + Y_F \geq 2$	[5]
$-X_4 + X_6 + Y_E \geq 6$	[6]
$-X_5 + X_6 + Y_G \geq 2$	[7]

also

$Y_A \leq 1$	[8]
$Y_B \leq 1$	[9]
$Y_C \leq 2$	[10]
$Y_D \leq 2$	[11]
$Y_E \leq 2$	[12]
$Y_F \leq 1$	[13]
$Y_G \leq 1$	[14]

and

$X_6 \leq 12$	[15]

All $X, Y \geq 0$

b.

Activity	Crash	Crashing Cost
C	1 day	$400
E	1 day	500
	Total	$900

c. Total Cost = Normal Cost + Crashing Cost
    $$= \$8,400 + \$900 = \$9,300$$

23.a.

Activity	Max Crash Days	Crash Cost/Day (000's)
A	2	10
B	3	5
C	1	4
D	2	15
E	1	10
F	0	—
G	2	7.5

min $100Y_A + 5Y_B + 4Y_C + 15Y_D + 10Y_E + 7.5Y_G$
s.t.

(event 2) $X_2 \geq 4 - Y_A$
(event 3) $X_3 \geq 6 - Y_B$
             $X_3 \geq X_2 + 2 - Y_C$
(event 4) $X_4 \geq X_2 + 6 - Y_D$
             $X_4 \geq X_3 + 3 - Y_E$
(event 5) $X_5 \geq X_4 + 5 - Y_G$
             $X_5 \geq X_3 + 3$

or

$X_2 + Y_A \geq 4$
$X_3 + Y_B \geq 6$
$-X_2 + X_3 + Y_C \geq 2$
$-X_2 + X_4 + Y_D \geq 6$
$-X_3 + X_4 + Y_E \geq 3$
$-X_4 + X_5 + Y_G \geq 5$
$-X_3 + X_5 \geq 3$

also

$Y_A \leq 2$
$Y_B \leq 3$
$Y_C \leq 1$
$Y_D \leq 2$
$Y_E \leq 1$
$Y_G \leq 2$
$X_5 \leq T$

All $X, Y \geq 0$.

b.   For $T = 12$ months

	Crash Activity	Number of Months	Cost
$Y_A = 1$	A	1	$ 10,000
$Y_G = 2$	G	2	$ 15,000
			$25,000

Critical Paths: A-D-G, B-E-G

24.a.

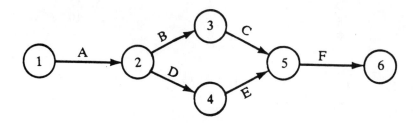

b.

Activity	Earliest Start	Latest Start	Earliest Finish	Latest Finish	Slack
A	0	0	10	10	0
B	10	10	18	18	0
C	18	18	28	28	0
D	10	11	17	18	1
E	17	18	27	28	1
F	28	28	31	31	0

c.   Activities A, B, C, and F are critical. The expected project completion time is 31 weeks.

d.

Crash Activities	Number of Weeks	Cost
A	2	$ 40
B	2	30
C	1	20
D	1	10
E	1	12.5
		$112.5

e.

Activity	Earliest Start	Latest Start	Earliest Finish	Latest Finish	Slack
A	0	0	8	8	0
B	8	8	14	14	0
C	14	14	23	23	0
D	8	8	14	14	0
E	14	14	23	23	0
F	23	23	26	26	0

All activities are critical.

f. Total added cost due to crashing $112,500 (see part d.)

25.a.

Let K_j = Cost to crash activity j one week
M_j = Maximum Crash time in weeks for activity j
Y_j = Number of weeks activity j is crashed
X_i = Time of occurrence of event i
T_j = Normal completion time for activity j

min $K_A Y_A + K_B Y_B + K_C Y_C + K_D Y_D + K_E Y_E + K_F Y_F + K_G Y_G + K_H Y_H + K_I Y_I + K_J Y_J$
s.t.

$$X_2 + Y_A \geq \tau_A$$
$$X_3 + Y_B \geq \tau_B$$
$$-X_3 + X_2 + Y_C \geq \tau_C$$
$$-X_3 + X_6 + Y_E \geq \tau_E$$
$$-X_3 + X_5 + Y_F \geq \tau_F$$
$$-X_6 + X_4 + Y_G \geq \tau_G$$
$$-X_2 + X_4 + Y_D \geq \tau_D$$
$$-X_6 + X_4 + Y_H \geq \tau_H$$
$$-X_4 + X_7 + Y_I \geq \tau_I$$
$$-X_5 + X_7 + Y_J \geq \tau_J$$

τ_j values can be computed from data given in problem 19. (See solution to problem 19.)

$Y_A \leq M_A$ $Y_F \leq M_F$
$Y_B \leq M_B$ $Y_G \leq M_G$
$Y_C \leq M_C$ $Y_H \leq M_H$
$Y_D \leq M_D$ $Y_I \leq M_I$
$Y_E \leq M_E$ $Y_J \leq M_J$

$X_7 < T$, where T is the desired project completion time.

b.   Information needed:

1. Maximum crash time for each activity (M_j)
2. Crashing cost for each activity (K_j)
3. Desired project completion time (T)

26.

Activity	Cost/Week	Activity	Cost/Week
A	15	F	1
B	8	G	20
C	1	H	5
D	20	I	2
E	2	J	1

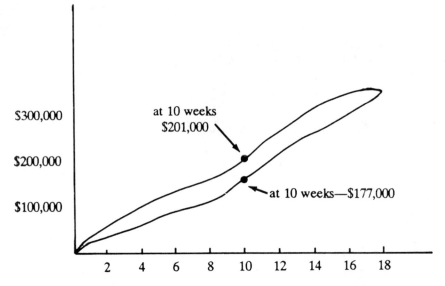

Biggest Range in Feasible
Budget Occurs at 7 weeks

($129,000 - $92,000) = $37,000

27.a.

Activity	Actual Cost	Budgeted Cost	Difference	
A	62	72	-10	
B	6	8	-2	
	68	80	-12	(underrun)

All looks good!

$$\frac{68 - 80}{80}(100) = -15\% \quad (\textit{underrun})$$

b.

Activity	Actual Cost	Budgeted Cost	Difference	
A	85	90	- 5	
B	16	16	0	
C	1	1	0	
D	100	80	20	*
E	4	6	- 2	
H	10	5	5	*
	216	198	18	(overrun)

Check activities D and H immediately.

Currently

$$\frac{216 - 198}{198}(100) = 9.1\% \quad (\textit{overrun})$$

c.

Activity	Actual Cost	Budgeted Cost	Difference	
A	85	90	- 5	
B	16	16	0	
C	3	3	0	
D	105	100	+ 5	
E	4	6	- 2	
F	3	2	+ 1	
G	55	60	- 5	
H	25	20	+ 5	
I	4	4	0	
	300	301	- 1	(underrun)

All looks in control. To date they have a $1,000 (0.3%) cost underrun. Activity *J* could cost as much as $3,000 and still keep the project within its budget.

28.a.

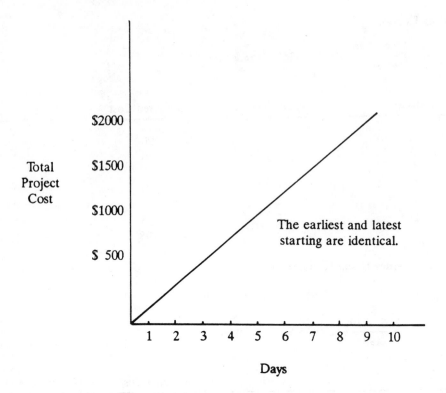

The above cost schedule is unusual, but can be expected to occur whenever all activities are critical.

b.

Activity	AC	BC	AC - BC	Cost Overrun
A	$ 800	$ 700	$ 100	✓
B	$ 100	$ 134	$- 34	
C	$ 450	$ 500	$- 50	
D	$ 250	$ 175	$ 75	✓
E	$ 0	$ 0	$ 0	
	$1600	$1509	$ 91	(overrun)

$$\% \; Overrun = \frac{AC - BC}{BC} = \frac{91}{1509} = 6\%$$

Follow-up desired on activity D.

29.a.

Activity	ES	LS	EF	LF	Slack	Critical Path
A	0	3	3	6	3	
B	3	6	5	8	3	
C	0	0	8	8	0	Yes
D	8	8	8	8	0	Yes
E	8	8	14	14	0	Yes
F	8	10	12	14	2	
G	14	14	19	19	0	Yes
H	14	18	15	19	4	
I	19	19	19	19	0	Yes
J	19	20	24	25	1	
K	19	19	25	25	0	Yes

Critical Path: C-D-E-G-I-K (25 weeks)

$$\text{Variance} = 2 + 0 + 1 + 0.4 + 0 + 0.6 = 4$$

$$z = \frac{26 - 25}{2} = 0.50 \therefore \text{Probability} = 0.6915$$

b. At 12th week, earliest start schedule = $58,000 and latest start schedule = $48,000.

30. Checking activity E we see that 50% completion should occur at week $8 + 0.50(6) = 11$. Thus activity E is one week behind schedule. Activity F is $10 + 0.75(4) = 13$, which is one week ahead of schedule.

Cost Status:

Activity	Actual Cost	Value $\left(\dfrac{P}{100}\right)B$	Difference
A	$ 5,000	$ 6,000	-$1,000
B	$ 4,000	$ 4,000	0
D	$18,000	$16,000	$2,000
E	$ 9,000	$ 9,000	0
F	$18,000	$15,000	$3,000
	$54,000	$50,000	$4,000

Cost Overrun $\dfrac{4,000}{50,000}(100) = 8\%$

Corrective action desired:
Activity E - 1 week behind schedule
Activity F - $3,000 cost overrun

Case Problem

a.   R.C. Coleman's Project Network

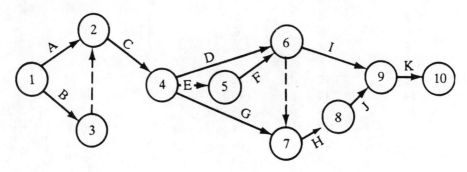

Activity	Expected Time	Variance
A	6	0.44
B	9	2.78
C	4	0.44
D	12	7.11
E	10	1.00
F	6	0.44
G	8	7.11
H	6	0.44
I	7	2.78
J	4	0.11
K	4	0.44

Activity	Earliest Start	Latest Start	Earliest Finish	Latest Finish	Slack	Critical Activity
A	0	3	6	9	3	
B	0	0	9	9	0	Yes
C	9	9	13	13	0	Yes
D	13	17	25	29	4	
E	13	13	23	23	0	Yes
F	23	23	29	29	0	Yes
G	13	21	21	29	8	
H	29	29	35	35	0	Yes
I	29	32	36	39	3	
J	35	35	39	39	0	Yes
K	39	39	43	43	0	Yes

The expected project completion time is 43 weeks. The critical path activities are B-C-E-F-H-J-K.
The variance of critical path activities is 5.67.

$$z = \frac{40 - 43}{\sqrt{5.67}} = -1.26$$

Appendix C
<u>Area</u>

0.3962

$$P(T \le 40) = 0.5000 - 0.3962 = 0.1038$$

Given the above calculations, we can conclude that there is about a 10% chance that the project can be completed in 40 weeks or less. Coleman should consider crashing project activities.

b.

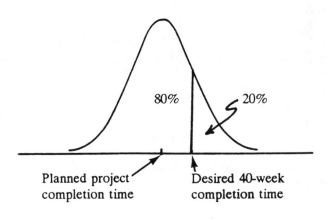

Planned project completion time

Desired 40-week completion time

For 80% chance,
$$z = +0.84$$
Thus

$$\frac{40 - E(T)}{\sqrt{5.67}} = 0.84$$

Solve for $E(T) = 38$ weeks.

R.C. Coleman should crash activities to reduce the expected project completion time to 38 weeks.

c.   In this section, we will use expected activity times as normal times and use a linear programming model based on expected times to make the crashing decisions.

LP Model
Let X_i = the time of occurrence of event (node) i
        Y_j = the amount of crash time for activity j

$$\text{min} \quad 450Y_A + 400Y_B + 600Y_C + 300Y_D + 1000Y_E +$$
$$550Y_F + 750Y_G + 700Y_H + 800Y_I + 400Y_J +$$
$$500Y_K$$

s.t.

	Activity
$X_2 + Y_A \geq 6$	A
$X_3 + Y_B \geq 9$	B
$-X_2 + X_4 + Y_C \geq 4$	C
$-X_4 + X_6 + Y_D \geq 12$	D
$-X_4 + X_5 + Y_E \geq 10$	E
$-X_5 + X_6 + Y_F \geq 6$	F
$-X_4 + X_7 + Y_G \geq 8$	G
$-X_7 + X_8 + Y_H \geq 6$	H
$-X_6 + X_9 + Y_I \geq 7$	I
$-X_8 + X_9 + Y_J \geq 4$	J
$-X_9 + X_{10} + Y_K \geq 4$	K
$-X_6 + X_7 \geq 0$	Dummy
$-X_3 + X_2 \geq 0$	Dummy
$X_{10} \leq 38$	Project Completion Time
$Y_A \leq 2$	
$Y_B \leq 2$	
$Y_C \leq 2$	
$Y_D \leq 4$	
$Y_E \leq 3$	
$Y_F \leq 2$	
$Y_G \leq 3$	
$Y_H \leq 2$	
$Y_I \leq 3$	
$Y_J \leq 1$	
$Y_K \leq 1$	

All X_i, $Y_j \geq 0$

The optimal crashing decisions are as follows:

Crash Activity	Weeks	Cost
B	2	800
F	1	550
J	1	400
K	1	500
	Total	2250

A revised activity schedule based on these crashing decisions is as follows:

Activity	Earliest Start	Latest Start	Earliest Finish	Latest Finish	Slack	Critical Activity
A	0	1	6	7	1	
B	0	0	7	7	0	Yes
C	7	7	11	11	0	Yes
D	11	14	23	26	3	
E	11	11	21	21	0	Yes
F	21	21	26	26	0	Yes
G	11	18	19	26	7	
H	26	26	32	32	0	Yes
I	26	28	33	35	2	
J	32	32	35	35	0	Yes
K	35	35	38	38	0	Yes

The student should comment on the fact that the crashing decisions may alter the variance in the project completion time. By defining revised optimistic, most probable, and pessimistic times for crashed activities B, F, J, and K, a revised variance in the project completion time can be found. Using this result, a revised probability of a 40-week completion time can be computed.

Answers to Questions for Quantitative Methods in Practice

1. The role of the investment banker in building projects is to develop a method of financing that will result in the owner receiving the necessary funds in a timely manner.

2. The major function of the hospital's investment banker is to arrange the timing of the financing in such a way that the proceeds of the bond issue can be made available within the time limit of the guaranteed-price construction bid.

3. Scheduled project completion time of 29.14 weeks. The activity schedule is shown below. Note that there are two critical paths: K-L-M-N-P-Q-R-S-U-W (the one shown in the application) and K-L-M-N-P-Q-R-S-U-V.

Activity	Earliest Start	Latest Start	Earliest Finish	Latest Finish	Slack	Critical Activity
A	0	11.00	4	15.00	11.00	
B	0	17.50	3	20.50	17.50	
C	0	18.00	2	20.00	18.00	
D	0	6.00	8	14.00	6.00	
E	4	15.00	8	19.00	11.00	
F	2	20.00	3	21.00	18.00	
G	8	14.00	12	18.00	6.00	
H	12	18.00	14	20.00	6.00	
I	8	19.00	10	21.00	11.00	
J	3	20.50	3.5	21.00	17.50	
K	0	0	20	20.00	0.00	Yes
L	20	20.00	21	21.00	0.00	Yes
M	21	21.00	22	22.00	0.00	Yes
N	22	22.00	21.14	22.14	0.00	Yes
O	22	23.86	22.28	24.14	1.86	
P	22.14	22.14	23.14	23.14	0.00	Yes
Q	23.14	23.14	24.14	24.14	0.00	Yes
R	24.14	24.14	24.14	26.14	0.00	Yes
S	26.14	26.14	26.14	26.14	0.00	Yes
T	26.14	29.00	29.00	29.14	2.86	
U	26.14	26.14	26.14	29.14	0.00	Yes
V	29.14	29.14	29.14	29.14	0.00	Yes
W	29.14	29.14	29.14	29.14	0.00	Yes

Chapter 14
Inventory Management: Independent Demand

Learning Objectives

1. Learn where inventory costs occur and why it is important for managers to make good inventory policy decisions.

2. Learn the economic order quantity (EOQ) model.

3. Know how to develop total cost models for specific inventory systems.

4. Be able to use the total cost model to make how-much-to-order and when-to-order decisions.

5. Extend the basic approach of the EOQ model to inventory systems involving production lot size, planned shortages, and quantity discounts.

6. Be able to make inventory decisions for single-period inventory models.

7. Know how to make order quantity and reorder point decisions when demand must be described by a probability distribution.

8. Learn about lead time demand distributions and how they can be used to meet acceptable service levels.

9. Be able to develop order quantity decisions for periodic review inventory systems.

10. Understand the following terms:

inventory holding costs	backorder
cost of capital	quantity discounts
ordering costs	goodwill costs
economic order quantity (EOQ)	independent demand
constant demand rate	probabilistic demand
reorder point	lead time demand distribution
lead time	service level
lead time demand	single-period inventory model
cycle time	periodic review
safety stock	

Solutions

1. a. $$Q^* = \sqrt{\frac{2DC_0}{C_h}} = \sqrt{\frac{2(3600)(20)}{0.25(3)}} = 438.18$$

   b. $$r = dm = \frac{3600}{250}(5) = 72$$

   c. $$T = \frac{250Q^*}{D} = \frac{250(438.18)}{3600} = 30.43 \; days$$

   d.

   $$TC = \frac{1}{2}QC_h + \frac{D}{Q}C_0$$
   $$= \frac{1}{2}(438.18)(0.25)(3) + \frac{3600}{438.18}(20) = \$328.63$$

2. Annual Holding Cost

   $$\frac{1}{2}QC_h = \frac{1}{2}(438.18)(0.25)(3) = \$164.32$$

   Annual Ordering Cost

   $$\frac{D}{Q}C_0 = \frac{3600}{438.18}(20) = 164.32$$
   $$Total \; Cost = \$328.64$$

3. $$Q^* = \sqrt{\frac{2DC_0}{C_h}} = \sqrt{\frac{2(5000)(32)}{2}} = 400$$

   $$d = \frac{D}{250} = \frac{5000}{250} = 20 \; units \; per \; day$$

   a. $r = dm = 20(5) = 100$

   Since $r \le Q^*$, both inventory position and inventory on hand equal 100.

   b. $r = dm = 20(15) = 300$

   Since $r \le Q^*$, both inventory position and inventory on hand equal 300.

   c. $r = dm = 20(25) = 500$

   Inventory position reorder point = 500. One order of $Q^* = 400$ is outstanding. The on-hand inventory reorder point is 500 - 400 = 100.

d. $r = dm = 20(45) = 900$

Inventory position reorder point = 900. Two orders of $Q^* = 400$ are outstanding. The on-hand inventory reorder point is 900 - 2(400) = 100.

4. a. $Q^* = \sqrt{\dfrac{2DC_0}{C_h}} = \sqrt{\dfrac{2(12,000)25}{(0.20)(2.50)}} = 1095.45$

   b. $r = dm = \dfrac{12000}{250}(5) = 240$

   c. $T = \dfrac{250Q^*}{D} = \dfrac{250(1095.45)}{12,000} = 22.82$

   d. Holding: $\dfrac{1}{2}QC_h = \dfrac{1}{2}(1095.45)(0.20)(2.50) = \$273.86$

   Ordering:

   $$\dfrac{D}{Q}C_0 = \dfrac{12,000}{1095.45}(25) = 273.86$$
   $$\text{Total Cost} = \$457.72$$

5. For $Q = 1000$
   $$TC = 1/2(1000)(0.20)(2.50) + (12,000/1000)(25)$$
   $$= 250 + 300 = \$550$$

   The cost increase of using $Q = 1000$ is only $550 - $547.72 = $2.28. Thus the order quantity of 1000 is acceptable.

   $r = dm = \dfrac{12,000}{250}(5) = 240$ *(unchanged)*

6. a. $D = 12 \times 20 = 240$

   $Q^* = \sqrt{\dfrac{2DC_0}{C_h}} = \sqrt{\dfrac{2(240)(70)}{0.22(600)}} = 15.95$

   b. Holding: $\dfrac{1}{2}QC_h = \dfrac{1}{2}(15.95)(0.22)(600) = \$1,053.00$

   Ordering: $\dfrac{D}{Q}C_0 = \dfrac{240}{15.95}(70) = \$1,053.00$
   $$\text{Total Cost} = \$2,106.00$$

c. $\dfrac{D}{Q} = \dfrac{240}{15.95} = 15.04$

d. $T = \dfrac{250Q}{D} = \dfrac{250(240)}{15.95} = 16.62 \; days$

7. $Q^{\bullet} = \sqrt{\dfrac{2DC_0}{C_h}} = \sqrt{\dfrac{2DC_0}{IC}} \qquad Q' = \sqrt{\dfrac{2DC_0}{I'C}}$

Where Q' is the revised order quantity for the new carrying charge I'. Thus

$$Q'/Q^{\bullet} = \dfrac{\sqrt{2DC_0/I'C}}{\sqrt{2DC_0/IC}} = \sqrt{\dfrac{I}{I'}}$$

$$\therefore Q' = \sqrt{\dfrac{I}{I'}} Q^{\bullet}$$

$$Q' = \sqrt{\dfrac{0.22}{0.27}} \, (80) = 72$$

8. Annual Demand D = (5/month)(12 months) = 60
Ordering Cost = Fixed Cost per class = \$22,000
Holding Cost = (\$1,600/month)(12 months)
      = \$19,200 per year for one driver

$$Q^{\bullet} = \sqrt{\dfrac{2DC_0}{C_h}} = \sqrt{\dfrac{2(60)(22,000)}{(19,200)}} = 11.73$$

Use 12 as the class size.

$$\dfrac{D}{Q^{\bullet}} = \dfrac{60}{12} = 5 \; \text{classes per year}$$

Driver holding cost = $1/2QC_h$ = 1/2(12)(19,200) = \$115,200
Class holding cost = $(D/Q)C_0$ = (60/12)(22,000) = 110,000
                          Total Cost = \$225,200

9. a. $Q^{\bullet} = \sqrt{\dfrac{2DC_0}{C_h}} = \sqrt{\dfrac{2(5000)(80)}{(0.25)(20)}} = 400$

b. $r = dm = \dfrac{5000}{250} (12) = 240$

c. $r = dm = \dfrac{5000}{250}(35) = 700$

d. Since $r = 700$ and $Q^* = 400$, one order will be outstanding when the reorder point is reached. Thus the inventory on hand at the time of reorder will be $700 - 400 = 300$.

10. This is a production lot size model. However, the operation is only six months rather than a full year. The basis for analysis may be for periods of one month, 6 months, or a full year. The inventory policy will be the same. In the following analysis we use a monthly basis.

$$Q^* = \sqrt{\dfrac{2DC_0}{1 - D/P)C_h}} = \sqrt{\dfrac{2(1000)(150)}{\left(1 - \dfrac{1000}{4000}\right)(0.02)(10)}} = 1414.21$$

$$T = \dfrac{20Q}{D} = \dfrac{20(1414.21)}{1000} = 28.28 \ days$$

$$\text{Production run length} = \dfrac{Q}{P/20} = \dfrac{1414.21}{4000/20} = 7.07 \ days$$

11. $$Q^* = \sqrt{\dfrac{2DC_0}{(1 - D/P)C_h}} = \sqrt{\dfrac{2(6400)(100)}{\left(1 - \dfrac{6400}{P}\right)2}}$$

$P = 8,000$	$Q^* = 1789$
$P = 10,000$	$Q^* = 1333$
$P = 32,000$	$Q^* = 894$
$P = 100,000$	$Q^* = 827$

EOQ Model:

$$Q^* = \sqrt{\dfrac{2DC_0}{C_h}} = \sqrt{\dfrac{2(6400)100}{2}} = 800$$

a. Production Lot Size Q^* is always greater than EOQ Q^* model with the same D, C_0, and C_h values.

b. As the production rate P increases, the recommended Q^* decreases, but always remains greater than the EOQ Q^*.

12. $$Q^* = \sqrt{\dfrac{2DC_0}{1 - D/P)C_h}} = \sqrt{\dfrac{2(2000)300}{\left(1 - \dfrac{2000}{8000}\right)1.60}} = 1000$$

Current total cost using $Q = 500$ is as follows:

$$TC = \frac{1}{2}(1 - D/P)QC_h + D/QC_0$$

$$= \frac{1}{2}\left(1 - \frac{2000}{8000}\right)500(1.60) + \frac{2000}{500}300$$

$$= 300 + 1200 = \$1500$$

Proposed Total Cost using $Q^* = 1000$ is as follows:

$$TC = \frac{1}{2}\left(1 - \frac{2000}{8000}\right)1000(160) + \frac{2000}{1000}300$$

$$= 600 + 600 = \$1200.$$

Savings of \$300/year

$300/1500 = 20\%$ of current policy.

$\therefore$ Make change to $Q^* = 1000$.

13.a.
$$Q^* = \sqrt{\frac{2DC_0}{(1 - D/P)C_h}} = \sqrt{\frac{2(7000)(150)}{(1 - 7200/25000)(0.18)(14.50)}} = 1078.12$$

b. Number of production runs $= \dfrac{D}{Q^*} = \dfrac{7200}{1078.12} = 6.68$

c. $T = \dfrac{250Q}{D} = \dfrac{250(1078.12)}{7200} = 37.43 \ days$

d. Production run length $= \dfrac{Q}{P/250} = \dfrac{1078.12}{25000/250} = 10.78 \ days$

e. Maximum Inventory

$$\left(1 - \frac{D}{P}\right)Q$$

$$= \left(1 - \frac{7200}{25000}\right)(1078.12) = 767.62$$

f. Holding Cost

$$\frac{1}{2}\left(1 - \frac{D}{P}\right)QC_h$$

$$= \frac{1}{2}\left(1 - \frac{7200}{25000}\right)(1078.12)(0.18)(14.50)$$

$$= \$1001.74$$

Ordering cost $\quad = \dfrac{D}{Q}C_0 = \dfrac{7200}{1078.12}(150) = \$1001.74$

Total Cost $\quad = \$2,003.48$

g. $\quad r = dm = \left(\dfrac{D}{250}\right)m = \dfrac{7200}{250}(15) = 432$

14. $\quad C$ = current cost per unit
$\quad C' = 1.23\, C$ new cost per unit

$$Q^* = \sqrt{\dfrac{2DC_0}{(1 - D/P)C_h}} = \sqrt{\dfrac{2DC_0}{(1 - D/P)IC}} = 5000$$

Let Q' = new optimal production lot size

$$Q' = \sqrt{\dfrac{2DC_0}{(1 - D/P)IC'}}$$

$$\dfrac{Q'}{Q^*} = \dfrac{\sqrt{\dfrac{2DC_0}{(1 - D/P)IC'}}}{\sqrt{\dfrac{2DC_0}{(1 - D/P)IC}}} = \dfrac{\sqrt{\dfrac{1}{C'}}}{\sqrt{\dfrac{1}{C}}} = \sqrt{\dfrac{C}{C'}}$$

$$= \sqrt{\dfrac{C}{1.23C}} = \sqrt{\dfrac{1}{1.23}} = 0.9017$$

$\quad Q' = 0.9017(Q^*) = 0.9017(5000) = 4509$

15.a. $\quad Q^* = \sqrt{\dfrac{2DC_0}{C_h}\left(\dfrac{C_h + C_b}{C_b}\right)} = \sqrt{\dfrac{2(12000)(25)}{0.50}\left(\dfrac{0.50 + 5}{0.50}\right)} = 1148.91$

b. $\quad S^* = Q^*\left(\dfrac{C_h}{C_h + C_b}\right) = 1148.91\left(\dfrac{0.50}{0.50 + 5}\right) = 104.45$

c. $\quad$ Max inventory $= Q^* - S^* = 1044.46$

d. $\quad T = \dfrac{250Q^*}{D} = \dfrac{250(1148.91)}{12000} = 23.94$

e.   Holding $\dfrac{(Q - S)^2}{2Q} C_h = \$237.38$

     Ordering $\dfrac{D}{Q} C_0 = 261.12$

     Backorder $\dfrac{S^2}{2Q} C_b = 23.74$

Total Cost $\$522.24$

The total cost for the EOQ model in problem 4 was $547.72. Allowing backorders reduces the total cost.

16. $r = dm = \left(\dfrac{12000}{250} \right) 5 = 240$

With backorder allowed the reorder point should be revised to

     $r = dm - S = 240 - 104.45 = 135.55$

The reorder point will be smaller when backorders are allowed.

17.   EOQ Model

$$Q^* = \sqrt{\dfrac{2DC_0}{C_h}} = \sqrt{\dfrac{2(800)(150)}{3}} = 282.84$$

Total Cost

$$= \dfrac{1}{2} QC_h + \dfrac{D}{Q} C_0$$

$$= \left(\dfrac{282.84}{2} \right) 3 + \dfrac{800}{282.84} (150) = \$848.53$$

Planned Shortage Model

$$Q^* = \sqrt{\dfrac{2DC_0}{C_h} \left(\dfrac{C_h + C_b}{C_b} \right)} = \sqrt{\dfrac{2(800)(150)}{3} \left(\dfrac{3 + 20}{20} \right)} = 303.32$$

$$S^* = Q^* \left(\dfrac{C_h}{C_h + C_b} \right) = (303.32) \left(\dfrac{3}{3 + 20} \right) = 39.56$$

Total Cost $= \dfrac{(Q - S)^2}{2Q} C_h + \dfrac{D}{Q} C_0 + \dfrac{S^2}{2Q} C_b$

                     $= 344.02 + 395.63 + 51.60 = \$791.25$

Cost Reduction with Backorders allowed

$848.53 - 791.25 = \$57.28$ (6.75%)

Both constraints are satisfied:

1. $\quad \dfrac{S}{Q} = \dfrac{39.56}{303.32} = 0.13$

Only 13% of units will be backordered.

2. $\quad$ Length of backorder period $= \dfrac{S}{d} = \dfrac{39.56}{800/250} = 12.4$ *days*

18. $\quad$ Reorder points:

$\quad$ EOQ Model: $\qquad\qquad r = dm = \dfrac{800}{250}(20) = 64$

$\quad$ Backorder Model: $\qquad r = dm - S = 24.44$

19.a. $\qquad\qquad Q^* = \sqrt{\dfrac{2DC_0}{C_h}} = \sqrt{\dfrac{2(480)15}{(0.20)(60)}} = 34.64$

$\quad$ Total Cost:

$$= \dfrac{1}{2}QC_h + \dfrac{D}{Q}C_0$$
$$= 207.85 + 207.85 = \$415.70$$

b. $\qquad\qquad Q^* = \sqrt{\dfrac{2DC_0}{C_h}\left(\dfrac{C_h + C_b}{C_b}\right)} = \sqrt{\dfrac{2(480)(15)}{0.20(60)}\left(\dfrac{0.20(60) + 45}{45}\right)} = 39$

$$S^* = Q^*\left(\dfrac{C_h}{C_h + C_b}\right) = 8.21$$

$\quad$ Total Cost:

$$= \dfrac{(Q - S)^2}{2}C_h + \dfrac{D}{Q}C_0 + \dfrac{S^2}{2Q}C_b$$
$$= 145.80 + 184.68 + 38.88 = \$369.36$$

c. $\quad$ Length of backorder period $= \dfrac{S}{d} = \dfrac{8.21}{480/300} = 5.13$ *days*

d. $\quad$ Backorder case since the maximum wait is only 5.13 days and the cost savings is

$\quad$ $415.70 - 369.36 = \$46.34$ (11.1%)

e.   EOQ: $r = dm = \left(\dfrac{480}{300}\right)6 = 9.6$

Backorder: $r = dm - S = 1.39$

20. $Q = \sqrt{\dfrac{2DC_0}{C_h}}$

$Q_1 = \sqrt{\dfrac{2(120)(20)}{0.25(30)}} = 25.30$ $Q_1 = 25$

$Q_2 = \sqrt{\dfrac{2(120)(20)}{0.25(28.5)}} = 25.96$ $Q_2 = 50$ to obtain 5% discount

$Q_3 = \sqrt{\dfrac{2(120)(20)}{0.25(27)}} = 26.67$ $Q_3 = 100$ to obtain 10% discount

Category	Unit Cost	Order Quantity	Holding Cost	Order Cost	Purchase Cost	Total Cost
1	30.00	25	93.75	96	3600	$3,789.75
2	28.50	50	178.13	48	3420	$3,646.13
3	27.00	100	337.50	24	3240	$3,601.50

$Q = 100$ to obtain the lowest total cost.
The 10% discount is worthwhile.

21. $Q = \sqrt{\dfrac{2DC_0}{C_h}}$

$Q_1 = \sqrt{\dfrac{2(500)(\$40)}{0.20(10)}} = 141.42$

$Q_2 = \sqrt{\dfrac{2(500)(\$40)}{0.20(9.7)}} = 143.59$

Since Q_1 is over its limit of 99 units, Q_1 cannot be optimal (see problem 23). Use $Q_2 = 143.59$ as the optimal order quantity.
Total Cost

$$= \dfrac{1}{2}QC_h + \dfrac{D}{Q}C_0 + DC$$
$$= 139.28 + 139.28 + 4,850.00 = \$5,128.56$$

22. $D = 4(500) = 2,000$ per year
       $C_0 = \$30$
       $I = 0.20$
       $C = \$28$

Annual cost of current policy: ($Q = 500$ and $C = \$28$)

$$TC = 1/2(Q)(C_h) + (D/Q)C_0 + DC$$
$$= 1/2(500)(0.2)(28) + (2000/500)(30) + 2000(28)$$
$$= 1400 + 120 + 56,000 = 57,520$$

Evaluation of Quantity Discounts

$$Q^* = \sqrt{\frac{2DC_0}{C_h}}$$

Order Quantity	C_h	Q_*	Q to obtain Discount	TC
0-99	(0.20)(36) = 7.20	129	*	—
100-199	(0.20)(32) = 6.40	137	137	64,876
200-299	(0.20)(30) = 6.00	141	200	60,900
300 or more	(0.20)(28) = 5.60	146	300	57,040

*Cannot be optimal since $Q^* > 99$.

Reduce Q to 300 pairs/order. Annual savings is \$480; note that shoes will still be purchased at the lowest possible cost (\$28/pair).

23. $$TC = \frac{1}{2}QIC + \frac{D}{Q}C_0 + DC$$

At a specific Q (and given I, D, and C_0), since C of category 2 is less than C of category 1, the TC for 2 is less than TC for 1. Thus

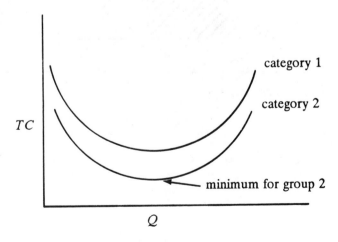

$\therefore$ If the minimum cost solution for category 2 is feasible, there is no need to search category 1. From the graph we can see that all *TC* values of category 1 exceed the minimum cost solution of category 2.

24.a.

$$c_0 = 1.50$$
$$c_h = 3.00 - 1.50 = 1.50$$
$$P\,(D \le Q^*) = \frac{c_u}{c_u + c_0} = \frac{1.50}{1.50 + 1.50} = 0.50$$

Order the mean demand of 500

b.

$$c_0 = 1.50 - 1.00 = 0.50$$
$$P\,(D \le Q^*) = \frac{c_u}{c_u + c_0} = \frac{1.50}{1.50 + 0.50} = 0.75$$

For area 0.25, $z = 0.67$
$$Q = 500 + 0.67(120) = 580.4$$

25.a.

$$c_0 = 80 - 50 = 30$$
$$c_u = 125 - 80 = 45$$
$$P\,(D \le Q^*) = \frac{c_u}{c_u + c_0} = \frac{45}{45 + 30} = 0.60$$

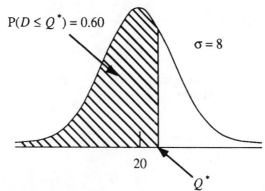

For an area of 0.60 below Q^*, $z = 0.25$

$$Q^* = 20 + 0.25(8) = 22$$

b. $P(\text{Sell All}) = P(D \ge Q^* = 1 - 0.60 = 0.40$

26.a.

$$c_0 = 0.35$$
$$c_u = 0.50 - 0.35 = 0.15$$
$$P(D \leq Q^*) = \frac{c_u}{c_u + c_0} = \frac{0.15}{0.15 + 0.35} = 0.30$$

For 0.30 area in the left tail, $z = -0.53$

$$Q = 450 - 0.53(100) = 397$$

b. $P(D \geq 397) = 1 - 0.30 = 0.70$

c.
$$c_u = \text{Lost Profit} + \text{Goodwill Cost}$$
$$= (0.50 - 0.35) + 0.50 = 0.65$$
$$P(D \leq Q^*) = \frac{c_u}{c_u + c_0} = \frac{0.65}{0.65 + 0.35} = 0.65$$

For 0.65 area to the left of Q^*, $z = 0.39$

$$Q = 450 + 0.39(100) = 489$$
$$P(D \geq 489) = 1 - 0.65 = 0.35$$

27.a.

$$c_0 = 1.19 - 1.00 = 0.19$$
$$c_u = 1.65 - 1.19 = 0.46$$
$$P(D \leq Q^*) = \frac{c_u}{c_u + c_0} = \frac{0.46}{0.46 + 0.19} = 0.7077$$

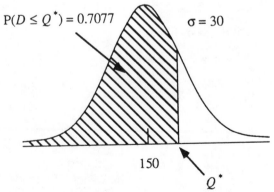

For a 0.7077 area below Q^*, $z = 0.55$

$$Q^* = 150 + 0.55(30) = 166.5$$

b.　$P(\text{Stockout}) = P(D \geq Q^*) = 1 - 0.7077 = 0.2923$

c.

$$c_0 = 1.19 - 0.25 = 0.94$$

$$P(D \leq Q^*) = \frac{c_u}{c_u + c_0} = \frac{0.46}{0.46 + 0.94} = 0.3286$$

For a 0.3286 area in the left tail, $z = -0.45$

$$Q^* = 150 - 0.45(30) = 136.50$$

The higher rebate increases the quantity that the supermarket should order.

28.a.

$$c_0 = 8 - 5 = 3$$
$$c_u = 10 - 8 = 2$$
$$P(D \leq Q^*) = \frac{c_u}{c_u + c_0} = \frac{2}{2 + 3} = 0.40$$

Q^* is 40% of way between 700 and 800

$$Q^* = 200 + 0.40(600) = 440$$

b.　$P(\text{stockout}) = P(D \geq Q^*) = 1 - 0.40 = 0.60$

c.　$P(D \leq Q^*) = 0.85$　$P(\text{Stockout}) = 0.15$

$$Q^* = 200 + 0.85(600) = 710$$

d.　Let g = goodwill cost

$$c_u = \text{lost profit} + \text{goodwill cost}$$

$$= (10 - 8) + g = 2 + g$$

$$P(D \leq Q^*) = \frac{c_u}{c_u + c_0} = 0.85$$

Solve for $c_u = 17$

$$c_u = 2 + g = 17$$
$$g = 15$$

29.a.　$r = dm = (200/250)15 = 12$

b.　$\dfrac{D}{Q} = \dfrac{200}{25} = 8$ orders/year

The limit of 1 stockout per year menas that
$$P(\text{Stockout/cycle}) = 1/8 = 0.125$$

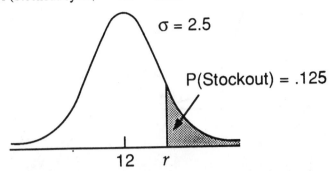

$\sigma = 2.5$

$P(\text{Stockout}) = .125$

12   r

For area in tail $= 0.125$, $z = 1.15$

$$z = \frac{r - 12}{2.5} = 1.15$$

or

$$r = 12 + 1.15(2.5) = 14.875 \approx 15$$

c.   Safety Stock $= 3$ units
Added Cost $= 3(\$5) = \$15/\text{year}$

30.a. $P(\text{Stockout/cycle}) = 2/8 = 0.25$

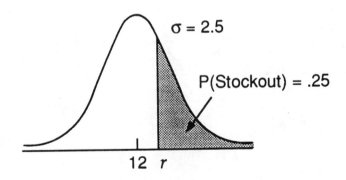

$\sigma = 2.5$

$P(\text{Stockout}) = .25$

12 r

For area $= 0.25$, $z = 0.67$

$$z = \frac{r - 12}{2.5} = 0.67$$

or

$$r = 12 + 0.67(2.5) = 13.675 \approx 14$$

b.

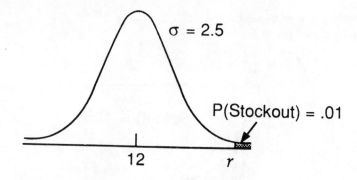

For an area in tail = 0.01, z = 2.33

$$r = 12 + 2.33(2.5) = 17.825 \approx 18$$

c. Safety Stock (a) = 14 - 12 = 2   Cost = 2($5) = $10
    Safety Stock (b) = 18 - 12 = 6   Cost = 6($5) = $30

31.a. $Q^* = \sqrt{\dfrac{2DC_0}{C_h}} = \sqrt{\dfrac{2(1000)(25.5)}{8}} = 79.84$

b.

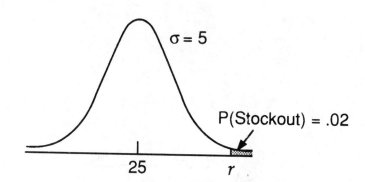

For area in tail = 0.02, z = 2.05

r = 25 + 2.05(5) = 35.3 ≈ 35
Safety Stock = 35 - 25 = 10
Safety Stock Cost = (10)($8) = $80/year

c.

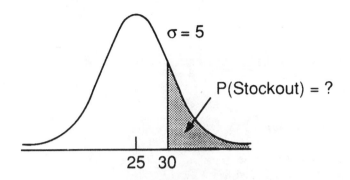

$$z = \frac{r - 25}{5} = \frac{30 - 25}{5} = 1$$

Area in tail at $z = 1$ is $0.5000 - 0.3413 = 0.1587$

P(Stockout/cycle) $= 0.1587$
Number of Stockouts/year $= 0.1587$ (Number of Orders)
$= 0.1587 \, D/Q = 2$

32.a. $Q^* = \sqrt{\dfrac{2DC_0}{C_h}} = \sqrt{\dfrac{2(300)(5)}{(0.15)(20)}} = 31.62$

b. $\dfrac{D}{Q^*} = 9.49$ orders per year

P(Stockout) $= \dfrac{2}{D/Q^*} = 0.2108$

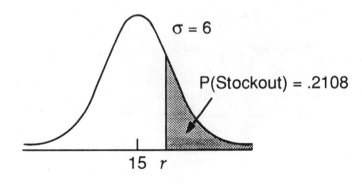

For area in tail $= 0.2108$, $z = 0.81$
$$r = 15 + 0.81(6) = 19.86 \approx 20$$

c.   Safety Stock $= 20 - 15 = 5$
Safety Stock Cost $= 0.5(0.15)(20) = \$15$

33.a. $1/52 = 0.0192$

b. $M = \mu + z\sigma = 60 + 2.07(12) = 85$

c. $M = 35 + (0.9808)(85\text{-}35) = 84$

34.a. $P(\text{Stockout}) = 0.01 \quad z = 2.33$

      $r = \mu + z\sigma = 150 + 2.33(40) = 243$

b.   Safety Stock $= 243 - 150 = 93$ units
Annual Cost $= 93(0.20)(2.95) = \$54.87$

c. $M = \mu + z\sigma = 450 + 2.33(70) = 613$ units

d.   Safety Stock $= 613 - 450 = 163$ units
Annual Cost $= 163(0.20)(2.95) = \$96.17$

e.   The periodic review model is more expensive ($96.17 - $54.87) = $41.30 per year. However, this added cost may be worth the advantage of coordinating orders for multi products. Go with the periodic review system.

f.   Unit Cost = $295   Annual Difference = $4,130
Use continuous review for the more expensive items.

35.a. $z = \dfrac{24 - 18}{6} = 1.00$

      From z table, $P(\text{Stockout}) = 0.5000 - 0.3413 = 0.1587$

b.   For 2.5%, $z = 1.96$
$M = \mu + z\sigma = 18 + 1.96(6) = 29.76$
Use $M = 30$.
The manager should have ordered $Q = 30 - 8 = 22$ units.

36.a. $\mu =$ Week 1 demand + Week 2 demand + Lead Time demand
      $= 16 + 16 + 8 = 40$

b. $\sigma^2 =$ Var (Week 1) + Var (Week 2) + Var (Lead Time)
      $= 25 + 25 + 12.25 = 62.25$

      $\sigma = \sqrt{62.25} = 7.9$ units

c.   26 orders per year
$P(\text{Stockout}) = 1/26 = 0.0385$ per replenishment
$z = 1.77$
$M = \mu + z\sigma = 40 + 1.77(7.9) = 54$

d. $54 - 18 = 36$

Case Problem

1. Holding Cost

Cost of capital		14.0%
Taxes/Insurance (24,000/600,000)		4.0%
Shrinkage (9,000/600,000)		1.5%
Warehouse overhead (15,000/600,000)		2.5%
	Annual rate	22.0%

2. Ordering Cost

2 hours at $28.00		$56.00
Other expenses (2,375/125)		19.00
	Cost per order	$75.00

3. Set-up Cost

> 8 Hours at $50.00
> $400 per set-up

4. & 5.
   a. Order from Supplier - EOQ model

$$C_h = IC = 0.22(\$18.00) = \$3.96$$

$$Q^* = \sqrt{\frac{2DC_0}{C_h}} = \sqrt{\frac{2(3,200)75}{3.96}} = 348 \; units$$

Number of orders $= D/Q = 9.2/year$

Cycle time $= \dfrac{250(Q)}{D} = \dfrac{250(348)}{3200} = 27 \; days$

Reorder Point:

$$P(\text{Stockout}) = \frac{1}{9.2} = 0.11$$

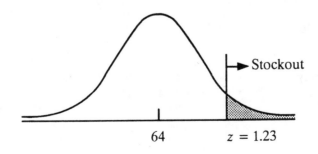

64          $z = 1.23$

$r = 64 + 1.23(10) = 76$

Safety stock	$= 76 - 64 = 12$
Maximum inventory	$= Q + 12 = 360$
Average inventory	$= Q/2 + 12 = 186$
Annual holding cost	$= 186(3.96) = \$737$
Annual ordering cost	$= 9.2(75) = \$690$
Purchase cost	$= 3,200(\$18) = \$57,600$
Total annual cost	$= \$59,027$

b. Manufacture - Production lot size model

$$C_h = IC = 0.22(\$17.00) = \$3.74$$
$$P = 1000(12) = 12,000/\text{year}$$

Note: The five-month capacity of 5,000 units is sufficient to handle annual demand of 3,200 units.

$$Q^* = \sqrt{\frac{2DC_0}{(1 - D/P)C_h}} = \sqrt{\frac{2(3200)(400)}{(1 - 3200/12000)3.74}} = 966$$

Number of production runs $= D/Q = 3.3/\text{year}$

$$\text{Cycle Time} = \frac{250(Q)}{D} = \frac{250(966)}{3200} = 75 \text{ days}$$

Reorder point:

$$P(\text{Stockout}) = \frac{1}{3.3} = 0.30$$

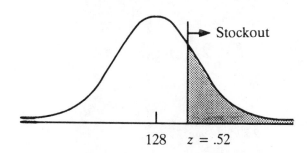

$$128 \quad z = .52$$

$r = 128 + 0.52(20) = 138$

Safety stock	$= 138 - 128 = 10$
Maximum inventory	$= (1 - 3200/12000)966 + 10 = 718$
Annual holding cost	$= 364(3.74) = \$1361$
Annual set up cost	$= 3.3(400) = \$1320$
Manufacturing cost	$= 57,081$

6.   Recommend manufacturing the part

Savings: $59,027 - 57,081 = $1,946 (3.3%)

Chapter 15
Inventory Management:
Dependent Demand

Learning Objectives

1. Understand the difference between independent and dependent demand for inventory items.

2. Know the inputs to a Material Requirements Planning (MRP) system, the master production schedule, the bill of materials, and the inventory file.

3. Be able to construct an MRP worksheet given information concerning lead time, lot size, safety stock, and gross requirements.

4. Understand the difference between the fixed lot size and lot for lot rules. Be able to explain the effect of these rules on set up and holding costs.

5. Understand how safety stock affects the computation of net requirements in developing an MRP worksheet.

6. Know what a product structure tree is and understand how lead times for items higher up in the tree influence the timing of order releases for items lower in the tree.

Solutions

1. a.

WHEEL SUBASSEMBLY	Lead Time: 2		Week					
Lot Size: 400	Safety Stock: 0		1	2	3	4	5	6
Gross Requirements				250		300		260
Scheduled Receipts				400				
Projected Balance		80	80	230	230	330	330	70
Net Requirements						70		
Planned Order Receipts						400		
Planned Order Releases				400				

b.

WHEEL SUBASSEMBLY	Lead Time: 2		Week					
Lot Size: 400	Safety Stock: 0		1	2	3	4	5	6
Gross Requirements				250		300		260
Scheduled Receipts				400				
Projected Balance		180	180	330	330	30	30	170
Net Requirements								230
Planned Order Receipts								400
Planned Order Releases						400		

c.

WHEEL SUBASSEMBLY	Lead Time: 2		Week					
Lot Size: 500	Safety Stock: 0		1	2	3	4	5	6
Gross Requirements				250		300		260
Scheduled Receipts				400				
Projected Balance		80	80	230	230	430	430	170
Net Requirements						70		
Planned Order Receipts						500		
Planned Order Releases				500				

2. a.

WHEEL SUBASSEMBLY Lead Time: 1		Week					
Lot Size: 400 Safety Stock: 0		1	2	3	4	5	6
Gross Requirements			250		300		260
Scheduled Receipts			400				
Projected Balance	80	80	230	230	330	330	70
Net Requirements					70		
Planned Order Receipts					400		
Planned Order Releases				400			

b.

WHEEL SUBASSEMBLY Lead Time: 3		Week					
Lot Size: 400 Safety Stock: 0		1	2	3	4	5	6
Gross Requirements			250		300		260
Scheduled Receipts			400				
Projected Balance	80	80	230	230	330	330	70
Net Requirements					70		
Planned Order Receipts					400		
Planned Order Releases		400					

c.   The different lead times have no effect on the inventory level. The projected balance is the same in parts a and b above.

3. a.

WHEEL SUBASSEMBLY Lead Time: 2		Week					
Lot for lot Safety Stock: 0		1	2	3	4	5	6
Gross Requirements			250		300		260
Scheduled Receipts			400				
Projected Balance	80	80	230	230	0	0	0
Net Requirements					70		260
Planned Order Receipts					70		260
Planned Order Releases			70		260		

b.

WHEEL SUBASSEMBLY Lead Time: 2		Week					
Lot for lot Safety Stock: 0		1	2	3	4	5	6
Gross Requirements			250		300		260
Scheduled Receipts			400				0
Projected Balance	180	180	330	330	30	30	230
Net Requirements							230
Planned Order Receipts							230
Planned Order Releases					230		

4. a.

DRAWER Lead Time: 1		Week					
Lot Size: 500 Safety Stock: 0		1	2	3	4	5	6
Gross Requirements		450		300	250		500
Scheduled Receipts		500					
Projected Balance	0	50	50	250	0	0	0
Net Requirements				250			500
Planned Order Receipts				500			500
Planned Order Releases			500			500	

b.

DRAWER Lot Size: 500	Lead Time: 1 Safety Stock: 0		Week					
			1	2	3	4	5	6
Gross Requirements			450		300	250		500
Scheduled Receipts			500					
Projected Balance		120	170	170	370	120	120	120
Net Requirements					130			380
Planned Order Receipts					500			500
Planned Order Releases				500			500	

c.

Drawer Lot Size: 800	Lead Time: 1 Safety Stock: 0		Week					
			1	2	3	4	5	6
Gross Requirements			450		300	250		500
Scheduled Receipts			500					
Projected Balance		0	50	50	550	300	300	600
Net Requirements					250			200
Planned Order Receipts					800			800
Planned Order Releases				800			800	

d. The inventory holding cost will be higher with the larger lot size. The projected balance in part c is larger than in part a for weeks 3 through 6 and the same in weeks 1 and 2. The lot size in part c will, over the long run, result in fewer production runs and, hence, fewer setups. It would be preferred when setup cost is high relative to inventory holding cost.

5.

DRAWER Lead Time: 2		Week					
Lot Size: 500 Safety Stock: 0		1	2	3	4	5	6
Gross Requirements		450		300	250		500
Scheduled Receipts		500					
Projected Balance	0	50	50	250	0	0	0
Net Requirements				250			500
Planned Order Receipts				500			500
Planned Order Releases		500			500		

6. a.

DRAWER Lead Time: 1		Week					
Lot for lot Safety Stock: 0		1	2	3	4	5	6
Gross Requirements		450		300	250		500
Scheduled Receipts		500					
Projected Balance	0	50	50	0	0	0	0
Net Requirements				250	250		500
Planned Order Receipts				250	250		500
Planned Order Releases			250	250		500	

b.

DRAWER Lead Time: 1		Week					
Lot for lot Safety Stock: 0		1	2	3	4	5	6
Gross Requirements		450		300	250		500
Scheduled Receipts		500					
Projected Balance	120	170	170	0	0	0	0
Net Requirements				130	250		500
Planned Order Receipts				130	250		500
Planned Order Releases			130	250		500	

c. The net requirements in a period are equal to the planned order releases in the period one lead time earlier.

d. The lot for lot rule results in a lower inventory holding cost. Note that the inventory balance is zero for weeks 3,4,5, and 6 using this rule. It is 370, 120, 120, and 120 for the same weeks when a fixed lot size of 500 is used (See 4b where the beginning projected balance is also 120).

7. a.

DRAWER	Lead Time: 1	Week					
Lot size: 500	Safety Stock: 30	1	2	3	4	5	6
Gross Requirements		450		300	250		500
Scheduled Receipts		500					
Projected Balance	0	50	50	250	500	500	500
Net Requirements				280	30		30
Planned Order Receipts				500	500		500
Planned Order Releases			500	500		500	

It causes larger projected balances and, therefore, increases the inventory holding cost.

b.

DRAWER	Lead Time: 1	Week					
Lot size: 500	Safety Stock: 100	1	2	3	4	5	6
Gross Requirements		450		300	250		500
Scheduled Receipts		500					
Projected Balance	120	170	170	370	120	120	120
Net Requirements				230			480
Planned Order Receipts				500			500
Planned Order Releases			500			500	

The projected balances are the same as in 4b so there would be no increase in holding cost. However, over a longer planning period we could expect holding costs to be higher; the projected balance could not drop below 100.

8. a.

BASE	Lead Time: 1	Week					
Lot size: 400	Safety Stock: 0	1	2	3	4	5	6
Gross Requirements		200	250	200	200	150	200
Scheduled Receipts		150					
Projected Balance	150	100	250	50	250	100	300
Net Requirements			150		150		100
Planned Order Receipts			400		400		400
Planned Order Releases		400		400		400	

b.

BASE	Lead Time: 1	Week					
Lot for lot	Safety Stock: 0	1	2	3	4	5	6
Gross Requirements		200	250	200	200	150	200
Scheduled Receipts		150					
Projected Balance	150	100	0	0	0	0	0
Net Requirements			150	200	200	150	200
Planned Order Receipts			150	200	200	150	200
Planned Order Releases		150	200	200	150	200	

c. The fixed lot size rule in part a results in higher inventory holding cost. If inventory holding costs are high, relative to setup costs, the lot for lot rule would be preferable. However, the fixed lot size rule of part a results in fewer production runs and less set up cost. For expensive items, holding costs will be high, thus the lot for lot rule is more desirable.

9. a.

BASE	Lead Time: 1	Week					
Lot size: 400	Safety Stock: 100	1	2	3	4	5	6
Gross Requirements		200	250	200	200	150	200
Scheduled Receipts		150					
Projected Balance	150	100	250	450	250	100	300
Net Requirements			250	50			200
Planned Order Receipts			400	400			400
Planned Order Releases		400	400			400	

b.

BASE	Lead Time: 1	Week					
Lot for lot	Safety Stock: 100	1	2	3	4	5	6
Gross Requirements		200	250	200	200	150	200
Scheduled Receipts		150					
Projected Balance	150	100	100	100	100	100	100
Net Requirements			250	200	200	150	200
Planned Order Receipts			250	200	200	150	200
Planned Order Releases		250	200	200	150	200	

c.   Safety stock increases inventory holding costs because it requires larger amounts of inventory on hand. Nevertheless, safety stock is often carried to avoid having to shut production down because of lack of components required in an assembly. This can happen when lead times fluctuate and/or there are defective parts found. Safety stock is often carried for end items because of variability in customer demand.

10.a.

B	Lead Time: 3	Week					
Lot size: 500	Safety Stock: 0	21	22	23	24	25	26
Gross Requirements			450		600		400
Scheduled Receipts			500				
Projected Balance	150	150	200	200	100	100	200
Net Requirements					400		300
Planned Order Receipts					500		500
Planned Order Releases		500		500			

b.

D	Lead Time: 1	Week			
Lot for lot	Safety Stock: 0	20	21	22	23
Gross Requirements			500		500
Scheduled Receipts					
Projected Balance	50	50	0	0	0
Net Requirements			450		500
Planned Order Receipts			450		500
Planned Order Releases		450		500	

11.a.

E	Lead Time: 1	Week					
Lot size: 300	Safety Stock: 0	11	12	13	14	15	16
Gross Requirements			250	200	280	250	230
Scheduled Receipts		200					
Projected Balance	80	280	30	130	150	200	270
Net Requirements				170	150	100	30
Planned Order Receipts				300	300	300	300
Planned Order Releases			300	300	300	300	

b.

B	Lead Time: 2	Week				
Lot size: 400	Safety Stock: 0	11	12	13	14	15
Gross Requirements			300	300	300	300
Scheduled Receipts						
Projected Balance	400	400	100	200	300	0
Net Requirements				200	100	
Planned Order Receipts				400	400	
Planned Order Releases		400	400			

c.

A	Lead Time: 1	Week				
Lot for lot	Safety Stock: 0	11	12	13	14	15
Gross Requirements			600	600	600	600
Scheduled Receipts						
Projected Balance	500	500	0	0	0	0
Net Requirements			100	600	600	600
Planned Order Receipts			100	600	600	600
Planned Order Releases		100	600	600	600	

12.a.

Gross requirement	1250
Engine assemblies on hand	450
Net requirement	800

b. Subtracting the lead times for the engine assembly (4 weeks) and the air cleaner subassembly (1 week), we see that we must plan for an order release in week 15.
The gross requirement for the air cleaner subassembly equals the net requirement for the engine assembly: 800 units. Since there is no inventory on hand and the lot for lot rule is being used, the order will be for 800 units.

c. The lead time for the filter housing is 2 weeks. So we must plan for an order release of 800 units in week 13.

13.a.   The net requirement for the wheel assemblies is 350 = 800 - 450. With a lead time of 2 weeks we have a planned order release for 350 wheel assemblies at the beginning of week 20.

    b.   The lead time for wheels is 1 week, so we must plan an order release at the beginning of week 19.

        There are 2 wheels required in each wheel assembly; thus the order must be for 700 = (350)(2) wheels.

    c.   The lead time for the blade assembly is 2 weeks, so the order must be released at the beginning of week 18. The gross requirement is for 350 blade assemblies, and 200 are on hand; thus, an order will be released for 150.

14.

Quantity of Lawn Spreaders to be produced:	3,000
Gross requirements, Base Assemblies:	3,000
Base Assemblies in inventory:	1,000
Net requirements, Base Assemblies:	2,000
Gross requirements, Wheel Subassemblies:	2,000
Wheel Subassemblies in inventory:	1,500
Net requirements, Wheel Subassemblies:	500
Gross Requirements, Tires:	1,000 (2 tires per wheel assembly)
Tires in inventory:	800
Net requirements, Tires:	200

15.

Complete order for Base Assemblies:	15
Minus lead time of Base Assemblies:	2
Place an order for Base Assemblies:	13
Complete order for Wheel Subassemblies:	13
Minus lead time of Wheel Subassemblies:	4
Place an order for Wheel Subassemblies:	9
Complete order for Tires:	9
Minus lead time of Tires:	5
Place an order for Tires:	4

Chapter 16
Waiting Line Models

Learning Objectives

1. Be able to identify where waiting line problems occur and realize why it is important to study these problems.

2. Know the difference between single-channel and multiple-channel waiting lines.

3. Understand how the Poisson distribution is used to describe arrivals and how the exponential distribution is used to describe services times.

4. Learn how to use formulas to identify operating characteristics of waiting lines.

5. Know how to incorporate economic considerations to arrive at decisions concerning the operation of a waiting line.

6. Understand how waiting line problems may be solved by simulation.

7. Understand the following terms:

queuing theory	mean service rate
queue	queue disicipline
single-channel	steady state
multiple-channel	utilization factor
mean arrival rate	operating characteristics

Solutions

1. a. $\lambda = 5(0.4) = 2$ per five minute period

   b. $P(x) = \dfrac{\lambda^x e^{-\lambda}}{x!} = \dfrac{2^x e^{-2}}{x!}$

x	$P(x)$
0	0.1353
1	0.2707
2	0.2707
3	0.1804

   c. $P(\text{Delay Problems}) = P(x > 3) = 1 - P(x \le 3) = 1 - 0.8571 = 0.1429$

2. a. $\mu = 0.6$ customers per minute

   $P(\text{service time} \le 1) = 1 - e^{-(0.6)1} = 0.4512$

   b. $P(\text{service time} \le 2) = 1 - e^{-(0.6)2} = 0.6988$

   c. $P(\text{service time} > 2) = 1 - 0.6988 = 0.3012$

3. a. $P_0 = 1 - \dfrac{\lambda}{\mu} = 1 - \dfrac{0.4}{0.6} = 0.3333$

   b. $L_q = \dfrac{\lambda^2}{\mu(\mu - \lambda)} = \dfrac{(0.4)^2}{0.6(0.6 - 0.4)} = 1.3333$

   c. $L = L_q + \dfrac{\lambda}{\mu} = 1.3333 + \dfrac{0.4}{0.6} = 2$

   d. $W_q = \dfrac{L_q}{\lambda} = \dfrac{1.3333}{0.4} = 3.3333$ min.

   e. $W = W_q + \dfrac{1}{\mu} = 3.3333 + \dfrac{1}{0.6} = 5$ min.

   f. $P_w = \dfrac{\lambda}{\mu} = \dfrac{0.4}{0.6} = 0.6667$

4. $$P_n = \left(\frac{\lambda}{\mu}\right)^n P_0 = \left(\frac{0.4}{0.6}\right)^n (0.3333)$$

n	P_n
0	0.3333
1	0.2222
2	0.1481
3	0.0988

$$P(n > 3) = 1 - P(n \leq 3) = 1 - 0.8024 = 0.1976$$

5. a. $$P_0 = 1 - \frac{\lambda}{\mu} = 1 - \frac{10}{12} = 0.1667$$

b. $$L_q = \frac{\lambda^2}{\mu(\mu - \lambda)} = \frac{10^2}{12(12 - 10)} = 4.1667$$

c. $$W_q = \frac{L_q}{\lambda} = 0.4167 \; hours$$

d. $$W = W_q + \frac{1}{\mu} = .5 \; hours \quad (30 \; minutes)$$

e. $$P_w = \frac{\lambda}{\mu} = \frac{10}{12} = 0.8333$$

6. a. $$P_0 = 1 - \frac{\lambda}{\mu} = 1 - \frac{12}{18} = 0.3333$$

b. $$L_q = \frac{\lambda^2}{\mu(\mu - \lambda)} = \frac{12^2}{18(18 - 12)} = 1.3333$$

c. $$W_q = \frac{L_q}{\lambda} = 0.1111 \; hours \quad (6.67 \; minutes)$$

d. $$P_w = \frac{\lambda}{\mu} = 0.6667$$

7. a. $L_q = \dfrac{\lambda^2}{\mu(\mu - \lambda)} = \dfrac{6^2}{8(8 - 6)} = 2.25$

$L = L_q + \dfrac{\lambda}{\mu} = 2.25 + \dfrac{6}{8} = 3$

b. $W_q = \dfrac{L_q}{\lambda} = 0.375 \ days \quad (3 \ hours)$

c. $W = W_q + \dfrac{1}{\mu} = 0.5 \ days$

8. $\lambda = 1 \ and \ \mu = 1.25$

$P_0 = 1 - \dfrac{\lambda}{\mu} = 1 - \dfrac{1}{1.25} = 0.20$

$L_q = \dfrac{\lambda^2}{\mu(\mu - \lambda)} = \dfrac{1}{1.25(0.25)} = 3.2$

$L = L_q + \dfrac{\lambda}{\mu} = 3.2 + \dfrac{1}{1.25} = 4$

$W_q = \dfrac{L_q}{\lambda} = \dfrac{3.2}{1} = 3.2 \ \text{min.}$

$W = W_q + \dfrac{1}{\mu} = 3.2 + \dfrac{1}{1.25} = 4 \ \text{min.}$

$P_w = \dfrac{\lambda}{\mu} = \dfrac{1}{1.25} = 0.80$

Even though the services rate is increased to $\mu = 1.25$, this system provides slightly poorer service due to the fact that arrivals are occurring at a higher rate. The average waiting times are identical, but there is a higher probability of waiting and the number waiting increases with the new system.

9. a. $P_0 = 1 - \dfrac{\lambda}{\mu} = 1 - \dfrac{2.2}{5} = 0.56$

b. $P_1 = \left(\dfrac{\lambda}{\mu}\right)P_0 = \dfrac{2.2}{5}(0.56) = 0.2464$

c. $P_2 = \left(\dfrac{\lambda}{\mu}\right)^2 P_0 = \left(\dfrac{2.2}{5}\right)^2 (0.56) = 0.1084$

d.　$P_3 = \left(\dfrac{\lambda}{\mu}\right)^3 P_0 = \left(\dfrac{2.2}{5}\right)^3 (0.56) = 0.0477$

e.　P(More than 2 waiting) = P(More than 3 are in system)
$$= 1 - (P_0 + P_1 + P_2 + P_3) = 1 - 0.9625 = 0.0375$$

f.　$L_q = \dfrac{\lambda^2}{\mu(\mu - \lambda)} = \dfrac{2.2^2}{5(5 - 2.2)} = 0.3457$

$W_q = \dfrac{L_q}{\lambda} = 0.157\ hours \quad (9.43\ minutes)$

10.a.

	$\lambda = 2$	$\mu = 3$	$\mu = 4$
Average number waiting (L_q)		1.3333	0.5000
Average number in system (L)		2.0000	1.0000
Average time waiting (W_q)		0.6667	0.2500
Average time in system (W)		1.0000	0.5000
Probability of waiting (P_w)		0.6667	0.5000

b.　New mechanic = $15(L) + $7
$$= 15(2) + 7 = $37\ per\ hour$$
Experienced mechanic = $15(L) + $10
$$= 15(1) + 10 = $25\ per\ hour$$

∴ Hire the experienced mechanic

11.a.　$\lambda = 2.5 \quad \mu = \dfrac{60}{10} = 6\ customers\ per\ hour$

$L_q = \dfrac{\lambda^2}{\mu(\mu - \lambda)} = \dfrac{(2.5)^2}{6(6 - 2.5)} = 0.2976$

$L = L_q + \dfrac{\lambda}{\mu} = 0.7143$

$W_q = \dfrac{L_q}{\lambda} = 0.1190\ hours \quad (7.14\ minutes)$

$W = W_q + \dfrac{1}{\mu} = 0.2857\ hours$

$P_w = \dfrac{\lambda}{\mu} = \dfrac{2.5}{6} = 0.4167$

b. No; $W_q = 7.14$ minutes. Firm should increase the mean service rate (μ) for the consultant or hire a second consultant.

c. $\mu = \dfrac{60}{8} = 7.5$ *customers per hour*

$$L_q = \frac{\lambda^2}{\mu(\mu - \lambda)} = \frac{(2.5)^2}{7.5(7.5 - 2.5)} = 0.1667$$

$$W_q = \frac{L_q}{\lambda} = 0.0667 \text{ } hours \text{ } (4 \text{ } minutes)$$

The service goal is being met.

12. $$P_0 = 1 - \frac{\lambda}{\mu} = 1 - \frac{15}{20} = 0.25$$

$$L_q = \frac{\lambda^2}{\mu(\mu - \lambda)} = \frac{15^2}{20(20 - 15)} = 2.25$$

$$L = L + \frac{\lambda}{\mu} = 3$$

$$W_q = \frac{L_q}{\lambda} = 0.15 \text{ } hours \text{ } (9 \text{ } minutes)$$

$$W = W_q + \frac{1}{\mu} = 0.20 \text{ } hours \text{ } (12 \text{ } minutes)$$

$$P_w = \frac{\lambda}{\mu} = \frac{15}{20} = 0.75$$

With $W_q = 9$ minutes, the checkout service needs improvements.

13. Average waiting time goal: 5 minutes or less.

a. One checkout counter with 2 employees

$\lambda = 15$ $\mu = 30$ *per hour*

$$L_q = \frac{\lambda^2}{\mu(\mu - \lambda)} = \frac{15^2}{30(30 - 15)} = 0.50$$

$$W_q = \frac{L_q}{\lambda} = 0.0333 \text{ } hours \text{ } (2 \text{ } minutes)$$

b.   Two channel-two counter system

$\lambda = 15$ $\mu = 20$ *per hour for each*

From Table 12.5, $P_0 = 0.4545$

$$L_q = \frac{(\lambda/\mu)^2 \lambda\mu}{1!(2(20) - 15)^2} P_0$$

$$= \frac{(15 / 20)^2 (15)(20)}{(40 - 15)^2} (0.4545) = 0.1227$$

$$W_q = \frac{L_q}{\lambda} = 0.0082 \; hours \;\; (0.492 \; minutes)$$

c.   Recommend one checkout counter with two people. This meets the service goal with $W_q = 2$ minutes. The two counter system has better service, but has the added cost of installing a new counter.

14.a. $$P_0 = 1 - \frac{\lambda}{\mu} = 1 - \frac{10}{12} = 0.1667$$

b. $$L_q = \frac{\lambda^2}{\mu(\mu - \lambda)} = \frac{10^2}{12(12 - 10)} = 4.1667$$

$$L = L_q + \frac{\lambda}{\mu} = 5$$

c. $$W_q = \frac{L_q}{\lambda} = 0.4167 \; hours \;\; (25 \; minutes)$$

d. $$P_w = \frac{\lambda}{\mu} = \frac{10}{12} = 0.8333$$

e.   No, the service is very poor.

15. $k = 2$, $\lambda = 10$, $\mu = 12$

Using Equation 12.11, $P_0 = 0.4118$

$$L_q = \frac{(\lambda/\mu)^2 \lambda\mu}{(1!)(k\mu - \lambda)^2} P_0 = 0.1751$$

$$L = L_q + \frac{\lambda}{\mu} = 1.0084$$

$$W_q = \frac{L_q}{\lambda} = 0.0175 \ hours \quad (1.05 \ minutes)$$

This system provides a big improvement. The average number of cars in the system is reduced to $L = 1$ and the average waiting time is reduced to $W_q = 1.05$ minutes.

16.a. $P_0 = 1 - \dfrac{\lambda}{\mu} = 1 - \dfrac{5}{10} = 0.50$

b. $L_q = \dfrac{\lambda^2}{\mu(\mu - \lambda)} = \dfrac{5^2}{10(10 - 5)} = 0.50$

c. $W_q = \dfrac{L_q}{\lambda} = 0.1 \ hours \quad (6 \ minutes)$

d. $W = W_q + \dfrac{1}{\mu} = .2 \ hours \quad (12 \ minutes)$

e.   Yes, unless $W_q = 6$ minutes is considered too long.

17.a.   From Table 16.3, $P_0 = 0.60$

b. $L_q = \dfrac{(\lambda/\mu)^2 \lambda\mu}{1!(k\mu - \lambda)^2} P_0 = 0.0333$

c. $W_q = \dfrac{L_q}{\lambda} = 0.0067 \ hours \quad (24.12 \ seconds)$

d. $W = W_q + \dfrac{1}{\mu} = 0.1067 \quad (6.4 \ minutes)$

e.   This service is probably much better than necessary with average waiting time only 24 seconds. Both channels will be idle 60% of the time.

18.a. $\dfrac{\lambda}{\mu} = \dfrac{6}{10} \doteq 0.6$

From Table 12.5, $P_0 = 0.5385$

b. $L_q = \dfrac{(\lambda/\mu)^2 \lambda\mu}{1!(2\mu - \lambda)^2} P_0 = 0.0593$

c. $W_q = \dfrac{L_q}{\lambda} = 0.0099 \; hours \quad (0.59 minutes)$

d. $W = W_q + \dfrac{1}{\mu} = 0.1099 \; hours \quad (6.59 \; minutes)$

e. $P_0 = 0.5385$

$$P_1 = \dfrac{(\lambda/\mu)^1}{1!} P_0 = 0.6(0.5385) = 0.3231$$

$P(\text{wait}) = P(n \geq 2) = 1 - P(n \leq 1)$
$$= 1 - 0.8616 = 0.1384$$

19.a. $k = 2 \quad \lambda/\mu = 14/10 = 1.4$

From Table 12.5, $P_0 = 0.1765$

b. $L_q = \dfrac{(\lambda/\mu)^2 \lambda\mu}{1!(2\mu - \lambda)^2} P_0 = \dfrac{(1.4)^2(14)(10)}{(20 - 14)^2}(0.1765) = 1.3453$

$L = L_q + \dfrac{\lambda}{\mu} = 1.3453 + \dfrac{14}{10} = 2.7453$

c. $W_q = \dfrac{L_q}{\lambda} = \dfrac{1.3453}{14} = 0.961 \; hours$

d. $W = W_q + \dfrac{1}{\mu} = 0.0961 + \dfrac{1}{10} = 0.1961 \; hours$

e. $P_0 = 0.1765$

$$P_1 = \dfrac{(\lambda/\mu)^1}{1!} P_0 = \dfrac{14}{10}(0.1765) = 0.2471$$

$P(\text{wait}) = P(n \geq 2) = 1 - P(n \leq 1)$
$$= 1 - 0.4236 = 0.5764$$

20.a.   From Table 12.5, $P_0 = 0.2360$

$$L_q = \frac{(\lambda/\mu)^3 \lambda\mu}{2!(3\mu - \lambda)} = \frac{(1.4)^3(14)(10)}{2(30 - 14)^2}(0.2360) = 0.1771$$

$$L = L_q + \frac{\lambda}{\mu} = 1.5771$$

$$W_q = \frac{L_q}{\lambda} = \frac{0.1771}{14} = 0.0127 \; hours$$

$$W = W_q + \frac{1}{\mu} = 0.0127 + \frac{1}{10} = 0.1127 \; hours$$

b. $k = 2$ $P(\text{wait}) = 0.5764$

$k = 3$ $P_0 = 0.2360$

$$P_1 = \frac{(\lambda/\mu)^1}{1!}P_0 = (1.4)(0.2360) = 0.3304$$

$$P_2 = \frac{(\lambda/\mu)^2}{2!}P_0 = \frac{(1.4)^2}{2}(0.2360) = 0.2313$$

$$P(\text{wait}) = P(n \geq 3) = 1 - P(n \leq 2)$$
$$= 1 - 0.7977 = 0.2023$$

∴ Prefer the three-channel system.

21.   From question 11, a service time of 8 minutes has $\mu = 60/8 = 7.5$

$$L_q = \frac{\lambda^2}{\mu(\mu - \lambda)} = \frac{(2.5)^2}{7.5(7.5 - 2.5)} = 0.1667$$

$$L = L_q + \frac{\lambda}{\mu} = 0.50$$

Total Cost $= \$25L + \$16$
$$= 25(0.50) + 16 = \$28.50$$

Two channels: $\lambda = 2.5$ $\mu = 60/10 = 6$

Using equation 12.11 $P_0 = 0.6552$

$$L_q = \frac{(\lambda/\mu)^2 \lambda\mu}{1!(2\mu - \lambda)^2}P_0 = 0.0189$$

$$L = L_q + \frac{\lambda}{\mu} = 0.4356$$

Total Cost = 25(0.4356) + 2(16) = $42.89

Use the one consultant with an 8 minute service time.

22. $\lambda = 24$

Characteristic	System A $(k = 1, \mu = 30)$	System B $(k = 1, \mu = 48)$	System C $(k = 2, \mu = 30)$
P_0	0.2000	0.5000	0.4286
L_q	3.2000	0.5000	0.1524
L	4.0000	1.0000	0.9524
W_q	0.1333	0.0200	0.0063
W	0.1667	0.0417	0.0397
P_w	0.8000	0.5000	0.2286

System C provides the best service.

23.   Service Cost per Channel

System A:	6.50	+	20.00	= $26.50/hour
System B:	2(6.50)	+	20.00	= $33.00/hour
System C:	6.50	+	20.00	= $26.50/hour

Total Cost = $c_1, L + c_2 k$

System A:	25(4)	+	26.50(1)	= $126.50
System B:	25(1)	+	33.00(1)	= $ 58.00
System C:	25(0.9524)	+	26.50(2)	= $ 76.81

System B is the most economical.

24. $\lambda = 2.8$, $\mu = 3.0$, $W_q = 30$ minutes

a. $\lambda = 2.8/60 = 0.0466$

      $\mu = 3/60 = 0.0500$

b. $L_q = \lambda W_q = (0.0466)(30) = 1.4$

c. $W = W_q + 1/\mu = 30 + 1/0.05 = 50$ minutes

      $\therefore$ 11:00 a.m.

25. $\lambda = 4$, $W = 10$ minutes

   a. $\mu = 1/2 = 0.5$

   b. $W_q = W - 1/\mu = 10 - 1/0.5 = 8$ minutes

   c. $L = \lambda W = 4(10) = 40$

26.a.   Express λ and μ in mechanics per minute

        $\lambda = 4/60 = 0.0667$ mechanics per minute

        $\mu = 1/6 = 0.1667$ mechanics per minute

        $L_q = \lambda W_q = 0.0667(4) = 0.2668$

        $W = W_q + 1/\mu = 4 + 1/0.1667 = 10$ minutes

        $L = \lambda W = (0.0667)(10) = 0.6667$

   b. $L_q = 0.0667(1) = 0.0667$

        $W = 1 + 1/0.1667 = 7$ minutes

        $L = \lambda W = (0.0667)(7) = 0.4669$

   c.   One-Channel

             Total Cost $= 20(0.6667) + 12(1) = \$25.33$

        Two-Channel

             Total Cost $= 20(0.4669) + 12(2) = \$33.34$

        One-Channel is more economical.

27.a.   2/8 hours $= 0.25$ per hour

   b.   1/3.2 hours $= 0.3125$ per hour

   c. $L_q = \dfrac{\lambda^2 \sigma^2 + (\lambda/\mu)^2}{2(1 - \lambda/\mu)} = \dfrac{(0.25)^2(2)^2 + (0.25/0.3125)^2}{2(1 - 0.25/0.3125)} = 2.225$

   d. $W_q = \dfrac{L_q}{\lambda} = \dfrac{2.225}{0.25} = 8.9$ *hours*

   e. $W = W_q + \dfrac{1}{\mu} = 8.9 + \dfrac{1}{0.3125} = 12.1$ *hours*

f.   Same at $P_w = \dfrac{\lambda}{\mu} = \dfrac{0.25}{0.3125} = 0.80$

80% of the time the welder is busy.

28. $\lambda = 5$

a.

Design	μ
A	$60/6 = 10$
B	$60/6.25 = 9.6$

b.   Design A with $\mu = 10$ jobs per hour.

c. $3/60 = 0.05$ for A $0.6/60 = 0.01$ for B

d.

Characteristic	Design A	Design B
P_0	0.5000	0.4792
L_q	0.3125	0.2857
L	0.8125	0.8065
W_q	0.0625	0.0571
W	0.1625	0.1613
P_w	0.5000	0.5208

e.   Design B is slightly better due to the lower variablility of service times.

System A: $W = 0.1625$ hrs   (9.75 minutes)
System B: $W = 0.1613$ hrs   (9.68 minutes)

29.

Characteristic	$\sigma = 1$ M/M/1	$\sigma = 0.5$ M/G/1
P_0	0.25	0.2500
L_q	2.25	1.4063
L	3.00	2.1563
W_q	3.00	1.8751
W	4.00	2.8751
P_w	0.75	0.7500

The lower service time variability of the new system is preferred. L_q, L, W_q, and W all improve.

Case Problem

1.   Single-Channel Waiting Line Analysis

The analysis that follows is based upon the assumptions of Poisson arrivals and exponential service times. With one call every 3.75 minutes, we have an average arrival rate of

$$\lambda = 60/3.75 = 16 \text{ calls per hour}$$

Similarly, with an average service time of 3 minutes, we have a service rate of

$$\mu = 60/3 = 20 \text{ calls per hour}$$

The operating characteristics of a single channel system with $\lambda = 16$ and $\mu = 20$ are as follows:

$$P_0 = \left(1 - \frac{\lambda}{\mu}\right) = 1 - \frac{16}{20} = 0.20$$

$$L_q = \frac{\lambda^2}{\mu(\mu - \lambda)} = \frac{16^2}{20(20 - 16)} = 3.2$$

$$L = L_q + \frac{\lambda}{\mu} = 3.2 + \frac{16}{20} = 4$$

$$W_q = \frac{L_q}{\lambda} = \frac{3.2}{16} = 0.20 \text{ hours} = 12 \text{ minutes}$$

$$W = W_q + \frac{1}{\mu} = 0.20 + \frac{1}{20} = 0.25 \text{ hours} = 15 \text{ minutes}$$

$$P_w = \frac{\lambda}{\mu} = \frac{16}{20} = 0.80$$

Operating the telephone reservation service with only one ticket agent appears unacceptable. With 80% of incoming calls waiting ($P_w = 0.80$) and an average waiting time of 12 minutes ($W_q = 12$), the company clearly needs to consider using two or more agents.

2.   Multiple-Channel Waiting Line Analysis

Since Regional's management team agreed that an acceptable service goal was to immediately answer and process at least 85% of the incoming calls, the probability of waiting must be 15% or less. Computing P_q for $k = 2$ agents and $k = 3$ agents provides the following.

$$P_w = \frac{1}{k!}\left(\frac{\lambda}{\mu}\right)^k \frac{k\mu}{k\mu - \lambda} P_0$$

For $k = 2$

$$P_w = \frac{1}{2!}\left(\frac{16}{20}\right)^2 \frac{2(20)}{2(20) - 16}(0.4286) = 0.2286$$

For $k = 3$

$$P_w = \frac{1}{3!}\left(\frac{16}{20}\right)^3 \frac{3(20)}{3(20) - 16}(0.4472) = 0.0520$$

Based on the value of P_w, 3 ticket agents will be required to meet the service goal. Other operating characteristics of the 3-ticket-agent system are as follows:

$P_0 = 0.4472$

$L_q = 0.0189$

$L = 0.8189$

$W_q = 0.0012$ hours $= 0.07$ minutes

$W = 0.0512$ hours $= 3.07$ minutes

3. We would need to know the average arrival rate for each hourly period throughout the day. An analysis similar to the one above would determine the recommended number of travel agents each hour. This information could then be used to develop full-time and part-time shift schedules which would meet the service goals.

Answers to Questions for Quantitative Methods in Practice

1. Goodyear decides to replace the manual system with a computer controlled system due primarily to a need to develop a computerized data base that could be analyzed to improve the maintenance function.

2. The arrivals were known to differ from the Poisson distribution. In addition, there were a number of other complicating factors that precluded the use of the waiting line models introduced in this chapter.

Chapter 17
Computer Simulation

Learning Objectives

1. Understand what simulation is and how it aids in the analysis of a problem.

2. Learn why computer simulation is a significant problem-solving tool.

3. Understand the simulation process.

4. Identify the important role probability distributions, random numbers, and the computer play in implementing simulation models.

5. Realize the relative advantages and disadvantages of computer simulation models.

6. Understand the following terms:

    simulation   pseudo-random numbers
    Monte Carlo simulation   simulator

Solutions

1. a.

Sales	Relative Frequency
0	0.08
1	0.12
2	0.28
3	0.24
4	0.14
5	0.10
6	0.04
	1.00

b. Use the following table to generate sales values.

Sales	Associated Interval of Random Numbers
0	00-07
1	08-19
2	20-47
3	48-71
4	72-85
5	86-95
6	96-99

Using the first 10 random numbers from row 4 of Appendix B, we obtain the following sales for ten days of simulated operation.

Day	Random Number	Sales
1	46	2
2	27	2
3	68	3
4	74	4
5	53	3
6	44	2
7	79	4
8	06	0
9	71	3
10	22	2

2. a.

Number of Arrivals	Relative Frequency
0	0.12
1	0.24
2	0.37
3	0.19
4	0.08
	1.00

b.   Use the following table to generate arrivals.

Number of Arrivals	Associated Interval of Random Numbers
0	00-11
1	12-35
2	36-72
3	73-91
4	92-99

Time	Random Number	Arriving Customers
9:00-9:05	08	0
9:05-9:10	61	2
9:10-9:15	22	1
	Total	3

3. a.   The following table shows the relative frequencies and associated intervals of random numbers used to generate demand.

Rental Demand	Relative Frequency	Interval of Random Numbers
7	0.08	00-07
8	0.20	08-27
9	0.32	28-59
10	0.28	60-87
11	0.12	88-99
	1.00	

Day	Random Number	Simulated Demand
1	15	8
2	48	9
3	71	10
4	56	9
5	90	11

b.   Note that no more than 9 cars can be rented each day because that is all that are available.

Average Rentals = $\dfrac{8 + 9 + 9 + 9 + 9}{5}$ = $\dfrac{44}{5}$ = 8.8 *cars*

c.   There will be 1 lost on day 3 and 2 lost on day 5.

d.   Expected daily demand is computed as follows.

Expected daily demand = 7(.08) + 8(.20) + 9(.32) + 10(.28) + 11(.12)
                      = 9.16

e.   Average daily demand $\dfrac{8 + 9 + 10 + 9 + 11}{5}$ = $\dfrac{47}{5}$ = 9.4

The average daily demand for the 5 days simulated is greater than the expected daily demand. This is because the simulation was only for 5 days. The longer the simulation is run the closer the average simulated daily demand will come to the expected demand. This is why simulation models should be run over a large number of periods.

4. a.

5-Minute Intervals	Random Number	Arriving Customers
1	01	0
2	09	0
3	26	1
4	05	0
5	33	1
6	14	1

b.   Average Number of Arrivals = $\dfrac{0 + 0 + 1 + 0 + 1 + 1}{6}$ = 0.5

c.   No, with a sample of only 6 intervals I would not feel comfortable estimating the average number of arrivals.

d.   Expected Number of Arrivals = 0(0.12) + 1(0.24) + 2(0.37) + 3(0.19) + 4(0.08)
                                 = 1.87 per 5-minute period.

This is much higher than the average computed from the small sample of 6 simulated arrivals.

5. a.

Number of Employees Absent	Relative Frequency
1	0.10
2	0.20
3	0.35
4	0.15
5	0.10
6	0.10
	1.00

b. Use the following table to generate the number of employees absent.

Number of Employees Absent	Associated Interval of Random Numbers
1	00-09
2	10-29
3	30-64
4	65-79
5	80-89
6	90-99

Simulation results will vary depending upon the random numbers used.

6. a.

Number of Sales	Relative Frequency
0	0.04
1	0.10
2	0.16
3	0.44
4	0.20
5	0.06
	1.00

b.

Number of Sales	Associated Interval of Random Numbers
0	00-03
1	04-13
2	14-29
3	30-73
4	74-93
5	94-99

For example, if the first random number drawn from Appendix B is 78, we would set weekly sales at 4 cars.

7.   To generate the number of failures for each year of simulated operation use the following table.

Number of Failures	Associated Interval of Random Numbers
0	00-79
1	80-94
2	95-98
3	99

The answer to the question will depend upon the random numbers used. However, most 25 year simulations will contain a few periods of 5 consecutive years of operation without failure. Using the given relative frequencies, the probability of 5 years without a failure is $(0.80)^5 = 0.32768$.

8.

Period	Random Number	Number of New Customers	Is Service Area Available	Random Number	Order Size	Service Periods	Number Lost Customer	Number Waiting	Was Service Completed This Period	Profit
1	20	1	Yes	71	Medium	2	0	0	No	—
2	15	0	No	—	—	—	0	0	Yes	1.50
3	56	1	Yes	09	Small	1	0	0	Yes	0.75
4	29	1	Yes	43	Medium	2	0	0	No	—
5	07	0	No	—	—	—	0	0	Yes	1.50

Total Customers Served = 3
Total Profit = 3.75

17-7

9. a.

Model	Associated Interval of Random Numbers
X100	00-59
Y200	60-99

Time of Service Call For X100	Associated Interval of Random Numbers
25	00-49
30	50-74
35	75-89
40	90-99

Time of Service Call For Y200	Associated Interval of Random Numbers
20	00-39
25	40-79
30	80-89
35	90-99

b. Simulation results will again vary depending on the random numbers used. Average or expected values show about 12 calls for X100 and about 8 calls for Y200. Total service time for the 20 calls should be around 5 minutes.

10.

Weekly Demand for Bath Landscaping	Associated Interval of Random Numbers
10	00-19
15	20-54
20	55-84
25	85-94
30	95-99

Weekly Demand for Pittsford Landscaping	Associated Interval of Random Numbers
30	00-19
40	20-59
50	60-89
60	90-99

Most simulations will show a beginning inventory of 70 does not satisfy demand 95% of the time. Therefore a beginning inventory of 80 cubic yards is recommended. The recommendation will vary depending on the random numbers selected because only 20 weeks of operation are being simulated. In a full scale simulation, many beginning inventory levels would be considered and the simulation period would be expanded beyond 20 weeks.

11.a.

Next Purchase	Probability	Interval of Random Numbers
Super Z	0.7	00-69
Devco	0.1	70-79
Floorgreen	0.2	80-99

b.

Next Purchase	Probability	Interval of Random Numbers
Super Z	0.3	00-29
Devco	0.5	30-79
Floorgreen	0.2	80-99

c.

Next Purchase	Probability	Interval of Random Numbers
Super Z	0.1	00-09
Devco	0.1	10-19
Floorgreen	0.8	20-99

d.

Random Number	Next Purchase
04	Super Z
23	Super Z
74	Devco
68	Devco

e.

Random Number	Next Purchase
04	Super Z
23	Super Z
74	Devco
68	Devco

f.   It definitely is not. We did not see any purchases from Floorgreen.

12.a   To generate an answer to a house called on, use the following table.

Response to Call	Relative Frequency	Associated Interval of Random Numbers
No Answer	0.30	00-29
Answer	0.70	30-99

To generate whether a man or woman answers use the following table.

Sex	Relative Frequency	Associated Interval of Random Numbers
Male	0.20	00-19
Female	0.80	20-99

To generate the number of subscriptions if a woman answers the door, use the following table. Note that no purchase has a 0.85 probability.

Number of Subscriptions Sold	Relative Frequency	Associated Interval of Random Numbers
0	0.850	000-849
1	0.090	850-939
2	0.045	940-984
3	0.015	985-999

To generate number of subscriptions if a man answers use the following table. Note that the probability of no subscription is 0.75.

Number of Subscriptions Sold	Relative Frequency	Associated Interval of Random Numbers
0	0.750	000-749
1	0.025	750-774
2	0.100	775-874
3	0.075	875-949
4	0.050	950-999

For example, begin by selecting a number at random to generate a call. Say we choose 68 from Appendix B. This corresponds to a house that answers. Next, we generate a random number to determine if a man or woman answers. Say we next get a random number of 19. This corresponds to a man answering. If the next random number selected is 37, we would associate this with a sale of no subscriptions. Hence, the salesman would realize no profit calling on this house.

b.   The expected total profit from 25 calls is $10.85. Simulation results will vary from the value based on the random numbers selected for the specific simulation.

c. The expected number of subscriptions sold during 100 calls is 21.7. The expected total daily profit is $43.40. Again simulation results will vary from these values based on the random numbers selected for a specific simulation.

13.a. Random numbers for simulating activity times:

Activity	Interval	Time
A	00-24	5
	25-54	6
	55-84	7
	85-99	8
B	00-19	3
	20-74	5
	75-99	7
C	00-09	10
	10-34	12
	35-74	14
	75-94	16
	95-99	18
D	00-59	8
	60-99	10

Again simulation results will vary around the expected or average project completion time of 33-34 weeks.

b. Again results depend upon the specific simulation run. However, the probability of 35 days should exceed 0.50 with most simulation results.

14.

Interval	Number of Newspapers
00-09	150
10-39	175
40-69	200
70-89	225
90-99	250

Simulated solutions should approximate the analytical solution which is as follows:

Order Size	Expected Daily Profit
200	$26.88
225	26.25
250	24.38

An order size of 200 is preferred.

15.   Follow the development in the text with the following modification for generating demand values.

Demand (units)	Associated Interval of Random Numbers
0	00-24
1	25-74
2	75-89
3	90-94
4	95-99

16.   To generate weekly demand use the following table.

Demand per Week	Associated Interval of Random Numbers
0	00-19
1	20-69
2	70-79
3	80-89
4	90-94
5	95-99

To generate lead time use the following table.

Lead Time (Weeks)	Associated Interval of Random Numbers
1	00-09
2	10-34
3	35-94
4	95-99

17.

Daily Demand	Realtive Frequency	Interval of Random Numbers
0	0.05	00-04
1	0.10	05-14
0	0.05	15-19
3	0.10	20-29
4	0.15	30-44
5	0.30	45-74
6	0.15	75-89
7	0.05	90-94
8	0.05	95-99
	1.00	

Ten-Day Simulation Results for a Production Quantity of $x = 3$

Day	Generated Daily Demand d	Daily Profit	Total Profit ($)
1	5	7.50	7.50
2	1	1.50	9.00
3	6	7.50	16.50
4	3	7.50	24.00
5	4	7.50	31.50
6	4	7.50	39.00
7	8	7.50	46.50
8	0	-1.50	45.00
9	5	7.50	52.50
10	6	7.50	60.00

Ten-Day Simulation Results for Various Production Quantities

Production Size	Ten-Day Simulated Profit ($)
1	25
2	44
3	60
4	79
5	90
6	93
7	91
8	89

A production size of 6 per day provides the best simulation results. Profit = $93.

18.a.   Order Quantity = 15 and Reorder Point = 10

Week	Beg. Inv.	Units Rcvd.	Rndm. Numb.	Units Sold	End Inv.	Holding Cost	Order Cost	Short Cost	Total Cost
1	20	0	88	4	16	320	0	0	320
2	16	0	54	3	13	260	0	0	260
3	13	0	70	3	10	200	50	0	250
4	10	0	98	5	5	100	0	0	100
5	5	0	96	5	0	0	0	0	0
6	0	15	95	5	10	200	50	0	250
7	10	0	43	3	7	140	0	0	140
8	7	0	67	3	4	80	0	0	80
9	4	15	91	4	15	300	0	0	300
10	15	0	15	2	13	260	0	0	260
11	13	0	08	1	12	240	0	0	240
12	12	0	30	3	9	180	50	0	230
			Average Cost for 12 Simulated Weeks:			190	12.50	0	202.50

19.a.   Random number assignments are as follows:

	Previous Trip		
Next Trip	(A) Marimont Interval	(B) Harrison Interval	(C) Hinton Interval
Marimont	00-69	00-19	00-14
Harrison	70-79	20-79	15-19
Hinton	80-99	80-99	20-99

b.

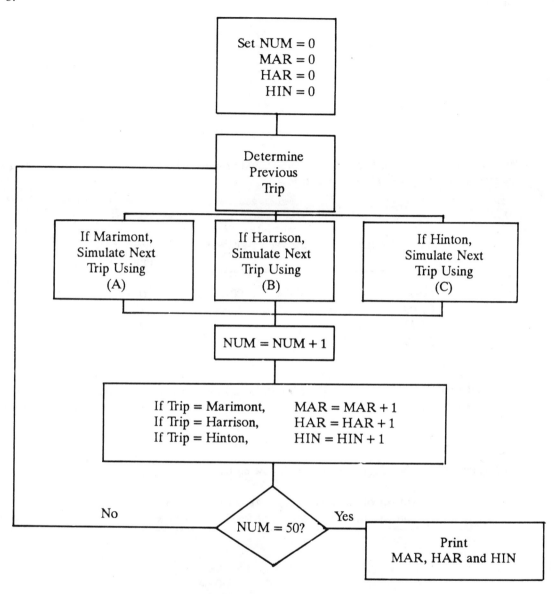

c. & d.   Hinton Hotels should be the most popular chain.

20.   First Ball:

Interval	Number of Pins
00-02	6
02-09	7
10-29	8
30-59	9
60-99	10

Use the results from the first ball to determine how to simulate the results for the second ball. Use the random number intervals as shown below.

If First Ball				Second Ball
6	7	8	9	
Interval	Interval	Interval	Interval	Number of Pins
00-00	00-03	00-04	00-14	0
01-03	04-13	05-29	15-99	1
04-23	14-49	30-99		2
24-49	50-99			3
50-99				4

The simulation program requires the programmer to know and be able to program a bowling scoring system. Random numbers and the above tables will simulate the number of pins downed on each ball.

21.   To generate the number if arrivals, use the following table.

Number of Arrivals in One Minute	Associated Interval of Random Numbers
0	00-09
1	10-29
2	30-64
3	65-94
4	95-99

To generate the type of service, use the following table.

Type of Service	Associated Interval of Random Numbers
Self Service	00-69
Full Service	70-99

To generate the time for self service customers, use the following table.

Service Time (Minutes)	Associated Interval of Random Numbers
2	00-09
3	10-29
4	30-89
5	90-99

To generate the time for full service customers, use the following table.

Service Time (Minutes)	Associated Interval of Random Numbers
3	00-19
4	20-49
5	50-84
6	85-94
7	95-99

22. A simulation model could be used to simulate the laboratory operation with any given number of x-ray units. By considering the arrivals of patients at the laboratory and the time of the x-ray process, the simulator can project patient waiting times and equipment utilization rates. The decision maker can then use the model's output to determine the number of x-ray units that provide a reasonably low waiting time and a reasonably high equipment utilization rate.

23. The objective would be to find the location that will minimize the average travel time from the station to the fires. After collecting data on fire frequency in each of many sections of the city, we could use a simulator to randomly select locations for a sequence of fires. For each trial location selected, we could estimate the travel time to each fire. The location with the smallest average travel time would be the primary location to be considered for the new station.

24. A simulator could be used to compute the number of customers getting on and off the bus at each location. By tracking the number of people on the bus, the simulation model could reject new customers if the bus was full. Repeated simulations of the bus route operation show total customers carried by a regular and a mini-bus. Thus a profit can be computed for each type of bus and the bus selection decision made.

Case Problem

1. Machine downtime for each machine
    Time spent working by each technician
    Total number of breakdowns
    Total Cost (cost of downtime and technicians)

2. Flowchart appears on the following page

3. The following probability distributions can be used to simulate the process.

Interval	Breakdown?
00-89	No
90-99	Yes

Interval	Repair Time
00-19	1
20-54	2
55-79	3
80-94	4
95-99	5

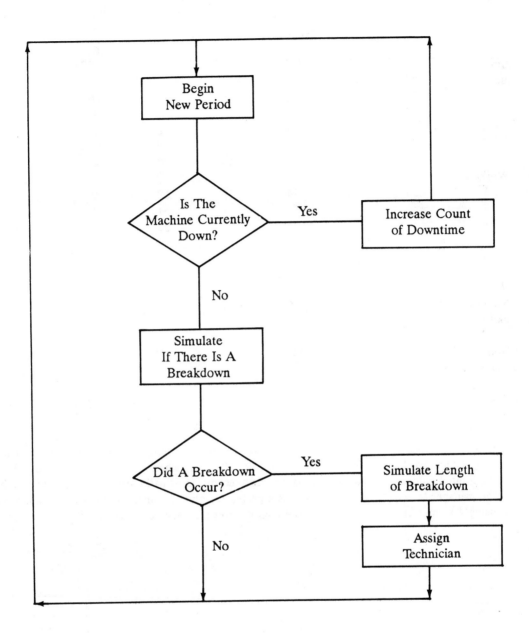

4.   The following results were obtained for simulation runs of 100 hours.

	Number of Technicians					
	1	2	3	4	5	6
Downtime						
Machine 1	35	23	39	15	20	20
2	57	33	30	16	31	31
3	53	38	40	38	39	39
4	54	18	25	43	26	26
5	51	54	28	17	15	15
6	86	50	19	44	40	40
Time Working						
Tech. 1	96	86	74	69	69	69
2		68	51	51	51	51
3			38	36	32	32
4				15	14	14
5					5	5
6						0
Total Number of Breakdowns	39	61	66	66	67	67
Total Hours of Repair Time	101	159	171	171	172	172
Total Cost (thousands)	35.8	23.8	20.3	19.5	19.3	19.3

Based upon these results we see that six technicians are not required since the sixth technician is not assigned any work. The lowest total cost of $19,300 occurs when 5 technicians are used. However, the limited number of repair hours that the fifth technician actually spends working (5) might lead the manager to select four technicians as a preferred solution, since the total cost associated with using 4 technicians is only $200   more than the cost if 5 technicians are used.

Answers to Questions for Quantitative Methods in Practice

1. An integrated pulp and paper mill is a facility in which wood chips and chemicals are processed in order to produce paper products or dried pulp. To begin with, wood chips are cooked and bleached in the pulp mill; the resulting pulp is piped directly into storage tanks. From the storage tanks the pulp is routed to one or more paper machines which produce the finished paper products. Alternatively, the pulp is sent to a dryer, and the dried pulp is then sold to other paper mills which do not have the capability of producing their own pulp.

2. The primary reason why Champion conducted a study of their integrated pulp and paper facility was to determine whether or not it would be worthwhile to invest in improvements which would increase the capacity of the dryer. One of the first questions to be answered in the study was, "How much additional pulp could be produced and dried, given each possible capacity increase on the dryer?"

3. An analysis of average flows is inadequate because it ignores the day-to-day deviations from the average.

4. The sample of actual downtimes could be used to develop a probability distribution of downtimes. Then a random number of pseudo-random numbers could be used to randomly select a downtime from this probability distribution.

5. A complex process was able to be studied where analytical procedures were inappropriate.

Chapter 18
Multicriteria Decision Problems

Learning Objectives

1.   Understand the concept of multicriteria decision making and how it differs from situations and procedures involving a single criterion.

2.   Be able to develop a goal programming model of a multiple criteria problem.

3.   Know how to use the goal programming graphical solution procedure to solve goal programming problems involving two decision variables.

4.   Understand how the relative importance of the goals can be reflected by altering the weights or coefficients foe the decision variables in the objective function.

5.   Know how to develop a solution to a goal programming model by solving a sequence of linear programming models using a general purpose linear programming package.

6.   Know how to apply the analytic hierarchy process (AHP) to solve a problem involving multiple criteria.

7.   Understand how the AHP utilizes pairwise comparisons to establish priority measures for both the criteria and decision alternatives.

8.   See how Expert Choice Software package can be used to implement the AHP on a microcomputer.

9.   Understand the following terms:

multicriteria decision problem	pairwise comparison matrix
goal programming	synthesization
deviation variables	consistency
priority levels	consistency ratio
goal equation	Expert Choice (EC)
preemptive priorities	
analytic hierarchy process (AHP)	
hierarchy	

Solutions

1. a.

Raw Material	Amount Needed to Achieve Both P_1 Goals
1	$\frac{2}{5}(30) + \frac{1}{2}(15) = 12 + 7.5 = 19.5$
2	$\frac{1}{5}(15) = 3$
3	$\frac{3}{5}(30) + \frac{3}{10}(15) = 18 + 4.5 = 22.5$

Since there are only 21 tons of Material 3 available, it is not possible to achieve both goals.

b. Let

x_1 = the number of tons of fuel additive produced

x_2 = the number of tons of solvent base produced

d_1^+ = the amount by which the number of tons of fuel additive produced exceeds the target value of 30 tons

d_1^- = the amount by which the number of tons of fuel additive produced is less than the target of 30 tons

d_2^+ = the amount by which the number of tons of solvent base produced exceeds the target value of 15 tons

d_2^- = the amount by which the number of tons of solvent base is less than the target value of 15 tons

$$
\begin{aligned}
\min \quad & d_1^- + d_2^- \\
\text{s.t.} \quad & \\
\tfrac{2}{5}\, x_1 + \tfrac{1}{2}\, x_2 & \le 20 \quad \text{Material 1} \\
\tfrac{1}{5}\, x_2 & \le 5 \quad \text{Material 2} \\
\tfrac{3}{5}\, x_1 + \tfrac{3}{10}\, x_2 & \le 21 \quad \text{Material 3} \\
x_1 \qquad\quad - d_1^+ + d_1^- & = 30 \quad \text{Goal 1} \\
x_2 - d_2^+ + d_2^- & = 15 \quad \text{Goal 2} \\
x_1,\ x_2,\ d_1^+,\ d_1^-,\ d_2^+,\ d_2^- & \ge 0
\end{aligned}
$$

c. In the graphical solution shown below, point A minimizes the sum of the deviations form the goals and thus provides the optimal product mix.

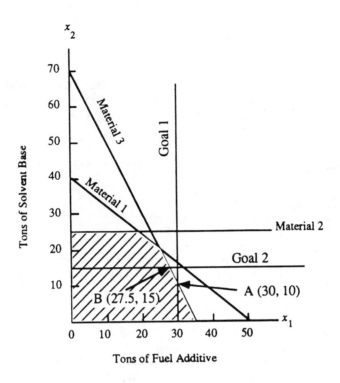

Tons of Fuel Additive

d. In the graphical solution shown above, point B minimizes $2d_1^- + d_2^-$ and thus provides the optimal product mix.

2. a. Let

   x_1 = number of shares of AGA Products purchased
   x_2 = number of shares of Key Oil purchased

<u>To obtain an annual return of exactly 9%</u>

$$0.06(50)x_1 + 0.10(100)x_2 = 0.09(50,000)$$
$$3x_1 + 10x_2 = 4500$$

<u>To have exactly 60% of the total investment in Key Oil</u>

$$100x_2 = 0.60(50,000)$$
$$x_2 = 300$$

Therefore, we can write the goal programming model as follows:

$$\min P_1(d_1^-) \quad + \quad P_2(d_2^+)$$

s.t.

$$
\begin{array}{rcll}
50x_1 \; + \; 100x_2 & \leq & 50{,}000 & \text{Funds Available} \\
3x_1 \; + \; 10x_2 \; - \; d_1^+ \; + \; d_1^- & = & 4{,}500 & P_1 \text{ Goal} \\
x_2 \; - \; d_2^+ \; + \; d_2^- & = & 300 & P_2 \text{ Goal} \\
x_1, \, x_2, \, d_1^+, \, d_1^-, \, d_2^+, \, d_2^- \geq 0
\end{array}
$$

b.   In the graphical solution shown below, $x_1 = 250$ and $x_2 = 375$.

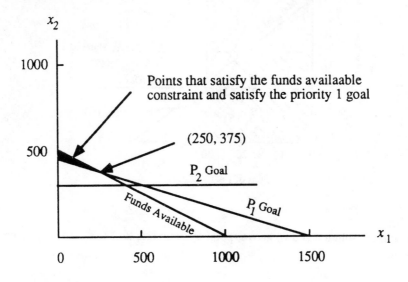

3. a.   Let

x_1 = number of units of product 1 produced
x_2 = number of units of product 2 produced

$$\min \quad P_1(d_1^+) \quad + \quad P_1(d_1^-) \quad + \quad P_1(d_2^+) \quad + \quad P_1(d_2^-) \quad + \quad P_2(d_3^-)$$

s.t.

$$
\begin{array}{rcll}
1x_1 \; + \; 1x_2 \; - \; d_1^+ \; + \; d_1^- & = & 350 & \text{Goal 1} \\
2x_1 \; + \; 5x_2 \; - \; d_2^+ \; + \; d_2^- & = & 1000 & \text{Goal 2} \\
4x_1 \; + \; 2x_2 \; - \; d_3^+ \; + \; d_3^- & = & 1300 & \text{Goal 3} \\
x_1, \, x_2, \, d_1^+, \, d_1^-, \, d_2^+, \, d_2^-, \, d_3^-, \, d_3^+ \geq 0
\end{array}
$$

b.   In the graphical solution shown below, point A provides the optimal solution. Note that with $x_1 = 250$ and $x_2 = 100$, this solution achieves goals 1 and 2, but underachieves goal 3 (profit) by \$100 since $4(250) + 2(100) = \$1200$.

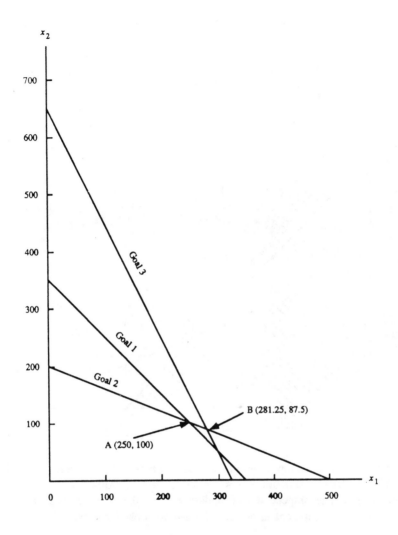

c.

$$\max \ 4x_1 \ + \ 2x_2$$
s.t.
$$
\begin{aligned}
1x_1 \ + \ 1x_2 \ &\leq \ 350 \ \text{Dept. A} \\
2x_2 \ + \ 5x_2 \ &\leq \ 1000 \ \text{Dept. B} \\
x_1, \ x_2 \ &\geq \ 0
\end{aligned}
$$

The graphical solution shown below indicates that there are four extreme points. The profit corresponding to each extreme point is as follows:

Extreme Point	Profit
1	$4(0) + 2(0) = 0$
2	$4(350) + 2(0) = 1400$
3	$4(250) + 2(100) = 1200$
4	$4(0) + 2(250) = 500$

Thus, the optimal product mix is $x_1 = 350$ and $x_2 = 0$ with a profit of $1400.

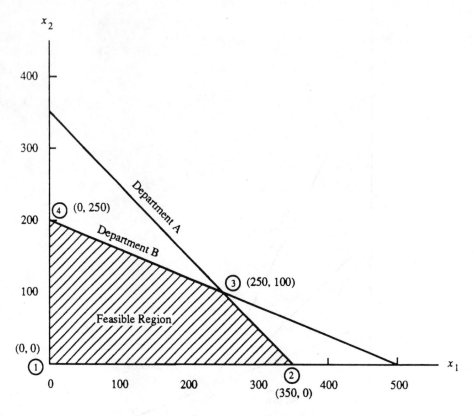

d. The solution to part (a) achieves both labor goals, whereas the solution to part (b) results in using only $2(350) + 5(0) = 700$ hours of labor in department B. Although (c) results in a $100 increase in profit, the problems associated with underachieving the original department labor goal by 300 hours may be more significant in terms of long-term considerations.

e. Refer to the graphical solution in part (b). The solution to the revised problem is point B, with $x_1 = 281.25$ and $x_2 = 87.5$. Although this solution achieves the original department B labor goal and the profit goal, this solution rises $1(281.25) + 1(87.5) = 368.75$ hours of labor in department B, which is 18.75 hours more than the original goal.

4. a.   Let

> x_1 = number of gallons of IC-100 produced
> x_2 = number of gallons of IC-200 produced

$$\min \; P_1(d_1^-) \; + \; P_1(d_2^+) \; + \; P_2(d_3^-) \; + \; P_2(d_4^-) \; + \; P_5(d_5^-)$$

s.t.

$20x_1$	+	$30x_2$	- d_1^+	+ d_1^-	=	4800	Goal 1
$20x_1$	+	$30x_2$	- d_2^+	+ d_2^-	=	6000	Goal 2
x_1			- d_3^+	+ d_3^-	=	100	Goal 3
		x_2	- d_4^+	+ d_4^-	=	120	Goal 4
x_1	+	x_2	- d_5^+	+ d_5^-	=	300	Goal 5

x_1, x_2, all deviation variables ≥ 0

b.   In the graphical solution shown below, the point x_1 = 120 and x_2 = 120 is optimal.

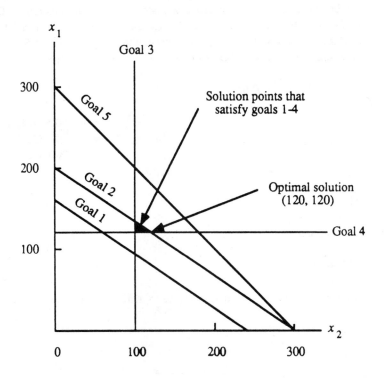

5. a.

$$\min \; P_1(d_1^-) \; + \; P_1(d_2^-) \; + \; P_2(d_3^+)$$

s.t.

$\tfrac{2}{5}x_1$	+ $\tfrac{1}{2}x_2$			$\leq$	20	Material 1
	$\tfrac{1}{5}x_2$			$\leq$	5	Material 2
x_1		- d_1^+	+ d_1^-	=	30	Goal 1
	x_2	- d_2^+	+ d_2^-	=	15	Goal 2
$\tfrac{3}{5}x_1$	+ $\tfrac{3}{10}x_2$	- d_3^+	+ d_3^-	=	21	Goal 3

x_1, x_2, d_1^+, d_1^-, d_2^+, d_2^-, d_3^+, $d_3^- \geq 0$

b. Optimal Solution is $x_1 = 30$, $x_2 = 15$

c. $d_3^+ = 1.5$ tons

6. a. Note that getting at least 10,000 customers from group 1 is equivalent to $x_1 = 40,000$ (25% of 40,000 = 10,000) and getting 5,000 customers is equivalent to $x_2 = 50,000$ (10% of 50,000 = 5,000). Thus, to satisfy both goals, 40,000 + 50,000 = 90,000 letters would have to be mailed at a cost of 90,000($1) = $90,000.

Let

x_1 = number of letters mailed to group 1 customers
x_2 = number of letters mailed to group 2 customers
d_1^+ = number of letters mailed to group 1 customers over the desired 40,000
d_1^- = number of letters mailed to group 1 customers under the desired 40,000
d_2^+ = number of letters mailed to group 2 customers over the desired 50,000
d_2^- = number of letters mailed to group 2 customers under the desired 50,000
d_3^+ = the amount by which the expenses exceeds the target value of $70,000
d_3^- = the amount by which the expenses falls short of the target value of $70,000

$$\min \ P_1(d_1^-) \ + \ P_1(d_2^-) \ + P_2(d_3^+)$$
s.t.

$$
\begin{array}{lll}
x_1 \qquad\qquad\quad - \ d_1^+ + \ d_1^- \qquad\qquad\qquad\qquad = 40,000 & \text{Goal 1} \\
\qquad\quad x_2 \qquad\qquad\qquad\qquad - 1d_2^+ + 1d_2^- = 50,000 & \text{Goal 2} \\
1x_1 \ + \ 1x_2 \ - \ d_3^+ \ + \ d_3^- \qquad\qquad\qquad = 70,000 & \text{Goal 3} \\
x_1, x_2, d_1^+, d_1^-, d_2^+, d_2^-, d_3^+, d_3^- \geq 0
\end{array}
$$

b. Optimal Solution: $x_1 = 40,000$, $x_2 = 50,000$

c. Objective function becomes

$$\min \ P_1(d_1^-) \ + \ P_1(2d_2^-) \ + P_2(d_3^+)$$

Optimal solution does not change since it is possible to achieve both goals 1 and 2 in the original problem.

7. a.   Let

x_1 = number of TV advertisements
x_2 = number of radio advertisements
x_3 = number of newspaper advertisements

$$\min \ P_1(d_1^-) + P_2(d_2^-) + P_3(d_3^+) + P_4(d_4^+)$$
s.t.

x_1					$\leq$	10	TV
	x_2				$\leq$	15	Radio
		x_3			$\leq$	20	Newspaper
$20x_1$ +	$5x_2$ +	$10x_3$ -	d_1^+ + d_1^-	=	400	Goal 1
$0.7x_1$ -	$0.3x_2$ -	$0.3x_3$ -	d_2^+ + d_2^-	=	0	Goal 2
$-0.2x_1$ +	$0.8x_2$ -	$0.2x_3$ -	d_3^+ + d_3^-	=	0	Goal 3
$25x_1$ +	$4x_2$ +	$5x_3$ -	d_4^+ + d_4^-	=	200	Goal 4

$$x_1, x_2, x_3, d_1^+, d_1^-, d_2^+, d_2^-, d_3^+, d_3^-, d_4^+, d_4^- \geq 0$$

b.   Optimal Solution: $x_1 = 9.474$, $x_2 = 2.105$, $x_3 = 20$

Rounding down leads to a recommendation of 9 TV advertisements, 2 radio advertisements, and 20 newspaper advertisements. Note, however, that rounding down results in not achieving goals 1 and 2.

8. a.   Let

x_1 = first coordinate of the new machine location
x_2 = second coordinate of the new machine location
d_i^+ = amount by which x_1 coordinate of new machine exceeds x_1 coordinate of machine i.
d_i^- = amount by which x_1 coordinate of machine i exceeds x_1 coordinate of new machine
e_i^+ = amount by which x_2 coordinate of new machine exceeds x_2 coordinate of machine i
e_i^- = amount by which x_2 coordinate of machine i exceeds x_2 coordinate of new machine

The goal programming model is given below.

$$\min \quad d_1^- + d_1^+ + e_1^- + e_1^+ + d_2^- + d_2^+ + e_2^- + e_2^+ + d_3^- + d_3^+ + e_3^- + e_3^+$$
s.t.

x_1	+ d_1^- - d_1^+				=	1
	x_2	+ e_1^- - e_1^+			=	7
x_1		+ d_2^- - d_2^+			=	5
	x_2		+ e_2^- - e_2^+		=	9
x_1			+ d_3^- - d_3^+		=	6
	x_2			+ e_3^- - e_3^+	=	2

$$x_1, x_2, d_1^-, d_1^+, e_1^-, e_1^+, d_2^-, d_2^+, e_2^-, e_2^+, d_3^-, d_3^+, e_3^-, e_3^+ \geq 0$$

b. The optimal solution is given by

$$x_1 = 5$$
$$x_2 = 7$$
$$d_1^+ = 4$$
$$e_2^- = 2$$
$$d_3^- = 1$$
$$e_3^+ = 5$$

The value of the solution is 12.

9. a.
x_1 = first coordinate of new location
x_2 = second coordinate of new location
d_i^+ = amount by which x_1 coordinate of new outlet exceeds x_1 coordinate of population center i.
d_i^- = amount by which x_1 coordinate of population center i exceeds x_1 coordinate of new outlet.
e_i^+ = amount by which x_2 coordinate of new outlet exceeds x_2 coordinate of population center i.
e_i^- = amount by which x_2 coordinate of population center i exceeds x_2 coordinate of new outlet.

min $d_1^- + d_1^+ + e_1^- + e_1^+ + d_2^- + d_2^+ + e_2^- + e_2^+ + d_3^- + d_3^+ + e_3^- + e_3^+$
s.t.

$$
\begin{aligned}
x_1 \quad + d_1^- - d_1^+ &&&&&&&&&= 2 \\
x_2 \quad + e_1^- - e_1^+ &&&&&&&&&= 8 \\
x_1 \quad\quad\quad + d_2^- - d_2^+ &&&&&&&&&= 6 \\
x_2 \quad\quad\quad + e_2^- - e_2^+ &&&&&&&&&= 6 \\
x_1 \quad\quad\quad\quad + d_3^- - d_3^+ &&&&&&&&&= 1 \\
x_2 \quad\quad\quad\quad\quad + e_3^- - e_3^+ &&&&&&&&&= 1 \\
\end{aligned}
$$

$$x_1, x_2, d_1^+, d_1^-, d_2^+, d_2^-, d_3^+, d_3^-, e_1^+, e_1^-, e_2^+, e_2^-, e_3^+, e_3^- \geq 0$$

The solution is
$$x_1 = 2$$
$$x_2 = 6$$
$$e_1^- = 2$$
$$d_2^- = 4$$
$$d_3^+ = 1$$
$$e_3^+ = 5$$

Value of objective function is 12.

b. The constraints remain the same but the weights change in the objective function. The new objective is given below.

min $4d_1^- + 4d_1^+ + 4e_1^- + 4e_1^+ + 2d_2^- + 2d_2^+ + 2e_2^- + 2e_2^+ + d_3^- + d_3^+ + e_3^- + e_3^+$

The new solution is
$$x_1 = 2$$
$$x_2 = 8$$
$$d_2^- = 4$$
$$e_2^+ = 2$$
$$d_3^+ = 1$$
$$e_3^- = 7$$

Value of the objective function is 20.

10. Synthesization

Step 1: Column totals are 8, 10/3, and 7/4

Step 2:

Price	Car A	Car B	Car C
Car A	1/8	1/10	1/7
Car B	3/8	3/10	2/7
Car C	4/8	6/10	4/7

Step 3:

Price	Car A	Car B	Car C	Row Average
Car A	0.125	0.100	0.143	0.123
Car B	0.375	0.300	0.286	0.320
Car C	0.500	0.600	0.571	0.557

Consistency Ratio

Step 1:

$$0.123 \begin{bmatrix} 1 \\ 3 \\ 4 \end{bmatrix} + 0.320 \begin{bmatrix} 1/3 \\ 1 \\ 2 \end{bmatrix} + 0.557 \begin{bmatrix} 1/4 \\ 1/2 \\ 1 \end{bmatrix}$$

Weighted Sum

$$\begin{bmatrix} 0.123 \\ 0.369 \\ 0.492 \end{bmatrix} + \begin{bmatrix} 0.107 \\ 0.320 \\ 0.640 \end{bmatrix} + \begin{bmatrix} 0.139 \\ 0.279 \\ 0.557 \end{bmatrix} = \begin{bmatrix} 0.369 \\ 0.968 \\ 1.689 \end{bmatrix}$$

Step 2: 0.369/0.123 = 3.000
0.968/0.320 = 3.025
1.689/0.557 = 3.032

Step 3: $\lambda_{max} = (3.000 + 3.025 + 3.032)/3 = 3.019$

Step 4: CI = (3.019 - 3)/2 = 0.010

Step 5: CR = 0.010/0.58 = 0.017

Since CR = 0.017 is less than 0.10, the degree of consistency exhibited in the pairwise comparison matrix for price is acceptable.

11. **Synthesization**

Step 1: Column totals are 11, 17/4, and 9/6
Step 2:

MPG	Car A	Car B	Car C
Car A	1/11	1/17	1/9
Car B	4/11	4/17	2/9
Car C	6/11	12/17	6/9

Step 3:

MPG	Car A	Car B	Car C	Row Average
Car A	0.091	0.059	0.111	0.087
Car B	0.364	0.235	0.222	0.274
Car C	0.545	0.706	0.667	0.639

Consistency Ratio

Step 1:

$$0.087 \begin{bmatrix} 1 \\ 4 \\ 6 \end{bmatrix} + 0.274 \begin{bmatrix} 1/4 \\ 1 \\ 3 \end{bmatrix} + 0.639 \begin{bmatrix} 1/6 \\ 1/3 \\ 1 \end{bmatrix}$$

$$\begin{bmatrix} 0.087 \\ 0.348 \\ 0.522 \end{bmatrix} + \begin{bmatrix} 0.069 \\ 0.274 \\ 0.822 \end{bmatrix} + \begin{bmatrix} 0.107 \\ 0.213 \\ 0.639 \end{bmatrix} = \begin{matrix} \text{Weighted} \\ \text{Sum} \\ \begin{bmatrix} 0.263 \\ 0.835 \\ 1.983 \end{bmatrix} \end{matrix}$$

Step 2: 0.263/0.087 = 3.023
0.835/0.274 = 3.047
1.983/0.639 = 3.103

Step 3: $\lambda_{max} = (3.023 + 3.047 + 3.103)/3 = 3.058$

Step 4: $CI = (3.058 - 3)/2 = 0.029$

Step 5: $CR = 0.029/0.58 = 0.05$

Since $CR = 0.05$ is less than 0.10, the degree of consistency exhibited in the pairwise comparison matrix for MPG is acceptable.

12. **Synthesization**

Step 1: Column totals are 17/4, 31/21, and 12

Step 2:

Style	Car A	Car B	Car C
Car A	4/17	7/31	4/12
Car B	12/17	21/31	7/12
Car C	1/17	3/31	1/12

Step 3:

Style	Car A	Car B	Car C	Row Average
Car A	0.235	0.226	0.333	0.265
Car B	0.706	0.677	0.583	0.655
Car C	0.059	0.097	0.083	0.080

Consistency Ratio

Step 1:

$$0.265 \begin{bmatrix} 1 \\ 3 \\ 1/4 \end{bmatrix} + 0.655 \begin{bmatrix} 1/3 \\ 1 \\ 1/7 \end{bmatrix} + 0.080 \begin{bmatrix} 4 \\ 7 \\ 1 \end{bmatrix}$$

$$\begin{bmatrix} 0.265 \\ 0.795 \\ 0.066 \end{bmatrix} + \begin{bmatrix} 0.218 \\ 0.655 \\ 0.094 \end{bmatrix} + \begin{bmatrix} 0.320 \\ 0.560 \\ 0.080 \end{bmatrix} = \begin{matrix} \text{Weighted} \\ \text{Sum} \\ \begin{bmatrix} 0.803 \\ 2.010 \\ 0.240 \end{bmatrix} \end{matrix}$$

Step 2: $0.803/0.265 = 3.030$
$2.010/0.655 = 3.069$
$0.240/0.080 = 3.000$

Step 3: $\lambda_{max} = (3.030 + 3.069 + 3.000)/3 = 3.033$

Step 4: $CI = (3.033 - 3)/2 = 0.017$

Step 5: $CR = 0.017/0.58 = 0.29$

Since $CR = 0.029$ is less than 0.10, the degree of consistency exhibited in the pairwise comparison matrix for style is acceptable.

13.a.

Reputation	School A	School B
School A	1	6
School B	1/6	1

b. Step 1: Column totals are 7/6 and 7
   Step 2:

Reputation	School A	School B
School A	6/7	6/7
School B	1/7	1/7

Step 3:

Reputation	School A	School B	Row Average
School A	0.857	0.857	0.857
School B	0.143	0.143	0.143

14.a. Step 1: Column totals are 47/35, 19/3, 11
      Step 2:

Desirability	City 1	City 2	City 3
City 1	35/47	15/19	7/11
City 2	7/47	3/19	3/11
City 3	5/47	1/19	1/11

Step 3:

Desirability	City 1	City 2	City 3	Row Average
City 1	0.745	0.789	0.636	0.723
City 2	0.149	0.158	0.273	0.193
City 3	0.106	0.053	0.091	0.083

b. Step 1:

$$0.723 \begin{bmatrix} 1 \\ 1/5 \\ 1/7 \end{bmatrix} + 0.193 \begin{bmatrix} 5 \\ 1 \\ 1/3 \end{bmatrix} + 0.083 \begin{bmatrix} 7 \\ 3 \\ 1 \end{bmatrix}$$

Weighted
Sum

$$\begin{bmatrix} 0.723 \\ 0.145 \\ 0.103 \end{bmatrix} + \begin{bmatrix} 0.965 \\ 0.193 \\ 0.064 \end{bmatrix} + \begin{bmatrix} 0.581 \\ 0.249 \\ 0.083 \end{bmatrix} = \begin{bmatrix} 2.269 \\ 0.587 \\ 0.250 \end{bmatrix}$$

Step 2: 2.269/0.723 = 3.138
0.587/0.193 = 3.041
0.250/0.083 = 3.012

Step 3: λ_{max} = (3.138 + 3.041 + 3.012)/3 = 3.064

Step 4: CI = (3.064 - 3)/2 = 0.032

Step 5: CR = 0.032/0.58 = 0.055

Since CR = 0.055 is less than 0.10, the degree of consistency exhibited in the pairwise comparison matrix is acceptable.

15.a. Step 1: Column totals are 4/3 and 4
Step 2:

	A	B
A	3/4	3/4
B	1/4	1/4

Step 3:

	A	B	Row Average
A	0.75	0.75	0.75
B	0.25	0.25	0.25

b. The individual's judgements could not be inconsistent since there are only two programs being compared.

16.a.

Flavor	A	B	C
A	1	3	2
B	1/3	1	5
C	1/2	1/5	1

b.   Step 1: Column totals are 11/6, 21/5, and 8
     Step 2:

Flavor	A	B	C
A	6/11	15/21	2/8
B	2/11	5/21	5/8
C	3/11	1/21	1/8

Step 3:

Flavor	A	B	C	Row Average
A	0.545	0.714	0.250	0.503
B	0.182	0.238	0.625	0.348
C	0.273	0.048	0.125	0.149

c.   Step 1:

$$0.503 \begin{bmatrix} 1 \\ 1/3 \\ 1/2 \end{bmatrix} + 0.348 \begin{bmatrix} 3 \\ 1 \\ 1/5 \end{bmatrix} + 0.149 \begin{bmatrix} 2 \\ 5 \\ 1 \end{bmatrix}$$

Weighted
Sum

$$\begin{bmatrix} 0.503 \\ 0.168 \\ 0.252 \end{bmatrix} + \begin{bmatrix} 1.044 \\ 0.348 \\ 0.070 \end{bmatrix} + \begin{bmatrix} 0.298 \\ 0.745 \\ 0.149 \end{bmatrix} = \begin{bmatrix} 1.845 \\ 1.261 \\ 0.471 \end{bmatrix}$$

Step 2: 1.845/0.503 = 3.668
         1.261/0.348 = 3.624
         0.471/0.149 = 3.161

Step 3: λ_{max} = (3.668 + 3.624 + 3.161)/3 = 3.484

Step 4: CI = (3.484 - 3)/2 = 0.242

Step 5: CR = 0.242/0.58 = 0.417

Since CR = 0.417 is less than 0.10, the individual's judgements are not consistent.

17.a.

Flavor	A	B	C
A	1	1/2	5
B	2	1	5
C	1/5	1/5	1

b. Step 1: Column totals are 16/5, 17/10, and 11
    Step 2:

Flavor	A	B	C
A	5/16	5/17	5/11
B	10/16	10/17	5/11
C	1/16	2/17	1/11

Step 3:

Flavor	A	B	C	Row Average
A	0.313	0.294	0.455	0.354
B	0.625	0.588	0.455	0.556
C	0.063	·0.118	0.091	0.091

c. Step 1:

$$0.354 \begin{bmatrix} 1 \\ 2 \\ 1/5 \end{bmatrix} + 0.556 \begin{bmatrix} 1/2 \\ 1 \\ 1/5 \end{bmatrix} + 0.091 \begin{bmatrix} 5 \\ 5 \\ 1 \end{bmatrix}$$

Weighted
Sum

$$\begin{bmatrix} 0.354 \\ 0.708 \\ 0.071 \end{bmatrix} + \begin{bmatrix} 0.278 \\ 0.556 \\ 0.111 \end{bmatrix} + \begin{bmatrix} 0.455 \\ 0.455 \\ 0.091 \end{bmatrix} = \begin{bmatrix} 1.087 \\ 1.719 \\ 0.273 \end{bmatrix}$$

Step 2: $1.087/0.354 = 3.071$
$1.719/0.556 = 3.092$
$0.273/0.091 = 3.000$

Step 3: $\lambda_{max} = (3.071 + 3.092 + 3.000)/3 = 3.054$

Step 4: $CI = (3.054 - 3)/2 = 0.027$

Step 5: $CR = 0.027/0.58 = 0.047$

Since $CR = 0.047$ is less than 0.10, the individual's judgements are consistent.

18.a.   Let   D = Dallas
               S = San Francisco
               N = New York

Location	D	S	N
D	1	1/4	1/7
S	4	1	1/3
N	7	3	1

b.   Step 1: Column totals are 12, 17/4, and 31/21
       Step 2:

Location	D	S	N
D	1/12	1/17	3/31
S	4/12	4/17	7/31
N	7/12	12/17	21/31

Step 3:

Location	D	S	N	Row Average
D	0.083	0.059	0.097	0.080
S	0.333	0.235	0.226	0.265
N	0.583	0.706	0.677	0.655

c.   Step 1:

$$0.080 \begin{bmatrix} 1 \\ 4 \\ 7 \end{bmatrix} + 0.265 \begin{bmatrix} 1/4 \\ 1 \\ 3 \end{bmatrix} + 0.655 \begin{bmatrix} 1/7 \\ 1/3 \\ 1 \end{bmatrix}$$

Weighted
Sum

$$\begin{bmatrix} 0.080 \\ 0.320 \\ 0.560 \end{bmatrix} + \begin{bmatrix} 0.066 \\ 0.265 \\ 0.795 \end{bmatrix} + \begin{bmatrix} 0.094 \\ 0.218 \\ 0.655 \end{bmatrix} = \begin{bmatrix} 0.240 \\ 0.803 \\ 2.010 \end{bmatrix}$$

Step 2: $0.240/0.080 = 3.000$
          $0.803/0.265 = 3.030$
          $2.010/0.655 = 3.069$

Step 3: $\lambda_{max} = (3.000 + 3.030 + 3.069)/3 = 3.033$

Step 4: $CI = (3.033 - 3)/2 = 0.017$

Step 5: $CR = 0.017/0.58 = 0.029$

Since $CR = 0.029$ is less than 0.10, the manager's judgements are consistent.

19.a. Step 1: Column totals are 94/21, 33/4, 18, and 21/12
Step 2:

Performance	1	2	3	4
1	21/94	12/33	7/18	4/21
2	7/94	4/33	4/18	3/21
3	3/94	1/33	1/18	2/21
4	63/94	16/33	6/18	12/21

Step 3:

Performance	1	2	3	4	Row Average
1	0.223	0.364	0.389	0.190	0.292
2	0.074	0.121	0.222	0.143	0.140
3	0.032	0.030	0.056	0.095	0.053
4	0.670	0.485	0.333	0.571	0.515

b. Step 1:

$$0.292 \begin{bmatrix} 1 \\ 1/3 \\ 1/7 \\ 3 \end{bmatrix} + 0.140 \begin{bmatrix} 3 \\ 1 \\ 1/4 \\ 4 \end{bmatrix} + 0.053 \begin{bmatrix} 7 \\ 4 \\ 1 \\ 6 \end{bmatrix} + 0.515 \begin{bmatrix} 1/3 \\ 1/4 \\ 1/6 \\ 1 \end{bmatrix}$$

$$\begin{bmatrix} 0.292 \\ 0.097 \\ 0.042 \\ 0.876 \end{bmatrix} + \begin{bmatrix} 0.420 \\ 0.140 \\ 0.035 \\ 0.560 \end{bmatrix} + \begin{bmatrix} 0.371 \\ 0.212 \\ 0.053 \\ 0.318 \end{bmatrix} + \begin{bmatrix} 0.172 \\ 0.129 \\ 0.086 \\ 0.515 \end{bmatrix} = \begin{bmatrix} 1.255 \\ 0.578 \\ 0.216 \\ 2.269 \end{bmatrix}$$

Step 2: $1.255/0.292 = 4.298$
$0.578/0.140 = 4.129$
$0.216/0.053 = 4.075$
$2.269/0.515 = 4.406$

Step 3: $\lambda_{max} = (4.298 + 4.129 + 4.075 + 4.406)/4 = 4.227$

Step 4: CI = (4.227 - 4)/3 = 0.076

Step 5: CR = 0.076/0.90 = 0.084

Since CR = 0.084 is less than 0.10, the judgements regarding performance are consistent.

20.a.

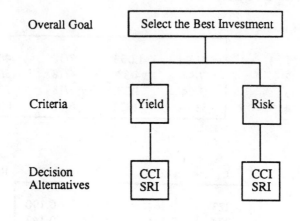

b.

Criterion	Yield	Risk
Yield: 0.667	CCI: 0.750	CCI: 0.333
Risk: 0.333	SRI: 0.250	SRI: 0.667

c.

	Criterion	
Alternative	Yield	Risk
CCI	0.750	0.333
SRI	0.250	0.667

Overall Priority for CCI

0.667(0.750) + 0.333(0.333) = 0.500 + 0.111 = 0.611

Overall Priority for SRI

0.667(0.250) + 0.333(0.667) = 0.167 + 0.222 = 0.389

21.a.

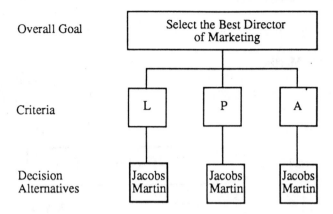

	Overall Goal	Select the Best Director of Marketing

Overall Goal — Select the Best Director of Marketing

Criteria — L, P, A

Decision Alternatives — Jacobs/Martin, Jacobs/Martin, Jacobs/Martin

b.   The priorities for the criteria are computed as follows:

Step 1: Column totals are 8, 11/6, and 13/4
Step 2:

Criterion	L	P	A
L	1/8	2/11	1/13
P	3/8	6/11	8/13
A	4/8	3/11	4/13

Step 3:

Criterion	L	P	A	Row Average
L	0.125	0.182	0.077	0.128
P	0.375	0.545	0.615	0.512
A	0.500	0.273	0.308	0.360

The priorities for the alternatives are shown below:

Leadership (L)	Personal (P)	Administrative (A)
Jacobs: 0.800	Jacobs: 0.250	Jacobs: 0.667
Martin: 0.220	Martin: 0.750	Martin: 0.333

c.

Alternative	L	P	A
Jacobs	0.800	0.250	0.667
Martin	0.200	0.750	0.333

Overall Priority for Jacobs

$$0.128(0.800) + 0.512(0.250) + 0.360(0.667) = 0.471$$

Overall Priority for Martin

$$0.128(0.200) + 0.512(0.750) + 0.360(0.333) = 0.529$$

22.a.

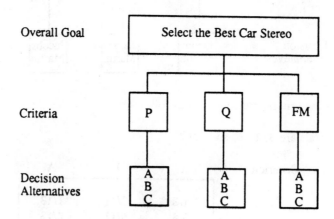

| Overall Goal | Select the Best Car Stereo | | |

b. **Priorities for Criterion**

Step 1: Column totals are 19/12, 13/3, and 8
Step 2:

Criterion	P	Q	FM
P	12/19	9/13	4/8
Q	4/19	3/13	3/8
FM	3/19	1/13	1/8

Step 3:

Criterion	P	Q	FM	Row Average
P	0.632	0.692	0.500	0.608
Q	0.211	0.231	0.375	0.272
FM	0.158	0.077	0.125	0.120

For Price

Step 1: Column totals are 14/8, 8, and 10/3
Step 2:

Price	A	B	C
A	8/14	4/8	6/10
B	2/14	1/8	1/10
C	4/14	3/8	3/10

Step 3:

Price	A	B	C	Row Average
A	0.571	0.500	0.600	0.557
B	0.143	0.125	0.100	0.123
C	0.286	0.375	0.300	0.320

For Quality

Step 1: Column totals are 7, 9/2, and 19/12
Step 2:

Quality	A	B	C
A	1/7	1/9	3/19
B	2/7	2/9	4/19
C	4/7	6/9	12/19

Step 3:

Quality	A	B	C	Row Average
A	0.143	0.111	0.158	0.137
B	0.286	0.222	0.211	0.240
C	0.571	0.667	0.632	0.623

For FM Reception

Step 1: Column totals are 14/8, 6, and 4
Step 2:

FM	A	B	C
A	8/14	4/6	2/4
B	2/14	1/6	1/4
C	4/14	1/6	1/4

Step 3:

FM	A	B	C	Row Average
A	0.571	0.667	0.500	0.579
B	0.143	0.167	0.250	0.187
C	0.286	0.167	0.250	0.234

	Criterion		
Alternative	P	Q	FM
A	0.557	0.137	0.579
B	0.123	0.240	0.187
C	0.320	0.623	0.234

Alternatives	Overall Priority
A	0.608(0.557) + 0.272(0.137) + 0.120(0.579) = 0.445
B	0.608(0.123) + 0.272(0.240) + 0.120(0.187) = 0.163
C	0.608(0.320) + 0.272(0.623) + 0.120(0.234) = 0.392

Case Problem

Let

x_{11} = number of EZ-190 trailers produced in March
x_{12} = number of EZ-190 trailers produced in April
x_{21} = number of EZ-250 trailers produced in March
x_{22} = number of EZ-250 trailers produced in April
s_{11} = EZ-190 ending inventory in March
s_{12} = EZ-190 ending inventory in April
s_{21} = EZ-250 ending inventory in March
s_{22} = EZ-250 ending inventory in April

P_1 Goal: Meet demand for the EZ-250

March: $\quad 300 + x_{21} - s_{21} - d_1^+ + d_1^- = 1000$ \hfill (1)

April: $\quad s_{21} + x_{22} - s_{22} - d_2^+ + d_2^- = 1200$ \hfill (2)

P_2 Goal: Meet demand for the EZ-190

March: $\quad 200 + x_{11} - s_{11} - d_3^+ + d_3^- = 800$ \hfill (3)

April: $\quad s_{11} + x_{12} - s_{12} - d_4^+ + d_4^- = 600$ \hfill (4)

P_3 Goal: Limit labor fluctuations from month to month to at most 1000

March:

$$5300 \le 4x_{11} + 6x_{21} \le 7300$$
$$4x_{11} + 6x_{21} - d_5^+ + d_5^- = 5300 \tag{5}$$
$$4x_{11} + 6x_{21} - d_6^+ + d_6^- = 7300 \tag{6}$$

April:

$$(4x_{11} + 6x_{21}) - 1000 \le 4x_{12} + 6x_{22} \le (4x_{11} + 6x_{21}) + 1000$$
$$4x_{12} + 6x_{22} = [(4x_{11} + 6x_{21}) - 1000] + d_7^+ - d_7^-$$

or

$$4x_{12} + 6x_{22} - 4x_{11} - 6x_{21} - d_7^+ + d_7^- = -1000 \tag{7}$$

$$4x_{12} + 6x_{22} = [(4x_{11} + 6x_{21}) + 1000] + d_8^+ - d_8^-$$

or

$$4x_{12} + 6x_{22} - 4x_{11} - 6x_{21} - d_8^+ + d_8^- = 1000 \tag{8}$$

The complete goal programming model is

$$\min \quad P_1(d_1^-) + P_1(d_2^-) \quad + \quad P_2(d_3^-) \quad + P_2(d_4^-) + P_3(d_5^-) + P_3(d_6^+) + P_3(d_7^+) + P_3(d_8^+)$$

s.t.

		x_{21}			$- s_{21}$			$-$	d_1^+	$+$	d_1^-	$=$	800
			x_{22}		$+ s_{21}$	$-$	s_{22}	$-$	d_2^+	$+$	d_2^-	$=$	1200
x_{11}				$-s_{11}$				$-$	d_3^+	$+$	d_3^-	$=$	600
	x_{12}			$+s_{11} - s_{12}$				$-$	d_4^+	$+$	d_4^-	$=$	600
$4x_{11}$		$+6x_{21}$						$-$	d_5^+	$+$	d_5^-	$=$	5300
$4x_{11}$		$+6x_{21}$						$-$	d_6^+	$+$	d_6^-	$=$	7300
$-4x_{11}$	$+ \ 4x_{12}$	$-6x_{21}$	$+6x_{22}$					$-$	d_7^+	$+$	d_7^-	$=$	-1000
$-4x_{11}$	$+ \ 4x_{12}$	$-6x_{21}$	$+6x_{22}$					$-$	d_8^+	$+$	d_8^-	$=$	1000

all variables ≥ 0

Information Needed for the Managerial Report

1.

	March	April
EZ-190	775	425
EZ-250	800	1200

2.   No changes since the ending inventories for the optimal production schedule are as follows:

	March	April
EZ-190	175	0
EZ-250	0	0

3.   The following constraints must be added to the model:

April ending inventory

$$s_{12} \geq 100$$
$$s_{22} \geq 100$$

Maximum storage of 300 units in each month

$$s_{11} \leq 300$$
$$s_{12} \leq 300$$
$$s_{21} \leq 300$$
$$s_{22} \leq 300$$

The new optimal production schedule is:

	March	April
EZ-190	900	400
EZ-250	800	1300

The corresponding ending inventories are:

	March	April
EZ-190	300	100
EZ-250	0	100

4. The new optimal production schedule is:

	March	April
EZ-190	625	275
EZ-250	800	1200

The corresponding ending inventories are:

	March	April
EZ-190	25	0
EZ-250	0	0